ADVANCES
IN CHILD DEVELOPMENT
AND BEHAVIOR

VOLUME 14

Contributors to This Volume

C. K. Crook

Lauren Julius Harris

Marion Perlmutter

Ian St. James-Roberts

Daniel S. P. Schubert

Herman J. P. Schubert

Ellen A. Strommen

Mazie Earle Wagner

John S. Werner

ADVANCES
IN
CHILD DEVELOPMENT
AND
BEHAVIOR

edited by

Hayne W. Reese
Department of Psychology
West Virginia University
Morgantown, West Virginia

Lewis P. Lipsitt
Department of Psychology
Brown University
Providence, Rhode Island

VOLUME 14

 1979

ACADEMIC PRESS • New York • San Francisco • London
A Subsidiary of Harcourt Brace Jovanovich, Publishers

ACADEMIC PRESS, INC.
111 Fifth Avenue, New York, New York 10003

United Kingdom Edition published by
ACADEMIC PRESS, INC. (LONDON) LTD.
24/28 Oval Road, London NW1 7DX

LIBRARY OF CONGRESS CATALOG CARD NUMBER: 63–23237

ISBN 0–12–009714–1

PRINTED IN THE UNITED STATES OF AMERICA

79 80 81 82   9 8 7 6 5 4 3 2 1

Contents

Development of Visual Memory in Infants

JOHN S. WERNER AND MARION PERLMUTTER

Sibship-Constellation Effects on Psychosocial Development, Creativity, and Health

MAZIE EARLE WAGNER, HERMAN J. P. SCHUBERT, AND DANIEL S. P. SCHUBERT

The Development of Understanding of the Spatial Terms Front and Back

LAUREN JULIUS HARRIS AND ELLEN A. STROMMEN

The Organization and Control of Infant Sucking

C. K. CROOK

Neurological Plasticity, Recovery from Brain Insult, and Child Development

IAN ST. JAMES-ROBERTS

List of Contributors

Numbers in parentheses indicate the pages on which the author's contributions begin.

C. K. CROOK
Department of Psychology, Science Laboratories, Durham University, Durham DH1 3LE, England (209)

LAUREN JULIUS HARRIS
Department of Psychology, Michigan State University, East Lansing, Michigan 48824 (149)

MARION PERLMUTTER
Institute of Child Development, University of Minnesota, Minneapolis, Minnesota 55455 (1)

IAN ST. JAMES-ROBERTS
University of London, Institute of Education, Department of Child Development, London WC1H OAL England (253)

DANIEL S. P. SCHUBERT
Department of Psychiatry, Case Western Reserve University School of Medicine and Cleveland Metropolitan General Hospital, Cleveland, Ohio 44109 (57)

HERMAN J. P. SCHUBERT
Graduate Study and Research, State University College, Buffalo, New York 14222 (57)

ELLEN A. STROMMEN
Department of Psychology, Michigan State University, East Lansing, Michigan 48824 (149)

MAZIE EARLE WAGNER
Emeritus Director of Counseling, State University College, Buffalo, New York 14222 (57)

JOHN S. WERNER
Department of Psychology, University of Colorado, Boulder, Colorado 80309 (1)

Preface

The amount of research and theoretical discussion in the field of child development and behavior is so vast that researchers, instructors, and students are confronted with a formidable task in keeping abreast of new developments within their areas of specialization through the use of primary sources, as well as being knowledgeable in areas peripheral to their primary focus of interest. Moreover, there is often simply not enough journal space to permit publication of more speculative kinds of analyses which might spark expanded interest in a problem area or stimulate new modes of attack on the problem.

The serial publication *Advances in Child Development and Behavior* is intended to ease the burden by providing scholarly technical articles serving as reference material and by providing a place for publication of scholarly speculation. In these documented critical reviews, recent advances in the field are summarized and integrated, complexities are exposed, and fresh viewpoints are offered. They should be useful not only to the expert in the area but also to the general reader.

No attempt is made to organize each volume around a particular theme or topic, nor is the series intended to reflect the development of new fads. Manuscripts are solicited from investigators conducting programmatic work on problems of current and significant interest. The editors often encourage the preparation of critical syntheses dealing intensively with topics of relatively narrow scope but of considerable potential interest to the scientific community. Contributors are encouraged to criticize, integrate, and stimulate, but always within a framework of high scholarship. Although appearance in the volumes is ordinarily by invitation, unsolicited manuscripts will be accepted for review if submitted first in outline form to the editors. All papers—whether invited or submitted—receive careful editorial scrutiny. Invited papers are automatically accepted for publication in principle, but may require revision before final acceptance. Submitted papers receive the same treatment except that they are not automatically accepted for publication even in principle, and may be rejected.

We wish to acknowledge with gratitude the aid of our home institutions, West Virginia University and Brown University, which generously provided time and facilities for the preparation of this volume. We also wish to thank Drs. Charles J. Brainerd, Nancy Datan, Allan C. Kerckhoff,

Kathleen A. McCluskey, John A. Meacham, and Robert Y. Moore for their editorial assistance.

Hayne W. Reese
Lewis P. Lipsitt

ADVANCES
IN CHILD DEVELOPMENT
AND BEHAVIOR

VOLUME 14

DEVELOPMENT OF
VISUAL MEMORY IN INFANTS

John S. Werner[1]

UNIVERSITY OF COLORADO

and
Marion Perlmutter[2]

UNIVERSITY OF MINNESOTA

[1] John S. Werner was supported, during the writing of this manuscript, by a USPHS Training Grant in Child Psychology to Brown University.

[2] Marion Perlmutter was supported, in part, during the writing of this manuscript, by NICHHD grant 5R01 HD 11776-01.

ADVANCES IN CHILD DEVELOPMENT
AND BEHAVIOR, VOL. 14

I. Introduction

Memory refers to conservation of the past and may be manifest in a number of ways. For example, humans apparently retain an autobiographical record of specific experiences, referred to as episodic memory by Tulving (1972) and as figurative knowledge by Piaget (1968; Piaget & Inhelder, 1973). Some information-processing theorists have also postulated that past experiences are abstracted into a generalized system of world knowledge, referred to as semantic knowledge (Tulving, 1972). Similarly, Piaget has suggested that memory, in a broad sense, involves all of the operations of intelligence, including logicomathematical or operative knowledge (Piaget, 1968; Piaget & Inhelder, 1973).

In this paper we will examine the earliest evidence of episodic memory, infant visual recognition. While there are now several reviews of specific aspects of infant memory (e.g., Cohen & Gelber, 1975; Fagan, 1975; Fantz, Fagan & Miranda, 1975), the literature has not yet been well synthesized, nor has it been integrated with other work on memory. Moreover, methodological considerations that could account for apparent experimental inconsistencies have not been widely considered. In this review data collected in many different laboratories are examined. Hypotheses are offered as to why certain methodological variations can be expected to produce different experimental results. Indeed, in some instances this examination leads to conclusions differing from those previously drawn. We shall attempt to assess whether available infant data provide evidence of developmental changes in retention capacity and, where possible, to integrate infant data with those from older children and adults.

II. Framework for Interpreting Memory Data

Two theoretical perspectives presently guiding most research on memory development are information processing and Piagetian points of view. While these conceptualizations differ on some important dimensions, they may be viewed largely as complementary to one another. Very briefly, the information-processing perspective conceptualizes memory as the transfer of information within a cognitive system. This involves encoding, retention, and retrieval of information. A data base evolves as a result of encoding and retention and may be remembered through recall and/or recognition. The Piagetian perspective is quite different. Piaget posits that memory should not be regarded as a separate cognitive function, but that it should be conceived of as integrally bound to intelligence.

While most information-processing theorists would agree that memory is, in some sense, inseparable from other cognitive functions, the emphasis is not comparable to the Piagetian perspective. Information-processing theorists generally analyze component processes of memory as they relate to children's increasing repertoire of, and proficiency at, memory skills. Piagetians, in contrast, focus on development of intelligence, and this has led them to examine the ways in which changing cognitive structures affect children's memory. Researchers with an information-processing orientation generally study the mechanisms of memory, expecting this to illuminate understanding of cognition; conversely, Piagetians usually concentrate on developmental changes in intelligence, expecting this to illuminate understanding of the contents of memory.

The conceptualization of memory used throughout this paper is rooted within both of these perspectives; however, questions concerning the ontogenesis of mechanisms involved in effective and efficient retention of previous experiences will be central. That is, we view the child as an information processor and examine developmental changes in the ways in which information is encoded, retained, and retrieved.

In interpreting research on infant memory it is important to distinguish between recall and recognition. This distinction concerns whether or not a stimulus must be physically present in order for the infant to remember it. According to information-processing models (see Crowder, 1976; Kintsch, 1970; Klatzky, 1975) recognition involves one processing stage, while recall involves recognition plus some other stage. For recall it is assumed that items are implicitly generated and then submitted to tests of recognition; self-generated representations are matched with memory representations. For recognition, however, the items are provided, and tests of recognition are all that are required; perceptual representations are matched with memory representations.

According to Piaget, recognition is a primitive process, found even in lower vertebrates. It occurs in the presence of an object and consists of perceiving the object as something that has been experienced in the past. In other words, recognition is "a double utilization of that figurative mechanism which we designate as perception" (Piaget & Inhelder, 1973, p. 13). It requires only a match between current perceptual activity and prior perceptual activity. However, Piaget views recall, or evocative memory, as specific to higher primates. It involves the impression, in the absence of a model, that an object or event has been experienced or perceived at a prior moment in time. It is said to "involve the use of a memory image . . . that is, a figurative cum semiotic mechanism or a purely semiotic mechanism" (Piaget & Inhelder, 1973, p. 13). Since no external stimulus is available during recall, it must rely on symbolic representation.

In general, Piaget's distinction between recognition and recall is based upon his view that perceptual schemata are the instruments of recognition, whereas internalized images are the instruments of recall. This then accounts for Piaget's observation that recognition is present during the first months of life, but that recall is not evidenced until later in development. Since "recognition can rely on perception and sensorimotor schemes alone, while evocation requires mental imagery or language, that is some form of symbolic function" (Piaget, 1968, p. 11), the infant would not be expected to evidence recall. According to Piaget, symbolic functions (i.e., mental imagery and language) are not available until about 1–2 years of age. The development of recall after recognition thus reflects a more basic aspect of cognitive development. The infant, equipped with perceptual schemata, is capable of recognition. Only after symbolic functions are developed does the child become capable of recall. For Piaget, then, a major cognitive developmental accomplishment, the growth of symbolic functions, is reflected in an important mnemonic feat, the emergence of recall.

In the review that follows, we shall concentrate primarily on studies of recognition memory in infants simply because infant recall memory has not been widely studied. Our emphasis, then, does not necessarily reflect an agreement with Piaget's view that infant memory skills are limited to recognition; rather, it acknowledges the current range of infant memory research. Indeed, as shall be seen, some recent data indicate that infant memory skills may be more extensive than has been theorized by Piaget.

III.   Methodological Considerations

A.   PARADIGMS

The methods developed to assess memory in mature humans have been extensive. For example, college students have been given diverse and complex verbal instructions and tested on a number of response measures, many of which have required linguistic skills. Of course, it is obvious that preverbal infants, with limited response systems, cannot be tested in the same manner. Indeed, the development of methodologies for assessing infants' memory and cognitive skills has been far from easy.

The origin of most commonly used infant testing procedures perhaps can be traced to the turn of the century, when Marsden (1903), Valentine (1913–1914), and others reported that human infants were differentially responsive to their visual worlds. Their method involved simultaneous presentation of two visual stimuli and measurement of an infant's differential fixation. If the infant looked at one stimulus more than another, then discrimination between the two stimuli could be inferred.

In spite of the great interest in infants and young children engendered in the late 1920s and early 1930s, the differential-looking technique was not widely used. In the late 1950s, however, the technique was resurrected. Fantz (1956, 1958, 1967) successfully used the differential-looking technique to investigate early form discriminations and visual acuity and then modified it so that he could also study memory. His procedure (Fantz, 1964) involved simultaneous presentations of two stimuli for specified lengths of time. One of the paired stimuli was the same throughout all trials (familiar), while the other stimulus was different in each successive trial (novel). If infants attended differentially to the novel and familiar stimuli, then it was inferred that they had remembered the familiar one.

While Fantz was one of the first to suggest that such differential responsiveness to novelty (i.e., recognition memory) was within the capabilities of infants, much subsequent research has been conducted to examine this phenomenon. Yet, general statements about infants' memory are difficult to make and must be highly qualified. Part of the problem lies in the fact that different investigators have used different methods, employing different procedures, stimuli, response measures, and subject-selection criteria. Although these differences obviate direct interstudy comparison, we believe that careful analysis of the differences between methods can clarify some of the apparent inconsistencies in experimental findings.

The general procedures used in most studies of infant visual recognition memory are shown in the flow chart in Fig. 1. The experiment begins with stimulus familiarization. Then, a novel stimulus is introduced. Differential responsiveness to the familiar stimulus, relative to the novel one, is attributed to memory for the familiar one. In most studies the novelty test has immediately followed familiarization, thus providing evidence of immediate recognition memory. However, as can be seen in the figure, the procedures can be modified to study delayed recognition or interference.

While the procedures used in most studies of infant recognition conform to this generalized schema, many variations may be noted. For example, it has been customary to distinguish between the Fantz-type differential-looking paradigm and the habituation–dishabituation paradigm. As already discussed, Fantz's differential-looking procedure involves familiarization for a fixed-time interval and simultaneous testing of familiar and

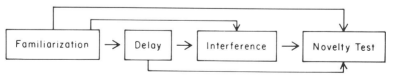

Fig. 1. Schematic of experimental procedures for investigating visual recognition memory in preverbal infants.

novel stimuli. In contrast, the habituation–dishabituation procedure involves familiarization until habituation occurs and separate testing of familiar and novel stimuli. Habituation is defined as a decrement in responding to repeated presentations of a stimulus that cannot be accounted for by effects of fatigue or sensory adaptation (Harris, 1943). Fatigue and adaptation are ruled out by assessing responding after the introduction of novel stimuli (Thompson & Spencer, 1966). If fatigue or sensory adaptation has occurred, responding should remain at a low level; however, if habituation has occurred, the introduction of a novel stimulus should produce an increase in responding, referred to as dishabituation. An even more convincing procedure for assessing habituation involves introduction of a novel stimulus that is weaker (i.e., of lower intensity, complexity, etc.) than the familiar stimulus. Fatigue or sensory adaptation explanations of response decrements would predict even greater decrements following the introduction of such stimuli (Jeffrey & Cohen, 1971).

The differential-looking and habituation–dishabituation techniques may be modified in a number of ways. For example, numerous independent variables may be manipulated, and many dependent variables may be assessed. To accommodate what we believe to be the most important variations, we have classified methods according to familiarization procedure (fixed vs. infant-controlled familiarization trials) and test procedure (simultaneous vs. successive presentations of familiar and novel stimuli). This two-way classification yields four basic paradigms for studying infant recognition memory. This classification provides a category for most existing methods; however, its major significance is that it defines dimensions that may contribute to differences in assessments of infant memory.

1. Familiarization: Fixed or Infant-Controlled Procedures

In both adults and children recognition accuracy improves when stimuli are presented for longer durations (e.g., Haith, Morrison, & Sheingold, 1970). Thus, it seems likely that infants' retention may also depend upon the amount of time stimuli are presented. In most studies of recognition memory, infants are provided with a fixed number of familiarization trials. It might be thought that the number, or length, of trials could be varied to determine the critical duration required for encoding at a particular age. This is probably not possible, however, since an experimenter is usually not able to control the infant's attention to the stimuli. Some investigators have used performance criteria of familiarization in order to accommodate individual differences in behavioral states, motivation, attention, etc. (see Clifton & Nelson, 1976). With such performance measures, the familiarization period continues until the infant's response to the stimulus decreases either to a specified absolute level or by a specified proportion relative to initial trials. With both fixed and infant-controlled familiarization procedures, immediate recognition, delayed recognition, and interference may be assessed in the same manner. Cohen (1972, 1975), and Horowitz and her colleagues (Horowitz, 1974; Horowitz, Paden, Bhana, & Self, 1972), have used performance measures of familiarization in which onset, length, and/or number of trials are controlled by the infant. In a typical study a trial began concurrently with the infant's fixation, rather than at an arbitrary point designated by the experimenter, and terminated when the infant terminated fixation. Thus, this procedure has been aptly named "infant control" of familiarization (Horowitz *et al.*, 1972b). Friedman (1972a; Friedman, Carpenter, & Nagy, 1970) and Siqueland (1969; Milewski & Siqueland, 1975) used infant-controlled procedures, but only the number, not the length, of trials was controlled by the infant.

On the surface it may appear that the difference between fixed and infant-controlled familiarization periods is subtle; however, results obtained with these two techniques differ substantially and thereby justify the distinction. For example, in infant-controlled studies in which high-amplitude sucking has been measured, developmental differences in infants' discrimination between familiar and novel stimuli have not been observed (Milewski & Siqueland, 1975; Werner & Siqueland, 1978). Such developmental stability is generally found when performance criteria for familiarization are used. Hunter and Ames (1975) reported that infants as young as 5 weeks old are responsive to stimulus novelty, and Friedman (1972a) demonstrated this effect in newborns. Yet it would be incorrect to conclude that age differences are never found in infants' memory. Cohen (e.g., Wetherford & Cohen, 1973; see Cohen & Gelber, 1975) consistently has failed to demonstrate retention in infants under about 2 months of age. Although this discrepancy has not yet been definitely resolved, we believe it may be related to whether or not infant-controlled procedures are utilized.

Infant-controlled familiarization procedures have also been used in studies which have provided some of the strongest evidence of interference effects in preverbal infants' memory (Stinson, 1971). This fact may reflect the greater control over encoding that is possible with infant-controlled familiarization techniques. Another important feature of infant-controlled familiarization procedures may be lower subject attrition compared with fixed-trial familiarization procedures. For example, Horowitz *et al.* (1972b) found that subject attrition decreased from 40% to 28% when infant-controlled procedures were incorporated into her studies, and Cohen (1975) reported that when he changed from fixed to infant-controlled familiarization periods subject attrition went from 40% to 25%. However, in other infant-controlled studies, subject attrition was still high. Milewski and Siqueland (1975) reported overall subject losses of about 52%, and for

Friedman (1972a) and DeLoache (1976) subject attrition was 56% and 49%, respectively.

2. *Novelty Tests: Simultaneous or Successive Comparisons*

Fagan (1970) has introduced a modification of the Fantz-type simultaneous differential-looking procedure to study immediate and delayed recognition memory. Following familiarization (presentation of identical stimuli on left and right sides), the familiar stimulus and a novel one are presented simultaneously. Differential fixation to the novel stimulus, relative to the familiar one, is taken as evidence of retention of the familiar one. Most other investigators have tested familiar and novel stimuli successively and have inferred retention from differential responsiveness to each. Successive testing may be done either by alternately presenting familiar and novel stimuli to the same infant (e.g., Caron & Caron, 1968; Wetherford & Cohen, 1973) or by comparing two groups, one receiving only a novel stimulus, the other receiving only a familiar one (e.g., Friedman, 1972a; Siqueland, 1969). As will be shown below, results obtained with successive versus simultaneous comparisons often differ considerably (also see Stinson, 1971).

Simultaneous comparisons of response to familiar and novel stimuli have often indicated retention even after relatively brief familiarization periods. For example, Fagan (1974) found significant discrimination of novel multidimensional stimuli in 5- to 6-month-old infants who were provided with only one 5-second familiarization period. Since habituation of comparable stimuli usually takes several minutes, Fagan's result suggests that some storage of information occurs well before habituation occurs. It appears that even after brief familiarization periods, retention will be evidenced if the infant is simultaneously presented familiar and novel stimuli. Simultaneous presentation procedures allow direct comparisons of familiar and novel items and are therefore probably more sensitive in detecting memory than are successive presentation procedures. That is, even if there is partial forgetting, the new stimulus will appear novel along some dimensions. Greater differential fixation would therefore be expected and retention concluded. Only if there is complete forgetting would one expect equal attention to simultaneously presented familiar and novel stimuli. In contrast when an incompletely remembered stimulus is tested with successive procedures, a change in response would be predicted and forgetting concluded. The two test methods therefore appear to be differentially sensitive to retention and forgetting. Simultaneous presentation procedures are probably more sensitive than successive procedures to retention but correspondingly less sensitive to forgetting. Evidence consistent with this view has been reported by Caron, Caron, Minichiello, Weiss, and Friedman (1977). After relatively brief familiarization periods, 14- and 20-week-old infants showed significant discrimination with simultaneous, but not successive, presentations of familiar and novel stimuli.

B. DEPENDENT MEASURES

Several different dependent measures have been used to study infant recognition memory. For example, total length of visual fixation is by far the most commonly used measure (e.g., Caron & Caron, 1968, 1969; Fantz, 1964; Horowitz, 1974; Lewis, 1967; Lewis, Goldberg, & Campbell, 1969; McGurk, 1970), but investigators have also examined length of first fixation (e.g., Kagan, Henker, Hen-Tov, Levine, & Lewis, 1966; Lewis, Kagan, & Kalafat, 1966), vocalizations and smiling (e.g., Kagan *et al.,* 1966), high-amplitude nonnutritive sucking (e.g., Siqueland, 1969), and cardiac deceleration (e.g., McCall & Kagan, 1967; McCall & Melson, 1969). Unfortunately, the data from different measures, even when obtained simultaneously, are not always consistent. For example, in several studies cardiac deceleration has been found to be more sensitive in assessing retention than is visual fixation (McCall & Kagan, 1967; Meyers & Cantor, 1967; McCall & Melson, 1969), while in another study no differences between the two measures were observed (McCall & Melson, 1970). The meaning of these different measures thus needs to be more extensively investigated. Additional research on the various measures of visual attention is also needed. For example, Judish (1969) has suggested that there are fundamental problems in interpreting visual fixation data because there are many components of fixation. Furthermore, there is apparently a lack of consistency among them. Judish videotaped 8- and 12-week-old infants' fixations during presentation of paired stimuli (faces, stripes, bull's eyes, and random dot patterns) using infrared corneal reflection photography. He found a lack of consistency among total binocular fixation time, proportion of binocular fixation time, total fixation time for each eye, length of first fixation for each eye, direction of first fixation by each eye, and number of fixations by each eye. These findings raise additional questions concerning interstudy comparisons. For example, some investigators assume fixation by a single eye is representative of binocular fixation and therefore a valid measure of overall visual attention. However, Judish reported that infants fixated binocularly only 26.5% of the time, compared to 40.6% and 44.2% monocular fixation by the left and right eyes, respectively. It is still unclear which fixation measure best represents infants' visual recognition. Yet it seems that dependent measures used in early studies have been chosen arbitrarily, with total fixation time most often employed.

The results of a series of reports by Cohen (1972, 1973, 1975) suggest that first fixation duration, mean fixation duration, number of fixations, and latency to first fixation may represent distinct attentional processes. Cohen (1972) suggested that infant looking involves two distinct attentional processes: an attention-getting process based on a "peripheral perceiver" that is primarily sensitive to movement, brightness, distance, and size of stimuli; and an attention-holding process that involves active information processing primarily governed by texture, contour, orientation, and pattern novelty. This dichotomy is similar to Neisser's (1966) model of recognition, which assumes a hierarchically arranged attentional–cognitive system. Neisser (1966) has proposed that preattentive processes provide a first level of feature analysis that is global and holistic and only can shift attention. This process is comparable to what William James (1890) referred to as "passive immediately sensorial attention." Neisser has argued that once preattentive processes have orientated the organism, focal attention takes over to bring in specific sequentially organized information. Cohen (1972) called this process attention holding. The basis for Cohen's distinction was an experiment (Cohen, 1972) in which 4-month-old infants were familiarized with red and white checkerboards varying in check number and size. Cohen used a performance criterion of familiarization. Prior to each trial, a light blinked on either the left or the right side of the testing chamber. When the infant fixated on the blinking light, an observer depressed a switch which terminated the light and activated a slide projector on the opposite side of the panel to present the familiarization stimulus, a checkerboard pattern. When the infant stopped fixating the familiarization stimulus, the trial was terminated; the stimulus went off, and a blinking

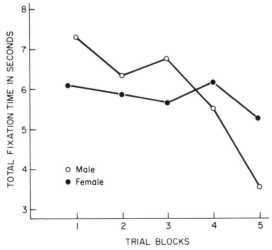

Fig. 2. Total fixation time during the habituation phase of Pancrantz and Cohen's (1970) study. Trial blocks are the average of two trials. (Reprinted with permission.)

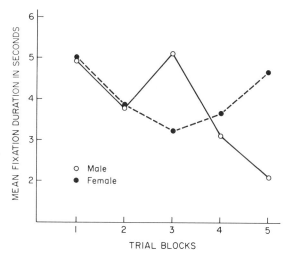

Fig. 3. *Mean fixation duration plotted as a function of trial blocks. (Data from Pancrantz and Cohen, 1970, as plotted by Cohen, 1973.) (Reprinted with permission.)*

light appeared until the infant fixated it and initiated another trial. Latency in turning to the checkerboard pattern was primarily related to check size, whereas duration of fixation was primarily a function of check number. These findings thus substantiate Judish's (1970) suggestion that different measures of visual fixation may be dissociated and also support Cohen's thesis that attention getting (turning to the stimulus) and attention holding (stimulus fixation) can be treated as separate processes.

To further support the notion of duality of attentional processes, Cohen (1973) reanalyzed data from a previous habituation study (Pancrantz & Cohen, 1970). The original dependent variable was total fixation time. As can be seen in Fig. 2, which shows total fixation time during the familiarization phase of Pancrantz and Cohen's (1970) study, there was evidence of habituation in males but not in females. When the data were replotted in terms of mean duration of fixation, as is shown in Fig. 3, there was again evidence of habituation in males, but not in females. However, when the data were plotted in still another way, mean number of fixations, there was no evidence of habituation in males or females (see Fig. 4). The fact that habituation is reflected only in fixation duration (attention holding), but not in number of fixations or in latency of turning toward patterns (attention getting), provides further evidence of the inconsistency between various fixation measures and of the duality of infant attentional processes.

Cohen (1973) has provided a tentative model to illustrate his interpretation of these data. This model is shown in the flow diagram in Fig. 5. It can be seen that environmental events that are of low intensity or duration do

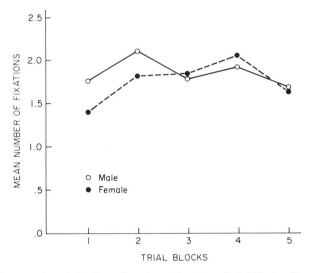

Fig. 4. Mean number of fixations plotted as a function of trial blocks. (Data from Pancrantz and Cohen, 1970, as plotted by Cohen, 1973.) (Reprinted with permission.)

not activate the peripheral perceiver (attention getting); however, if an environmental event is of high intensity or duration, the peripheral processor is activated and leads to an orienting response and fixation. Fixation then accomplishes two things. First, at the level of attention holding, information is processed on the basis of components such as color and form. Then, information is transmitted to memory, and to a comparator, where it is analyzed with respect to information already in memory. If incoming information matches information in memory, the process recycles, and presumably only short fixations occur. However, if the information is different from that already in memory, fixation continues until the new information can be represented in memory.

Although Cohen does not present physiological data, it is worth noting that his distinction between attention getting and attention holding is related, at least by analogy, to electrophysiological classifications of single cells in the visual system. At a very general level, attention getting and attention holding may be thought of in terms of the X and Y channels, respectively, which were first identified in cat retinal ganglion cells (Enroth-Cugell & Robson, 1966). X-Cells are characterized by receptive field tuning to high spatial frequencies, sustained firing for the duration of stimulus presentation, and relatively slow neural conduction velocities. Y-Cells, in contrast, conduct information rapidly, summate visual responses non-linearly, are tuned to low spatial frequencies, and fire transiently when visual stimuli are introduced or removed. X-Cells are found primarily in the central retina and Y-cells in the periphery (Fukuda & Stone, 1974).

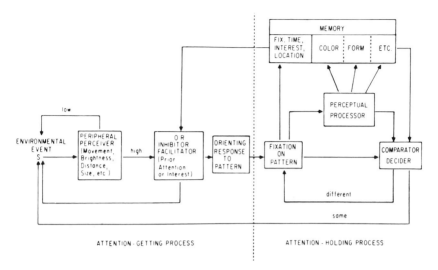

Fig. 5. Cohen's (1973) model of infant visual attention. (Reprinted with permission.)

These functional properties are maintained in separate channels from the retina to the superior colliculus and cortex (Hoffmann, 1973; Ikeda & Wright, 1975). The evolution of pattern processing mechanisms seems to be resident in the X channel, perhaps as in attention holding. The Y system, however, seems to be well suited for processing of movement and brightness information, such as that involved in attention getting. Thus, the physiological distinctions between the X and Y channels parallel the behavioral distinctions between attention holding and attention getting.

In summary, Cohen's (1973) model has some heuristic appeal and a modicum of supporting evidence (see also, Cohen, DeLoache, & Rissman, 1975); however, an adequate evaluation will have to await further experimentation. One optimistic note is that the apparent discrepancy in results obtained by various investigators may be reconcilable. The lack of agreement among different fixation measures is probably not random but related to different attentional processes. Thus, it is likely that investigators who have chosen different dependent measures have been tapping different processes.

IV. Experimental Findings

A. RETENTION CAPACITY

Adult humans are capable of retaining a great deal of information about pictures, even after very brief exposures. For example, Shepard (1967) successively presented 612 pictures to adults, for a few seconds each, and assessed memory with forced-choice recognition tests. He reported very accurate immediate performance (98%) and only slight decrements after 1 week (92%). In a similar experiment, Standing, Conezio, and Haber (1970) presented 2560 pictures over a 4-day period. Recognition accuracy exceeded 90%, and there was no significant difference in recognition of pictures presented on the first, compared to the fourth, day. Shaffer and Shiffrin (1972) presented 120 pictures, varying exposure duration (0.2 to 4 seconds) and time between items (1 to 4 seconds). They also found high levels of performance. Moreover, accuracy increased with exposure duration but was not affected by time between stimulus presentations. Potter and Levy (1969) used similar procedures, but their 128 pictures were presented at much faster rates, varying from 125 msec to 2 seconds. Accuracy increased monotonically from 16% at 125 msec to 93% at 2000 msec. Potter (1975) subsequently reported that median exposure duration for identification is about 125 msec, whereas for retention it is more than 300 msec. Thus, adults appear to be able to retain a great deal of information about pictures with high levels of accuracy, even after very brief stimulus presentations.

Perhaps more surprising than the extremely accurate retention observed in adults is the very proficient memory observed in young childen. For example, Kagan (1970) reported that a 4-year-old correctly recognized a large proportion of pictures taken from magazines he had previously seen. Subsequently Brown and Scott (1971) suggested that 3- to 5-year-olds' recognition performance approximates that of adults. They presented children 100 pictures and found that the probability of correct immediate recognition, even when 50 pictures intervened between presentation and test, was .98. Accuracy decreased with length of retention interval (1, 2, 7, or 28 days), but if children had seen the pictures twice, accuracy was .98 after 1 day and declined to .78 after 28 days. Von Wright (1973) examined recognition of 5-year-olds. He showed them 16 drawings of common objects for 3 seconds each and tested recognition either immediately or after 2 weeks. Recognition was 99% accurate for children tested immediately, and 85% correct for those tested after 2 weeks. Entwisle and Huggins (1973) examined recognition of first graders. They showed the children 40 colored slides of landscapes or cityscapes at a 10-second presentation rate. Two and one-half hours later their subjects' recognition accuracy averaged 86%, and after 1 week it was 80%. Brown and Campione (1972) also examined recognition in young children. They showed preschoolers complex pictures and then tested recognition with one of three types of test stimuli: new, old–identical, and old–similar. The old–similar items were pictures containing a character previously seen (therefore old) but shown in a new position. Test results showed that the children could discriminate identical and similar recurrences of a central character, even for a period of up to 7 days. They therefore concluded that the children initially stored considerable detail about the pictures and retained it for extended time intervals.

While each of these studies demonstrates rather remarkable recognition performance in young children, such proficient memory is not always observed in subjects of these ages. Moreover, these studies did not include multiple age groups. Thus, they could not be used to answer adequately the question of whether memory improves with age. Of course, many investigators have compared the memory performances of different age groups. In several of these studies no developmental differences were observed. For example, Nelson (1971) tested first, fourth, and seventh graders on a picture recognition task. He found equivalent immediate and delayed (2 weeks) retention over this 7- to 13-year age span. Brown (1973) tested 7-, 8-, 10-, and 18-year-olds on a recency judgment task. She also found no developmental trend in level of accuracy, or in pattern of errors. Yet these studies are the exception rather than the rule. In most developmental studies of memory, age differences are observed (see Flavell, 1977; Kail & Hagan, 1977; Ornstein, 1978). Still, memory performance probably reflects more than merely memory capacity. For example, familiarity with the stimuli, as well as knowledge of and skill at control processing, have been shown to affect memory performance.

A central question for understanding memory development is thus how each of these three components, (1) capacity, (2) knowledge, and (3) strategies, contributes to age differences. After reviewing experiments from a wide variety of approaches, Belmont and Butterfield (1969) concluded that "none of the studies gave any but highly questionable evidence that children mature in retention ability" (pp. 52–53). They argued that improved short-term memory, associated with increasing age and intelligence, is probably due to differences in acquisition or retrieval strategies but not to retention per se. For example, Belmont (1967) compared forgetting curves of retarded and normal subjects matched on mental or chronological age. Using a delayed brightness comparison task, which presumably minimized encoding and response requirements, he found no significant group differences in forgetting curves. Thus, once acquisition was equated, retention of retardates appeared comparable to normals. Brown (1975) reached a similar point of view in her more recent analysis of memory development. She proposed a taxonomy in which memory tasks could be classified in terms of whether or not they involved strategies and/or semantic knowledge and predicted that developmental differences would be minimal when strategies and mediating knowledge were not necessary or helpful. Similarly, in Chi's (1976) review of children's short-term memory (STM) she suggested that "increases in performance with age (1) need not imply similar increases in capacity of STM, (2) can be explained in terms of developmental changes in use of control processes, and (3) can also be accounted for by differences in complexity of the knowledge base" (p. 560).

Even recent evidence of age-related improvement in recognition performance (e.g., Dirks & Neisser, 1977; Fajnstztejn-Pollack, 1973; Hoffman & Dick, 1976; Mandler & Day, 1975; Mandler & Stein, 1974; Nelson & Kosslyn, 1976; Newcombe, Rogoff, & Kagan, 1977; Perlmutter & Myers, 1974, 1976a; Rogoff, Newcombe, & Kagan, 1974) is not counter to a "constant retention capacity" argument. For example, in their discussion of recognition memory, Perlmutter and Lange (1978) point out that age-related increases in accrued world knowledge, as well as developmental improvement in information-pickup skills (e.g., scanning, discrimination, and encoding) would lead to age-related improvement in recognition performance. Moreover, age-related changes in monitoring and response factors could contribute to developmental differences in older children's recognition performance, although this is probably not a factor in infants' recognition performance (see Perlmutter, in press). That is, in studies with older children, procedures have been used that involve considerably more response demands than those used with infants; in only two studies with verbal children have procedures comparable to those used with infants been employed (Daehler & Bukatko, 1977; Faulkender, Wright, & Waldron, 1974). While the infant studies (as well as the studies by Daehler and Bukatko and by Faulkender *et al.*) in which visual attention measures of recognition have been used do attest to the fact that subjects remember information, they do not demonstrate whether subjects are cognizant of that memory. The added demand of monitoring memory in recognition tests used with older children and adults could certainly contribute to age-related improvements in recognition performance.

It is evident, then, that much recent research on memory development suggests that the growth of knowledge and strategy contributes to age change in performance. However, capacity differences have not been well substantiated. Since this view is based largely on work with children over 5 years of age, it is still unclear whether there are age differences in preverbal infants' memory performance.

Of course, the question reserved for infancy researchers is: What is the youngest age at which humans demonstrate memory? Friedman and his colleagues have found decreased visual fixation to repeated trials in which checkerboard patterns were presented to newborns. While significant response decrements during familiarization were obtained in earlier studies (Friedman & Carpenter, 1971; Friedman, Nagy, & Carpenter, 1970), the more recent inclusion of novelty test procedures (Friedman, 1972a, 1972b; Friedman, Bruno, & Vietze, 1974) was what really substantiated the conclusion that infants had memory capacity from birth. Moreover, Werner and

Siqueland (1978) have extended this observation by demonstrating discrimination between familiar and novel stimuli in preterm newborns.

Yet reviews of research using the habituation and differential-looking techniques (Bond, 1972; Cohen & Gelber, 1975; Fantz *et al.,* 1975; Jeffrey & Cohen, 1971) mention many failures to demonstrate differential responsiveness to novel and familiar visual stimuli with infants less than 2 months of age. We believe that this discrepancy lies in the criteria used for familiarization. That is, when a fixed-familiarization period is used developmental differences may be observed, but not when infant-controlled familiarization methods are used. Indeed, studies using infant-controlled familiarization consistently fail to demonstrate developmental differences in the capacity for visual recognition. For example, in addition to the newborn data discussed, Siqueland (1969) demonstrated recovery of nonnutritive sucking with the introduction of novel color stimuli in infants as young as 3 weeks of age. Milewski and Siqueland (1975) found recognition memory of different color and/or form stimuli in 1-month-olds. Using visual attention as a dependent measure, Self (1974) also reported differential responsiveness to novel and familiar stimuli with infants as young as 5 weeks of age. Finally, the generalization that age differences are eliminated with infant-controlled familiarization methods also holds beyond 2 months, as has been demonstrated by McCall, Hogarty, Hamilton, and Vincent (1973). They failed to find developmental changes in recognition memory between 12 and 18 weeks of age when infants were presented color-pattern stimuli until reaching a performance criterion of familiarization. Thus, although infants of different ages may vary in rate of familiarization, when exposure to stimuli is varied to accommodate individual differences, recognition memory may be demonstrated from the first days of life.

It appears well documented, then, that age is not a relevant variable in the capacity to respond differentially to novel and familiar stimuli (Friedman, 1972a; Horowitz, 1974; Hunter & Ames, 1975; Milewski & Siqueland, 1975; Werner & Siqueland, 1978). Failures to demonstrate such differential responding in infants may be due to the stimuli used, which could have been too "complex" for young infants to encode, and/or to the use of fixed-trial familiarization procedures. A recent study with 5- to 6-week-olds (Hunter & Ames, 1975) supports this view. Hunter and Ames used infant-controlled familiarization of 2 × 2 checkerboard stimuli and found that an average of 13.5 familiarization trials was adequate for immediate recognition. In a second part of the study, they used 8 × 8 checkerboard stimuli and two groups of subjects. Infants in Group 1 received 13 trials, an amount that was likely to produce memory of 2 × 2 checkerboards, whereas for Group 2, infant-controlled familiarization was used. Only subjects in Group 2 (that is, those who had individual differences in familiarization rate taken into account) showed significant differential response to novel stimuli. Thus, Hunter and Ames (1975) demonstrated the importance of using infant-controlled familiarization procedures. It seems that when such methods are used, and the stimuli do not exceed infants' sensory ability to encode, there are no age differences in capacity for retention.

In summary, immediate recognition memory can be demonstrated at early ages; however, such demonstrations are constrained in that special considerations must be given to insure adequate familiarization. When the goal is to demonstrate retention capacity, it can be accomplished with simple stimuli and infant-controlled familiarization periods. When fixed-trial procedures are used, age differences emerge. It may be inferred, then, that age differences are related to encoding, not to retention capacity.

B. FAMILIARIZATION TIME

The child and adult memory literature indicates that the amount of familiarization is related to recognition. For example, Haith *et al.* (1970) presented outlined geometric forms to preschool and college students at exposure durations of 5, 10, 20, 30, and 40 msec. Performance of both age groups improved with increased exposure. Moreover, when accuracy was plotted as a function of exposure duration, the shape of the curve for 5-year-olds approximated that for adults; however, 5-year-olds reached maximum performance levels at exposure durations that were 5–10 msec longer than those for adults. Potter and Levy (1969) manipulated exposure durations for adults from 125 msec to 2 seconds and found recognition accuracy correspondingly varied from 15% to 90%. They suggested that the improvement in retention with increased familiarization time was related to the number of visual fixations. Indeed, Loftus (1972) has since shown that recognition accuracy is a positive function of fixation number and that when pictures are viewed for fixed amounts of time, memory is a function of number of fixations. Whether or not a similar relation holds for infants is unknown; however, limitations in their sensory capacities, and difficulties in motivating them to attend to stimuli, would lead one to predict the need for longer familiarization times. Furthermore, since there is no way to guarantee that infants will fixate on the "appropriate features" of a stimulus, determining the critical duration for encoding is difficult.

One way to conceptualize infant stimulus encoding is in terms of schema construction. Sokolov (1960, 1963) has provided a schema model of habituation that is useful for interpreting infant recognition memory data.

He suggests that response decrements during familiarization correspond to construction of cortical models, or engrams, of the stimuli. Incoming information that matches the neuronal model currently in operation is edited and filtered out, causing inhibition of the reticular activating system and response decrement. In contrast, incoming information that is novel (i.e., that does not match the neuronal model) stimulates the reticular activating system through corticoreticular connections. This produces an orienting response that Sokolov (1963) describes as "a system of reactions promoting directly, (cortical rhythm, ERG) or indirectly, (cerebral blood supply) the most favourable conditions for stimulus reception" (p. 285). Thus, during familiarization or habituation the reticular activating system is inhibited, but during novel stimulus presentations it is activated by discrepancies between incoming sensory information and the schema of the familiar stimulus. Although Sokolov's neuronal model is considered here in relation to memory, it is also more generally related to conditioning and perceptual learning.

Schema models make rather straightforward predictions relevant to infant memory. These predictions are that (1) more complex stimuli are associated with more complex schemata, and therefore require longer encoding times; and (2) younger infants, with less efficient encoding abilities, require longer periods of familiarization to form schema. These predictions are considered in this section and the next. A corollary, that familiarization time required for encoding is related to individual and group differences, is considered in later sections.

Developmental changes in some aspects of recognition memory are well documented. Our interpretation is that these changes are related to encoding. Wetherford and Cohen (1973), in agreement with Fantz (1964), reported habituation of visual fixation among 10- and 12-week-olds, but not among 6- to 8-week-olds, to geometric forms presented for a fixed number of trials. The substrate for this sudden change in habituation at 2 months of age is unknown, but it has been consistently observed with fixed-trial familiarization procedures. It has been suggested that the nature of this developmental change is maturational, not experiential. Fagan, Fantz, and Miranda (1971; Fantz *et al.*, 1975) tested preterm and full-term infants' differential response to simultaneously presented familiar and novel stimuli following 100 seconds of familiarization to achromatic forms. The tests were repeated at five intervals between 6 and 15 weeks postnatal age. The full-term infants evidenced reliable retention beginning at 11 weeks postnatal age, while the preterm infants did not show significant retention until about 1 month later. However, when the data were plotted as a function of conceptional age (i.e., gestational age plus postnatal age) there were no differences between the two groups. Thus, it appears that a change in processing takes place at about 51 weeks conceptional age, independently of postnatal visual experience. In another study with preterm and full-term infants, Fantz and Fagan (1975) reported consistent developmental changes in infants' differential looking at black and white checkerboards (varying size and number of checks). Although this study did not include tests of memory, it is relevant to the issue of familiarization and encoding. They found that both groups declined in total fixation from about 45 to 60 weeks conceptional age. Because the preterm infants had about 5 weeks more of visual experience, the results suggest that the age change in visual responsiveness may be maturational. Furthermore, these changes appear to continue through later postnatal development. Experiments by Lewis, using faces (Lewis, 1969) or a blinking light (Lewis, 1971; Lewis *et al.*, 1969), showed that the magnitude of response decrement during familiarization increased from 3 to 44 months of age. Thus, it appears that when encoding is constrained by a fixed number of trials, the ability to become adequately familiarized for recognition is age dependent.

Of course, not all age changes observed in fixed-familiarization trial experiments occur at 51 weeks conceptional age. Generalizations are complicated by length of familiarization and type of stimuli. For example, experiments by Miranda and Fantz (1974), using brief fixed-familiarization periods followed by simultaneous presentations of familiar and novel stimuli, suggest a developmental hierarchy of recognition memory for the following sets of stimuli: (1) multidimensional achromatic patterns, (2) face photographs, and (3) patterns varying only in element arrangement. This hierarchy can be recreated at a single age, simply by manipulating familiarization time. This fact suggests that the developmental progression is related to the encoding stage of memory, not to retention capacity. Fagan (1974) determined the familiarization time required for 5- to 6-month-old infants' recognition of four types of achromatic stimuli: (1) stimuli differing in form and amount of contour, (2) stimuli differing only in element arrangement, (3) photographs of faces, and (4) line drawings of faces. Familiarization time required for recognition systematically increased from stimulus types 1 to 4. Comparable differential looking for novel, relative to simultaneously presented familiar, stimuli was obtained with only 3.4 seconds of fixation to multidimensional stimuli, but with 17.1 seconds to stimuli that varied in arrangement of pattern elements. Moreover, comparable recognition of photographs required 22.4 seconds of visual attention, but 35 seconds were still inadequate for recognition of line drawings. These results indicate that the familiarization time required for recognition is affected by qualitative differences in stimulus information. Section IV, C reviews evidence showing that encoding time required for retention may also vary with quantitative variations within classes of stimulus information.

In addition to amount of decrement in responsiveness occurring within a fixed-familiarization period, rate of decrement has also been related to age. That is, within a given age, when subjects are grouped in terms of fast and slow habituators, it has been found that only fast habituators show significant differential responding to novel stimulus presentation (McCall & Kagan, 1970; McCall & Melson, 1969). This finding has prompted the suggestion that immediate memory is an important variable for assessing early cognitive development (Lewis, 1967; McCall, 1971). Without addressing the implications of this result, we feel that the memory components involved should be clarified. As with age differences, it appears that individual subject differences are related to encoding and not to retention capacity. Since fixed-trial procedures were used in these studies, it could not be determined whether slow habituators would have shown the same retention capacity as fast habituators, had the slow habituators been adequately familiarized. Indeed, these two groups do not appear to differ in retention capacity. When infant-controlled familiarization procedures were used (DeLoache, 1976; McCall *et al.,* 1973), no differences in the magnitude of response to novelty were observed between fast and slow habituators.

Taken together, these data suggest that the mechanisms mediating differences in infants' recognition memory are not related to retention capacity but to the ability to process and encode stimuli. If the findings discussed here are thought of as "main effects of age" on familiarization, the findings reviewed in Section IV, C, 1 may be considered "age × stimulus interactions." In that section we consider studies that demonstrate effects of stimulus complexity on infants' processing of information and that show further developmental trends in ability to encode information. Then we shall review memory studies that have manipulated stimuli on pattern and/or color dimensions and that suggest that stimulus variables are important determinants of familiarization.

C. STIMULUS DIMENSIONS

1. Complexity

Despite several attempts to develop a metric of form perception (e.g., Attneave & Arnoult, 1956; Corcoran, 1971; Gibson, 1961, 1966), the relevant dimensions of form are still unknown. As noted by Michels and Zusne (1965), form is a second-order variable with an unknown, but probably large, number of dimensions. One method of specifying form is in terms of bits of information; however, the value of this approach is limited because information in patterns does not always correlate with other physical parameters and does not predict adult recognition (see Corcoran, 1971).

An important dimension of form perception which is related to the pattern preferences of children and adults is "complexity" (Munsinger, Kessen, & Kessen, 1964). Usually complexity is defined operationally along one or two dimensions, but when adults are asked to rate random configurations for complexity, a number of dimensions seem to be utilized. The most important parameters are probably number of angles, symmetry, and contour (Attneave, 1957). A number of studies have examined the relations between complexity and infants' differential attention. Hershenson, Munsinger, and Kessen (1965) presented newborns "random" shapes, varying in number of angles. They found an inverted U-shaped function between visual attention and number of turns; however, the reliability of the inverted U was tentative, since only two of the three points differed by a statistically significant margin. In a replication, Munsinger and Weir (1967) studied 9- and 41-month-old infants' visual attention to stimuli with 5, 10, 20, and 40 turns. They found attention to be a monotonic function of increasing stimulus complexity. While these infants attended most to the complex stimuli, Hershenson (1964) found that newborns attended least to the complex stimuli. Since Hershenson (1964) defined complexity differently (number of checks in a checkerboard) than Munsinger and Weir (number of turns), the two studies cannot be directly compared. However, the results do suggest that there may be developmental changes in attention to differentially complex stimuli. A subsequent series of studies has begun to clarify the relation between age and attention to stimuli in which complexity is defined in terms of number of checks in a checkerboard pattern (Brennan, Ames, & Moore, 1966; Greenberg, 1971; Greenberg & Weizmann, 1971; Greenberg & O'Donnell, 1972). The results of these studies suggest that when visual attention is plotted as a function of number of checks in a checkerboard pattern (complexity), the function is best described as an inverted U. With increasing age, the function shifts along the axis of abscissae toward greater complexity. That is, with the exception of one study (Horowitz, Paden, Bhana, Aitchinson, & Self, 1972; however, see Greenberg & Blue, 1977), it has been found that as infants increase in age, they attend more to stimuli with more checks.

Karmel (1969; Karmel & Maisel, 1975) has offered an alternative explanation for these findings. He proposed that contour density, regardless of its spatial distribution, is the most important determinant of this age-related function. More specifically, Karmel has concluded that infants' visual attention is an inverted U-shaped function of the square root of contour density (specified with respect to visual angle), and that the function shifts toward greater contour density with age. One problem with this interpretation is that many of the studies considered by Karmel have confounded contour density with number of elements in the stimuli. When stimuli were equated in contour but differed in element number, or equated in element number but varied in contour density, it was found that both contour and number of pattern elements were important determinants of age changes in visual attention (Greenberg & Blue, 1975). Indeed, age changes in attention to differential complexity may be divided into at least two phases. At younger ages size seems to be of special importance, while at older ages number of elements is more important (Fantz & Fagan, 1975). Thus, the Fantz and Fagan results indicate that complexity may not be a necessary concept in describing infant visual attention; rather, simple objective dimensions suffice. Whatever the underlying stimulus dimensions, these developmental changes are indicative of infants' improving ability to process information and, we believe, are the basis for age changes in time required for familiarization.

Furthermore, there is evidence that age changes in familiarization (encoding) are dependent upon level of stimulus complexity. For example, Ames (1966) reported that habituation by $5\frac{1}{2}$- and 11-week-old infants was similar for a 2×2 checkerboard, but only the older group habituated to an 8×8 checkerboard. Martin (1975) defined complexity in terms of number of turns in colored forms and found that infants at 2, $3\frac{1}{2}$, and 5 months all looked longer at complex, relative to simple, stimuli. Amount of response decrement over familiarization trials was a function of age and inversely related to stimulus complexity.

Using a single age group, $3\frac{1}{2}$-month-olds, Caron and Caron (1968, 1969) have reported that response decrements during habituation are linear functions of number of checks (response decrement for $2 \times 2 > 12 \times 12 > 24 \times 24$). A comparable finding was obtained with infants of the same age by Greenberg, O'Donnell, and Crawford (1973), and with 17-week-old infants by Cohen *et al.* (1975). Likewise, Hunter and Ames (1975) familiarized 5- to 6-week-old infants for 13 trials with either a 2×2 or an 8×8 checkerboard, but only the 2×2 checkerboard was remembered when assessed by successive comparisons of visual responsiveness to familiar and novel stimuli. It appears that the 8×8 stimulus requires more encoding time. Indeed, when an additional group of infants of the same age was tested following infant-controlled familiarization, the 8×8 stimulus was recognized, although twice as much familiarization time was needed for the 8×8 (mean of 52 trials) as for the 2×2 checkerboard (mean of 26 trials). Thus, the rate at which infants encode information appears to be a function of both stimulus complexity and age. Over and above the fact that infants can encode more rapidly with age, stimulus variables influence rate of encoding at each age. These data also support two notions germane to the present viewpoint: (1) Schema models, suggesting that encoding time is a function of stimulus complexity, accurately predict infant visual recognition memory data; and (2) developmental differences in infant visual recognition memory may be primarily a matter of encoding or familiarization, not of retention. Additional data are needed to clearly rule out retention effects, although the data available so far support this contention.

If we are correct, the infant memory literature is consistent with some other developmental data which indicate a lack of age difference in retention when learning is controlled. For example, a study by Hulicka and Weiss (1965) is illustrative of studies on memory aging that have found that age differences in retention are eliminated when initial learning is equated (e.g., Moenster, 1972; Wimer & Wigdor, 1958). These investigators had younger and older adults learn paired associates under three conditions: equal number of training trials, learning to criterion, and overlearning. Older subjects learned less with equal exposures and required more trials to criterion; however, once they had learned the material, they retained it as well as younger subjects. Perlmutter (1978) found a comparable effect when she examined recognition performance of 20- and 60-year-olds. For one list of stimuli the subjects were given intentional instructions to remember the items, and for another they were given instructions to generate associations. This latter condition presumably directed all subjects to encode stimuli in a similar manner. While there was a sizeable age difference in retention following intentional instructions, this was eliminated with associative instructions. It is interesting that when retention was tested with recall rather than with recognition procedures, age differences persisted in both encoding conditions. This is not too surprising, however, since uncontrolled age differences in retrieval processes would be expected to affect recall, but not recognition. Similar findings have been demonstrated with children. For example, Geis and Hall (1976) tested first, third, and fifth graders for free recall following semantic, acoustic, and orthographic orienting tasks. As would be predicted from a levels of processing view of memory (see Craik & Lockhart, 1972), they found that semantic encoding led to better retention than acoustic or orthographic encoding. Moreover, they observed no age differences. When orienting tasks directed encoding, retention of 7- to 11-year-olds was constant. In contrast, in a similar study with $2\frac{1}{2}$- to 5-year-olds, Perlmutter, Schork, and Lewis (1978) found that a semantic orienting task enhanced retention relative to a nonsemantic (perceptual) orienting task. However, they failed to find attenuation of age differences. Since their retention measures were free and cued recall, which require retrieval, their results are not counter to those with infants. That is, preschool children, particularly very young ones, undoubtedly suffer from inefficient retrieval skills, which preclude competent recall even if acquisition and retention are proficient. It is worth noting that most of these studies with older children and adults have attempted to answer the question: What constitutes efficient encoding? In contrast, research with infants has not yet addressed this issue.

2. Pattern and Color

In many early studies of immediate recognition in infants investigators have concentrated on form and pattern discrimination, rather than on color discrimination. However, Siqueland (1969) reported significant increases of high-amplitude sucking in response to novel color stimuli with infants 1 and 4 months of age. Using visual fixation as the dependent measure, Bornstein (1976) demonstrated memory for monochromatic lights with 4-month-old infants. Throughout the remainder of this review, *color discrimination* refers to discriminations based on either hue, saturation, or brightness, since no infant memory study has used stimuli in which only one of these variables clearly has been responsible for recognition (see Werner & Wooten, 1979).

One question of interest is whether information about colored forms is stored as a color–form compound or as separate color and form components. Milewski and Siqueland (1975) investigated this question with 1-month-olds. They used an infant-controlled familiarization procedure and successive comparisons of familiar and novel stimuli. The novel stimuli differed from the familiar in either color, form, or both. Recovery of responding to changes in only color, or in only form, would of course indicate retention of these dimensions. Moreover, additivity of color and form effects could provide a hint about how information is stored in memory. If color and form are stored in separate memory loci, then stimulus changes along both dimensions may result in greater response to novelty than changes in only one dimension. The assumption here is that two storage bins are being tapped. In contrast, additivity failure is ambiguous with respect to how information is stored. A hypothesis based upon storage of color and form as a compound would lead to the prediction of additivity failure. However, it is always possible that ceiling effects associated with particular dependent variables mask additivity effects. Milewski and Siqueland (1975) found significant recovery of nonnutritive sucking to each novelty condition; however, there was no suggestion that the novelty effect of color and form was additive. That is, changes in both color and form did not produce greater recovery of response than did change in only one dimension. These results thus suggest that 1-month-olds retain information about both color and form; however, it is still unclear whether this information is stored as a compound.

While additivity was not found in this study of nonnutritive sucking in 1-month-olds, the results of other studies measuring fixation time in older infants have indicated additivity of color–form novelty. In two independent experiments, in which fixed-familiarization periods and simultaneous presentations of familiar and novel stimuli were used, identical results were obtained. Saayman, Ames, and Moffett (1964) presented a stimulus to 3-month-olds for 4.5 minutes and tested for recovery of fixation to stimuli

that were novel with respect to color, form, or both. There was no significant differential attention to novel stimuli with a change in color or form
alone, but there was significant differential attention to novel stimuli with
changes in both color and form. As Saayman *et al.* note, one problem with
their experiment was that the infants were familiarized to stimuli for which
differential attention was exhibited in a pretest, thereby leaving open the
possibility that some of the results were related to regression toward the
mean. However, Welch (1974) reported essentially the same results with
stimuli that were fully counterbalanced to prevent confoundings of initial
differences in attention.

Cohen, Gelber, and Lazar (1971), using the habituation–dishabituation
paradigm, found additivity of color and form novelty. Four-month-olds
were familiarized to simple geometric color stimuli for 12 15-second trials.
Successive comparisons of fixation recovery were made for two test trials
with the same stimuli and for two test trials with each of three other
stimuli, varying in either color, form, or both. The results (shown in Fig. 6)
indicated significant habituation and recovery to changes in color or form.
Additionally, recovery to novel stimuli that changed in both color and
form was significantly greater than the other conditions. This result was
also obtained by Fagan (1977b) with infants ranging in age from $5\frac{1}{2}$ to $7\frac{1}{2}$
months. After a brief familiarization period (30–90 seconds), differential
fixation between simultaneously presented familiar and novel stimuli was
observed. There was singificantly greater fixation to novel stimuli that differed from the familiar in either color or form. However, fixation was even
greater for novel stimuli that differed in both color and form. These data
are consistent with a hypothesis of separate storage of color and form.

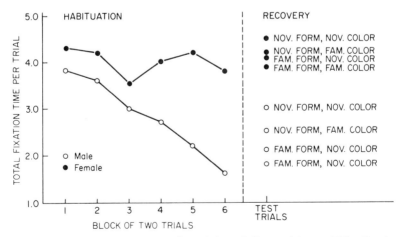

Fig. 6. Habituation and recovery data from Cohen, Gelber, and Lazar (1971). (Reprinted
with permission.)

COMPOUND VS COMPONENT EXPERIMENT

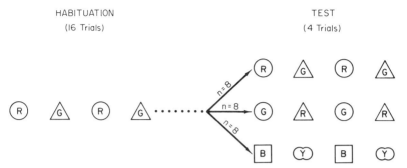

Fig. 7. Cohen's (1973) design of compound vs. component experiment. (Reprinted with permission.)

Still, the conclusion of separate storage of color and form is quite speculative. It is possible that additivity was due simply to summation of dishabituation to features within a single memory store, rather than within independent systems. Cohen (1973) has carried out another experiment which suggests that this is not the case. Figure 7 illustrates his experimental design. During 16 habituation trials infants were exposed to two compound stimuli. For the example shown in Fig. 7, the stimuli were a red circle alternated with a green triangle. Following familiarization, independent groups were tested with one of three sets of stimuli. One group was exposed to stimuli shown in the top row of the figure. This group was the no-change control included to rule out spontaneous increases in fixation. The stimuli illustrated in the second row were presented to another group. These stimuli consisted of the same color and form components as used in familiarization but they were arranged in new compounds. In contrast, the stimuli shown in the bottom row were novel whether viewed as components or as compounds. The rationale for Cohen's experiment was that if infants store information as separate color and form components, then response recovery to stimuli in the middle row should be about the same as to the no-change stimuli (top row); there was no change in the component elements of either stimulus. If infants store information as compounds, however, then recovery should be comparable for stimuli in the middle and bottom rows; the compounds in both cases were different from familiarized stimuli. The mean fixation time for the stimuli shown in the top, middle, and bottom rows was 1.9, 2.2, and 4.1 seconds, respectively. Statistically speaking, response to stimuli in the top row was not different from that for the middle row. However, response to stimuli in the bottom row was significantly different from that for the other two. Thus, these findings support the view that infants store color and form as independent components. Although these data are provocative and suggest additional studies, we must wait for more research before strongly concluding that color and form are stored in separate memory loci.

A comparable question, that of component versus compound encoding, has had a long history in research on children's discrimination learning (see Kendler & Kendler, 1975; Tighe & Tighe, 1972; Zeaman & House, 1974). Several investigators, most notably Tighe and Tighe (1972), have suggested that ontogenetic changes in discriminative shift behavior may be attributable to differential attention to, or perception of, stimulus components and compounds. Older subjects seem to respond on the basis of dimensional components, while younger subjects, and nonhumans, respond more to compounds. Of course, the demands of discrimination learning problems are likely to play an important role in determining how information is encoded. For example, since solutions are in fact based on shared components of successively presented compounds, it is not surprising that more mature subjects appear to encode in terms of components. Using a recognition task, which is more comparable to the procedures used with infants, Perlmutter (1977) found that 4-year-olds were similar to college students with respect to remembering stimuli as components and compounds. Subjects were shown pictorial stimuli that contained either one or two common objects and then tested for recognition with (1) single and compound stimuli that were identical to the original stimuli, (2) single items from the original compounds, (3) compounds of the original single items, and (4) single and compound stimuli that were completely new. They found that all subjects usually retained veridical memory representations; compound stimuli were responded to as if they were represented as integrated units, and single stimuli were responded to as if they were represented as individual units. Apparently young children and adults can both integrate information in compound stimuli and encode and retain individual objects as separate components.

D. DELAY

Research with young children indicates that immediate recognition memory is very good. Moreover, as with adults, recognition accuracy decreases as retention intervals increase, and recognition remains far above chance, even after long delays. Brown and Scott (1971) found 3- to 5-year-olds correctly recognized over three-quarters of 100 pictures, after 4 weeks. Brown and Campione (1972) found that when old and new test items were very similar, preschool children's recognition accuracy was 85% after 1 week. Entwistle and Huggins (1973) found that 7-year-olds correctly recognized 80% of 40 pictures shown a week before, and von Wright (1973) found that 5-year-olds correctly recognized 85% of 16 drawings of common objects shown 2 weeks before. Tests with preverbal infants, however, are more ambiguous with respect to length of accurate retention.

Fagan conducted a series of studies that provide evidence of long-term retention in preverbal infants. His first experiment (Fagan, 1970) involved a 2-minute familiarization period, followed by immediate and delayed recognition tests in which the familiar and a novel stimulus were presented simultaneously. Infants ranging from 3 to 6 months of age retained information about achromatic patterns for at least 2 hours. That is, there was greater than 50% fixation to the novel stimulus on both immediate and delayed tests. In addition, there were strong trends suggesting traces of retention after 24 hours. Fagan (1971) replicated this experiment with infants ranging from 15 to 33 weeks of age (median = 5 months), using three retention tasks. Each of the tasks involved three achromatic stimuli; infants were familiarized with one for 2 minutes and subsequently tested for differential fixation during two 10-second presentations of the familiar and novel stimuli. The three tasks were administered successively with 30 seconds between them. Novelty tests were conducted so that delays of 1, 4, or 7 minutes intervened between familiarization and testing. The results indicated that there was significant immediate and delayed retention. Moreover, even longer delayed recognition was shown in a later experiment using the same methods. Fagan (1973) found significant retention of multidimensional achromatic patterns and patterns differing only in element arrangement after delays of 24 and 48 hours. Thus, these experiments establish that preverbal infants can encode relatively brief perceptual experiences and maintain the information in storage for a matter of hours.

Perhaps more ethologically valid stimuli for infants are human faces. Fagan (1972) reported seven experiments demonstrating that 5- to 6-month-olds could discriminate two upright faces but not two faces rotated 180°, and that discrimination of upright facial stimuli was facilitated by increasing the similarity to real human faces. Moreover, the infants demonstrated immediate recognition memory of face photographs, as well as retention over delays of 3 hours to 2 weeks (Fagan, 1973). In contrast, when three-dimensional face masks, more akin to human faces, were used, recognition was found to decline over 3 hours. This suggests possible effects of interference.

Fagan used a fixed-familiarization period. It should be noted that with infant-controlled familiarization periods recognition of faces may be demonstrated even earlier in development (Young-Browne, Rosenfeld, & Horowitz, 1977). Also, Fagan's tests of retention involved simultaneous comparisons of fixation to familiar and novel stimuli. Loss of memory was inferred when there was a lack of differential fixation for the novel stimulus. With this paired comparison procedure, even if there was partial forgetting, a preference for novelty would be expected. In contrast, when a previously familiarized stimulus is tested alone, if there is partial forgetting, novelty of the forgotten features would be expected to lead to an increase in fixation. Thus, although Fagan demonstrated retention after 2 weeks, it is possible that it occurred in spite of some memory loss. If this is correct, successive comparisons of familiar and novel stimuli may show forgetting, even with shorter delays. However, such procedures would be correspondingly less sensitive in demonstrating partial retention. Indeed, besides Fagan's experiments, there is little evidence that infants remember visual stimuli for more than a few minutes.

One exception to the above generalization is an experiment reported by Martin (1975). In this study infants of 2, $3\frac{1}{2}$, and 5 months of age were familiarized for a fixed number of trials (totaling 4.5 minutes) and tested for response to novelty. These procedures were repeated on the following day. Fixation of familiarized stimuli was significantly lower on Day 2, relative to Day 1. Although the decrease was greater for older infants, it was reliable for each of the three age groups. Since this decreased responsiveness was found only for previously familiarized stimuli, and not for the novel stimuli, the effect could not be attributed to an overall change in visual responsiveness. Thus, these results suggest retention for 24 hours in infants as young as 2 months.

Yet most studies have shown retention for only a matter of seconds or minutes. Caron and Caron (1968, 1969) presented checkerboards to $3\frac{1}{2}$-month-old infants using a habituation procedure and, following exposure to three novel stimuli (presented for 20 seconds each), re-presented the familiarization stimulus. Since response to the familiar stimulus was at habituation level, it could be inferred that infants retained information during the 1-minute intervals. In a similar type of study with 6- and 12-month-olds, Schaffer and Parry (1969) showed significant recognition memory of three-dimensional objects after $1\frac{1}{2}$-minute delays. Although these two studies did not test for maximum retention time, several other studies using similar methods have reported maximum retention intervals, with 4-month-old infants, to be less than 1 minute (Pancrantz & Cohen, 1970; Stinson, 1970, 1971). Pancrantz and Cohen presented a familiarization stimulus to 4-month-olds for 10 15-second trials, and following intervals of either 15 seconds or 5 minutes they successively presented familiar and novel stimuli. They found significant retention after 15 seconds, but not after 5 minutes. Stinson (1971) used an infant-controlled familiarization procedure with nonnutritive sucking as the dependent measure. Retention tests were conducted with four delay intervals: 1, 15, 30, and 75

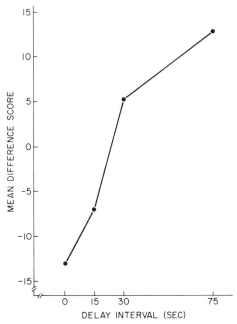

Fig. 8. Forgetting function for 4-month-old infants. Mean test segment difference score plotted for each of the four delay groups. (From Stinson, 1971.) (Reprinted with permission.)

seconds. Stinson's data are presented in Fig. 8, in the form of difference scores plotted as a function of delay (the mean response rate during the last 2 minutes of familiarization was subtracted from the mean response rate during the 5 minutes of the test phase). It can be seen that with increased delay intervals there was a corresponding increase in forgetting. Retention was reliable after 0- and 15-second delays, but not after 30- and 75-second delays. These data represent the first available forgetting function for preverbal infants.

Pancrantz and Cohen's and Stinson's studies clearly show that forgetting begins shortly after exposure to visual stimuli and is statistically significant after about 15 seconds. As noted earlier in this section, tests involving successive presentations of familiar and novel stimuli are likely to provide information about when forgetting begins. In contrast, simultaneous comparisons of responsiveness to familiar and novel stimuli would be expected to be more sensitive to partial retention, thereby providing better indicators of the temporal limits of retention. At the same time, it is recognized that investigators using these two methods often differ in their choice of stimuli. Since evidence cited earlier has shown that recognition is related to stimulus variables, we must temper our conclusion that most differences are procedural. Nevertheless, when data from the different methods are considered together, we are led to the conclusion that for infants forgetting begins within 15 seconds (or less) after stimulus encoding, but memory traces may last for hours and sometimes even weeks.

Although the question of possible developmental change in the course of retention duration is certainly of interest, there are presently not sufficient data to make reasonable conjectures about this for infants. However, Fajnsztejn-Pollack (1973) found that when degree of learning was controlled, rate of loss from memory was invariant across age, from 5 to 16 years. Sophian and Perlmutter's (1978) findings suggest that this generalization can be extended to younger ages, and Wicklegren's (1975) data indicate that it can be extended to older ages. Sophian and Perlmutter found comparable forgetting rates in 3- and 5-year-olds, and Wicklegren found that while acquisition functions changed over childhood and adulthood, the form and rate of retention functions were the same for three age groups between 9 and 68 years of age. He tentatively concluded that "storage dynamics appear to be invariant with age" (p. 165).

E. INTERFERENCE

It has generally been assumed that interference, rather than simply passage of time, importantly contributes to forgetting (see Cermak, 1972; Spear, 1976). A number of studies with adults substantiate this claim (e.g., Norman, 1966; Reitman, 1971). Reitman reported forgetting of verbal stimuli during 15-second retention intervals during which subjects engaged in syllabic detection tasks, but not during tonal detection tasks. He concluded that stimulus interference, not decay, is responsible for forgetting in short-term memory, and that interference is specific to the stimuli being encoded (in his study, linguistic items). Posner and Konick (1966) found interference was a function of the number of interfering items, as well as of their similiarity to the original items. Thus, effects of interference appear to be dependent on both stimulus similarity and number of stimuli.

Although questions concerning interference in children's memory have not received widespread attention in the recent upsurge of research on memory development, Goulet (1968) concluded that "children are certainly subject to interference effects, but there is little evidence regarding the changes in such interference as a function of age or age-related variables" (p. 365). More recently, Reese (1977) has suggested that additional research is needed to assess the effects of imagery on interference in children's memory. Finally, many studies of recognition memory in children suggest that when distractor and presentation items are very different, recognition performance is good, but that when they are similar it is worse (e.g., Bach

& Underwood, 1970; Cramer, 1972, 1973, 1974; Felzen & Ainsfeld, 1970; Hall, 1969; Hall & Halpern, 1972; Hall & Ware, 1968; Kilburg & Siegel, 1973; Kosslyn & Bower, 1974; Perlmutter & Myers, 1976b; Siegel, Babich, & Kirasic, 1974; Siegel, Kirasic, & Kilburg, 1973; von Wright, 1973). While this effect is probably related to response stages of recognition performance, and thus should not be interpreted as analogous to effects of interference on familiarization items, it does suggest that disruption of recognition performance may be produced by similar stimuli.

Figure 1 shows how habituation and differential-looking procedures can be modified to study effects of interference on infants' retention. Only quite recently have experiments been designed to study these effects. Yet experimental manipulations relevant to this issue were employed in some earlier studies. For example, Caron and Caron (1968, 1969) interspersed three highly discrepant stimuli (multicolored abstract art), for 20 seconds each, between familiarization trials. They found that this manipulation did not significantly affect infants' response decrement to checkerboard stimuli. Martin (1975), who tested $3\frac{1}{2}$ and 5-month-olds, also reported that three novel stimuli, presented for 30 seconds each, did not lead to a change in visual fixation of familiarized stimuli. Fagan (1971) tested infants on three different recognition tasks in succession. Statistical tests indicated that serial position of the three tasks did not significantly influence acquisition or retention. The close temporal succession of the tasks might have provided sufficient opportunity for proactive and/or retroactive interference, yet no evidence of either was found. It may be worth noting that in these three studies the potentially interfering stimuli were substantially different from the familiarization stimulus. In contrast, Pancrantz and Cohen (1970) used an interfering stimulus that was similar to their familiarization stimuli. During 15-second and 5-minute delays they presented a black star stimulus to 4-month-olds who had been familiarized to other simple colored forms (e.g., blue triangle, red square). The interfering stimulus had no effect on recognition after the 15-second delay, but it might have been a factor in the recognition failure that was observed after 5 minutes. In contrast, with 4-month-olds Bornstein (1976) found no decrement in retenton following a 3-minute interference period in which stimuli varying along the same (color) or different (mother–infant contact) dimensions as the encoded items were presented. Thus, these studies show that infant recognition memory is not easily affected by subsequent presentations of other visual stimuli.

Some convincing evidence of interference of infants' memory was, however, provided by Stinson (1971). He examined nonnutritive high-amplitude sucking in 4-month-olds. After an infant-controlled familiarization period, interfering stimuli were presented during a 20-second retention interval. The familiarization stimulus was a red circle on a white

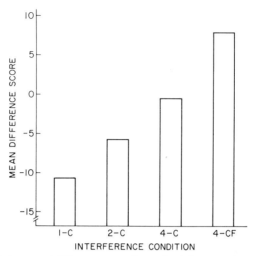

Fig. 9. Mean test segment difference score for each of four interference conditions: 1–C, one novel color stimulus; 2–C, two novel color stimuli; 4–C, four novel color stimuli; 4–CF, four novel stimuli varying in both color and form. (From Stinson, 1971.) (Reprinted with permission.)

background. Four different interference conditions were used: (1) one novel color stimulus, (2) two novel color stimuli, (3) four novel color stimuli, and (4) four novel stimuli varying in both color and form. Stinson's results are shown in Fig. 9. Difference scores (response to the familiarized stimulus after interference relative to response in the last two trials before interference) are plotted for each interference condition. These data show that response to the familiarized stimulus increased as a function of increasing stimulus interference. Stinson (1971) concluded that forgetting was a function of the amount of interference between encoding and retention. This conclusion is consistent with his data; however, it must be reconciled with the results of such studies as those conducted by Caron and Caron (1968, 1969). In Caron and Caron's studies similar interference conditions were used, but forgetting was not indicated. One possible explanation for this difference is that Stinson (1971), as well as Pancrantz and Cohen (1970), used familiarization and interference stimuli that were from the same class (colored geometric forms). This was not true of the Caron and Caron studies (1968, 1969). Thus, interfering stimuli may facilitate forgetting, but the magnitude of forgetting is probably dependent on their similarity to familiarized stimuli, the number of stimuli presented (Stinson, 1971), and the length of exposure (Pancrantz & Cohen, 1970).

Other investigators have emphasized the possibility that failure to demonstrate interference of infant memory may be related to inadequate encoding of the interference stimuli. DeLoache (1976) presented interference stimuli to $4\frac{1}{2}$-month-olds until a habituation criterion was reached or until eight trials were completed. This interference condition was associated with forgetting of the previously familiarized stimulus. DeLoache concluded that for interfering stimuli to be effective the infant must receive enough trials to become familiarized with the interfering items, perhaps even to the point of habituation. An apparent contradiction to this conclusion was reported by Cohen, DeLoache, and Pearl (1977). These investigators presented infants a face photograph during familiarization trials and then presented interfering stimuli for eight trials, followed by tests of recognition. The results of their two experiments suggested that interference had little or no effect on subsequent recognition. Even when data from only infants who habituated to the interfering items were considered, there was no evidence of forgetting. However, their criterion for habituation to the familiarization stimulus was different from their criterion for habituation to the interfering stimuli. It could be that the habituation criterion for interfering stimuli was not sufficiently stringent ["infants whose looking time decreased by 2 sec. or more from the first to the last interference trials" (p. 94)]. McCall, Kennedy, and Dodds (1977) examined data of infants evidencing decline in fixation over interference trials and found significant losses of memory for the previously familiarized stimulus. Thus, they concluded that: "Under conditions of maximum encoding of the distracting stimulus, interference was essentially total" (p. 85). To our list of qualifications, then, we must add that infants must clearly encode interfering stimuli in order for interference to be observed. The amount of encoding of the interference stimulus necessary to disrupt retention is probably proportional to the amount of encoding of the previously presented familiarization stimulus. That is, experiments using longer familiarization periods probably require longer interference periods to disrupt retention.

In three studies (Cohen, DeLoache, & Pearl, 1977; DeLoache, 1976; McCall, Kennedy, & Dodds, 1977), attempts were made to examine the relation between forgetting and similarity of familiarization and interference stimuli. In each study similarity appeared to be irrelevant. When interference was observed, it was observed for all stimulus conditions. However, since presentation time for interfering items was not varied, we cannot accept the conclusion that similarity is unimportant. It is quite possible that the critical exposure duration is less when interfering stimuli are similar to familiarization stimuli than it is when they are dissimilar.

In most of the above studies, interfering stimuli were introduced after relatively long familiarization periods. This may account for the difficulty in demonstrating the effect of interference on retention. Olson and Strauss (1974) demonstrated interference with 4-month-olds by successively presenting five stimuli, for 15 seconds each, and testing recognition with simultaneous comparisons of a novel and one of the five familiar stimuli. Recognition was found only for the stimulus in the fifth serial position (a recency effect); that is, the first four items presented were not recognized, but the final item was. While the results of this study provided no evidence of proactive interference (at least for the stimulus in the fifth serial position), the data were consistent with an interpretation based on retroactive interference. Further, the interference might have been related to the high similarity among the five familiarization stimuli. This interpretation is consistent with the results of several of Fagan's (1973, 1977a) studies in which similar procedures were used.

Fagan (1973, 1977a) found significant retroactive interference with 5- to 6-month-olds. His method consisted of 2 minutes of familiarization followed by immediate and/or delayed recognition tests with simultaneous presentations of the familiar and a novel stimulus. One of the first indications (Fagan, 1973; experiment 3) that interference might be important was the observation that after a 3-hour delay infants recognized familiarized achromatic patterns and face photographs but not familiarized three-dimensional face masks. As Fagan suggested, one explanation for this finding is that intervening exposure to human faces interfered with retention of the highly similar three-dimensional face masks, but not with less similar face photographs. Fagan (1973; Experiment 4) subsequently conducted an experiment in which delayed recognition tests (60 seconds) were preceded by exposure to interfering stimuli of either high (face photographs of proper orientation), medium (face photographs rotated 180°), or low (line drawings of faces) degrees of similarity to the familiarized stimulus (face photograph). The results showed that only the medium similarity stimulus had a significant interfering effect on recognition. In a replication in which five different kinds of interfering stimuli were presented to $5\frac{1}{2}$-month-olds, Fagan (1977a; Experiment 2) found that stimuli of both high and moderate similarity produced significant interference.

Fagan also examined the temporal relation between familiarization and effective interference. In one experiment (Fagan, 1973; Experiment 5) two groups of infants were tested for recognition of photographs after a 3-hour delay. Interfering stimuli were presented to one group (rotated face photographs) immediately after familiarization, and the other group saw the same stimuli at the end of the 3-hour delay, just prior to the recognition test. Only subjects in the former group, who experienced interference immediately following familiarization, suffered memory loss. Yet Fagan (1977a, Experiment 3) found that it was possible to offset effects of interference by providing additional exposure to the familiarization stimulus.

We conclude that in at least a few instances, factors influencing recognition in older children and adults have similar effects on preverbal infants.

When infants are "thoroughly" familiarized to visual stimuli, there is substantial resistance to interference. In contrast, interference is readily demonstrated after brief familiarization periods. From these observations, we suggest that interference is a function of (1) the schema of the previously familiarized item(s), and (2) the extent of encoding of the interfering stimuli. Because the results of many of the studies have indicated minimal effects of interference, it is not surprising that the methods used have been insensitive to effects specifically related to stimulus similarity. However, when similarity is examined with conditions conducive to demonstrating interference, it emerges as an important variable. We suggest that with Fagan's (1973, 1977a) procedures, longer exposures to less similar interfering stimuli would also be effective in facilitating forgetting. Yet, Fagan is probably correct in suggesting that interference is more effective when the interfering stimuli are similar to the familiarization stimuli. This might be clarified by determining the critical duration for similar and nonsimilar interfering stimuli following familiarization procedures such as those used by Cohen *et al.* (1977) and McCall *et al.* (1977). Finally, there are too few data to allow conjectures about whether there are developmental changes in the effects of interference. However, since there is an ontogenetic progression with respect to encoding, parallel effects on interference may be expected. More parametric research is needed to resolve these issues.

V. Relations between Infant Visual Recognition Memory and Later Cognitive Development

Piaget and Inhelder (1973) pointed out that development of memory functions is not independent of changes in cognitive structures. This position is consistent with a number of other perspectives on memory and cognition. For example, similar issues are addressed by Bartlett's (1932) schema theory, contemporary information-processing models (e.g., Neimark, 1970), and infant developmental theory (Fagan, 1975; Greenberg, 1971; Lewis *et al.,* 1969; McCall, 1971; Miranda, 1976). Moreover, it has frequently been suggested that memory is related to intelligence, and developmental psychologists have suggested that individual differences in infants' recognition memory may both reflect the current status of their cognitive skills and also be predictive of later perceptual and cognitive ability. Previous attempts to predict cognitive development using sensorimotor schedules (e.g., Bayley, 1955) have failed, but perhaps early visual attention is a more relevant index. A stable behavioral index that is predictive of later intellectual abilities would be important for both basic and applied science, although most emphasis has centered on the utility that such assessments would have for earlier and more specific intervention with high-risk infants.

Fantz and Nevis (1967a, 1967b) have suggested that infants' selective attention to their environment is probably necessary for normal cognitive development. They conducted a longitudinal study with groups of infants expected to show large differences in intellectual performance in later life. That is, rather than picking random samples of infants and waiting to measure correlations between differential looking and later IQs, Fantz and Nevis (1967a) compared development of differential looking in two groups that were classified a priori. One group consisted of 10 infants of university faculty, and the other of 10 foundlings from an institution. Differential visual attention to paired stimuli was recorded every week for infants 2–16 weeks of age and biweekly from age 18 through 24 weeks. In addition, infants were rated on clusters of items from the Griffiths Mental Development Scale (Griffiths, 1954). They found 21 significant differences in performance favoring the homereared infants, and only four favoring institutionalized infants. Moreover, within each group most of the stimulus pairs were sensitive to developmental progressions, with 12 showing differences before 3 months of age. Figure 10 illustrates the developmental trends of

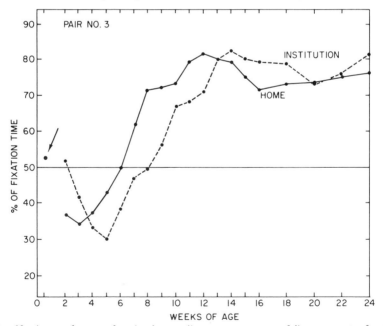

Fig. 10. Age preferences for circular vs. linear arrangement of line segments, for two samples of infants in Fantz and Nevis's (1967a) study. (Reprinted with permission.)

home-reared and institutionalized infants which Fantz and Nevis (1967b) observed for one stimulus pair. It can be seen that both groups went through the same developmental sequence; however, institutionalized infants did so at a later age. These tests were more sensitive to group differences than was the Griffiths Mental Development Scale. The Griffiths scale did not show significant differences between the two groups until 15 weeks of age, while the visual attention tests showed differences much earlier. Thus, measures of selective visual attention appear quite sensitive for differentiating between groups of infants who are likely to differ cognitively in later life. Further justification for this conclusion was obtained by comparing visual attention in normal and Down's syndrome infants (Fantz *et al.,* 1975). Developmental differences in differential looking at pattern stimuli were even larger for these two groups than those reported by Fantz and Nevis. This would, of course, be predicted from the greater intellectual deficits that are virtually certain to exist in Down's syndrome infants.

If spontaneous selective visual attention is a sensitive index of developing capacities to process information, it might also be expected that recognition memory performance could differentiate between populations. As Hagen, Jongeward, and Kail (1975) note, tests of memory have always been a part of intelligence assessment. One of the first comparisons of visual recognition in normal and Down's syndrome infants was reported by Miranda (1970). Infants were familiarized to multidimensional achromatic patterns for 60 seconds and tested for immediate memory with simultaneous presentations of familiar and novel stimuli. At 8 months of age both groups showed greater attention to novel than to familiar stimuli. The failure to differentiate between the two groups was attributed to "ceiling effects." That is, the stimulus novelty was discriminated too easily and thereby insensitive to group differences in information-processing abilities. Indeed, at 8 months, subjects in the two groups were shown to differ in selective attention in ways that could not be attributed to differences in visual acuity (Miranda & Fantz, 1973). The results of a subsequent study by Miranda and Fantz (1974) provided a more comprehensive evaluation of developmental differences in memory between Down's syndrome and normal infants. Recognition memory was tested at 8–16 weeks, 17–29 weeks, and 30–40 weeks. At each age immediate and delayed (30–120 seconds) recognition of three discrimination tasks were measured: (1) color and pattern stimuli, (2) face photographs, and (3) stimuli varying only in arrangement of pattern elements. In Fig. 11, the results for each group are plotted in terms of percentage of fixation to the novel stimulus. It can be seen that the first evidence of immediate memory of pattern stimuli in problem 1 was at 8–16 weeks for normal infants but at 17–29 weeks for Down's syndrome infants. At 17–29 weeks normal infants showed evidence of memory of face

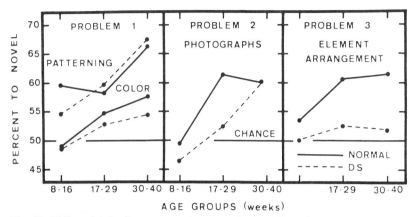

Fig. 11. *Differential fixation responses between paired novel and familiar stimuli, for normal and Down's syndrome infants at successive ages. (From Miranda and Fantz, 1974.) (Reprinted with permission.)*

photographs and element arrangement; however, Down's syndrome infants did not show the former until 30–40 weeks and did not show the latter even after 30–40 weeks. Thus, Down's syndrome and normal infants evidenced an overall developmental difference in memory performance of about 2 months.

The early differences in immediate memory of Down's syndrome and normal infants are perhaps not surprising, in view of the considerable intellectual differences observed between these groups throughout development. It would be valuable, however, to know whether infant recognition memory differentiates between groups of infants likely to show more subtle differences in later life. Preterm infants constitute such a group. Although generalizations are complicated by a number of factors (see Sameroff & Chandler, 1975), reviews of research with preterm infants show greater than average incidence of: (1) retarded physical development, (2) intellectual impairment, and (3) behavioral disorders (Benton, 1940; Wiener, 1962; Caputo & Mandell, 1970). Thus, the study of preterm infants may answer questions about how differences in infants' recognition memory predict later cognitive development. In addition, preterm infants are uniquely suited for testing hypotheses about effects of early experience on memory resulting from their greater postnatal visual experience relative to term infants of the same conceptional age.

Using brief, infant-controlled familiarization periods (100 seconds), Fagan *et al.* (1971) found that preterm infants lagged behind full-term infants by about 1 month in recognition memory onset. However, when the data for the two groups were plotted as a function of conceptional age, there were no differences. Thus, they concluded that visual recognition memory began at about 51 weeks conceptional age, irrespective of postnatal visual experience. In contrast, Sigman and Parmelee (1974) reported significant differences in recognition memory of preterm and full-term infants of the same conceptional age (58–59 weeks). They attributed the difference between their results and those of Fagan *et al.* (1971) to a higher incidence of abnormalities in the preterm infants tested in their study (which they inferred from differences in gestational ages of the preterm infants of the two studies). This conclusion, although quite speculative, suggests that infants on the end of a continuum of reproductive casualty may evidence differences in recognition memory.

These studies suggest that populations of infants that are likely to differ in later cognitive development may also differ in early visual recognition. An alternative approach is to examine relations between visual recognition and individual differences within populations. Werner and Siqueland (1978) correlated newborn preterm infants' relative response to visual stimulus novelty with contemporaneous perinatal variables. Since they used infant-controlled familiarization periods, the issue was not presence or absence of recognition but the magnitude of response to novelty. They reported significant negative correlations between relative response to novelty and mortality risk, number of medical complications, and hospitalization time, while there were significant positive correlations between relative response to novelty and birth weight, gestational age, and conceptional age. Thus, individual differences in visual recognition were related to individual differences in variables related to developmental risk.

Still other correlational data reported by Lewis (1967; Lewis *et al.,* 1969) suggest that individual differences in early recognition are related to later differences in perceptual-cognitive processes. Unfortunately, since dishabituation to novelty often was not demonstrated in these experiments, it is impossible to distinguish memory from other factors, such as sensory adaptation and fatigue. Nevertheless, the major findings were: (1) At 12 weeks, infants with Apgar scores of 10 showed significantly more response decrement over familiarization trials than infants with Apgar scores of less than 10; (2) there was a significant positive correlation between magnitude of response decrement at 1 year and IQ at $3\frac{1}{2}$ years; and (3) there was significant positive correlation between magnitude of response decrement at 1 year and higher performance on a concept formation task at $3\frac{1}{2}$ years.

Perhaps a more informative approach would be to conduct prospective studies that relate visual recognition memory with later cognitive performance. In one such study it was found that habituation ratios (see McCall & Kagan, 1970) at 4 months were significantly correlated with object concept performance at 14 months (Miller, Sinnott, Short, & Hains, 1976). Habituation ratios obtained at 2, 3, and 4 months were also correlated significantly with composite scores obtained from performance on five object concept tasks and three operational causality tasks (Miller, Ryan, Short, Ries, McGuire, & Culler, 1977).

In summary, the findings we have reviewed provide evidence that early deficits in visual recognition memory may be related to later cognitive deficits. There is also some evidence, albeit much weaker, that individual differences in cognitive processes of normal children may be related to responsiveness to visual stimulus novelty in infancy.

VI. Theoretical Considerations

We shall next briefly discuss how research on infant memory relates to information-processing and Piagetian points of view. Then, we shall discuss schema models, which are perhaps best suited for interpreting infant recognition memory data.

A. INFORMATION-PROCESSING PERSPECTIVE

The information-processing point of view maintains that memory is a critical component of essentially all cognition. Memory is conceptualized as the transfer of information within a cognitive system and is analyzed in terms of component processes of encoding, retention, and retrieval. In considering information-processing models it is important to note that they have been derived largely to explain and predict adults' verbal performance in specific experimental tasks. While the models surely can be applied usefully to children's, and perhaps infants', memories the ways in which they may need to be modified and/or extended have not yet been fully explored. In relating these models to infant research, perhaps the most obvious point is the apparent limitation in infants' information-processing skills. While adults have been found to have many processes at their command and are able to recall as well as recognize information, fewer processes have been demonstrated in infants; for example, they have only been shown to recognize, not recall, information. As is discussed further in Section VI, B, it is still not clear whether these limitations are in infants' capacities or in investigators' methodologies.

At present, adult information-processing models seem to be of limited applicability to infant data. Even models of adult recognition are not entirely appropriate for interpreting results of infant recognition studies. For example, we really do not know what pattern of data mature subjects would generate in such experimental tasks as those used with infants; we are ignorant concerning visual attention measures of memory in adults. Moreover, there is probably a lack of comparability in what is measured in studies of adult and infant recognition memory. While recognition tasks used with adults generally require a response whereby subjects indicate cognizance of their memory, those used with infants have no such requirement. That is, when adults say "yes" or "no" to each item in an item by item recognition test, or point to old items in a forced-choice recognition test, they must be cognizant or aware of having previously experienced the item and make a conscious decision about it. In contrast, when infants' recognition is assessed by measuring differences in response to old versus new stimuli, awareness and decisions about memory are probably not involved. More automatic matching processes would appear most relevant to infant memory. Perhaps elaboration of these processes will develop from infant work (e.g., Olson, 1976). This would be likely to provide a more complete understanding of recognition memory and thus contribute to adult models as well.

A further caution in adopting adult information-processing models for understanding infant memory concerns the nature of stimuli used in research with these different age groups. Adult information-processing models account for retention of primarily verbal stimuli. Even when applied to pictorial stimuli, the materials used with adults have been rich with semantic meaning. This contrasts sharply with stimuli used in infant studies. These have mainly been geometric patterns, devoid of semantic meaning. Since adult models stress the interaction of accrued world knowledge, or semantic memory, with more specific episodic memory, this difference may be of considerable import. Indeed, the suggestion that age differences in world knowledge contribute to age differences in memory performance of preschool (e.g., Myers & Perlmutter, 1978) and grade-school children (e.g., Brown, 1975; Chi, 1976), supports the view that retention depends upon how information is interpreted in the context of past experiences. It may well be, then, that retention of simple, nonmeaningful stimuli, as used in infant research, is based upon a memory system quite different from that understood to mediate retention of semantically meaningful stimuli, as used in adult research.

In spite of these substantive problems in applying current information-processing models to infant research, we believe the approach has much to offer. The information-processing conceptualization provides a rich general framework for interpreting memory data, and its task analysis approach is likely to lead to explicit and testable models that will enhance our understanding of infant recognition memory.

B. PIAGETIAN PERSPECTIVE

Piaget has not provided explicit process models of memory. Nevertheless, he has distinguished between recall and recognition, and he has discussed an explicit developmental progression of these types of memory. Specifically, Piaget (Piaget & Inhelder, 1973) has suggested that perceptual schemata are the instruments of recognition, whereas internalized images are the instruments of recall. Thus, he believes that recognition is possible during the first months of life, but that recall is not attainable before 1 or 2 years of age.

While the coverage of our review, which was essentially limited to infants' recognition memory, would seem to support Piaget's view that young infants are not capable of recall, we do not believe this is necessarily true. It is not at all clear that we presently have adequate techniques for determining the full range of infants' memory skills. For example, it is possible that infants do have recall capacities, although investigators have not yet discovered how to assess them. Indeed, some recent research that seems to have demonstrated deferred imitation in neonates (Meltzoff & Moore, 1977) suggests that we may well have underestimated infants' memory skills. Meltzoff and Moore found that neonates between 12 and 21 days of age imitated facial and manual gestures, even after the model was withdrawn. This seems to indicate that the neonates formed representations of the gestures. Even more remarkably, after the gestures were removed the infants apparently were able to re-present and read off memory representations. It is possible that the imitation observed by these investigators is the result of infants' reading off perceptual or short-term iconic representations, rather than what are more typically considered memory representations. For example, since it probably takes infants a considerable amount of time to execute responses, even after they are "programmed," the imitative responses may actually have been initiated when the stimuli were still perceptually available, or in a sensory buffer. While Meltzoff and Moore tried to control for this possibility, more research should be directed toward replicating and extending their findings. Specifically, the possibility that evocative memory is within the capacities of neonates should be explored more extensively.

C.   SCHEMA MODELS

Schema models perhaps have the most to offer to our understanding of infant visual recognition memory data. Since almost all contemporary schema models have intellectual roots in Bartlett's (1932) theory, it is worth considering what he intended. He wrote:

> "Schema" refers to an active organisation of past reactions, or of past experiences, which must always be supposed to be operating in any well-adapted organic response. That is, whenever there is any order or regularity of behaviour, a particular

response is possible only because it is related to other similar responses which have been serially organised, yet which operate, not simply as individual members coming one after another, but as a unitary mass. . . . All incoming impulses of a certain kind, or mode, go together to build up an active, organised setting. (p. 201)

Although contemporary theories such as those of Bruner and Piaget are consistent with Bartlett's ideas about schema formation, most infant memory discussions have been centered around Sokolov's schema model. Sokolov's model (as discussed in Section IV, B) conceives of response decrement during stimulus familiarization as corresponding to the construction of a schema for the incoming information. When processed information is discrepant from existing schema an orienting reaction occurs which serves to facilitate processing of the new stimulus.

Perhaps the most direct evidence of schema formation in information processing comes from studies with adults. Posner (1969) presented stimuli that were various distortions of a single prototype, to adult observers and tested recognition memory with previously presented stimuli, "new" stimuli, and a prototype of the familiarized stimuli. The observers were able to discriminate "old" and "new" items but tended to classify the prototype as previously presented. Thus, during familiarization with components of a prototype, they may have constructed a schema for the compound. Such a representation would therefore match the prototype and be classified as previously presented. A subsequent experiment by Franks and Bransford (1971) suggests that stimulus prototypes (schemas formed from viewing transformations of a prototype) may be "remembered" better than stimuli that subjects actually see during familiarization. In their studies, adults were shown a series of colored geometric figures and told to remember them. The figures presented were transformations of a prototype. In subsequent recognition tests the subjects were shown the originally presented patterns, new configurations, and the prototype. Recognition confidence ratings were highest for the prototype and progressively decreased with increasing transformational distance from the prototype. Thus, subjects were more confident in their recognition of a prototype that had not previously been presented than of transformations of the prototypes to which they had been exposed. These findings support the notion that recognition memory is based on the construction of schema.

A number of infant and adult memory models (e.g., Berlyne, 1960, 1967; Lewis, 1967, 1971; McCall, 1971; Vernon, 1952) have been based on schema formation. Unfortunately, the schema concept has usually been used as a vague theoretical construct. It is unfortunate that schema models have not led to more specific experimental tests, such as those reported by

Posner and by Franks and Bransford. For example, if infants form a schema during familiarization, does their novelty discrimination improve with increasing transformational distance from the familiarization stimulus? The advantage of schema models is that such questions can be addressed with both infants and adults using comparable methods as long as encoding of the stimuli does not depend upon previous experiences. Thus, schema models are probably the most age-independent models for the study of memory. They should, therefore, be explored in order to find continuity in memory abilities throughout development.

VII. Summary and Conclusions

Preverbal infants encode and retain some information about their visual world from the first hours of life. Even neonates demonstrate recognition memory. We have attempted to review and interpret infant visual recognition memory literature in terms of the particular methodologies used in each study, and believe this has helped reconcile many apparent experimental inconsistencies. Additionally, we have attempted to relate this literature to work on memory of older children and adults, and believe this has highlighted many consistencies that appear in the memory systems of infants and more mature subjects. Although clear conclusions about specific aspects of infant recognition memory are not possible at this time, some generalizations have emerged. These may perhaps best be summarized by a set of hypotheses. As with all hypotheses, they remain to be scrutinized by further empirical evidence.

1. Development of infant visual recognition is not the result of changing retention capacity but of changes in infants' ability to encode stimulus information. While memory performance follows a developmental pattern, there is no compelling evidence that retention per se (that is, capacity) changes with age. When infant-controlled familiarization procedures are used, there are no age differences in ability to retain information about pictures. We feel that it is clearly established that memory is possible from the first days of life. Unfortunately, adequate evidence for comparing the retention capacity of different age groups is not available. However, we suggest that if techniques could be developed to insure that infants encoded large numbers of visual stimuli, retention would not be constrained by capacity.

2. Rate of familiarization is a function of stimulus encoding. As information-processing abilities improve with age, less encoding time is required to demonstrate memory, but at any given age more familiarization time is needed to encode more complex stimuli.

3. The temporal course of infant forgetting is still unclear; however, it appears that memory loss begins within seconds of encoding, although traces of stored information may persist for at least days or weeks.

4. Preverbal infants are not special with respect to their susceptibility to retroactive interference, except insofar as they are limited in their ability to encode interfering material. Compared to older infants, younger infants require more time to become familiarized to visual stimuli and, subsequently, require more exposure to interfering items before retention is disrupted.

It is hoped that some investigators will find these hypotheses worthy of disproof. However, it seems likely that progress will require more refined methodologies, as well as more systematic variation of parameters, including familiarization time, retention interval, and type of stimuli. Additionally, it is hoped that future experiments will examine infants' retention in other sensory modalities and will also explore the possibility that infants have more complex mnemonic skills, including perhaps the ability to recall nonpresent information. Thus, while it is presently possible to conclude that infants retain information about their visual worlds, much about the ontogeny and organization of their memory systems remains to be charted.

REFERENCES

Ames, E. W. *Stimulus complexity and age of infants as determinants of the rate of habituation of visual-fixation*. Paper presented at meetings of the Western Psychological Association, Long Beach, Cal., April 1966.

Attneave, F. Physical determinants of the judged complexity of shapes. *Journal of Experimental Psychology,* 1957, **53**, 221–227.

Attneave, F., & Arnoult, M. D. The quantitative study of shape and pattern perception. *Psychological Bulletin,* 1956, **53**, 452–471.

Bach, M. J., & Underwood, B. J. Developmental changes in memory attributes. *Journal of Educational Psychology,* 1970, **61**, 292–296.

Bartlett, F. C. *Remembering: A study in experimental and social psychology*. London: Cambridge University Press, 1932.

Bayley, N. On the growth of intelligence. *American Psychologist,* 1955, **10**, 805–818.

Belmont, J. M. Perceptual short-term memory in children, retardates and adults. *Journal of Experimental Child Psychology,* 1967, **5**, 114–122.

Belmont, J. M., & Butterfield, E. C. The relations of short-term memory to development and intelligence. In L. P. Lipsitt & H. W. Reese (Eds.), *Advances in child development and behavior* (Vol. 4). New York: Academic Press, 1969.

Benton, A. L. Mental development of prematurely born children: A critical review of the literature. *American Journal of Orthopsychiatry,* 1940, **10**, 719–746.

Berlyne, D. E. *Conflict, arousal and curiosity*. New York: McGraw-Hill, 1960.

Berlyne, D. E. Arousal and reinforcement. In D. Levine (Ed.), *Nebraska Symposium on Motivation*. Lincoln: University of Nebraska Press, 1967.

Bond, E. K. Perception of form by the human infant. *Psychological Bulletin,* 1972, **77**, 225–245.

Bornstein, M. H. Infants' recognition memory for hue. *Developmental Psychology,* 1976, **12**, 185-191.

Brennan, W. M., Ames, E. W., & Moore, R. W. Age differences in infants' attention to pattern of different complexities. *Science,* 1966, **151**, 354-356.

Brown, A. L. Judgments of recency for long sequences of pictures: The absence of a developmental trend. *Journal of Experimental Child Psychology,* 1973, **15**, 473-480.

Brown, A. L. The development of memory: Knowing, knowing about knowing, and knowing how to know. In H. W. Resse (Ed.), *Advances in child development and behavior* (Vol. 10). New York: Academic Press, 1975.

Brown, A. L., & Campione, J. C. Recognition memory for perceptually similar pictures in preschool children. *Journal of Experimental Psychology,* 1972, **95**, 55-62.

Brown, A. L., & Scott, M. S. Recognition memory for pictures in preschool children. *Journal of Experimental Child Psychology,* 1971, **11**, 401-412.

Caputo, D. V., & Mandell, W. Consequences of low birth weight. *Developmental Psychology,* 1970, **3**, 363-383.

Caron, R. F., & Caron, A. J. The effects of repeated exposure and stimulus complexity on visual fixation in infants. *Psychonomic Science,* 1968, **10**, 207-208.

Caron, R. F., & Caron, A. J. Degree of stimulus complexity and habituation of visual fixation in infants. *Psychonomic Science,* 1969, **14**, 78-79.

Caron, A. J., Caron, R. F., Minichiello, M. D., Weiss, S. J., & Friedman, S. L. Constraints on the use of the familiarization-novelty method in the assessment of infant discrimination. *Child Development,* 1977, **48**, 747-762.

Cermak, L. S. *Human memory: Research and theory.* New York: Ronald, 1972.

Chi, M. T. H. Short-term memory limitations in children: Capacity or processing deficits? *Memory and Cognition,* 1976, **4**, 559-572.

Clifton, R. K., & Nelson, M. N. Developmental study of habituation in infants: The importance of paradigm, response system, and state. In T. J. Tighe & R. N. Leaton (Eds.), *Habituation: Perspectives from child development, animal behavior, and neurophysiology.* Hillsdale, N.J.: Erlbaum, 1976.

Cohen, L. B. Attention-getting and attention-holding processes of infant visual preferences. *Child Development,* 1972, **43**, 869-879.

Cohen, L. B. A two process model of infant visual attention. *Merrill-Palmer Quarterly,* 1973, **19**, 157-180.

Cohen, L. B. Infant visual memory: A backward look into the future. In N. R. Ellis (Ed.), *Aberrant development in infancy: Human and animal studies.* Hillsdale, N.J.: Lawrence Erlbaum, 1975.

Cohen, L. B., DeLoache, J. S., & Rissman, M. W. The effect of stimulus complexity on infant visual attention and habituation. *Child Development,* 1975, **46**, 611-617.

Cohen, L. B. DeLoache, J. S., & Pearl, R. A. An examination of interference effects in infants' memory for faces. *Child Development,* 1977, **48**, 88-96.

Cohen, L. B., Gelber, E. R., & Lazar, M. A. Infant habituation and generalization to differing degrees of stimulus novelty. *Journal of Experimental Child Psychology,* 1971, **11**, 379-389.

Cohen, L. B., & Gelber, E. R. Infant visual memory. In L. B. Cohen & P. Salapatek (Eds.), *Infant perception: From sensation to cognition.* New York: Academic Press, 1975.

Corcoran, D. W. J. *Pattern recognition.* Baltimore: Penguin, 1971.

Craik, F. I. M., & Lockhart, R. S. Levels of processing: A framework for memory research. *Journal of Verbal Learning and Verbal Behavior,* 1972, **11**, 671-684.

Cramer, P. A. A developmental study of errors in memory. *Developmental Psychology,* 1972, **7**, 204-209.

Cramer, P. A. Evidence for a developmental shift in the basis for memory organization. *Journal of Experimental Child Psychology,* 1973, **16,** 12–22.

Cramer, P. A. Idiodynamic sets as determinants of children's false recognition errors. *Developmental Psychology,* 1974, **10,** 86–92.

Crowder, R. G. *Principles of learning and memory.* Hillsdale, N.J.: Erlbaum, 1976.

Daehler, M. W., & Bukatko, D. Recognition memory for pictures in very young children: Evidence from attentional preferences using a continuous presentation procedure. *Child Development,* 1977, **48,** 693–696.

DeLoache, J. S. Rate of habituation and visual memory in infants. *Child Development,* 1976, **47,** 145–154.

Dirks, J., & Neisser, U. Memory for objects in real scenes: The development of recognition and recall. *Journal of Experimental Child Psychology,* 1977, **23,** 315–328.

Enroth–Cugell, C., & Robson, J. G. The contrast sensitivity of retinal ganglion cells of the cat. *Journal of Physiology (London),* 1966, **187,** 517–552.

Entwisle, D. R., & Huggins, W. H. Iconic memory in children. *Child Development,* 1973, **44,** 392–394.

Fagan, J. F. Memory in the infant. *Journal of Experimental Child Psychology,* 1970, **9,** 217–226.

Fagan, J. F. Infants' recognition memory for a series of visual stimuli. *Journal of Experimental Child Psychology,* 1971, **11,** 244–250.

Fagan, J. F. Infants' recognition memory for faces. *Journal of Experimental Child Psychology,* 1972, **14,** 453–476.

Fagan, J. F. Infants' delayed recognition memory and forgetting. *Journal of Experimental Child Psychology,* 1973, **16,** 424–450.

Fagan, J. F. Infant recognition memory: The effects of length of familiarization and type of discrimination task. *Child Development,* 1974, **45,** 351–356.

Fagan, J. F. Infant recognition memory as a present and future index of cognitive abilities. In N. R. Ellis (Ed.), *Aberrant development in infancy: Human and animal studies.* Hillsdale, N.J.: Erlbaum, 1975.

Fagan, J. F. Infant recognition memory: Studies in forgetting. *Child Development,* 1977, **48,** 68–78. (a)

Fagan, J. F. An attentional model of infant recognition. *Child Development,* 1977, **48,** 345–359. (b)

Fagan, J. F., Fantz, R. L., & Miranda, S. B. *Infants' attention to novel stimuli as a function of postnatal and conceptional age.* Paper presented at the meeting of the Society for Research in Child Development, Minneapolis, Minn., April 1971.

Fajnsztejn-Pollack, G. A developmental study of decay rate in long-term memory. *Journal of Experimental Child Psychology,* 1973, **16,** 225–235.

Fantz, R. L. Pattern vision in young infants. *The Psychological Record,* 1958, **8,** 43–47.

Fantz, R. L. Visual experience in infants: Decreased attention to familiar patterns relative to novel ones. *Science,* 1964, **146,** 668–670.

Fantz, R. L. Visual perception and experience in early infancy: A look at the hidden side of behavior development. In H. W. Stevenson, E. H. Hess, & H. L. Rheingold (Eds.), *Early behavior: Comparative and developmental approaches.* New York: Wiley, 1967.

Fantz, R. L., & Fagan, J. F. Visual attention to size and number of pattern details by term and preterm infants during the first six months. *Child Development,* 1975, **46,** 3–18.

Fantz, R. L., Fagan, J. F., & Miranda, S. B. Early visual selectivity as a function of pattern variables, previous exposure, age from birth and conception, and expected cognitive deficit. In L. B. Cohen & P. Salapatek (Eds.), *Infant perception: From sensation to cognition.* New York: Academic Press, 1975.

Fantz, R. L., & Nevis, S. Pattern preferences and perceptual-cognitive development in early infancy. *Merrill-Palmer Quarterly,* 1967, **13,** 77–108. (a)

Fantz, R. L., & Nevis, S. The predictive value of changes in visual preferences in early infancy. In J. Hellmuth (Ed.), *Exceptional infant: The normal infant* (Vol. 1). Seattle: Special Child Publications, 1967. (b)

Faulkender, P. J., Wright, J. C., & Waldron, A. Generalized habituation of conceptual stimuli in toddlers. *Child Development,* 1974, **45,** 351–356.

Felzen, E., & Anisfeld, M. Semantic and phonetic relations in the false recognition of words by 3rd and 6th grade children. *Developmental Psychology,* 1970, **3,** 163–168.

Flavell, J. H. *Cognitive development.* New York: Prentice-Hall, 1977.

Franks, J. J., & Bransford, J. D. Abstraction of visual patterns. *Journal of Experimental Psychology,* 1971, **90,** 65–74.

Friedman, S. Habituation and recovery of visual response in the alert human newborn. *Journal of Experimental Child Psychology,* 1972, **13,** 339–349. (a)

Friedman, S. Newborn visual attention to repeated exposure of redundant versus "novel" targets. *Perception and Psychophysics,* 1972, **12,** 291–294. (b)

Friedman, S., Bruno, L. A., & Vietze, P. Newborn habituation to visual stimuli: A sex difference in novelty detection. *Journal of Experimental Child Psychology,* 1974, **18,** 242–251.

Friedman, S., & Carpenter, G. C. Visual response decrement as a function of age of human newborn. *Child Development,* 1971, **42,** 1967–1973.

Friedman, S., Carpenter, G. C., & Nagy, A. N. Decrement and recovery of response to visual stimuli in the newborn infant. *Proceedings of the 78th Annual Convention, APA,* 1970, **5,** 273–274. (a)

Friedman, S., Nagy, A. N., & Carpenter, G. C. Newborn attention: Differential response decrement to visual stimuli. *Journal of Experimental Child Psychology,* 1970, **10,** 44–51. (b)

Fukuda, Y., & Stone, J. Retinal distribution and central projections of Y-, X-, and W-cells of the cat's retina. *Journal of Neurophysiology,* 1974, **37,** 749–772.

Geis, M. F., & Hall, D. M. Encoding and incidental memory in children. *Journal of Experimental Child Psychology,* 1976, **22,** 58–66.

Gibson, J. J. Ecological optics. *Vision Research,* 1961, **1,** 253–262.

Gibson, J. J. *The senses considered as perceptual systems.* Boston: Houghton-Mifflin, 1966.

Goulet, L. R. Verbal learning in children: Implications for developmental research. *Psychological Bulletin,* 1968, **69,** 359–376.

Greenberg, D. J. Accelerating visual complexity levels in the human infant. *Child Development,* 1971, **42,** 905–918.

Greenberg, D. J., & Blue S. Z. Visual complexity in infancy: Contour or numerosity? *Child Development,* 1975, **46,** 357–363.

Greenberg, D. J., & Blue S. Z. The visual-preference technique in infancy: Effect of number of stimuli presented upon experimental outcome. *Child Development,* 1977, **48,** 131–137.

Greenberg, D. J., & O'Donnell, W. J. Infancy and the optimal level of stimulation. *Child Development,* 1972, **43,** 639–645.

Greenberg, D. J., O'Donnell, W. J., & Crawford, D. Complexity levels, habituation, and individual differences in early infancy. *Child Development,* 1973, **44,** 569–574.

Greenberg, D. J., & Weizmann, F. The measurement of visual attention in infants: A comparison of two methodologies. *Journal of Experimental Child Psychology,* 1971, **11,** 234–243.

Griffiths, R. *The abilities of babies.* New York: McGraw-Hill, 1954.

Hagen, J. W., Jongeward, R. H., & Kail, R. V. Cognitive perspectives on the development of memory. In H. W. Reese (Ed.), *Advances in child development and behavior* (Vol. 10). New York: Academic Press, 1975.

Haith, M. M., Morrison, F. J., & Sheingold, K. Tachistoscopic recognition of geometric forms by children and adults. *Psychonomic Science,* 1970, **19**, 345-347.

Hall, J. W. Errors in word recognition and discrimination by children of two age levels. *Journal of Educational Psychology,* 1969, **60**, 144-147.

Hall, J. W., & Halperin, M. S. The development of memory-encoding processes in young children. *Developmental Psychology,* 1972, **6**, 181.

Hall, J. W., & Ware, W. B. Implicit associative responses and false rcecognition by young children. *Journal of Experimental Child Psychology,* 1968, **6**, 52-60.

Harris, J. D. Habituatory response decrement in the intact organism. *Psychological Bulletin,* 1943, **40**, 385-422.

Head, H. *Studies in neurology.* London: Hodder & Stoughton, 1920.

Hershenson, M. Visual discrimination in the human newborn. *Journal of Comparative and Physiological Psychology,* 1964, **58**, 270-276.

Hershenson, M., Munsinger, H., & Kessen, W. Preferences for shapes of intermediate variability in the newborn human. *Science,* 1965, **147**, 630-631.

Hoffman, C. D., & Dick, S. A demonstrated investigation of recognition memory. *Child Development,* 1976, **47**, 794-799.

Hoffmann, K-P. Conduction velocity in pathways from retina to superior colliculus in the cat: A correlation with receptive-field properties. *Journal of Neurophysiology,* 1973, **36**, 409-424.

Horowitz, F. D. Visual attention, auditory stimulation, and language discrimination in young infants. *Monographs of the Society for Research in Child Development,* 1974, **39** (5-6, Serial No. 158).

Horowitz, F. D., Paden, L., Bhana, K., Aitchison, R., & Self, P. Developmental changes in infant visual fixation to differing complexity levels among cross-sectionally and longitudinally studied infants. *Developmental Psychology,* 1972, **7**, 88-89. (a)

Horowitz, F. D., Paden, S., Bhana, K., & Self, P. An infant-control procedure for studying infant visual fixations. *Developmental Psychology,* 1972, **7**, 90. (b)

Hulicka, I. M., & Weiss, R. Age differences in retention as a function of learning. *Journal of Consulting Psychology,* 1965, **29**, 125-219.

Hunter, M. A., & Ames, E. W. *Visual habituation and preference for novelty in five-week-old infants.* Paper presented at the meetings of the Society for Research in Child Development, Denver, Col., 1975.

Ikeda, H., & Wright, M. J. Spatial and temporal properties of 'sustained' and 'transient' neurones in area 17 of the cat's visual cortex. *Experimental Brain Research,* 1975, **22**, 363-383.

James, W. *The principles of psychology.* New York: Holt, 1890.

Jeffrey, W. E., & Cohen, L. B. Habituation in the human infant. In H. W. Reese (Ed.), *Advances in child development and behavior* (Vol. 6). New York: Academic Press, 1971.

Judisch, J. M. Fixation and pattern preference in young infants. (Doctoral dissertation, Pennsylvania State University, 1969), *Dissertation Abstracts International,* 1970, **30**, 3407-B. (University Microfilms No. 70-680).

Kagan, J. The determinants of attention in the infant. *American Scientist,* 1970, **58**, 298-306.

Kagan, J., Henker, B. A., Hen-Tov, A., Levine, J., & Lewis, M. Infants' differential reactions to familiar and distorted faces. *Child Development,* 1966, **37**, 519-532.

Kail, R. V., & Hagen, J. W. (Eds.). *Perspectives on the development of memory and cognition.* Hillsdale, N.J.: Erlbaum, 1977.

Karmel, B. Z. The effect of age, complexity, and amount of contour on pattern preferences in human infants. *Journal of Experimental Child Psychology,* 1969, **7**, 339-354.

Karmel, B. Z., & Maisel, E. B. A neuronal activity model for infant visual attention. In L. B. Cohen & P. Salapatek (Eds.), *Infant perception: From sensation to cognition.* New York: Academic Press, 1975.

Kendler, H. H., & Kendler, T. S. From discrimination learning to cognitive development: A neobehavioristic odyssey. In W. K. Estees (Ed.), *Handbook of learning and cognitive processes.* Hillsdale, N.J.: Erlbaum, 1975.

Kilburg, R. R., & Siegel, A. W. Differential feature analysis in the recognition memory of reflective and impulsive children. *Memory and Cognition,* 1973, **1,** 413–419.

Kintsch, W. *Learning, memory and conceptual processes.* New York: Wiley, 1970.

Klatzky, R. L. *Human memory: Structures and processes.* San Francisco: Freeman, 1975.

Kosslyn, S. M., & Bower, G. H. The role of imagery in sentence memory: A developmental study. *Child Development,* 1974, **45,** 30–38.

Lewis, M. *Infant attention: Response decrement as a measure of cognitive processes, or what's new, Baby Jane?* Paper presented at meetings of the Society for Research in Child Development, New York, March 1967.

Lewis, M. Infants' responses to facial stimuli during the first year of life. *Developmental Psychology,* 1969, **1,** 75–86.

Lewis, M. Individual differences in the measurement of early cognitive growth. In J. Hellmuth (Ed.), *Exceptional infant: Studies in abnormalities* (Vol. 2). New York: Brunner/Mazel, 1971.

Lewis, M., Goldberg, S., & Campbell, H. A developmental study of information processing within the first three years of life: Response decrement to a redundant signal. *Monographs of the Society for Research in Child Development,* 1969, **34** (9, Serial No. 133).

Lewis, M., Kagan, J., & Kalafat, J. Patterns of fixation in the young infant. *Child Development,* 1966, **37,** 331–341.

Loftus, G. R. Eye fixations and recognition memory for pictures. *Cognitive Psychology,* 1972, **3,** 525–551.

Mandler, J. M., & Day, J. Memory for orientation of forms as a function of their meaningfulness and complexity. *Journal of Experimental Child Psychology,* 1975, **20,** 430–443.

Mandler, J. M., & Stein, N. L. Recall and recognition of pictures by children as a function of organization on distractor similarity. *Journal of Experimental Psychology,* 1974, **102,** 657–669.

Marsden, R. E. Discussion and apparatus. A study of the early color sense. *Psychological Review,* 1903, **10,** 37–47.

Martin, R. M. Effects of familiar and complex stimuli on infant attention. *Developmental Psychology,* 1975, **11,** 178–185.

McCall, R. B. Attention in the infant: Avenue to the study of cognitive development. In D. N. Walcher & D. L. Peters (Eds.), *Early childhood: The development of self-regulatory mechanisms.* New York: Academic Press, 1971.

McCall, R. B., Hogarty, P. S., Hamilton, J. S., & Vincent, J. H. Habituation rate and the infant's response to visual discrepancies. *Child Development,* 1973, **44,** 280–287.

McCall, R. B., & Kagan, J. Stimulus-schema discrepancy and attention in the infant. *Journal of Experimental Child Psychology,* 1967, **5,** 381–390.

McCall, R. B., & Kagan, J. Individual differences in the distribution of attention to stimulus discrepancy. *Developmental Psychology,* 1970, **2,** 90–98.

McCall, R. B., Kennedy, C. B., & Dodds, C. The interfering effects of distracting stimuli on the infant's memory. *Child Development,* 1977, **48,** 79–87.

McCall, R., & Melson, W. H. Attention in infants as a function of magnitude of discrepancy and habituation rate. *Psychonomic Science,* 1969, **17,** 317–319.

McCall, R. B., & Melson, W. H. Complexity, contour, and area as determinants of attention in infants. *Developmental Psychology,* 1970, **3,** 343-349.

McGurk, H. The role of object orientation in infant perception. *Journal of Experimental Child Psychology,* 1970, **9,** 363-373.

Meltzoff, A. N., & Moore, M. K. Imitation of facial and manual gestures by human neonates. *Science,* 1977, **198,** 75-78.

Meyers, W. J., & Cantor, G. N. Observing and cardiac responses of human infants to visual stimuli. *Journal of Experimental Child Psychology,* 1967, **5,** 16-25.

Michels, K. M., & Zusne, L. Metrics of visual form. *Psychological Bulletin,* 1965, **63,** 74-86.

Milewski, A. E., & Siqueland, E. R. Discrimination of color and pattern novelty in one-month human infants. *Journal of Experimental Child Psychology,* 1975, **19,** 122-136.

Miller, D. J., Sinnott, J. P., Short, E. J., & Hains, A. A. Individual differences in habituation rates and object concept performance. *Child Development,* 1976, **47,** 528-531.

Miller, D. J., Ryan, E. B., Short, E. J., Ries, P. G., McGuire, M. D., & Culler, M. P. Relationships between early habituation and later cognitive performance in infancy. *Child Development,* 1977, **48,** 658-661.

Miranda, S. B. Response to novel visual stimuli by Down's Syndrome and normal infants. *Proceedings of the 78th Annual Convention of the American Psychological Association,* 1970, **6,** 275-276.

Miranda, S. B. Visual attention in defective and high-risk infants. *Merrill-Palmer Quarterly,* 1976, **22,** 201-228.

Miranda, S. B., & Fantz, R. L. Visual preferences of Down's Syndrome and normal infants. *Child Development,* 1973, **44,** 555-561.

Miranda, S. B., & Fantz, R. L. Recognition memory in Down's Syndrome and normal infants. *Child Development,* 1974, **45,** 651-660.

Moenster, P. A. Learning and memory in relation to age. *Journal of Gerontology,* 1972, **27,** 361-363.

Munsinger, H., Kessen, W., & Kessen, M. L. Age and uncertainty: Developmental variation in preference for variability. *Journal of Experimental Child Psychology,* 1964, **1,** 1-15.

Munsinger, H., & Weir, M. W. Infants' and young children's preference for complexity. *Journal of Experimental Child Psychology,* 1967, **5,** 69-73.

Myers, N. A., & Perlmutter, M. Memory in the years from two to five. In P. A. Ornstein (Ed.), *Memory development in children.* Hillsdale, N.J.: Erlbaum, 1978.

Neimark, E. D. Model for a thinking machine: An information-processing framework for the study of cognitive development. *Merrill-Palmer Quarterly,* 1970, **16,** 345-368.

Neisser, U. *Cognitive Psychology.* New York: Appleton, 1966.

Nelson, K. E. Memory development in children: Evidence from nonverbal tasks. *Psychonomic Science,* 1971, **25,** 346-348.

Nelson, K. E., & Kosslyn, S. M. Recognition of previously labeled or unlabeled pictures by 5-year olds and adults. *Journal of Experimental Child Psychology,* 1976, **21,** 40-45.

Newcombe, N., Rogoff, B., & Kagan, J. Developmental changes in recognition memory for pictures of objects and scenes. *Developmental Psychology,* 1977, **13,** 337-341.

Norman, D. A. Acquisition and retention in short-term memory. *Journal of Experimental Psychology,* 1966, **72,** 369-381.

Olson, G. M. An information processing analysis of visual memory and habituation in infants. In T. J. Tighe & N. Leaton (Eds.), *Habituation: Perspectives from child development, animal behavior, and neurophysiology.* Hillsdale, N.J.: Erlbaum, 1976.

Olson, G. M., & Strauss, M. S. *Short-term visual memory in infants.* Paper presented at the meetings of the Midwestern Psychological Association, Chicago, May 1974.

Ornstein, P. A. (Ed.). *Memory development in children.* Hillsdale, N.J.: Erlbaum, 1978.

Pancrantz, C. N., & Cohen L. B. Recovery of habituation in infants. *Journal of Experimental Child Psychology,* 1970, **9,** 208–216.

Perlmutter, M. *A developmental study of stimulus integration in recognition memory.* Unpublished manuscript, 1977.

Perlmutter, M. What is memory aging the aging of? *Developmental Psychology,* 1978, **14,** 330–345.

Perlmutter, M. Development of memory in the preschool years. In R. Greene & T. D. Yawkey (Eds.), *Childhood Development.* Lexington, Mass.: Lexington Press, in press.

Perlmutter, M., & Lange, G. A developmental analysis of recall-recognition distinctions. To appear in P. A. Ornstein (Ed.), *Memory development in children.* Hillsdale, N.J.: Erlbaum, 1978.

Perlmutter, M., & Myers, N. A. Recognition memory development in two- to four-year-olds. *Developmental Psychology,* 1974, **10,** 447–450.

Perlmutter, M., & Myers, N. A. Recognition memory in preschool children. *Developmental Psychology,* 1976, **12,** 271–272. (a)

Perlmutter, M., & Myers, N. A. A developmental study of semantic effects on recognition memory. *Journal of Experimental Child Psychology,* 1976, **22,** 438–453. (b)

Perlmutter, M., Schork, E., & Lewis, D. *The effects of color and category orienting tasks on preschool children's free and cued recall.* Unpublished manuscript, 1978.

Piaget, J. *On the development of memory and identity.* Barre, Mass.: Clark University Press, 1968.

Piaget, J., & Inhelder, B. *Memory and intelligence.* New York: Basic Books, 1973.

Posner, M. I. Abstraction and the process of recognition. In G. H. Bower & J. T. Spence (Eds.), *The psychology of learning and motivation* (Vol. 3), New York: Academic Press, 1969.

Potter, M. C. Meaning in visual search. *Science,* 1975, **187,** 965–966.

Potter, M. C., & Levy, E. I. Recognition memory for a rapid sequence of pictures. *Journal of Experimental Psychology,* 1969, **81,** 10–15.

Reese, H. W. Imagery and associative memory. In R. V. Kail & J. W. Hagen (Eds.), *Perspectives on the development of memory and cognition.* Hillsdale, N.J.: Erlbaum, 1977.

Reitman, J. S. Mechanisms of forgetting in short-term memory. *Cognitive Psychology,* 1971, **2,** 185–195.

Rogoff, B., Newcombe, N., & Kagan, J. Planfulness and recognition memory. *Child Development,* 1974, **45,** 972–977.

Saayman, G., Ames, E. W., & Moffett, A. Response to novelty as an indicator of visual discrimination in the human infant. *Journal of Experimental Child Psychology,* 1964, **1,** 189–198.

Sameroff, A. J., & Chandler, M. J. Reproductive risk and the continuum of caretaking casualty. In F. D. Horowitz, E. M. Hetherington, S. Scarr-Salapatek, & G. M. Siegel (Eds.), *Review of child development research* (Vol. 4). Chicago: University of Chicago Press, 1975.

Schaffer, H. R., & Parry, M. H. Perceptual-motor behaviour in infancy as a function of age and stimulus familiarity. *British Journal of Psychology,* 1969, **60,** 1–9.

Self, P. A. Control of infant visual attending by auditory and interspersed stimulation. In F. D. Horowitz (Ed.), Visual attention, auditory stimulation, and language discrimination in young infants. *Monographs of the Society of Research in Child Development,* 1974, **39**(5–6, Serial No. 158).

Shaffer, W. O., & Shiffrin, R. M. Rehearsal and storage of visual information. *Journal of Experimental Psychology,* 1972, **92,** 292–296.

Shepard, R. N. Recognition memory for words, sentences and pictures. *Journal of Verbal Learning and Verbal Behavior,* 1967, **6,** 156–163.

Siegel, A. W., Babich, J. M., & Kirasic, K. C. Visual recognition memory in reflective and impulsive children. *Memory and Cognition,* 1974, **2,** 379–384.

Siegel, A. W., Kirasic, K. C., & Kilburg, R. R. Recognition memory in reflective and impulsive preschool children. *Child Development,* 1973, **44,** 651–656.

Sigman, M., & Parmelee, A. H. Visual preferences of four-month-old premature and full-term infants. *Child Development,* 1974, **45,** 959–965.

Siqueland, E. R. *Further developments in infant learning.* Paper presented at the XIXth International Congress of Psychology, London, 1969.

Sokolov, E. N. Neuronal models and the orienting reflex. In M. A. B. Brazier (Ed.), *The central nervous system and behavior.* New York: Josiah Macy, Jr. Foundation, 1960.

Sokolov, E. N. *Perception and the conditioned reflex.* London: Pergamon, 1963.

Sokolov, E. N. The neuronal mechanisms of the orienting reflex. In E. N. Sokolov & O. S. Vinogradova (Eds.), *Neuronal mechanisms of the orienting reflex.* Hillside, N.J.: Erlbaum, 1975.

Sophian, C., & Perlmutter, M. *Short-term forgetting in preschool children.* Paper presented at the meetings of the Midwest Psychological Association, Chicago, 1978.

Spear, N. E. Retrieval of memories: A psychobiological approach. In W. K. Estees (Ed.), *Handbook on learning and cognitive processes* (Vol. 4). Hillsdale, N.J.: Erlbaum, 1976.

Standing, L., Conezio, J., & Haber, R. N. Perception and memory for pictures: Single-trial learning of 2500 visual stimuli. *Psychonomic Science,* 1970, **19,** 73–74.

Stinson, F. S. *A study of visual novelty with four-month infants in an operant visual reinforcement paradigm.* Unpublished Master's thesis, Brown University, 1970.

Stinson, F. S. Visual short-term memory in four-month infants. (Doctoral dissertation, Brown University, 1971). *Dissertation Abstracts International,* 1973, **33,** 3998–3999–B. (University Microfilms No. 73–2340).

Thompson, R. F., & Spencer, W. A. Habituation: A model phenomenon for the study of neuronal substrates of behavior. *Psychological Review,* 1966, **73,** 16–43.

Tighe, T. J., & Tighe, L. S. Stimulus control in children's learning. In A. D. Pick (Ed.), *Minnesota Symposia on Child Psychology* (Vol. 6). Minneapolis: University of Minnesota Press, 1972.

Tulving, E. Episodic and semantic memory. In E. Tulving & W. Donaldson (Eds.), *Organization and Memory.* New York: Academic Press, 1972.

Valentine, C. W. The colour perception and colour preferences of an infant during its fourth and eighth months. *British Journal of Psychology,* 1913–1914, **6,** 363–386.

Vernon, M. D. *A further study of visual perception.* London and New York: Cambridge University Press, 1952.

von Wright, J. M. Relation between verbal recall and visual recognition of the same stimuli in young children. *Journal of Experimental Child Psychology,* 1973, **15,** 481–487.

Waugh, N. C., & Norman, D. A. Primary memory. *Psychological Review,* 1965, **72,** 89–104.

Welch, M. J. Infants' visual attention to varying degrees of novelty. *Child Development,* 1974, **45,** 344–350.

Werner, J. S., & Siqueland, E. R. Visual recognition memory in the preterm infant. *Infant Behavior and Development,* 1978, **1,** 79–94.

Werner, J. S., & Wooten, B. R. Human infant color vision and color perception. *Infant Behavior and Development,* 1979, **2,** 241–274.

Wetherford, M. J., & Cohen, L. B. Developmental changes in infant visual preferences for novelty and familiarity. *Child Development,* 1973, **44,** 416–424.

Wicken, C. D. Temporal limits of human information processing: A developmental study. *Psychological Bulletin,* 1974, **81,** 739–756.

Wicklegren, W. A. Age and storage dynamics in continuous recognition memory. *Developmental Psychology,* 1975, **11,** 165-169.

Wiener, G. Psychological correlates of premature birth: A review. *Journal of Nervous and Mental Diseases,* 1962, **134,** 129-144.

Wimer, R. E., & Wigdor, B. T. Age differences in retention of learning. *Journal of Gerontology,* 1958, **13,** 291-295.

Young-Browne, G., Rosenfeld, H. M., & Horowitz, F. D. Infant discrimination of facial expression. *Child Development,* 1977, **48,** 555-562.

Zeaman, D., & House, B. J. Interpretations of developmental trends in discriminative transfer effects. In A. D. Pick (Ed.), *Minnesota Symposia on Child Psychology* (Vol. 8). Minneapolis: University of Minnesota Press, 1974.

SIBSHIP-CONSTELLATION EFFECTS ON PSYCHOSOCIAL DEVELOPMENT, CREATIVITY, AND HEALTH[1]

Mazie Earle Wagner and Herman J. P. Schubert

STATE UNIVERSITY COLLEGE, BUFFALO

and

Daniel S. P. Schubert

CASE-WESTERN RESERVE MEDICAL SCHOOL

AND

CLEVELAND METROPOLITAN GENERAL HOSPITAL

[1] Daniel Schubert contributed the sections on creativity, health, and physical characteristics and helped with the overall organization and planning of this article. The editor's suggestions were most helpful in enhancing clarity and readability, for which we are grateful. The authors thank Rose Gardner for her painstaking preparation of the manuscript. Supported in part by a grant from NICHD, #2 R01 HD07551-03.

57

I. Introduction

The study of the effects of sibship variables on child development resulted in findings vital to family and population planning and to child rearing, education, and therapy. For example, knowing that the only child usually develops superior intellect, social success, self-esteem, and responsibility can free couples to have an only child by choice. An ultimate aim of investigating sibship-variable effects is to maximize in the family, school, and clinic the positive consequences of each sibship category while reducing the negative. To know that wide spacing between siblings, even in sibships of two, makes stronger characters for both children is a help in family planning. Similarly, for parents having two closely spaced boys, knowing that individualized treatment from the beginning is necessary for good personality development would prompt them to make every effort to give differential treatment.

The reader will find in this contribution a summary and integration of the abundant research findings culled from over 2000 articles. The contribution reviews the effects of each of the sibship variables: sibship size, ordinal position, and sibling age spacing with regard to intelligence, achievement, creativity, personality, and health. All descriptions included are based on at least one reported research finding. Speculative literature is consistently excluded. Each section is planned and written so as to be a unit which may be read separately. The first section gives an account of the development of the body of knowledge and the means by which it grew. A section is devoted to the effects of each of the above sibship variables, and a special one each to their effects on creativity, health, and physical characteristics. The reviewers are cognizant of the consequential effects on personality of such factors as the sibship category of parent, socioeconomic status, lack of intactness of family, and father absence, and they regret the lack of time and space that precluded adequate treatment of these influences.

II. Basic Advances in Research on Sibship Effects

Research on the personality traits characteristic of each of the sibship categories has advanced greatly as understanding of the interactional effects of the various sibship variables increased. Research design was improved by (1) contrasting unique sibship categories, (2) holding influencing demographic and familial factors constant, and (3) using personality-trait measurement resulting in the unique trait descriptions of each sibship pattern.

During the nineteenth century and approaching the middle of the twentieth century, the major emphasis was on primogeniture: the firstborn were contrasted with the laterborn. Then, investigators began to divide firstborn into onlies (onlyborn) and eldests, a productive procedural advance because, in spite of eldests and onlies resembling each other considerably in verbal ability and academic achievement, in other respects, their similarity is limited. The next refining step divided laterborn into intermediates and lastborn. So now four ordinal positions are studied. Adler (1924, 1930) was among the first to emphasize the differences between these four ordinal positions.

In 1954–1955 Helen Koch refined research in the area of sibship variables by a precision of at least one significant figure. In epoch-making research she compared 5- and 6-year-old boys in sibships of two, divided into four categories: *B* B (the index case being the older boy with a younger brother), B *B* (younger boy with older brother), *B* G (older boy with younger sister), and G *B* (younger boy with older sister); each category is divided into three subgroups by age interval separating the siblings, namely, less than 2 years, 2–4 years, and over 4 years. She demonstrated that, when studying sibship-constellation effects, error variance is reduced by holding constant sibship size, age of index case, sex of sibling, age spacing, and ordinal position, in addition to race, socioeconomic status, and degree of urbanness. It took some time for researchers to realize the value of her paradigm but in time the white, suburban, middle-class sibship of two was being investigated with exactitude. Rosenberg and Sutton-Smith (1964), Bigner (1972), and Cicirelli (1974) intensively studied sex-of-sibling effects in the two-child sibship. Unfortunately, however, comparisons of all firstborn with all laterborn continue to appear with accompanying persistent underreporting, that is, with either ordinal position or sibship size omitted. The best report is a grid (Belmont & Marolla, 1973; Schachter, 1963) of sibship size by ordinal (rank) position from which essential measures may be computed. Chen and Cobb (1960) urged comparison of percentages of oldest and youngest mentioning that, in complete families, they would theoretically be the same. Subsequently, Price and Hare (1969) and Hare and Price (1970) pointed out that, when a population is growing, the percentage of firstborn will be disproportionately higher than of each other ordinal position.

Using the experimental approach, Schachter (1959) compared the behavior of subjects in different ordinal positions, rather than determining the frequency of their appearance in a specific sample. His use of the observational technique to determine whether ordinal position influences behavior resulted in the finding that under stress eldest women tend to seek the presence of others for reassurance. He started a new approach.

Having available the sibship data of birth order and sibling spacing in addition to intelligence measurements of nearly 400,000 young men, Belmont and Marolla (1973) showed, among other things, that intellectual performance decreases with sibship size and with birth order. By grouping these same subjects by both sibship size and birth rank, Belmont, Stein, and Susser (1975) were able to plot for each family size a curve of intelligence against birth order. Using Belmont and Marolla's data, Zajonc and Markus (1975) developed a confluence model that explains the relation of birth order, sibship size, and age spacing to intelligence. They derived a regression equation that accounts for 97% of the variance, a generalization regrettably limited to men. Zajonc (1976) presented some indirect evidence that age-spacing effects could account for the different curves of intelligence by birth rank produced by data from the Netherlands, United States, France, and Scotland which show that lastborn have the highest intelligence scores. Investigators have become increasingly aware of the complexities in the number of sibship variables affecting personality development, of the interaction between the sibship variables, and of the influence of numerous demographic variables interacting with the sibships variables. In general research-design terms, such awareness has meant that researchers are becoming more careful and diligent in (1) searching for the sibship factors affecting personality development; (2) analyzing distinguishable groups separately, for instance, onlyborn, eldest, middleborn, and youngest by size of sibship; (3) keeping as many factors, both sibship and demographic, as constant as possible; (4) seeking to determine the characteristics of the exceptions not having the noted effect and of those falling below the mean of the control group; and (5) carrying out crosscultural, including cross-socioeconomic, studies.

III.   Sibship Size[2]

The most intensely researched area among sibship variables is size of family or sibship. Terhune's (1974) timely and valuable review of the effects of family size, containing abstracts of about 250 articles, is recommended reading. He included studies concerning effects not only on the sibship members, but also on their parents, whose life style changed with an increase of the number of children. Fathers tend to become more involved as the family size increases, especially with the eldest (Clausen, 1966; Nuttall & Nuttall, 1975), and the involvement places more stress on the father (Nye, Carlson, & Garrett, 1970), resulting in hypertension and gastric ulcers (Omran, 1974). Mothers of large families are more affectionately demonstrative but spank more (Sears, Maccoby, & Levin, 1957) and they find a brood of children fairly close in age, with the turmoil of their interaction, a considerable burden (Clausen, 1966). Further, women with high parity have more hypertension (Omran, 1974). As might be expected from the increased stress on both parents, marital adjustment frequently declines as the sibship size increases (Farber & Blackman, 1956; Nuttall & Nuttall, 1975; Omran, 1974).

In contrast to small sibships, large families tend to spend more time socializing together while smaller families spend more time at restaurants, at movies, and with others (Nuttall & Nuttall, 1975). Members of large families tend to be more authoritarian, less ideationally flexible, and more distrustful of others (Schooler & Scarr, 1962), to value responsibility over independence training, conformity over self-expression, cooperation and obedience over individualism (Rosen, 1961), and organization and leadership, in practice, relying on the older siblings for care and control of younger ones (Clausen, 1966; Sears, Maccoby, & Levin, 1957). They tend to increase control over high-school-aged girls while decreasing control over high-school-aged boys, to use more rules and corporal punishment (Elder, 1962b; Nye, Carlson, & Garrett, 1970), and to apply more discipline of the "unconcerned" type—exposure to which leads to poor performance on IQ tests, to apathy, to lack of spontaneity, and to a tendency to give up quickly when failure is imminent (Kent & Davis, 1957).

These effects of family size on family rule vary greatly with sex and ordinal position of the child and with social class. The negative effects of large sibships are less drastic on girls than on boys. The most asocial warping of personality occurs in the "unacculturated" lower-lower class irrespective of race.

---

[2] Presented in part at the InterAmerican Congress of Psychology, Miami Beach, 1974.

A.   INTELLIGENCE

Numerous investigations, including several large-scale studies, have cor-
roboratively established the effects of sibship size on intelligence. Schooler
(1972) studied 1101 men representative of all employed men in the United
States and found that large sibships are related to poor intellect. Breland
(1972) studied over 680,000 merit scholars in the United States, and Belmont and Marolla (1973) studied over 400,000 19-year-old men, the total
population born between 1944 to 1947 in the Netherlands. Both obtained
the usual finding of an inverse relation between intelligence and both size
of sibship and ordinal rank in the sibship. Nisbet (1953) found a higher
relation between sibship size and verbal performance than between sibship
size and nonverbal performance. Among Selective Service mental rejectees
at fifth-grade level or less, 70% came from families of five or more children
(Lieberman, 1964). In a study of all men called up for military service in
Sweden in 1954, intelligence was inversely related to the number of younger
siblings (Quensel, 1958). In a large sample of Baltimore births, risk of mental deficiency increased with sibship size (Lilienfeld & Pasamanick, 1956).
Lower school readiness scores were shown by 2- to 3-year-old children
from large disadvantaged families than by those from smaller families. A
group intelligence test administered to 70,805 Scottish 11-year-olds yielded
a correlation of $-.28$ with family size and, for a subsample, an r of $-.32$
(Maxwell, 1954). Recently, Zajonc (1976) predicted correctly that the intelligence of United States college students would decrease as a result of the
post-Second World War baby boom. He now predicts an increase in
college-student intelligence as a consequence of the decrease in the 1960s
birth rate.

Several researchers report that the effects of sibship-size on intelligence
are most conspicuous for the middle class. Belmont and Marolla (1973)
found that, when they divided their 19-year-olds into nonmanual, manual,
and farm groups, the intelligence test scores decreased with increase in sibship size but that the relationship was distinctly less pronounced in the
farm-reared group. Long ago, Maxwell and Huestis (1930) found that
among college students the negative correlation between intelligence and
sibship size presented itself only among those from middle socioeconomic-
status categories. Kennett and Cropley (1970) found that the inverse relationship between family size and intelligence diminished to nonsignificance
for a sample of 170 upper-middle-class and upper-class children and more
recently Kennett (1973) established that in upper-class homes, children
from large families were more creative than those from smaller families,
although verbal ability measures showed the usually found negative relationship between sibship size and intelligence for other socioeconomic

levels (see also Section VI). Wagner and H. Schubert (1977a) supported Kennett's (1973) finding that in upper- and upper-middle-classes a large sibship does not necessarily lead to diminished ability. United States presidents, contenders for the presidency, and eminent military leaders usually come from large (mean family size 5.7, 4.9, and 5.2, respectively) upper-middle- and upper-class families. Using statistically highly sophisticated methods, Marjoribanks (1976), Marjoribanks and Walberg (1975), Marjoribanks, Walberg, and Bargen (1975), and Walberg and Marjoribanks (1976) found that at least half the variance in verbal ability can be accounted for by family size plus father's occupational level.

B.   ACADEMIC ACHIEVEMENT

Given that intelligence is inversely related to sibship size, at least in the middle class, it should not be astonishing to find that academic and professional achievement are similarly related to sibship size. Wahl's (1956b) data for 100,000 United States Navy recruits, whose mean schooling was eleventh grade, produce a mean sibship size of 4.0. Schachter's sets of data (1963) yield a mean sibship size for 651 high-school students of 3.6; for 4013 University of Minnesota psychology students, 3.15; and for 199 graduate students in psychology, 2.8. Thus, sibship size decreased with increase of educational level. Datta (1967), studying 536 science merit students, obtained an average sibship size of 2.6. Cobb and French (1966) found that 192 Columbia College undergraduates who tended to come from upper- and upper-middle-class homes, the mean sibship size was 2.4. For freshmen entering the State College at Buffalo in 1958, Wagner (1960) calculated for 264 men an average sibship size of 3.0, and for 616 women, 3.1. The student body at this college is lower-middle and middle-middle class in origin. Using the data from these studies, educational level and sibship size are inversely related to the extent indicated by an r of $-.56$.

The smaller the family and the higher the socioeconomic status the higher the verbal ability, the educational and vocational success, the achievement motivation, and the upward mobility. Family size and socioeconomic level are highly correlated. Both seem to contribute to coping level. As suggested by Marjoribanks (1976), 50% of the variance in verbal ability is accounted for by family size plus father's occupational level. Rosen (1961) found that parents of small families plan ambitiously for their children who have strong achievement motivation. Barger and Hall (1966) concluded that family size is more strongly related to educational and vocational achievement than is ordinal position. Among 1893 British couples both intergenerational and personal mobility are inversely related to family size (Berent, 1952), also, among 457 high-status families, upward mobility was inversely related to family size (Tomasson, 1966). With social origin held constant among 3128 individuals, males from sibships of five or more were more liable to downward mobility than those from smaller families (Svalastoga, 1959). The question remains whether it is indeed the socioeconomic and cultural status that determines not only family size but also verbal ability, success, motivation, and general upward mobility.

C.   PERSONALITY TRAITS

On the whole, smaller families provide psychological advantages for children. Krout (1939) stated that the filial value of an individual is inversely proportional to the number of children, particularly of the same sex, already in the family. Fifth-graders from small families are better adjusted than those from larger families on tests of personality (Hawkes, Burchinal, & Gardner, 1958; Lessing & Oberlander, 1967) and on teachers' ratings (Blatz & Bott, 1927), are more extraverted and brighter, have parents who are more interested in them (Eysenck & Carlson, 1970), and have greater moral knowledge and honesty (Maller, 1931). Conversely viewed, children from larger families have a poorer self-concept (Sears, 1970), more family tension, resentment, and discouragement in their youth (Moore & Holtzman, 1965), more suicides (Chen & Cobb, 1960), more need for approval (Masterson, 1971), and, among college students, less stability and dominance (Stagner & Katzoff, 1936).

Some authors specifically assert that the two-child family is optimal. Herbst (1954) found that the average degree of "tension" was lowest in the sibship of two and, from several studies, Lieberman (1970) concluded that the two-child family is advantageous both to parents and children. Yet, harmonious and facilitative one-child as well as large families can and do produce capable, productive, and socialized adults. Many only children become well-adjusted, outgoing, and cooperative (see Section IV, B). In many cases, large families produce altruistic (Krebs, 1970; Ribal, 1963), cooperative (Maller, 1931), and creative individuals (Kennett, 1973; Wagner & H. Schubert, 1977a). Walberg and Marjoribanks (1976) showed that socioeconomic status has little effect on intellect in sibships of two but has a major effect on sibships of three and over.

Researchers have done extensive surveys on the frequency of gross maladjustment by sibship size. Diagnostically different maladjustments occur in the small as contrasted with the larger families. In the small family, anxiety in male children is higher than in the large family (Rosenberg & Sutton-Smith, 1964); neurosis is more frequent especially among oldest (Riess, 1976; Rutter & Graham, 1970; Tuckman & Regan, 1967); neurotic delinquents are also overrepresented in small families (Riess, 1976); "personality and emotional problems" that cause gross discomfort but not dysfunction occur more frequently in small sibships (Levy, 1931); and schizophrenia during childhood is higher in small rather than large sibships (Mintz, 1965). Hollingshead and Redlich (1958) found that neurosis is more prevalent in the middle socioeconomic class at which level smaller families are more common. Small sibships, then, produce self-controlled, anxious, neurotic persons who suffer anguish rather than foisting disturbance on others when pressure mounts. Large sibships have an overrepresentation of juvenile delinquents according to several broad samples (Clausen, 1966; Glueck & Glueck, 1950; Levy, 1931; Reiss, 1952; Schindler, 1974). Among 1297 referred children, those from large families are overrepresented in having school problems, antisocial behavior, and doing poor school work (Tuckman & Regan, 1967). Prisoners convicted of more serious crimes come from larger families than people convicted of lesser offenses (Koller & Castanos, 1970). Alcoholics and antisocial adults (Riess, 1976; Smart, 1963) are more likely to come from large rather than small sibships, and especially from the latter half of large sibships. Related to such personality disorders and delinquency is the finding that children from large families take more risks (Jamieson, 1969), that adolescents from larger families are much less adjusted to parents than those from smaller sibships (Nye, 1952), and that antisocial children tend to come from large sibships (Rutter & Graham, 1970).

Wahl (1956b) found that schizophrenics in the Navy, compared with Navy recruits in general, tend to come from significantly larger sibships, the means of which are 4.4 and 4.0, respectively. Granville-Grossman (1966) reported a family size of 4.1 for 652 female and 4.2 for 540 male schizophrenics, but had no comparison control. Large sibships are more likely than small ones to set the stage for learned withdrawal from family relationships, especially from mother figures, and thus predispose the siblings to social disarticulation and schizophrenia (Alkire, Brunse, & Houlihan, 1974). Wahl (1956a), who widely investigated the topic both clinically and by survey, felt that a large number of siblings leads to increased difficulty in identification, owing to little time with parents, intensified sibling rivalry for limited parental time, greater economic privation, and increased intrapsychic anxiety and hostility with resultant guilt engendered by intrafamilial striving. Lewandowski and Graham (1972) found in a psychiatric population on the Minnesota Multiphasic Personality Inventory (MMPI) that those with high 46/64 scales have signifantly more siblings, that is, that large families produce more suspicious, guarded, manipulative opportunists.

The present researchers found in middle-class families (1) a greater prevalence of maladjustment among large-family, college-going middleborn girls especially when closely spaced, than among middle girls from families of three (see Section V); (2) increased feminine interests with increasing family size among college girls (Wagner, 1975); and (3) more homosexuality among large-family rather than small-family outpatient males (H. Schubert, Wagner, & Riess, 1976). Overrepresentation of in- and out-patient psychiatric men from all-male sibships also was found (Wagner & H. Schubert, 1976).

D.   DISCUSSION

Several cautionary notes need emphasis: First, empirical evidence for sibship size effects is available almost exclusively for the middle-middle, lower-middle, and upper-lower socioeconomic classes and is practically nonexistent for upper, upper-middle, and lower-lower socioeconomic levels and rural populations; second, not all the studies cited had the best methodology nor do all differences reported reach statistical significance. Yet the consistency of the main results gathered, using a wide variety of procedures and samples and by many different researchers, greatly heightens reliability and confidence in the findings. Finally, even significant findings are based on means and distributions that involve overlapping of groups. For instance, on any measure for which the mean for large exceeds that for small families, the former will still have cases below the mean for small families and, vice versa, among the small families will be some with values above the mean for the large families. The differences are more or less, not all or none.

Finally, the negative concomitants of the large family may not hold for that small minority whose finances, energies, and management abilities are sufficient to assure the full development of each child. Yet the large sibship is primarily the domain of those not only financially poor but also lacking in foresight, favorable cultural attitudes regarding progress, knowledge of good child-rearing procedures, physical stamina, and information regarding salubrious health practices. As it stands, then, it would seem that if a people, a country, or a community wishes to increase its standard of living, its intellectual growth, its occupational achievement, and its social and emotional health, a most effective move would be to decrease its birth rate to a level approaching the two-child sibship.

IV.   Ordinal Position

Among persistently repeated experiences, resulting in overlearning, are those related to one's ordinal position among siblings, the effects of which endure throughout life and even influence longevity (Beeton & Pearson, 1901). The over 2000 scientific articles on sibship-constellation effects (D. Schubert, Wagner, & H. Schubert, 1976, 1980) indicate the persistence of the scientific belief that effects of sibship constellation exist and can, by diligent research, be identified. The high reliability of the retrospective data on sibship constellation adds to its appeal. In this section we will review and update findings on the unique characteristics of each major ordinal position (the only born, eldest, middleborn, and youngest), briefly consider the parent–child relation by ordinal position and sex, and suggest relevant research.

A.   PARENT–CHILD RELATIONS

1. Ordinal Position

In much of the research concerning differences in child treatment of the first- and laterborn, the onlyborn and oldest are combined. This is quite proper here, since until the advent of a second, the two groups would presumably, though not necessarily, be treated similarly. What, then, is being compared is the behavior of primiparous and multiparous mothers. How do mothers treat their firstborn differently from laterborn?

Rothbart (1971) concluded that the mother identifies more with her firstborn daughter than with any of her other children. Other researchers found more caretaker interaction with firstborn 2-week-old infants, as contrasted with the laterborn children (McBride, 1974), more social, affectionate, and caretaking interactions with 3-month-old firstborn sons and daughters (Jacobs & Moss, 1976), decreasing interactive vocalization with increasing birth order (Judd & Lewis, 1976), and more smiling at the firstborn by mothers (Barker & Lewis, 1975). Both bottle-feeding and nonfeeding attention time are longer for firstborn, although they actually consume less food than laterborn siblings (Thoman, Turner, Lieberman, & Barnett, 1970).

On the less positive side, firstborn as contrasted with laterborn are more dominated, more pressured to conform and achieve, and more anxiously intruded upon (Lasko, 1954; Rothbart, 1971; Sears, Maccoby, & Levin, 1957). Whether breast- or bottle-fed, infant firstborn are more interrupted and dominated by their mothers while secondborn are treated more permissively and with more warmth and are more frequently fed on a self-demand schedule (Gerwitz, 1948). Nurses do not show differential treatment by ordinal position (Thoman, Lieberman, & Olson, 1972; Thoman, Turner, Lieberman, & Barnett, 1970). Parental treatment toward the eldest is more restrictive, involves more disciplinary friction, and carries less warmth than toward secondborn, with whom parents seem more relaxed (Lasko, 1954). Laterborn also receive less attention at bedtime, less restriction in play, and less concern regarding health, being treated generally more casually than are firstborn (Gerwitz, 1948). More firstborn are referred to child guidance clinics, and, as described by parents, have more problems (Shrader & Leventhal, 1968). The present reviewers suggest that this maladjustment may be due to the greater inexperience and anxiety of parents with their first children. As parents gain experience and security, altered perceptions and treatment of children follow. Mothers of firstborn daughters especially pressure their children for achievement (Rothbart, 1971). Mothers of firstborn sons are more demanding, exacting, intrusive, and cautious than they are with their younger children (Cushna, 1966). Parents' anxiety and inexpertise, as well as their greater involvement, seem to convert into differential interactions with their firstborn.

Bartlett and Smith (1966) felt that the achievement tendencies of many firstborn are due to the relatively greater parental involvement, encouragement, and urging. Gerwitz (1948) found that upwardly mobile parents allow more self-demand feeding but are more punitive regarding aggression. Elder (1962a, b) concluded, from his extensive study of adolescents, that in high socioeconomic-status families, the eldest receives more parental encouragement, has higher aspirations, and is more likely to achieve, while in lower socioeconomic families, it is the youngest who benefits similarly from his ordinal position. However, among 8- to 10-year-old boys, there are more firstborn with high achievement needs and each mother more often expresses disappointment with unsatisfactory behavior and less often rewards by telling how much she loves her son (Bartlett & Smith, 1966). Several investigators (Elder, 1962a; Hancock, 1965; Sampson, 1962; Sampson & Hancock, 1967) reported that firstborn show a greater need for achievement. In constrast Rosenfeld (1966) found that laterborn girls have more need for academic success than elderborn, though onlyborn girls have more success than those with siblings. The weight of the evidence is that firstborn have a greater need to achieve than laterborn. This trend may account for their observed greater achievement, that is, their more frequent college (Altus, 1965a, 1966; Forbes, 1970b; Nisbett, 1968; Purpura, 1971; Schachter, 1963; Wagner, 1960), medical school (Cobb & French, 1966), and graduate school attendance (Schachter, 1963), in their being more often applicants for merit science scholarships (Datta, 1968), and in their greater frequency among the eminent, the creative, and those with unusual problem-solving ability (Apperly, 1939; Burnand, 1973; Roe, 1953; D. Schubert, Wagner, & H. Schubert, 1977c; Wagner & Schubert, 1977a, 1979; Zweigenhaft, 1975).

2. Age Spacing

Two researchers investigated the relationship of age spacing between siblings to parental treatment of the child (Lasko, 1954; Nuttall & Nuttall, 1975). The former found that mothers treat two closely spaced (7–20 months) children very much alike, talking with and reacting to the two relatively at the same time and in much the same way, thus making the older child with a closely spaced siblings suffer by being held to the speed of the younger. White (1974) wrote about the closely spaced younger child: "To be a nine-month old *only* child means to live in a world that is full of happiness, sweetness, pleasant interpersonal relations. . . . To have an older sibling at home who is two almost invariably means being on the receiving end of genuine hatred from time to time. . . . The older child is having a very tough time. . . . The younger one . . . may be experiencing things that I do not think anyone should have to experience" (p. 9). The older child intermediately spaced (21–36 months) to the next (Lasko, 1954) receives the least attention and becomes aggressive and disturbed. The child widely spaced (over 3 years) usually has many interests and many friends in school groups and seems to be least disadvantaged by his displacement. Lasko concluded that it is easier to meet the needs of children who are widely spaced. The Nuttalls found that children closely spaced to next oldest report being less accepted by both parents than those with at least a 30-month interval. These investigators found that closely spaced children report that their mothers used firm discipline and that those spaced 18–30 months report that the mother used least hostile psychological control. Generally, intermediate- and far-spaced children thought that the mothers were more lax in their discipline.

3. Sex of Sibling

There are indications that the sex of an oldest child or older children affects the welcome of subsequent children, and presumably their treatment. Westoff, Potter, and Sagi (1963) found that following a boy and a girl the average number of additional children was less than when a couple had two boys or two girls, and they added a supporting statement indicating a greater desire for further children when parents already had a same-sexed pair. Bigner (1975) states that couples who have a girl firstborn will attempt a subsequent quick conception hoping for a boy. Sears, Maccoby, and Levin (1957) found that when a family had only girls, a boy was treated more warmly than in any other combination of previous children. Findings are less clear regarding an additional girl. Research seems to support the current lore that parents want a boy first, then a girl, and that boys are generally more welcome than girls. When a family has two, three, or more same-sexed children, does the decreased welcome accorded one of that same sex reduce the self-esteem, productivity, and so on of the laterborn?

4. Discussion

We have previously stated that in the average home the firstborn, whether only or eldest, wins more welcome and attention than the laterborn. Parental anxiety and variability in handling, exhibited in the inexperienced treatment of the firstborn, should be much the same (or is it?) for onlyborn and eldest. Research is needed to see whether onlyborn are at this early stage treated by parents differently from those with subsequent siblings. Are such differences as are found between onlies and eldest already determined during their first weeks or months of life, or are these differences largely due to displacement versus lack of it, as shown in subsequent treatment (by parents, siblings, and others) through years lived within the parental home?

Schaefer (1973), in a comprehensive review of the effects of various family variables on child development and behavior, concluded that parental acceptance, control, and involvement are significantly related to the child's behavior, achievement, and adjustment; that, indeed, the father may have as much influence on the child's development as does the mother; and that a low level of paternal acceptance and involvement has all-pervasive negative effects upon the child. Schaefer also reported that poor husband and wife relations may be the best indicator of antisocial behavior in boys and that children from unhappy intact families are more maladjusted than children from some broken homes. Other studies (e.g., Krumholtz & Krumholtz, 1972; Schaefer, 1974) indicate that changes in parental behavior can produce substantial positive or negative changes in child behavior.

B.   THE ONLYBORN

The great variability of levels of personality and coping of onlyborn children is related to the great variability in parental acceptance and treatment. The degree of acceptance and the desire for an only child are associated, as are nature of treatment, parental emotional problems, and child-rearing inexperience. An onlyborn may be an only for many reasons: (1) illegitimacy, (2) premarital conception, (3) incompatability of parents, resulting in early termination of the marriage, (4) physical incapacity of the couple to have more children, (5) overanxiety of the couple concerning having more children, (6) the situation of a working mother without adequate facilities for child care, (7) upward mobility of parents without the wherewithall for adequate child care, support, and education of additional children, (8) the early death of a parent, or (9) the parental belief that one child is an optimal number. As suggested by Mitchell and Schroers (1973) from observation of monkeys, parental emotional disturbance may result in particularly harsh treatment of firstborn. Parental inexperience in child care and associated high anxiety lead to inconsistency and mistakes in rearing of firstborn. Such variability in acceptance and treatment of onlyborn makes them notably variable in behavior and personality traits (Campbell, 1933; LaVoie, 1973; Ogburn, 1930; Wisdom & Walsh, 1975).

Over 40 years ago Campbell (1934) reviewed 75 articles on the only child and concluded, as most recent reviewers also have, that onlyborn are not seriously disadvantaged. He wrote, " 'Onliness' *per se* is not the environmental specter so widely assumed" (p. 200). Falbo (1976) found that non-onlies think onlies suffer more from onliness than onlies themselves think. Still Americans—public and scientists alike—persist in believing that the only child is disadvantaged, destined to be arrogant, selfish, inadequate, and unmotivated (Cutts & Moseley, 1954; Griffith, 1973; Peck & Senderowitz, 1974; Russo, 1976; Solomon, Clare & Westoff, 1956; Thompson, 1974). Such ideology may be in part due to the onlyborn's variability in coping, with negative deviations being particularly remembered.

To answer the question of whether onlyborn are disadvantaged the present reviewers analyzed studies that give (1) percentage frequencies of onlyborn in various normal, successful, and poorly coping groups, and (2) comparisons of onlyborn with non-onlyborn on various personality traits, intelligence, and achievement.

Tables I through IV, based on close to 100 investigations, show the percentage of onlyborn, eldest, middleborn, and youngest in general-population, college-attending, successful professional, and socially malfunctioning groups. The mean percentage of onlyborn in all groups is slightly over 10% (*SD* = 6.4%) with both the mode and median at 10%. The mean percentage of onlyborn for all general-population and control samples (Table I) is just under 9% (*SD* = 6.0%) and for the eight large, white, general-population samples is 8.9% (*SD* = 1.0%). Using 2 standard deviations (2 × 1.0 = 2.0) in both directions from the general-population normal-group mean as cut-off points, any sample with a percentage over 11 or under 7% can be taken as having, respectively, an over- or underrepresentation of the onlyborn.

1. Intellect and Achievement

Intellectually the only child stands slightly below his peers from sibships of two, about equal to eldest of three, but exceeds the firstborn of sibships of four and over and laterborn (Belmont & Marolla, 1973; Breland, 1972). The

TABLE I

Percentages of Onlyborn, Eldest, Middleborn, and Youngest and Sibship Size in Nondeviant (Control) Samples

Size and type of sample	Sex	Sibship size	Only	Oldest	Middle	Youngest
386,114 19-Year-old draftees, Netherlands (Belmont & Marolla, 1973)	M	4.4	5.1	26.4	46.7	22.7
670 Normative sample for merit scholars (Breland, 1972)	B[a]	2.8	11.8	37.0	25.2	26.0
156 University nonprofessional staff (Chen & Cobb, 1958)	B	[b]	11.5	28.6	30.8	28.8
50 Normal controls for ulcer patients (Hamilton, 1950)	M		14.0	22.0	42.0	22.0
250 Controls for ulcered children (Kellock, 1951)	M		4.8	21.6	48.8	24.8
500 General hospitalized patients (Norton, 1952)	B		8.4	23.4	45.5	24.1
650 Controls for coronary-heart-disease decedents (Paffenbarger, Wolf, Notkin, & Thorne, 1966)	M		15.0			
495 Controls for Schizophrenic patients (Patterson & Zeigler, 1941)	B		9.1	25.7	44.8	20.4
495 Controls for Schizophrenic (Plank, 1953)	M		9.1	25.7	44.8	20.4
651 High-school students in Minnesota (Schachter, 1963)	B	3.6	8.0	27.2	36.2	28.6

3315 Random sample, West German, ages 16–65 (Schachter 1963)	B	4.5	9.1	23.8	45.5	21.9
968 Veteran Administration Hospital patients 1951–1968 (Schubert, 1970)	M	4.4	12.4	22.5	43.3	21.8
396 Black general population (H. Schubert & Wagner, 1976)	F	5.3	5.6	18.7	61.1	14.6
106 Black general population (H. Schubert & Wagner, 1976)	M	5.0	6.0	26.0	50.0	18.0
172 Blue-collar, white general population (H. Schubert & Wagner, 1976)	B	4.5	6.8	22.3	48.2	22.7
78 Black golden agers (H. Schubert & Wagner, 1976)	B	5.6	1.3	25.6	62.8	10.3
144 White golden agers (H. Schubert & Wagner, 1976)	B	4.6	7.0	23.6	48.7	20.8
782 High-school students (Sletto, 1934)	B			22.0	52.0	26.0
106 Medical patients used as controls for schizophrenics (Smith & McIntyre, 1963)	B	5.5	3.8	24.6	52.8	18.8
144 Controls for retarded children (Tizard & Hemming, 1970)	B		9.7	34.0	22.2	34.0
100,000 Navy recruits (Wahl, 1956b)	M	4.0	9.0	27.0	34.0	27.0

[a] B equals both and female.
[b] When blank, sibship size not given by author.

TABLE II

Percentages of Onlyborn, Eldest, Middleborn, and Youngest and Sibship Size by Academic Success

Size and type of sample	Sex	Sibship size	Only	Oldest	Middle	Youngest
College samples						
300 Queens College (Abernethy, 1940)	F	2.0[a]		63.0		
689 University of California at Santa Barbara (Altus, 1965a)	M	2.0[a]		63.0		
518 University of California at Santa Barbara (Altus, 1965a)	M	3.0[b]		50.0		
1,128 University of California at Santa Barbara (Altus, 1965a)	F	2.0[a]		63.0		
781 University of California at Santa Barbara (Altus, 1965a)	F	3.0[b]		51.0		
441 Superior high-school students (Bradley & Sanborn, 1969)	B[c]	2.0[a]		63.0		
428 Superior high-school students (Bradley & Sanborn, 1969)	B	3.0[b]		45.0		
1,147 Commended merit scholars in 1962 (Breland, 1972)	B	2.6	15.8	51.8	15.2	17.9
81,175 Project Talent scholars (Claudy, 1976)	M	[d]	10.9			
81,175 Project Talent scholars (Claudy, 1976)	F		10.2			
192 Medical-school students (Cobb & French, 1966)	M	2.9	11.1	52.3	26.8	21.8

74

Group	Sex[c]	Sibship size[d]				
804 College students (Forbes, 1970b)	B		9.8	40.0	25.6	24.6
78 Mt. Holyoke women (Hayes, 1938)	F	2.0[a]		58.0		
106 Mississippi State 1968 undergraduates (McGlynn, 1969)	B	2.0[a]		59.0		
2,410 Columbia undergraduates (Nisbett, 1968)	M	2.4	18.4	43.7	12.6	25.2
265 Columbia students who play dangerous sports (Nisbett, 1968)	M	2.8	14.7	37.0	21.2	26.3
4,013 University of Minnesota students taking psychology in 1959–1961 (Schachter, 1963)	B	3.2	10.4	40.0	24.8	25.1
199 Graduate students in psychology at University of Minnesota in 1961 (Schachter, 1963)	B	2.8	21.0	37.0	18.0	24.0
44 Nursing students (D. Schubert, 1976)	F		6.8	27.3	47.7	18.2
284 White 1958 college students (Wagner, 1960)	M	2.6	26.0	32.4	20.1	20.4
615 White 1958 college students (Wagner, 1960)	F	3.1	18.0	40.3	22.4	20.9
Reading and mental retardates						
42 Reading disabilities (Siegel, 1951)	B	2.2	19.0	21.5	21.5	38.0
54 Mental (IQ) retardates (Tizard & Hemming, 1970)	B		9.3	18.5	38.9	33.3
84 Reading retardates (Tizard & Hemming, 1970)	B		6.0	20.2	42.8	31.0

[a] Data restricted to families of two siblings where 50% would be expected.

[b] Data restricted to families of three siblings where 33% would be expected.

[c] B equals combined male and female.

[d] When blank, sibship size was not given by author.

TABLE III

Percentages of Onlyborn, Eldest, Middleborn, and Youngest and Family Size for Highly Successful Men and Women by Profession

Size and type of sample	Sex	Sibship size	Only	Oldest	Middle	Youngest
Athletes						
15 Baseball players (Chen & Cobb, 1960)	M	[a]	0	0	47.0	53.0
Composers and writers						
75 Writers and poets (Bliss, 1970)	M		9.1	28.6	29.9	32.4
30 Autobiographers (Burnand, 1973)	B[b]		6.7	10.0	36.7	46.7
47 Autobiographers who also were writers (Burnand, 1973)	B		10.6	40.4	25.5	23.3
80 Eminent composers (D. Schubert, Wagner, & H. Schubert, 1977a)	B	4.0	20.0	24.0	27.0	29.0
Illustrious men and women						
261 Eminent Americans (Bowerman, 1947)	M		3.8	28.0	54.0	14.2
37 Eminent biographees (Burnand, 1973)	B		10.8	27.1	48.7	13.4
215 Distinguished Americans on covers of *Time* (Toman & Toman, 1970)	M		27.0	27.4	21.9	24.0
38 Distinguished Americans on covers of *Time* (Toman & Toman, 1970)	F		18.9	37.0	15.8	23.7
283 Actors (Zillich, Wagner, & H. Schubert, 1980)	M	3.2	25.0	22.0	19.8	33.2
186 Actresses (Zillich, Wagner, & H. Schubert, 1980)	F	2.8	25.7	33.5	11.2	29.6

Politicians and military

128 Candidates for Illinois Legislature in 1970 (Forbes, 1971)			8.0	32.0	32.0	29.0
100 Boston lawyers (Very & Prull, 1970)	M		3.0	66.0	23.0	8.0
48 United States military leaders (Wagner & H. Schubert, 1977b)	M	5.2	4.2	27.1	45.8	22.9
29 Contenders for United States presidency (Wagner & H. Schubert, 1977a)	M	3.8	10.0	25.0	40.0	25.0
38 United States presidents (Wagner & H. Schubert, 1977a)	M	5.6	2.6	34.1	47.3	16.0
133 United States senators and representatives (Zweigenhaft, 1975)	B	3.7	9.0	38.3	29.3	23.3
Scientists						
2,450 Science doctorates (Bayer, 1967)		2.0		56.0		
855 American scientists (Cattell & Brimhall, 1921)	M	4.5	7.3	33.3	38.8	20.6
112 High science-attainment, high-school seniors (Datta, 1967)	B	2.6	11.6	50.0	15.2	17.8
137 Middle science-attainment, high-school seniors (Datta, 1967)	B	2.7	10.2	50.4	10.2	25.5
287 Low science-attainment, high-school seniors (Datta, 1967)	B	2.6	16.4	46.7	13.9	18.8
40 American scientists (Eiduson, 1962)	M		12.5	47.5	17.5	22.5
99 English scientists (Galton, 1874)	M	6.3	22.2	26.3	36.4	15.1
506 American scientists (Hart, 1960)	M		15.6	33.4	25.1	25.9
906 Top American scientists, many Nobel prize winners (Visher, 1948)	M	4.6	8.0	33.5		
57 American scientists (West, 1960)		2.0[c]		57.0		

(continued)

TABLE III (continued)

Size and type of sample	Sex	Sibship size	Only	Oldest	Middle	Youngest
Social scientists, educators, and scholars						
930 American Rhodes Scholars (Apperly, 1939)	M	3.6	8.4	38.9	25.9	26.8
235 American Rhodes Scholars (Apperly, 1939)		2.0[c]		61.0		
230 American Rhodes Scholars (Apperly, 1939)		3.0[d]		44.0		
309 British geniuses (Ellis, 1926)	B			30.4	47.9	21.7
93 Educational administrators (Havighurst & Wagner, 1977)	M	3.8	9.7	31.2	36.6	22.5
150 Social scientists (Havighurst & Wagner, 1977)	M	3.9	14.9	30.5	33.8	21.0
134 Social scientists (Havighurst & Wagner, 1977)	F	3.6	9.0	44.0	32.0	15.0

[a] When blank, sibship size was not given by author.
[b] B equals combined men and women.
[c] Data restricted to families of two siblings where 50% would be expected.
[d] Data restricted to families of three siblings where 33% would be expected.

TABLE IV

Percentages of Onlyborn, Eldest, Middleborn, and Youngest and Family Size among Cigarette Smokers, Alcoholics, Social Deviants, Delinquents, and Psychiatric Patients

Size and type of sample	Sex	Sibship size [b]	Only	Oldest	Middle	Youngest
Cigarette smokers						
228 Students who smoked (Forbes, 1970b)	B[a]		6.1	35.6	27.6	30.7
Alcoholics						
110 Alcoholics (police records) (Bakan, 1949)	M		9.1	21.8	35.5	33.6
50 Alcoholics in workhouse (Feeney, Mindlin, Minear, & Short, 1955)	M		6.0	26.0	46.0	22.0
50 Alcoholic patients (clinic) (Feeney, Mindlin, Minear, & Short, 1955)	M		18.0	18.0	34.0	30.0
90 Alcoholic outpatients (Lisansky, 1957)	B		13.3	28.9	28.9	28.9
32 Alcoholics, Federal state farm (Lisansky, 1957)	M		18.8	31.2	21.9	28.1
230 Hospitalized patients (Navratil, 1956)	M		6.0	17.0	47.0	30.0
274 Alcoholics, middle class (Olson, 1958)	B		12.4	31.0	38.3	18.3
242 Alcoholic clinic patients (Smart, 1963)		4.2	8.6	28.9	43.4	19.1
109 Alcoholics (Wahl, 1956a)	M		13.0	25.0	40.0	21.0
Social deviants						
43 Neurotic children (Rutter & Graham, 1970)	B		14.0	41.8	27.9	16.3
42 Children with clinic problems (Siegel, 1951)	B	2.2	17.0	46.0	14.0	24.0
294 Unwed mothers (Horn & Turner, 1975)	F	3.0	8.2	38.4	27.9	25.5
136 Unwed mothers (Horn & Turner, 1975)	F	2.9	14.0	41.2	24.2	20.6
81 Homosexual outpatients (H. Schubert, Wagner, & Riess, 1976)	M	3.4	8.6	33.3	26.0	32.1
35 Strippers (Skipper & McCaghy, 1970)	F		14.0	74.0		

(continued)

TABLE IV (continued)

Size and type of sample	Sex	Sibship size	Only	Oldest	Middle	Youngest
Delinquents						
3,692 Delinquents, mean age 14 (Biles, 1971)	B	4.6	4.3	23.7	48.8	23.2
467 Australian delinquents (Ogden, De, & Horn,	M	5.8	1.4	24.2	68.3	6.1
31 Delinquent antisocial children (Rutter & Graham, 1970)	B		0	25.8	32.3	41.9
35 Delinquent nonsocialized children (Rutter & Graham, 1970)	B		2.0	37.1	43.6	11.4
1,048 Juvenile delinquents (Sletto, 1934)	B		10.0	21.0	51.0	18.0
Psychiatric patients						
271 Mental patients (Eisenman & Taylor, 1966)			13.6	23.6	34.6	28.2
518 Schizophrenics (Granville-Grossman, 1966)	M		11.3	21.2	37.1	30.3
622 Schizophrenics (Granville-Grossman, 1966)	F		11.6	26.9	36.8	24.6
549 Schizophrenics (Gregory, 1958)	B		5.0	23.0	49.0	26.0
158 Schizophrenics (Grosz, 1958)	B		4.5	35.3	25.0	35.3
500 Psychiatric patients (Norton, 1952)	B		9.0	19.2	46.8	25.0
442 Schizophrenics (Patterson & Zeigler, 1941)	B		5.2	22.2	53.8	18.8
53 Schizophrenics (Plank, 1953)	M		9.4	26.4	51.0	13.2
2,447 Psychiatric outpatients (Riess & Safer, 1973)	B	2.8	15.6	31.7	20.1	32.3
568 Schizophrenics in United States Navy (Wahl, 1956b)	M	4.4	14.0	18.0	42.0	26.0
231 Schizophrenics (Wahl, 1956a)	M	4.1				

[a] B equals combined male and female.
[b] When blank, sibship size not given by author.

positive effects of acting as interlocutor between parents and younger siblings is thought to account for the onlyborn's lack of superiority over eldest of sibships of two and three (Breland, 1974; Kammeyer, 1967).

Onlyborn were underrepresented among retardates and school underachievers among over 200,000 male 19-year-olds (Belmont, Stein, & Wittes, 1976) and among reading retardates in 2,199 Isle of Wight school children, and had a tendency for underrepresentation among the intellectually retarded (Tizard & Hemming, 1970).

Onlyborn and eldest have higher academic achievement than all laterborn (Guilford & Worcester, 1930; Jones, 1954; Lees & Stewart, 1957; Oberlander & Jenkin, 1967; Skovholt, Moore, & Wellman, 1973).

Along with eldest, onlyborn, when contrasted with other sibship categories, are more upwardly mobile (Berger & Ivancevich, 1973) and have higher achievement needs (Angelini, 1967; Edwards & Braunburger, 1973; Sampson & Hancock, 1967). No difference was found by one author (Rosenfeld, 1966). They are more likely (see Table II) to be merit scholars (Breland, 1972), to attend college and graduate school (Bayer, 1966; Farley, Smart, & Brittain, 1974; Nisbett, 1968; Schachter, 1963; Wagner, 1960), to be superior and voracious readers (Farley, Smart, & Brittain, 1974; Levinson, 1963), to have high reading-readiness scores (Rubin, Balow, & Dorle, 1975) and to have an IQ over 170 (Sheldon, 1954).

Using the general-population mean percentage plus two SDs as an expected upper cut-off point (11% or higher), onlyborn are considerably overrepresented (see Table III) among eminent scientists (Eiduson, 1962; Galton, 1874; Hart, 1960; Roe, 1953), merit scholars (Breland, 1972), and high-school seniors with attainment in science (Datta, 1967). Onlyborn are also overrepresented among 92 literary biographees (24%), among 75 artistic biographees (20%) (Goertzel, Goertzel, & Goertzel, 1978), and among 80 renouned composers (D. Schubert, Wagner, & H. Schubert, 1977a), as well as among 215 illustrious men and 35 outstanding women who appeared on the cover of *Time* (Toman & Toman, 1970), and among 77 autobiographers (Burnand, 1973). Early studies showed onlyborns as underrepresented among eminent Americans (Bowerman, 1947) and among Rhodes Scholars (Apperly, 1939), possibly due to being born in an earlier era when the percentage of onlyborns was overall low.

Onlyborn have average representation in a sample of eminent male educational administrators (see Table III), but high representation in a sample of male social scientists (Havighurst & Wagner, 1977). Among firemen onlyborn and oldests more often take leadership roles (Smith & Goodchilds, 1963). Onlyborn occur at the average frequency or are underrepresented among eminent politicians, lawyers, and military men (Forbes, 1971; Wagner & H. Schubert, 1977a; Zweigenhaft, 1975). Of the 37 United States presidents, one, F. D. Roosevelt, was considered an only child, although he had a half-brother 28 years his senior. In a study of 77 eminent political biographees only 6.5% were onlyborn (Goertzel, Goertzel, Goertzel, 1978). Although onlyborn men seem to take some leadership roles, they do not seem to become politicians.

Onlyborn women are considerably overrepresented among actresses, especially when parents are separated and the mother is motivated toward the theatre (Wagner, Zillich, & H. Schubert, 1980). Eminent women social scientists are at about the average expected for their family size (Havighurst & Wagner, 1977).

2. *Personality Characteristics*

Onlyborn have higher self-esteem than non-onlyborn according to four researchers (Coopersmith, 1967; Fenton, 1928; Goodenough & Leahy, 1927; M. Rosenberg, 1965); but in contrast, laterborn have higher self-esteem than the onlyborn according to two other studies (Kaplan, 1970; Zimbardo & Formica, 1963). One author reported no difference in self-esteem (Kaplan, 1970) except that white male onlyborn with middle socioeconomic status did have higher self-esteem than corresponding non-onlyborn. Obviously more data are needed here with family size, sex, socioeconomic class, and possibly other characteristics of parents held constant. Further, as Falbo (1977) pointed out, ratings of onlyborn children and non-onlies need to be blind for ordinal position so that results are not contaminated by sterotypic judgments of raters.

As children, onlyborn are more self-confident, gregarious, affectionate, and aggressive with peers (Goodenough & Leahy, 1927), superior to non-onlyborn in social success (Bonney, 1944), more popular (Laosa & Brophy, 1970), more out-going (Rosenberg & Sutton-Smith, 1973), more likely than others to make a cooperative move (Falbo, 1976), and more autonomous though not so much as to be social isolates (Falbo, 1976). Onlyborn favor independent work and self-employment, and are more disinclined toward social work (Schiller, 1966).

Onlyborn are more adult-oriented (Guilford & Worcester, 1930), more frequently say parents were the most influential persons in their lives (Falbo, 1976), as volunteers are more likely than other ordinals to return questionnaires (Ebert, 1973), and as college students are more socially responsible but less rigid than eldests (MacDonald, 1971). Without sibling rivalry, onlyborn acquire a more trusting style of interaction than non-onlyborn (Sutton-Smith & Rosenberg, 1970).

Male onlyborn are above the average adolescent in conformity, though less affiliative (Sampson, 1962). Among Air Force Academy freshmen, on peer ratings, onlyborn are above average in leadership, personality, and compatability (Payne, 1971).

Onlyborn are not different from non-onlyborn in altruism (Friedrichs,

1960; Handlon & Gross, 1959; Harris, 1967), comparative competitive stance (Falbo, 1976), self-derogation (Kaplan, 1970), popularity as perceived by others (Simon, Sands, & Forman, 1971), or neuroticism (Farley, 1975).

The dependency of the onlyborn is repeatedly mentioned (Adler, 1931; Haeberle, 1958; Hilton, 1967), as is his and the eldest's need for affiliation (Adler, 1931; Forbes, 1970a; Hoyt & Raven, 1973; Radloff & Helmreich, 1968; Schachter, 1959). However, onlyborn have less need for affiliation than eldests (Connors, 1963; Falbo, 1976; Rosenfeld, 1966; Schutz, 1958), although more anxious than non-onlyborn (Rosenberg & Sutton-Smith, 1964).

Both male and female onlyborn show more feminine interests (Gormly, 1968; Lunneborg, 1969) and onlyborn women are more frequently lesbian than other women (Gundlach & Riess, 1967) in part due to their being more frequently raped as children by male relatives and acquaintances (Gundlach, 1977).

Among 200,000 19-year-old Netherlands draftees, onlyborn were rated by their physical-examining physicians as greater risks of psychiatric malfunction than eldest and youngest (Belmont, 1977). As combat pilots, onlyborn (along with eldest) were rated inferior in combat performance and, as divers, more frightened by time spent under water (Radloff & Helmreich, 1968). Onlyborn seem to rate poorly in the military.

3. Clinical Groups

In clinical samples, onlyborn girls exhibit the highest level of adjustment and onlyborn boys a poorer level, although both sexes had more problems than non-onlyborn. The mothers of onlyborn were more overprotective and visited the clinic more than mothers with larger families (Hough, 1932; Howe & Madgett, 1975; Ko & Sun, 1965; Landis, 1955). Onlyborn children were underrepresented (see Table IV) in four clinical groups (Blatz & Bott, 1927; Cornfield, 1968; Kurth & Schmidt, 1964; Tuckman & Regan, 1967), while overrepresented in one (Siegel, 1951). The question of the onlyborn's frequency in clinics is moot.

Two investigators found a sample of onlyborn children (with a high percentage of boys) overrepresented among delinquents (see Table IV) compared to the general-population mean (Burt, 1925; Parsley, 1933, girls); another found them slightly above average in frequency (Sletto, 1934), and two found them underrepresented (Biles, 1971; Rutter & Graham, 1970, two samples). Along with eldest, onlyborn girls are overrepresented among unwed mothers (Horn & Turner, 1975). It should be noted that earlier samples show overrepresentation, and more current ones, underrepresentation of onlyborn children.

Among nine samples of alcoholics, onlyborn are overrepresented compared to the general population mean in five samples, underrepresented in three, and near the average in the remaining one (see Table IV). The preponderance was in the direction of overrepresentation. Onlyborn rated higher than average in the use of tranquilizers but lower in the use of marijuana (Linder & Lerner, 1972a, b). Among student cigarette smokers only 6% were onlyborn (Forbes, 1970).

Firstborn, both onlyborn and eldest (see Table IV), as contrasted with laterborn, are more often obsessive (Ruff, Ayers, & Templer, 1975) and more frequently found among psychiatric outpatients (Riess & Safer, 1973). Onlyborn are more often discharged for psychiatric reasons from basic training in the military (Taintor, 1970), and are more often among childhood schizophrenics (Parsley, 1933), adult psychiatric patients (Granville-Grossman, 1966), and schizoprenics in the Navy (Wahl, 1956b), though underrepresented among one adult schizophrenic sample (Patterson & Zeigler, 1941). Onlyborn are averagely frequent among five schizophrenic samples (see Table IV). The frequency of the onlyborn among the greatly disturbed would seem to be, overall, average to somewhat above average with some variability in frequency due to the era and the mean sibship size of the samples.

In a study of 824 neuropsychiatric cases, using the MMPI scales (Marks & Seeman, 1963), onlies were not found to be higher on any scale than a total of all other ordinal groups, but were found to be lower on scales 2-7-4/2-4-7/4-7-2 combined, on 2-8/8-2 combined, and on K + . Such MMPI codes would indicate that onlyborn are lower on depression/psychopathy/psychaesthenia, on depression/schizophrenia, and on self-aggrandizement than other psychiatric patients (Carson, 1969; Dahlstrom, Welsh, & Dahlstrom, 1972, pp. 163–171).

4. Discussion

Although many of the studies reported above have flaws in methodology, report differences not reaching conventional statistical significance, and call for cross-validation, on the whole they support and validate each other and support the conclusion that the present stereotype of personality and behavior of onlyborn is not justified. Onlyborn can be and frequently are highly productive, intelligent, and creative. Their substantiated fortes are educational achievement, accomplishments in science and the arts, high sociability, and effectiveness as leaders. It is obvious that the historical, cultural stereotype concerning the shortcomings, the "spoiledness," of the onlyborn is unwarranted. This stereotype may have resulted from the considerable variability of onlyborn. As so often happens, the negative extreme attracts attention while the positive one is overlooked. Onlyborn have been described as more maladjusted in early American samples and among populations of the Netherlands (Belmont, 1977) and southern Germany (Adler, 1931; Toman, 1976), at times and places where larger families were the mode, and onlyborn children were accidentally conceived out-of-wedlock or came otherwise unwanted, and where expectations were more ingrained that onlyborn are "spoiled," self-centered, and uncooperative.

C.   THE ELDEST

This section describes what researchers found when they compared eldest with other ordinals. The earliest studies frequently compared all firstborn (oldest plus onlyborn) with all laterborn without examining for differences between onlyborn and eldest—differences that begin when the eldest shares his parents with another and perhaps at an earlier period. Despite this inequality between onlyborn and eldest, they do resemble each other in having high cognitive sophistication, intellectual acumen, academic achievement, and abstract interests (McClure, 1971; see also Table II).

1.   Establishing Normative Mean Percentages

The percentage of firstborn births (onlyborn plus eldest) varies in the United States with the time period, for example, from about 27% from 1950 to 1962 and 30% in 1923 to almost 43% in 1943 and again in 1947, when there were many new marriages. In the middle 1930s, when the birth rate was at an all-time low, the percentage of firstborn also ran high, close to 40%, due not to a bumper crop of marriages but to small families, resulting in few middleborn children. How to separate the onlyborn from the eldest in these percentages is a perplexing and as yet unsolved question. Knowing something about the relative size of the corresponding sibships helps. In the small families of the mid-1930s, the high percentage of firstborn might well contain a considerable quota of onlyborn, while in 1943 and 1947, when larger families were being started, eldest might well comprise a greater share. An additional variable affecting the percentage of eldest is family size because as sibship size increases, the percentage of eldest decreases. To develop a basis for setting normative percentages of eldest, the present researchers compiled from the literature percentages for each ordinal position in various general-population and special samples (see Tables I–IV).

For the over 100 samples culled from the literature for which percentages are available (Tables I–IV), the mean percentage of eldest is 29.7% (*SD* = 10%). The mean percentage of eldest for nine large general-population and control groups is 25.4% (*SD* = 2.1%) and for the six large, white, general-population samples, the mean percentage of eldest is 25% (*SD* = 2.0%). The higher mean percentage of eldest for the total of all samples studied as compared with that of the general-population and control samples is consistent with findings of greater variability or deviancy of eldests (Campbell, 1933; Ogburn, 1930). Using two standard deviations above and below the mean of the general population as cut-off points, any sample in which the percentage of eldest is 30% and over or 21% and less will be considered as containing, respectively, an over- or underrepresentation of such eldest. Over- and underrepresentation of eldest and comparisons of the personality traits of eldest and noneldest will be described under the rubrics of (1) intelligence and ability, (2) achievement and academic motivation, (3) popularity and leadership, dependency, affiliation need, and conformity, (4) pain and risk taking, (5) performance in the military, (6) neurotic behavior and delinquency, and (7) schizophrenia.

2. *Intellect and General Ability*

At all age levels, firstborn, on the average (see also Section III), have higher intelligence test scores than their laterborn siblings while eldest of two score even higher than the onlyborn (Belmont & Marolla, 1973; Breland, 1970). As children, the firstborn are likely to have high verbal ability (Sutton-Smith, Roberts, & Rosenberg, 1964), are more cognitively sophisticated (Rossiter & Robertson, 1974), and gain more connectness in thinking derived from talking to adults (Harris, 1964), which may reduce "freedom" leading to "creativity." Developmentally, eldest are superior among 12-week-olds (Lee-Painter & Lewis, 1976; Lewis & Gallas, 1976), at 15 months of age (Bayley, 1965), and among 1500 young children (Bradley & Sanborn, 1969).

Eldest are overrepresented in special programs for superior children (see Table II), among superior high-school students (Bradley & Sanborn, 1969), college students (Altus, 1966; Forbes, 1970b; Nisbett, 1968; Schachter, 1963; Wagner, 1960), and medical students (Cobb & French, 1966). Further eldest are overrepresented (see Table II) among British geniuses (Ellis, 1904/1926), National Merit normatives and finalists (Nichols, 1964), and graduate students (Montgomery & Puetz, 1975; Schachter, 1963); they also score higher, on the average, than other ordinals on the Miller's Analogies Test (Harris, 1964).

In small families, eldest are educationally advantaged, while in large families, especially in the lower socioeconomic class, youngest are (Blau & Duncan, 1967; Elder, 1962a) favored. Eldest are verbally superior because of playing the interlocutor role between parents and laterborn (Breland, 1974; Kammeyer, 1967), except when closely-spaced to the next younger. This effect of close spacing on verbal ability is similar to that for twins who have relatively the poorest verbal ability (Breland, 1974; Record, McKeown, & Edwards, 1970).

Eldest are underrepresented among mental retardates and have a low average of occurrence as reading retardates (Siegel, 1951; Tizard & Hemming, 1970).

3. *Achievement and Academic Motivation*

Firstborn, along with onlyborn, regularly average higher than laterborn on need for achievement, academic motivation, effort, and conscientiousness (Adams & Phillips, 1972; Bartlett & Smith, 1968; Elder, 1962a; Fakouri, 1974; Start & Start, 1974). If surpassed by the laterborn, eldest are likely to make great effort to reestablish their priority (Lees, 1952). They are, on the average, less fond of cuddling, easier to train, likely to work harder at school, are more serious, walk, talk, and read earlier than laterborn children, and set themselves higher standards than do noneldests (Price, 1969). Children of firstborn mothers progress faster in school than those of laterborn mothers (Rossi, 1965).

Eldest are likely to prefer working with ideas, showing noticeable proclivity for abstract verbal functioning (McClure, 1971), have higher reading-achievement test scores (Oberlander & Jenkin, 1967; Oberlander, Frauenfelder, & Heath, 1971), and read more (McClure, 1971); they have shown more concrete professional plans than noneldests (Schiller, 1966), higher achievement motivation scores on the Thematic Apperception Test, a projective device (Lompa, 1967), and higher problem solving potential in work groups of firemen (Smith & Goodchilds, 1963). Further eldest are likely to receive high parent-surrogate training and make strong identification with parents, show high conscientiousness, dependence, conformity, and affiliation (Sutton-Smith, Roberts, & Rosenberg, 1964), as adults they have high identification and affect in recalled attitudes toward parents (Rankin & Bahnson, 1976), and are likely to react to parents (and other authority figures) with dependence and productivity and to siblings (peers) with high power tactics (Sutton-Smith, 1968).

Eldest are overrepresented (Table III) among writers on diverse subjects including autobiographical material, but not among those who write only autobiographies (Burnand, 1979). Among illustrious women selected to appear on the cover of *Time* eldest are unduly frequent, but not among the men so selected (Toman & Toman, 1970). Goertzel, Goertzel, and Goertzel (1978) studied 306 illustrious biographees of whom 92 (30%) were eldest, a number slightly more than the number of middleborn and of youngest (27% each). They describe these firstborn, "for the most part as people with confidence, charisma, and presence, . . . distinctive, and original, their political beliefs strongly stated. . . . When on our side, we revere them; when they are not, we fear them. . . . They feel needed and accept what seems at times to be inappropriate responsibility" (pp. 85–86).

Eldest were significantly overrepresented (Table III) among 128 candidates for the Illinois legislature (Forbes, 1971), among the presidents of the United States (Wagner & H. Schubert, 1977a), and among 133 United States congressmen (Zweigenhaft, 1975) but only slightly above average among 29 contenders for the United States presidency and among 48 United States military leaders (Wagner & H. Schubert, 1977b).

Six of seven investigations regarding scientists (Table III) reported eldest considerably overrepresented (Cattell & Brimhall, 1921; Datta, 1967; Eiduson, 1962; Hart, 1960; Roe, 1953; Visher, 1948), whereas the seventh reported the frequency of eldest as average (Galton, 1874). Eldest are not unduly frequent among eminent anthropologists and psychologists (Roe, 1953). However, eldest are overrepresented among 93 outstanding educational administrators and 150 male and 125 female eminent social scientists (Havighurst & Wagner, 1977), 930 Rhodes scholars (Apperly, 1939), 309 British geniuses (Ellis, 1904/1926), and highly gifted students (Terman, 1925).

4. Popularity and Leadership

Perhaps because of being more "bossy" (Sutton-Smith, 1968), eldest are less popular than laterborn (Finneran, 1958; Schachter, 1964). They have more need for autonomy than noneldests (Hancock, 1965), display more leadership and compatability (Payne, 1971; Smith & Goodchilds, 1968), and are more often elected to class-leadership positions (Oswald, 1963). Girl eldest especially demonstrate such leadership ability (Sandler & Scalia, 1975). Eldest have more energy and exert more power than noneldest (Bakan, 1966; Gerstner, 1967) and have more organizational, as well as intellectual, interests and ability (Hall & Barger, 1964).

Eldest are more adult-oriented than noneldests (McArthur, 1956; Purpura, 1971; Singer, 1971), acquire more adult-role behavior (LaVoie, 1973), and as parent surrogates are guardians of law and order who value power to help others (Adler, 1927/1956). Eldest from small families are more socialized (Murrell, 1974), and are more empathetic with high-status persons. This empathy of eldest, is especially carried by verbal material (Stotland, Sherman, & Shaver, 1971).

5. Dependency, Affiliation Need, and Conformity

On the average, eldest girls are more traditional than noneldests (Kammeyer, 1966), more affiliative under stress (Schachter, 1959; Warren, 1966), especially when followed by one or two brothers (Sampson, 1962; Sampson & Hancock, 1967), and generally more in need of approval (Moran, 1967). Eldest college men are more serious, dependable, and conservative (Hall & Barger, 1964). In general, eldest are more susceptible to social pressure (Warren, 1966) and more dependent on the social evaluation of significant others (Alexander, 1968). As children, eldest are more dependent, fearful, worried, sensitive, and excitable (Dean, 1947), and keep promises and secrets better than noneldests (Wuebben, 1967).

Contrasted to those in other ordinal positions, eldest are more successful under authoritarian rule (Exner & Sutton-Smith, 1970), have role behavior for either high submission or high authority (Arrowood & Amoroso, 1965), and are more likely to be nurturant and to assume the parent-surrogate role (Adler, 1931). In general, eldest identify more than laterborn with parents and authority.

The preponderance of studies point toward eldest being more conforming than other ordinals. Purpura (1971) found eldest are more conforming than noneldest and Price (1969) that eldest are more methodological, law abiding, tidy, and less impulsive. Eldest with a cross-sexed sibling were found by Bragg and Allen (1970) to be more conforming than those with like-sexed siblings. Eldest of both sexes were found to show more feminine characteristics, possibly resulting in more conformity, than noneldest (Gormly, 1968). In contrast, Sampson (1962) found no difference between eldest and noneldest in conformity.

6. Pain, Risk, and the Militry Service

Eldest are more sensitive to and report more pain than noneldest (Carman, 1899; Johnson, Leventhal, & Dabbs, 1971; MacDonald, 1901). However, eldest in class experiments are least likely to avoid electric shock (Fischer & Winer, 1969).

Eldest are likely to avoid extreme risk (Winterbottom, 1958) and are underrepresented in baseball (Chen & Cobb, 1960; Wagner, H. Schubert, Zillich, & D. Schubert, 1980) and in dangerous college sports (Nisbett, 1968).

Air Force Academy peer-ratings place firstborn higher in leadership, personality, and compatibility than laterborn (Payne, 1971). In the military, all seven of the original astronauts were eldest, as were 12 of 15 candidates for the Gemini program, and 55% of helicopter pilot trainees as compared with 40% of nonvolunteers for such training (Perry, 1965). Sealab candidates had 16 eldest of 28 (57%) (Helmreich, 1968). As compared with 55% of random Air Force pilots, 65% of superior Navy jet pilots and 80% of Air Force military achievers were eldest versus 55% random Air Force men (Helmreich, 1968). Eldest in the military are overrepresented and, in general, are more successful (along with onlyborn) than are laterborn (Herrell, 1972), and were found to be more frequent among 49 eminent military leaders (Wagner & H. Schubert, 1977b).

7. Social and Emotional Problems

In the military, eldest are underrepresented among outpatients in basic training (Taintor, 1970) and among those committing violent crimes, such as assaulting an officer (Herrell, 1970). Eldest Vietnam soldiers, especially from small families, occurred with above average frequency among those who presented themselves as reactively disturbed by ongoing circumstances and obtained a resultant diagnosis of neurosis (Herrell, 1970).

Among children referred to guidance clinics, eldest are more often neurotic and less often antisocial (Rutter & Graham, 1970), and in two-child sibships eldest are more often referred for anxiety, severe symptoms, and difficulty in interpersonal relations (Tuckman & Regan, 1967).

Eldest are overrepresented among hospitalized depressives compared to middleborn (Grosz, 1968), among obsessive–compulsives in sibships of two (Kayton & Borge, 1967), and, in India, among depressive neurotic and schizophrenic patients (Sethi & Gupta, 1973).

The picture for personality disorder is inconsistent and complex. In two early studies, eldest scored frequently among delinquents (Armstrong, 1933; Breckenridge & Abbott, 1912), but, according to a recent study, are less likely to show psychopathic behavior than the laterborn (Murrell, 1974). Eldest boys with younger sisters are underrepresented among delinquents (Tolman, 1939). Finally, among 1110 delinquents, eldest are overrepresented, being the compliant and submissive adolescents from small families. Among 1200 Australilan delinquents, mostly committing crimes against property, eldest are underrepresented (Ogden, De, & Horne, 1974). Three samples (see Table IV) show eldests to occur with average frequency among delinquents.

Eldests are less likely than those in other ordinal positions to use drugs (Linder & Lerner, 1975-6). In nine samples of alcoholics (see Table IV) eldest are, in two studies each, over- and underrepresented, while in the remaining five they are at the average frequency.

Eldest women are overrepresented among unwed mothers (Horn & Turner, 1975) and strippers (Skipper & McCaghy, 1970). Eldest men are slightly overrepresented among homosexual outpatients, especially if they have a sister as the next youngest sibling (H. Schubert, Wagner, & Riess, 1976). Eldest are overrepresented among 42 children with clinical problems (Siegel, 1951), among 43 neurotic children (Rutter & Graham, 1970), and among psychiatric outpatients (Riess & Safer, 1973). These samples (Table IV) all come from relatively small sibships, which increase the relative frequency of eldest.

8. *Schizophrenia*
Among 11 investigations of schizophrenia by ordinal position (see Table IV), one showed an overrepresentation (Grosz, 1958), two a slight underrepresentation (Norton, 1952; Wahl, 1956b), and eight an average frequency. Birtchnell (1972) reported no ordinal position differences for mental-health patients.

Eldest have above average occurrence among schizophrenic outpatients, especially those from small sibships (Riess & Safer, 1973), and generally high occurrence among outpatients (Riess & Safer, 1973; Norton, 1957, reanalyzed by Riess & Safer, 1973). Generally sibship size is small for these two samples. Barry and Barry (1967) report that eldest from small families are overrepresented among schizophrenic inpatients though under-represented when all sizes of sibships are combined. Eldest women when followed by a sibling in less than 2 years or more than 4 years are over-represented among schizophrenic inpatients (Walker & Johnson, 1973).

Marks and Seeman (1963) report MMPI high-point scales by ordinal position for 270 men and 556 women hospitalized psychiatric patients. Eldestborn score deviantly high on $K+$, but not on any clinical scale. For eldest such scores would indicate no specific psychiatric diagnosis among psychiatric inpatients, only that they would tend to be guarded, intensely desirous of approval, inflexible particularly regarding nonconformist behavior, authority oriented, socially inept, and deficient in self-insight (Carson, 1969; Dahlstrom, Welsh, & Dahlstrom, 1972, pp. 163–171).

9. Discussion

In most areas of personality, data concerning the characteristics of eldest are amazingly consistent, a consistency evident in spite of many different approaches, lack of statistically significant differences in some studies, and poor design in earlier studies which used firstborn contrasted with later-born rather than eldest excluding onlyborn, contrasted with noneldest.

To reiterate, differences between ordinal groups—here firstborn or eldest from laterborn or noneldest—are not all or none. Among groups over-represented by eldest, there are noneldest, and among groups under-represented by eldest, eldest still occur. Although ordinal position, especially for eldest, is a strong factor in personality development, many other factors impinge on such development. One such factor considered below is the age spacing to the next sibling.

10. Suggested Research

Several questions that might prove worthy of further investigation follow: When the sex of the next sibling is held constant, will closely spaced eldest prove to be more affiliative, more dependent, more neurotic, or more personality disordered than widely spaced eldest? Are more widely spaced eldest better adjusted? What are the effects of the sex of the adjacent sibling on personality traits of eldest in families of three and over? Is the interval between marriage and the birth of the first child related to the adjustment of a firstborn? What effect does conception before marriage have on the firstborn, or being fathered by other than the household male parent? What effect does the early death of a first child have psychologically on the secondborn, who psychologically grows up as an eldest? The verbal ability and test intelligence of the eldest decreases with family size and increases with age spacing. Is there a similar negative relationship for eldest between various personality variables and sibship size?

D.   THE LASTBORN OR YOUNGEST

Youngest are the next most variable group in coping and behavior compared to eldest, with middleborn the least variable (LaVoie, 1973; Ogburn, 1930; Wisdom & Walsh, 1975). All the concomitants of parental response—from extreme rejection of the lastborn, which often increases with each successive child (Bumpass & Westoff, 1970), to extreme parental delight in the "golden baby" for one's late middle years—cause variability in the coping ability of the last child in the sibship. Where, then, are lastborn children underrepresented and where unexpectedly frequent among the normative and diagnostic groups investigated?

While the mean percentage of eldest in the available samples of general-normative and special-characteristics groups (Tables I–IV) was just under 30% ($SD = 10\%$), it was somewhat lower for the youngest—26% ($SD = 7\%$). The average difference between the mean percentage of eldest and youngest, about 4%, may be due mostly to the Price–Hare effects (an overrepresentation of eldest in a growing population) and to a higher death rate of laterborn children (Beeton & Pearson, 1901; Hare & Price, 1969; Jones, 1933; Price & Hare, 1969). Obviously, the percentage of eldest and youngest varies with the size of the sibship, from 50% of each in sibships of two, 33% of each in sibships of three, and so on. So, as the family size increases, the percentages of eldest and youngest decrease, while the percentage of the middleborn increases.

Eight investigators each provided a percentage of lastborn in a sizable sample for a general-population or normal-control group (Table I). These percentages ranged from 20 to 28.6%, with a mean of 24.6% ($SD = 2.7\%$). This mean is closely equivalent to the mean of all samples, namely 26%. Using a cut-off point of two standard deviations ($2 \times 2.7\% = 5.4\%$) above and below the mean of the general-population normal-control sample (24.6%), any percentage of youngest of 30% or over will be considered overrepresentation, and any of 19% or less, underrepresentation.

In addition to such deviations of the youngest from the normal mean, results of investigations will be discussed for comparisons of measured differences between youngest and nonyoungest (e.g., means on height or test intelligence) and for differences in frequency between youngest and eldest (since eldest and youngest should be roughly equivalent). An example of the latter might be the percentage of all youngest college freshmen enrolled in art versus the percentage of eldest so enrolled. These differences will be discussed under intelligence and achievement, creativity, sociability, self-destruction, and incidence rates in clinical populations.

1. Intellect, Achievement, and Motivation

Youngest are lowest on verbal intelligence, increasingly so as sibship size increases, among some 200,000 19-year-old males of the Netherlands born between 1944 and 1947 (Belmont & Marolla, 1973) and among merit-scholar high-school students (Breland, 1972a). They make lower grades as reported for a large group of Minneapolis high-school students (Schachter, 1963). They are also less upwardly mobile than nonyoungest (Srole & Fischer, 1973), and attend college, medical, and graduate school less frequently than eldest (Cobb & French, 1966; Forbes, 1970b; Nisbett, 1968; Schachter, 1963; Wagner, 1960).

Lastborn are at greater risk of school failure and of attendance at schools for mentally retarded than nonlastborn among the 200,000 19-year-old males from both manual and nonmanual social classes (Belmont, Stein, & Wittes, 1976). Lastborn are also more frequent among the mentally retarded (Tizard & Hemming, 1970; Tuckman & Regan, 1967), and among children with learning disabilities (Siegel, 1951); Lilienfeld and Pasamanick (1956) found mental deficiency increased with birth rank. However, in families of three, youngests are underrepresented among mental retardates (Vockell & Bennett, 1972).

According to investigations in the late 1920s, lastborn are given advantages over earlierborn (Arthur, 1926) and laterborn are more intelligent as ordinal rank increases among Chicago underprivileged public-school children in grades 1 through 12 (Steckel, 1930, p. 343). Youngest are more advantaged among working-class adolescents (Elder, 1962a) and among black fifth-grade boys have the best grades of all ordinal groups (Solomon, Hirsch, Scheinfeld, & Jackson, 1972). Among 4000 11-year-olds, although intelligence increased with sibship size, youngest average higher in intelligence than middleborn (Scottish Council of Research in Education, 1949). Zajonc (1976) showed that the Scottish children were more widely age spaced which is taken to explain the higher intelligence of the lastborn (see also Section V).

2. Creativity

Youngest, among Peace Corps teachers, are more successful and innovative in free planning than earlierborn (Exner & Sutton-Smith, 1970), and youngest girls are more persistent in creative problem solving (D. Schubert, Wagner, & H. Schubert, 1977c; see also Section VI for further discussion of creativity).

Youngest are more flexible, less rigid and, dogmatic (Kaplan, 1970;

Sutton-Smith, 1968; Wisdom & Walsh, 1975). Laterborn do not differ from firstborn in degree of intellect, but are more disconnected in thinking which is less meaningful to adults (Harris, 1964).

The laterborn occur more frequently among political leaders, United States presidents, vice presidents, and also-rans during peace, while eldest and onlyborn are preferred during periods of war (Stewart, 1970). Youngest are overrepresented among 75 male writers and poets (Bliss, 1970), among autobiographees who wrote nothing else (Burnand, 1973), among eminent male classical composers (below conventional statistical significance, D. Schubert, Wagner, & H. Schubert, 1977a), but underrepresented among eminent Americans (Bowerman, 1947; Burnand, 1973), English scientists (Galton, 1874), and American women writers, and randomly distributed among English women writers (D. Schubert, Wagner, & H. Schubert, 1979) and women social scientists (Havighurst & Wagner, 1977).

3. Sociability

Youngest, as compared with nonyoungest, are more popular with peers (Finneran, 1958; Miller & Maruyama, 1976; Schachter, 1964; Sells & Roff, 1963), more gregarious (Hall & Barger, 1964), more empathetic (Kaplan, 1970; Sutton-Smith, 1968; Wisdom & Walsh, 1975), and, in sibships of two, more rivalrous and envious (Stotland, Sherman, & Shaver, 1971), more affectionate, independent, physically aggressive toward peers (Dean, 1947), and more bossy toward a best friend (Sutton-Smith, 1968). The empathy of youngest as compared to nonyoungest is more often based on postural cues (Rosenberg, Sutton-Smith, & Griffiths, 1965) and more directed toward those similar to themselves (Stotland, Sherman, & Shaver, 1971). Laterborn are more affected by eldest than vice versa (Sutton-Smith, Roberts, & Rosenberg, 1964).

As compared with earlierborn, youngest communicate and identify less with parents (McArthur, 1956; Peterson & Sharpe, 1972; Purpura, 1971; Singer, 1971), are likely to find parents more strict (Sears, Maccoby, & Levin, 1957), yet run to parents and complain for help in stress (Sutton-Smith, 1968). Youngest are less frequently referred to a child guidance clinic than other ordinals and have fewer problems as rated by parents than nonyoungest (Shrader & Leventhal, 1968).

Youngest are less conforming than eldest (in sibships of two there is no difference for women) (Sampson & Hancock, 1967), less susceptible to social pressure (Warren, 1966), less needful of autonomy (Sandler & Scalia, 1975) and of approval (Moran, 1967), and less responsible, and more likely to expect their lives to be controlled by external forces (MacDonald, 1971). Youngest are lower in self-esteem than only born and eldest (Coopersmith,

1959), and youngest women show less leadership in church organizations (Sandler & Scalia, 1975).

Youngest are more versatile in their interests, confident, activity-oriented, and take more risks (Hall & Barger, 1964). They participate more in baseball (Chen & Cobb, 1960; Wagner, Zillich, H. Schubert, & D. Schubert, 1980) and in dangerous college sports (Nisbett, 1968).

4. Self-Destructiveness: Suicide, Alcohol, and Accidents

As noted above youngest take more risks than nonyoungest. They are also, as children, more accident-prone, along with other laterborn in large families (Krall, 1953), and are less likely to stop smoking (Jacobs, 1972).

Among prisoners (Koller & Castanos, 1969), physicians (Thomas & Duszynski, 1974), and alcoholics (Ritson, 1968), youngest commit suicide more frequently than nonyoungest, although among children who commit suicide they are underrepresented (Jan-Tausch, 1963).

Youngest are more frequent than firstborn in 20 of 27 studies of alcoholics (Blane & Barry, 1973) and are overrepresented among all alcoholics (Bakan, 1949), among alcoholics in large families (Smart, 1963), and among alcoholic men (Martenson-Larsen, 1956). Youngest are more physically dependent on alcohol and socially dependent on peers (Blane & Barry, 1973), and are more likely than nonyoungest to use heroin (Linder & Lerner, 1975-6).

5. Schizophrenia and Other Psychoses

Schizophrenics occur relatively more frequently among youngest than among other ordinal positions, especially in large families and among men (Barry & Barry, 1967; Granville-Grossman, 1966; Gregory, 1958; Grosz, 1958). Laterborn are more likely to recover from schizophrenia than earlyborn (Farina, Barry, & Garmezy, 1963).

Youngest in the military develop psychoses three times more frequently than do eldest and more often commit crimes of violence (Herrell, 1969). Youngest are also more frequent among nonschizophrenic neuropsychiatric patients than nonyoungest (Hare & Price, 1970). Lastborn are more frequent among middle-class psychotics; but firstborn psychotics are more frequent in working-class families (Schooler, 1961). Youngest are not different from controls among schizophrenics in three samples (Birtchnell, 1972; Gregory, 1958; Patterson & Zeigler, 1941) and relatively underrepresented in another four (Kay & Roth, 1961; Munro, 1966; Plank, 1953; Walker, Johnson, & Goolishian, 1973). Contributing to inconsistencies of relative frequency of schizophrenics among youngest are such design deficiencies as mixing men and women and racial and cultural groups. Regarding socioeconomic level schizophrenics show overrepresentations of youngest among women of all classes and among men of the middle class, whereas for men of the working class the picture is unclear.

6. Personality Disorders

Youngest are overrepresented among truants, but underrepresented among adolescents who commit crime against property (Tennent, 1970), and are relatively more frequent among antisocial children (Rutter & Graham, 1970). Younger girls from two-child Anglo-Saxon sibships are more often diagnosed as personality-disordered (Walker, Johnson, & Goolishian, 1973). Youngest are underrepresented among 1200 Australian delinquents (convicted mostly of crimes against property) (Ogden & Horne, 1976).

Among outpatients, youngest are overrepresented (Norton, 1957, reanalyzed by Riess & Safer, 1973); they are less depressed than nonyoungest (Grosz, 1958), and have poorer acculturation resources (Herrell, 1974).

Youngest are overrepresented among hysterics (Ruff, Ayers, & Templer, 1975), personality-disordered, manics, and hysterics (Riess, 1976), more likely to show psychopathic behavior than firstborn (Murrell, 1974), twice as likely as firstborn to be separated from Service as unfit (Herrell, 1969), and, in Navy basic training, more frequently diagnosed as having a personality disorder (Taintor, 1970).

Youngest are more frequent among homosexuals (Slater, 1962; H. Schubert, Wagner, & Riess, 1976), and more frequent among lesbians, especially if they come from large families (Gundlach, 1972).

As rated by physicians during physical examination, youngest among 200,000 19-year-old draftees were found at greater risk of psychiatric disorder than eldest, though less so than onlyborn (Belmont, 1977).

One author found no personality deviations by ordinal position among the mentally disordered and concluded that birth order was not a factor in mental health (Birtchnell, 1972).

Youngest tend to be higher on MMPI codes 4–7–2, 2–7–4, and 7–4–2 (Eisenman & Taylor, 1966; Marks & Seeman, 1963). Such codes indicate that youngest, especially when their coping mechanisms are faltering, are likely to be irresponsible and unproductive, free of many conventional restraints, inclined to seek pleasures of the moment, self-destructive and risk-taking, overaware of human frailties, skeptical of social mores and progress, anti-intellectual, and intermittently remorseful, worried, and agitated (Carson, 1969; Dahlstrom, Welsh, & Dahlstrom, 1972, pp. 257–266; Gilberstadt & Duker, 1965; Guthrie, 1949).

7. Discussion

Compared to other sibship patterns, youngest are, on the average, less verbally facile and less academically motivated and are at greater risk of being school retardates and of having learning difficulties. However, various demographic factors seem to confound the picture including socioeconomic status, sex, race, era, size of sibship, and spacing to and sex of siblings. The inclusion of these variables in the research design would likely result in sharper delineation of differences in intelligence and personality of youngest as compared to nonyoungest.

Since factors in addition to sibling constellation impinge on personality development, the above contrasts are by no means all-or-none. In groups in which youngest are overrepresented, other ordinals are also present; when underrepresented, some are still present. Although the various researchers use different methodologies as well as different populations, on the whole, there is considerable consistency of direction of results, adding to their reliability.

The problem for the development of the character and health of lastborn is how to treat youngest so that they develop self-esteem, responsibility, a strong ego, a life goal, and a positive identity. Parents and teachers should be as strongly committed to giving a youngest the same emotional support, warmth, and attention given to a firstborn. Only with such investment will the lastborn develop as he should.

E. THE INTERMEDIATE OR MIDDLEBORN

When one reviews the results of personality studies of the intermediate or middleborn of a sibship, one is struck by the relative paucity of research findings and the frequency of faulty research methodology. In general, the middleborn are less variable (Ogburn, 1930) and less likely than other ordinals to appear in exceptional or abnormal groups. Even though the middle- and lastborn have not been shown similar in personality, they are unwarrantedly grouped into one indiscriminate class, the laterborn. Because the percentage of intermediates varies with sibship size, from zero for two siblings to 77.8 for nine, the interactive effect of sibship size and intermediate position is very pronounced and requires the separate determination of the trait cluster of the middleborn by ordinal rank in each sibship size. Two ungrounded and simplistic suggestions have been offered as a means of establishing the trait clusters of middleborn. The first is the method of extrapolating the middleborn personality from those of sibships of two as practiced by Toman (1976). The second is the repeating cycle of first-, second-, and thirdborn trait clusters of Very and Prull (1970), by which the fourth child is given the personality of an eldest, the fifth of a second, and the sixth of a thirdborn. The middleborn are unique with unique characteristics, varying among themselves by family size, sex of siblings, and relative ordinal rank. Illustrations of correct procedure are the study which focuses on the closely spaced middle girl flanked by sisters on either side (Wagner & H. Schubert, 1974), and another (Wagner & H. Schubert, 1976a) which describes the middleborn in an all-male sibship.

For actual experimental data, among the just under 100 samples in the literature reporting ordinal-position frequencies in various groups (Tables I–IV), middleborn percentages vary from 0 to 51%. The mean percentage of middleborn is 34.2% (SD = 13%), just over that expected for a sibship of three. For the large general-population samples, the mean percentage of middleborn is 42.9% (SD = 7.4%) and the mean sibship size is 4.01. Because sibship size, affected as it is by era, social class, and other factors, varies from group to group as in Tables I–IV, one cannot justifiably compare the percentage of middleborn in such groups. The percentage differences will not be emphasized herein, rather attention will be given largely to comparisons of observed characteristics of the middleborn and nonmiddleborn.

Investigations concerning comparisons of middleborn with other ordinals will be described under parent–child relations, intellect and achievement, sociability and independence, delinquency and personality disorder, and psychoses and schizophrenia. Throughout the following discussion, it should be kept in mind that middleborn, on the average, come from larger sibships than do other ordinal groups and that the larger the sibship the greater overall disadvantage in intelligence, academic achievement, as well as parental attention, and probably, socioeconomic level.

1. Parent–Child Relations

Regarding parent–child relations (see also Section IV,A), multiparous mothers vocalize and socialize more with their infants, especially their daughters, than do primiparous mothers (Nagelbush, 1974) and show more affection, spank more, and assign more chores (Sears, Maccoby, & Levin, 1957).

The middleborn is more deprived of parental affection than the firstborn (Connors, 1963), and feels more painfully the uncertainty of his position at home (Hug-Hellmuth, 1921), though he probably feels less keenly his displacement than does the eldest (Rankin & Bahnson, 1976). The firstborn, on the average, gets full (although at times erratic, inconsistent, and overdemanding) attention from parents, and the youngest may get considerable attention or, as often as not, little (see Section IV,A). However, the middle child, though treated more permissively (Dean, 1947), is left considerably outside the innermost circle (McGurk & Lewis, 1972), and receives less parental attention than the eldest (Barker & Lewis, 1975; Jacobs & Moss, 1974; Judd & Lewis, 1975; McBride, 1974; Rothbart, 1971).

As a result of the less attention received from parents by the middleborn, as contrasted with the firstborn, the former identifies less with parents (Purpura, 1971; Rankin & Bahnson, 1976), and with adults in general (Singer, 1971), but more often models on his siblings (Sutton-Smith, 1968).

2. *Intellect and Achievement*

In direct relation to the size of his sibship and to the lateness of his sibship rank, the middleborn is less verbally facile (Altus, 1966; Belmont & Marolla, 1973; Breland, 1974; see Table II). Lilienfeld and Pasamanick (1956) found mental deficiency increases with birth rank. Laterborn are less cognitively sophisticated (Rossiter & Robertson, 1978); their difference in intellect from the firstborn is not so much one of degree as of kind—a greater disconnectedness, perhaps related to creativity with more nonverbal content (Harris, 1964).

Middleborn first-grade children are especially disadvantaged in reading readiness (Doren, 1973). Middleborn are least likely to further their education (Bayer, 1966; Purpura, 1971), have high test anxiety (Hansson, 1974), are consistently found less academically motivated and have fewer upward mobility aspirations (Elder, 1962a; Srole & Fischer, 1973; Toman & Toman, 1970; Wark & Swanson, 1971).

Middleborn were underrepresented (see Table III) among *Time* magazine's selection of distinguished persons (Toman & Toman, 1970), eminent women writers (D. Schubert, Wagner, & H. Schubert, 1979), classical composers (D. Schubert, Wagner, & H. Schubert, 1977a), United States senators and representatives (Zweigenhaft, 1975), and eminent scientists (Cattell & Brimhall, 1921; Datta, 1967; Eiduson, 1962).

3. *Sociability and Lack of Dependency*

Middleborn are more popular than firstborn (Finneran, 1958; Schachter, 1964), have greater social and affiliative skills (Miller & Maruyama, 1976; Zajonc & Markus, 1975), are more self-disclosing (Dimond & Munz, 1967), are more likely to join a fraternity (Baker & O'Brien, 1969), and yield more to social pressure (Langenmayr, 1966) than other ordinals. Middleborn are more interested in working with and among people and being active in groups than the nonmiddleborn (Klockars, 1968; Oberlander, Frauenfelder, & Heath, 1970). Of all females, secondborn are most socially active (Wark & Swanson, 1971).

Laterborn identify and empathize more with those similar to themselves while the eldest do so with parental figures (Stotland & Dunn, 1963), are more aware than firstborn of the communication value of postural cues, and are more able to use them (Rosenberg, Sutton-Smith, & Griffiths, 1968). Secondborn are more affectionate and physically aggressive toward

peers than are other ordinals (Dean, 1947). Laterborn are more independent (Dean, 1947; Haeberle, 1958; Zajonc, 1976), have less need for approval (Moran, 1967), as children handle their distress on their own by
thumb sucking (Johnson & Johnson, 1975), and are more successful under
free-planning and innovation than firstborn (Exner & Sutton-Smith, 1970).

4. Alcohol and Tobacco Usage, Accidents, and Suicide

Three of four authors (see Table IV) found a high percentage of mostly
male laterborn are alcoholic (Bakan, 1949; Martensen-Larsen, 1956;
Smart, 1963); one (O'Hallaren & Wellman, 1957) found only 15% middleborn among 738 alcoholics of both sexes.

One author (Simon, 1973) found laterborn men and women smoked
more cigarettes and another (Srole & Fischer, 1973) found middleborn
smoked intermediately in amount between eldest and youngest.

Laterborn use more drugs than firstborn (Linder & Lerner, 1975–6) and
in high school, middleborn and those from large families use more drugs
than nonmiddleborn and those from smaller families.

Middleborn are less happy than eldest and youngest (Peterson & Sharpe,
1972), are more likely to be depressed (Grosz, 1968), are more self-
derogatory than nonmiddleborn (Kaplan, 1970), evaluate their own performances as others evaluate them (Stotland & Dunn, 1963), yet do not
become obsessive–compulsive (Kayton & Borge, 1967). Accident-prone
children are more frequently late in birth order (Krall, 1953).

Among child suicides, there is a significant deficit of middleborn
children compared to nonmiddleborn (Jan-Tausch, 1963) and physicians
who commit suicide include no middleborn although 17% of the control
group committed suicide (Thomas & Duszynski, 1974).

Perhaps a partial explanation of the frequency of accident proneness,
drug usage, and depression, with low incidence of suicide, might be found
in the MMPI description of hospitalized middleborn. Although middleborn
male college students (Olson, 1973; Wagner, 1975) were found lower on all
clinical MMPI scales than other ordinal groups, middleborn, both men and
women, among neuropsychiatric patients (Eisenman & Taylor, 1966;
Marks & Seeman, 1963) are more frequent than other ordinals on codes
3-2-1, 2-3-1, and 2-1-3. From such MMPI codes (Carson, 1969;
Dahlstrom, Welsh, & Dahlstrom, 1972, pp. 257–266; Gilberstadt & Duker,
1965; Guthrie, 1949), middleborn are most likely to have some of the
following characteristics in one or another combination: outwardly
friendly, although at times demanding and quick tempered, usually in-
dustrious and trustworthy, and at the moment of crisis suppressing and/or
repressing the full negative import of the situations. Being nonintellectual
and unsophisticated, middleborn usually deny the presence of psycholog-

ical and emotional difficulties, yet, being suggestible, profit from reassurance and advice. Prolonged tension and worry lead middleborn to functional conversion and somatic complaints and to sudden manifest anxiety attacks shown by sweating, headache, or palpitation. Such symptoms under stress may be used as a partial solution to emotional problems, early learned as a way out. Among psychiatric patients, a small percentage of middleborn, likely the closely spaced laterborn from large families, who are likely to feel slighted by parents and siblings, are likely to have difficulty relating to others and react with feelings of being treated unfairly, by withdrawing, or by asocial behavior. Most of such individuals are overactive, excitable, and somewhat disorganized; a few are apathetic and inefficient.

5. *Delinquency and Personality Disorders*

Laterborn boys show less resistance to temptation than first- and earlyborn boys (LaVoie, 1973) and were more frequent in an English survey among truants and those who steal; the truants were psychologically more disturbed (Tennent, 1970).

Laterborn show more psychopathic behavior (Murrell, 1974), and are overrepresented among 1110 Cook County, Illinois delinquents with defective superegos, who are mostly from large families and broken homes (Reiss, 1952).

Middleborn are overrepresented (see Table IV) among delinquent English children (Lees & Newson, 1954), are at greater risk of delinquency (Ogden, De, & Horne, 1974), constitute a high percentage among 500 delinquent boys (Glueck & Glueck, 1950), and in families of three are most deviant (Nowicki, 1967).

In Service, laterborn who exhibit psychiatric problems in basic training are often character disordered and, among American soldiers in Vietnam who were psychiatrically disturbed, laterborn more often commit civilian crimes (e.g., theft) and violent crimes (e.g., assaulting an officer), and twice as often are hospitalized or separated as unfit for military service, three times as often develop psychoses (Herrell, 1969), and more often display psychopathic disorders than firstborn (Herrell, 1970, 1972).

In penitentiaries 50% of male and 35% of all inmates are middleborn (Sutker & Moan, 1973), which percentages do not seem above the average considering the reported family sizes of 3.6 for whites and 5.0 for blacks in prison population.

6. *Psychosis and Schizophrenia*

Laterborn among American soldiers in Vietnam more frequently develop psychoses than the earlierborn (Herrell, 1972). Middleborn are significantly more frequent among the 442 schizophrenic patients than among the 495 controls (Patterson & Zeigler, 1941). Among some 1000 psychiatric patients there are more middleborn schizophrenics than expected, especially from the last half of the birth order in large families (Barry & Barry, 1967) and such patients with a large number of older siblings are less likely to recover (Farina. Barry. & Garmezy, 1963).

7. Discussion

Conclusions regarding effects of being middleborn are less reliable than are those for other ordinals because (1) fewer investigations have been done with them; (2) poorer methodology has been used due to the large number of cases needed for analysis, the complexity of research procedures required, and the resulting greater cost of gathering data; and (3) middleborn effects interact strongly with size of family, race, and socioeconomic level so that findings are frequently contaminated each by the other factors.

Although middleborn are found in all walks of life, among good as well as poor copers, they are less frequent among the former, very likely because of their obvious origin in large families. They are neither upwardly mobile nor especially downwardly mobile, staying largely in the middle class from which they came.

V. Sibling-Spacing Effects

Of the sibling-constellation variables, sibling spacing presented here has been the least comprehensively investigated, although several exemplary studies have been made (Belmont & Marolla, 1973; Belmont, Stein, & Susser, 1975; Breland, 1972; Koch, 1953; Nuttall & Nuttall, 1975). The age of subjects studied varies from infancy (Lasko, 1954) to 5- and 6-year-olds (Koch, 1954, 1955), to adolescence (Nuttall & Nuttall, 1973), to 19-year-old males (Belmont and collaborators, 1973, 1975), and to age at death (Beeton & Pearson, 1901). Most of the investigators studied intelligence and achievement and a few investigated various personality characteristics.

Drawing sharply defined conclusions from the array of findings has been difficult because investigators have used widely varying definitions of near and far spacing. The near-spacing intervals have varied from under 18 to under 36 months, the far-spacing intervals from over 24 to over 72 months, and the intermediate-spacing intervals from 19 to 30 months for the lower values to 36 to 71 months for the higher values. Recommended standard age-spacing intervals are up to 18 months, then by 6-month intervals to 48 months, and, when necessary, additional broad intervals of 48–60 months and 60 months and over.

Sharp demarcations between developmental stages probably do not exist, eliminating the need for smaller interval steps than 6 months for the usual sibling-spacing range of 18–48 months. Whenever results for any two adjacent intervals are similar, they can be combined, that is, if inspection of data indicates essential similarity in verbal impairment for those spaced up to 18 months and those spaced 19–24 months, the short-gap limits would extend up to 24 months.

Lasko (1954) suggests that the interval before displacement has differential, negative effects depending on its length, that is, displacement before a 42- to 48-month period disadvantages the child in social and emotional adjustments, and displacement before 30 to 36 months is disadvantageous intellectually. White (1976) demonstrated that cognitive disability is particularly likely with early displacement, up to 30 months, and psychosocial handicap may still occur up to 48 months. After the latter time the child has developed environmental interests apart from the mother and is unlikely to be measurably traumatized by being displaced by a sibling.

Other pitfalls to be avoided in age-spacing studies include (1) combining pre- and postgaps in the analysis of effects, combining the postgaps of eldest and middleborn, and combining the pregaps of middleborn and youngest; (2) including with the wide gappers the ultrawide (5 years and over), those far-separated, "menopausal," unplanned, and unwanted lastborn; and (3) inattention to the interactional age-spacing effects with sibship size, sex of index case, ordinal position, and sex of adjacent siblings. Suggestive research indicates that sibling-spacing effects vary with socioeconomic status. All variables except the one under investigation need to be held constant.

A.   SIBLING–SPACING EFFECTS ON THE OLDER CHILD

Effects of sibling interval are divided into those for intelligence and those for emotional and social development. As with other sibship variables, more research has been done and more definitive results obtained in the area of intelligence. In each of the following sections, data are presented in order of age of subject.

1.   Effects of Sibling Spacing on Intelligence

Koch (1954), studying 5- and 6-year-olds, reported that long spacing is favorable to the cognitive development of boys, while close-spacing effects are minimal on girls, differences for the latter being inconsistent for subtests and often nonsignificant. Brim (1958), using Koch's data, found that close spacing reduces originality. Nuttall and Nuttall (1975) studied latency and early adolescent children in the suburbs of Boston. They found that spacing to the next-younger sibling is related to intelligence in both small and large sibships, though significant only for the large sibships. Intelligence is significantly higher for those far spaced to the next younger sibling. Spacing of less than 18 months is detrimental to the ability of both the older and the younger child. Wide spacing produces not only higher intelligence, but a greater tendency to go to college and better school records. Although narrow spacing leads to low school interest, it produces high involvement in athletics and a desire for a high-level occupation.

Breland (1972) in a study of over 300,000 merit-scholarship applicants near the end of high school, reported that the individual with an age spacing of 2 years or less from his next youngest sibling has reduced word usage, which does not occur with an age spacing of 3 years or more. For both boys and girls in three-child families, except for the younger brother with two older sisters or the younger sister with two older brothers, the top 22 of 34 positions in intelligence were held by either eldest or those with a wide gap to a preceding sibling. The last 14 rankings were occupied by those with a close younger sib. Breland goes on to say that differential parent–child interaction during early developmental years explains the higher verbal facility of eldest, onlyborn, those with wide spacing, and those from small families, as well as the low verbal ability of twins. The former have far greater opportunity for close one-to-one interaction and a higher level of such interaction than do twins, with all of which White (1976) concurred. Kammeyer (1967) added that the eldest, in playing an interlocutor role between parents and the laterborn, is in an excellent position for further development of verbal skills.

Rosenberg and Sutton-Smith (1969) stated that wide spacing has a positive effect on cognitive abilities for firstborn boys, but no significant effect on girls, which agrees with Koch (1954, see above). Dandes and Dow (1969) studied children in grades 1 to 9 and found that the larger the family and the more closely spaced the children, the lower the test intelligence. Zajonc (1975) remarked that wide spacing may partially mitigate negative effects on intelligence of large families. He reasoned that close spacing is more detrimental to the younger of the pair, since the closely spaced younger is exposed to a less mature speech model. This hypothetical detriment to the closely spaced younger is not entirely consistent with the empirical findings (see above) of Breland and of Nuttall and Nuttall.

Elliott and Elliott (1970) reported that a large gap to an older sibling leads to higher academic aspiration for the younger if the older was an oldest child and was achievement oriented. Levinson (1963) found that wide spacing (31 months or more) produces extremes in reading ability in the younger but has no effect, on the older. Yet Schoonover (1959) found that age spacing has no effect on intelligence or on the level of achievement of sibling pairs, but that the sex of the sibling does.

2. Psychosocial Effects: Emotions, Autonomy, Security, and General Adjustment

a. Short Gap after Displaced Older. Lasko (1954) found that the early-displaced child suffers more from a lack of warmth from its parents than the more widely spaced. As Stendler (1964) found, a "new arrival" is more traumatic upon the displaced child when the latter is still very dependent on the mother. Parents of adolescents that are spaced less than 2 years apart use more physical force to control their offspring (Edwards & Braunburger, 1973). Both Stout (1960) and Waldrop and Bell (1966) found that short spacing, especially in large families, leads to increased dependency in the child. Zucker and Van Horn (1972) found that closely spaced firstborn adolescent boys showed more oral behavior in smoking and problem drinking. Lasko did find (cross-validated by Judd & Lewis, 1976), that with age spacing of 18 months or less, the mother verbalizes simultaneously with both children treating them both as babies. Such reduced individualized vocalization and accompanying derogation of the older to the level of the younger child might be expected to have a demoralizing effect on the older. Breland (1972) and Kammeyer (1967) supported this conjecture with findings that twins average the poorest verbal ability of all spacing groups.

Koch reported that the displaced older sibling, with a close gap to the next child, especially if this is a cross-sexed sibling, recovers more slowly and less adequately from emotional upset. She also found that older boys, with spacing of less than 2 years, especially with a younger sister, are more passive, while with spacing of 24–48 months, older boys do not show such passivity. Boys closely spaced to a younger brother are more withdrawn, passive, and apprehensive than other boys (Koch, 1956a, b). Boys also have intense conflict and rivalry with their closely aged brothers (Toman, 1976), and frequently feel hatred for the younger brother (Adler, 1931). Toman and Preiser (1973) found more neurotic children among those displaced at less than 3 years, although among criminals there is an overrepresentation of those displaced at over 3 years. Differences are more extreme when the boy is displaced by a sister. From a study of college men, Grinker, Grinker, and Timberlake (1962) reported marginal adjustment in those separated from the next younger sibling by less than 33 months, fair adjustment in those separated 33–48 months, and very good adjustment in those displaced at 48 months or more. Wagner and H. Schubert (1974) found that middleborn college girls wedged closely between two siblings are less well adjusted psychosocially than when spaced farther apart in age. This difference is accentuated when both adjacent siblings are sisters. Beeton and Pearson (1901) found that men closely spaced to a younger sibling, do not live as long.

When a male child is displaced at an early age by a sister, he assigns more power to the female (Bigner, 1974), is more likely to become homosexual (H. Schubert, Wagner, & Riess, 1976), and becomes defeated and a women hater when surpassed by an early-developing sister.

If an older girl is displaced at an early age by a sister, she becomes tenacious and aggressive (Koch, 1956a, 1956b). Although at an early stage she may be handicapped in achievement, she comes to the fore in college (Cicirelli, 1967). When displaced by a brother, she is similarly more aggressive, but also more ambitious, enthusiastic, and less procrastinating than girls from other sibship patterns (Koch, 1956a).

b. Intermediate-Spaced Displacement.   The individual displaced after 20–24 months of age, but not by more than 36 months, has unique problems of psychological stress. Richer (1968) showed from age 2 years and after the child gradually becomes aware of the value of compliance to parental directives. As noted above, Lasko (1954) found that children displaced at this stage of development, generally, but especially the second of three, are treated with less warmth and attention and more friction, resulting in turmoil in the child. By 4 years of age, both mother and child handle the displacement much better. Lasko concluded that the mother better meets the needs of her children if they are widely separated. Further, Koch (1956a, 1956b) determined that those spaced by 2–4 years show more intersibling strain and find life generally more stressful. The displaced child with intermediate spacing generally shows more conflict and feels that the parents side more with the younger sibling. Associated with a cross-sexed 2-to 4-year-old younger child, her 5- and 6-year-old are more nervous. She further reported that girls displaced at this intermediate length of time are less curious and enthusiastic, strive more for adult attention, and tattle more. Boys displaced at this intermediate length are more quarrelsome, teasing, intense, and slow to recover from emotional upset. Nuttall and Nuttall (1975) found that among latency and early adolescent children the intermediate spaced are less intelligent than either those displaced earlier or later. Further, these children are less involved socially, but very obedient, work harder, and feel capable, Grinker, Grinker, and Timberlake (1962) found such intermediately displaced college men have fair adjustment, better than those with narrower spacing to next younger, but less than those spaced by 4 years or more.

Sibling spacing of between 24 and 40 months tends to result in stressful interaction with both parents and siblings, an emotional disturbance that leads to less adequate psychosocial adjustment. Spacing of less than 2 years often leaves the child somewhat apathetic, withdrawn, apprehensive, and psychosocially inept. The intermediate displacement results in a stressful childhood with poor adolescent and young adult adjustment. Careful research is needed to pinpoint more exactly the spacing lengths that lead to such difficulties, and indeed to determine more exactly the character of the difficulties themselves.

 c. Wide Spacing from Displaced to Next Younger Sibling. Regarding young children, Lasko (1954) reported that mother–child relations are much better when the spacing is 4 years or more. Koch (1956b) found widely spaced displaced boys are more aggressive and feel favored by their fathers. When displaced by a sister, they are less intense, quarrelsome, and jealous, more enthusiastic and responsible, but more apprehensive than when displaced by a brother. Koch also found (1956a, 1956b) that the widely spaced older girl dawdles less, is less quarrelsome, more sociable, and shows more liking for the younger sister than does the closely spaced older girl. However, when this older girl has a widely spaced younger brother, she is rated nervous.

 Nuttall and Nuttall (1975) reported that, when widely spaced, latency children and young adolescents are more intelligent, happy-go-lucky, controlled, and fervent, beginning to make substantial college plans. Widely spaced older girls have more friends in school than those more closely spaced to younger siblings.

 Cicirelli (1967) found that sixth-grade boys displaced by sisters after 4 years or more are more fluent and flexible; and Toman (1976) thought that boys so displaced accept their sisters better.

 Wide spacing somewhat mitigates the ill effects of large families on intelligence and achievement (Zajonc, 1976). Widely spaced middleborn girls in college are psychosocially better adjusted (MMPI) than those closely spaced (Wagner & Schubert, 1974).

 In summary, those individuals who are at least 40 months of age at displacement are better adjusted psychosocially, as well as more intelligent and achievement oriented, than individuals that are more closely spaced.

 B. SIBLING–SPACING EFFECTS ON THE YOUNGER CHILD

1. Effects of Sibling Age Spacing on Intelligence

Fewer findings are reported for the younger child with close spacing to an older brother and sister than for the older sibling in this relationship. The effects on the younger child are more closely related to both the sex of the individual and the sex of the other child, but generally seem less negative than for the displaced older sibling. Cicirelli (1967) reported that closely spaced youngers are more creative and that reading and arithmetic are enhanced by near spacing. Koch (1954, 1955) found that the younger with a closely spaced older brother averages higher on mathematics than when preceded by a sister. Lunneborg (1971) concluded that the closely spaced younger brother of two boys has higher mathematics ability than when preceded by a sister close in age, but that this differential effect of the sex of the older sibling decreases as the spacing increases.

For closely spaced younger girls from sibships of two, the findings about spacing effects are positive or negligible. Although secondborn do not excel firstborn in intelligence, Koch (1956b) showed that, emotionally and socially, close spacing assists the younger of two sisters. Cicirelli (1967) found that the younger of two sisters is most creative when close spaced and that reading and arithmetic skills are enhanced by narrow spacing in same-sexed siblings. Rosenberg and Sutton-Smith (1969) found that a close older sister raises cognitive ability.

Koch (1956b) showed that the younger of two siblings with intermediate spacing is likely to be more intelligent than the younger for whom the gap is close. Nuttall and Nuttall (1975) found that the younger of two intermediately spaced siblings is the more intelligent of the two, although less able than when either narrowly or widely spaced. Intermediately spaced youngers feel that their mothers are more lax and use less hostile psychological control than do closely spaced.

Studying latency and adolescent children, Nuttall and Nuttall (1975) noted that the widely spaced younger sibling is more intelligent than the closely spaced, corroborating the results obtained by Breland (1972) and Zajonc (1976). The latter felt that wide spacing partially mitigates the ill effects of large families. Elliott and Elliott (1970) found that in sibling pairs, the younger has higher academic aspirations when the older is widely spaced and has high achievement needs. Rosenberg and Sutton-Smith (1964) asserted that a wide interval has a positive effect on cognition, and McGurk and Lewis (1972) that the widely spaced are more like eldests who are consistently more able verbally.

2. Sibling-Spacing Effects on Psychosocial Traits of Younger Child

a. Close Spacing to Older Sibling. Close spacing seems less negative in its psychosocial than in its intellectual effects on the younger child, especially for girls, who actually may be advantaged. Bigner (1971a) reported that an older closely spaced sister increases the feminine activities of her younger brother and leads him to assign more power to girls, a behavior and attitude which decreases with an increase in age interval. Koch reported (1955) more originality, tenacity, and planfulness for the closely rather than for the intermediately spaced sibling.

A younger closely spaced boy with an older sister may display more feminine interests and behaviors, both of which are in addition to and not a substitution for more masculine ways (Bigner, 1971b). In contrast to the general finding of lack of negative effects on the closely spaced younger sibling, Chittenden, Foan, Zweil, and Smith (1968) reported that youngers of sibling pairs are more disadvantaged than elders among latency and early adolescent children.

b.   Intermediate Spacing to Older Siblings.   Only a few researchers divided age spacing into three categories, with an intermediately spaced group. However, the design is robust enough so that some significant replicated findings appear. Lasko (1954) reported less vocalizing for both the intermediately spaced older and the younger, a finding corroborated by Judd and Lewis (1976), who found that the mother's time is more distributed and difficult to manage with intermediately spaced children, a temporal problem that would affect both.

Koch (1956b) found more intersibling stress and more stress on the mother when the spacing is between 2 and 4 years. She found that the younger of two so spaced is less original, tenacious, and ambitious, but more procrastinating, and she feels that parents side more with the older sibling, as compared to the situation with closer spaced children. She found that such intermediately spaced children with an older brother are more quarrelsome, vengeful, competitive, and defensive, more seeking of adult help, and less able to take defeat. Boys with an intermediately spaced older brother are more pressured to keep up with the older brother; girls are more tomboyish.

Overall, researchers report that the younger of an intermediately spaced pair finds life more stressful, being consequently belligerent and searching more for adult support than those closely spaced. Compared to those at a greater spacing from older children, the intermediately spaced siblings are less poised and less emotionally controlled.

c.   Wide Spacing to Older Sibling.   Findings indicate fairly consistently that, overall, a wide spacing is beneficial for both the older and the younger child. Perhaps the older sibling is somewhat more severely disadvantaged by close or intermediate spacing than the younger, but the reports leave little doubt that the latter is also thrown into turmoil, though possibly less affected intellectually, than those more widely spaced. What is not clear is at what point in the spacing this psychological disturbance is overcome, certainly after a spacing of 4 years and possibly earlier.

In elucidating the advantages of wide spacing, Lasko (1954) and Judd and Lewis (1976) unequivocally state that the early mother–child relationship is considerably enhanced by a wide space of time between children in that it allows for better intercommunication and for the mother to be better able to meet the needs of both. Cicirelli (1973, 1974) found that the widely spaced younger child is more willing to accept and profit from the help and guidance of an older sibling than from that of a closer aged sibling, and that the former learns in a more inferential style rather than in the descriptive style used by the latter.

Psychosocially, Rosenberg and Sutton-Smith (1969) pointed out that wide spacing allows the youngest to "escape from overwhelming competition." Nuttall and Nuttall (1975) found that the greater the distance to the older child, the more happy-go-lucky, controlled, and vivacious is the younger child.

Wide spacing leads the younger child to be more enterprising, socially expansive, and socially effective (Koch, 1956b). For the younger of two boys, Koch found that the boy widely spaced from his brother is more friendly, less quarrelsome, less apprehensive, and less sensitive. With wider spacing, boys are more protected by their mothers and more supported by their fathers, and develop a greater liking for school and teachers. A cross-sexed sibling tends to elicit a more frequent rating of nervousness. Wide spacing to the older brother leads girls to increased femininity, a decrease of envy of the brother with less jealously and teasing, more cheerfulness and friendliness to adults, and a quicker recovery of poise after emotional upset. Reciprocally, Bigner (1971b) found younger boys with a distant older sister are more masculine than those more closely spaced.

Overall, wide spacing has possibly less effect on the intelligence of the younger of the two siblings than on the older. However, on emotional and social development, the researchers clearly agree that wide spacing has positive effects on the security, poise, gender identity, and general happiness of the younger child.

d. Very Widely Spaced Lastborn.   Very wide spacing of the lastborn seems to exert an inhibiting effect on those in this ordinal position. Datta (1968) reported lowered creativity among the "distant" younger brothers. Nuttall and Nuttall (1975) reported that such very widely spaced youngest feel the least self-sufficient. Walker, Johnson, and Goolishian (1973), found that very widely spaced secondborn are overrepresented among transient personality-disordered adolescents, while widely spaced firstborn occur with undue frequency among schizophrenic adolescents. Levinson (1963) reported that more very widely spaced as well as more closely spaced youngests occur among extremely poor readers. Very widely spaced (over 5 years) lastborn resemble firstborn more than other youngest (Collard, 1968; Helmreich, Kuiken, & Collins, 1968; Miller & Zimbardo, 1966) on anxiety and fear reactions and reaction to stress. The present researchers are inclined to think that the unhappy state of these distant youngest may largely be due to their being unexpected and unwanted. Zajonc suggests that there may be an optimal spacing.

C. SUMMARY AND CONCLUSIONS

Spacing of children has very extensive and powerful effects on their intelligence and psychosocial development. Age spacing in the neighborhood of 4 years seems best for the emotional development of the children and for the effectiveness of the mother's child-rearing endeavors. Sibling spacing has very powerful effects that persist throughout life. Because investigators have only recently begun to study birth spacing, many pressing questions remain to be resolved, questions that need careful, tight research design to obviate the interactional effects of sibship and demographic variables (i.e., sex, race, socioeconomic level, and intactness of the family), as well as the cultural variables of attitude and values.

Probably a first-order goal is to pinpoint exactly where the effects of various gap lengths begin and/or end. To what upper limit does the narrow gap extend—to 20, 24, 30, or 36 months or even farther—in its deleterious effects on the verbal ability of the older child? What also are the upper space limits of negative personality effects? Are eldest in sibships of two as compared to eldest in large sibships and girls compared to boys better able to tolerate a narrow gap to the next sibling? How much does the strength, aggressivity, or sex of the second child effect tolerance of short birth spacing? Then come the extrawide gap effects. Some such youngest become excellent copers; other do not. What other characteristics of the early environment impinge on the successful copers and on those not successful? What are the upper gap limits of intermediate sibling spacing that develop the tumultuous, irracible, emotionally disturbed older child? What are the lower limits?

Research on sibling spacing, as for other sibship variables, is especially needed for the larger families—those of three, four, and more children—since the sibship of two has been more fully examined.

A summary of the major research findings on sibling spacing follows:

1. Both the displaced and displacing child are seriously disturbed by close spacing—the displaced child showing the greatest disturbance. These negative effects are less evident in sibships of two, and for girls.

2. Early displacement leads to early and persistent cognitive effects on intelligence and psychosocial development. The early displaced child is at greater risk than the later-in-life displaced of becoming unmotivated, ineffectual, dependent, passive, apprehensive, withdrawn, and shorter lived, with less emotional resilience. All of these probably are due to less warmth, acceptance, and attention.

3. The intermediately displaced child is less affected intellectually than the close spaced but has distinct, sizable psychosocial handicaps such as explosiveness, obstinacy, quarrelsomeness, and lack of stamina.

4. Displacement after 36 to 54 months, in contrast to other gaps to the next sibling, leads to higher intelligence, greater poise, enterprise, and responsibility.

5. While still negative, close spacing between siblings has less effect on the younger, displacing child than on the older child. Some of the closely spaced younger succeed against difficulties by being tenacious and less bound by hampering rules, and thus become distinctly creative.

6. The intermediately spaced younger is frequently less handicapped intellectually and in achievement than either the closely or very widely spaced younger. Having tenacity and enterprise, some intermediately spaced younger achieve much. However, the intermediately spaced younger are often procrastinating, quarrelsome, and vengeful, with long-lasting emotional difficulties.

7. The child separated by a fairly wide gap from his next older sibling develops well intellectually and in personality. He is effective, cooperative, and happy-go-lucky.

8. Very widely spaced youngest may be handicapped intellectually and psychosocially perhaps because they are unexpected and unwanted by their parents. Some are well adjusted.

9. Wide spacing tends to mitigate the negative effects of the large sibship and of later ranking in the sibship.

VI. Creativity and Sibship Variables

The findings of previous investigators have shown notable consistency in the relations between sibship patterns and such creativity indices as interest in creativity, ratings of creative ability, artistic creativity, eminence in creative production, and problem solving. This section presents the findings of the relationships with each creativity index and gives suggested research hypotheses and approaches to adding more definitive knowledge.

A.   STUDIES BY CREATIVITY CRITERIA

1. Interest in Creativity
Four studies (Brim, 1958; Gandy, 1973; Koch, 1956b; Sutton-Smith, Roberts, & Rosenberg, 1964) indicate that an individual with a cross-sexed sibling is more likely to have creative interests. However, one study pointed to the enhancement (statistically nonsignificant) of creative interest by older same-sexed siblings (Leventhal, 1970). Onlyborn do not elect college courses aimed at increasing creative potential (D. Schubert, Wagner, & H. Schubert 1977c).

2. Rated Creativity

Four studies involved ratings of creative ability as the criterion measure in investigating the effects of sibship variables; two (Brim, 1958; Datta, 1968) indicate that both sex of and age spacing between the siblings affect creativity. In an extended analysis of Koch's data (1955), Brim discovered that the sex of sibling and age-spacing effects on creativity are limited to certain sibship categories. Both boys and girls with 2 years or less spacing to an older sibling, regardless of sex, showed low originality. Girls with a sister 2–4 years older and boys with a brother 4–6 years older were high in originality. All other sibship categories showed no such differential effect. Datta (1968) showed that in a sibship of two boys, a younger brother with close spacing is more creative than one with distant spacing. Helson (1971) found that creative women mathematicians tend not to have brothers.

3. Artistic Creativity

Studies involving judgments of artistic creativity and of eminence are likely to suffer a paucity of cases and lack of a control group; however, diligent search of archival sources can net a sizable sample and incidence of each sibship category in the general population and normal groups can serve as relative frequencies with which those of creative groups may be contrasted.

Four studies indicate that firstborn children, and onlyborn in particular, occur relatively more frequently among musicians (Raychaudhuri, 1965, 1966; Mikol, 1975; D. Schubert, Wagner, & H. Schubert, 1977a). According to the latter study, onlyborn children are distinctly overrepresented among composers accounting for 20%, although onlyborn account for approximately 10% of the general population (Chen & Cobb, 1960; see also Section IV,B). Wallbrown, Wallbrown, and Wherry (1975) showed that older children and children from small families are overrepresented among painters. However, youngest and near-youngest appear disproportionately more often among poets and writers (Bliss, 1970).

4. Eminence

All except one of the studies investigating the correlates of eminence with sibship patterns have involved samples of scholars and scientists. Among the lettered and learned, firstborn, particularly eldest, are overrepresented (Eiduson, 1962; Ellis, 1904/1926; Galton, 1874; McCurdy, 1957; Roe, 1953; Terman, 1925). However, among renowned baseball players (Cobb, 1950), there were no firstborn. Some evidence indicates that youngest (Bliss, 1970; Ellis, 1904/1926) and secondborn (McCurdy, 1957) may appear relatively frequently among eminent artists. Coming from a small family contributes to giftedness (Terman, 1925). Coming from an all-male sibship (Wagner & H. Schubert, 1977a, 1977b) increases the likelihood of eminence in politics and the military.

5.   Problem Solving

The problem-solving area of creativity has generated more research than other areas, partly because standard problems may be given to subjects without waiting for a spontaneous, elaborate creation such as a work of art, and scoring may then be done in a repeatable standardized fashion. Because of the large number of studies available, particularly on position among siblings and sibship size, creative problem solving will be divided into studies with single-answer problems and those with multiple-answer problems.

   a.   Birth Order and Single-Answer Problem Solving.   The single-answer type of problem-solving test is frequently used as a general achievement measure and at times as part of an estimate of intelligence. Such single-answer tests are included here because of their similarity along some dimensions to multiple-answer problem-solving tests, as well as their suggestiveness of some of the results in other areas of the interrelationship between sibship constellation and creativity. The multiple-answer problem is a test of what Guilford (1967) would describe as divergent thinking. Divergent thinking tests including those devised by Guilford (1967) are more closely linked in the literature to creativity than the single-answer problem.

   Firstborn or earlierborn generally (Table V) do better than those in other sibling positions on single-answer verbal problems. On the Raven Progressive Matrices, the average scores decrease both with the size of the sibship and with ordinal rank, with the exception that those in sibships of two surpass onlyborn. When the task was that of finding embedded figures, youngest men with brothers only or with sisters only did better than eldest men in sibships that were otherwise similar.

   b.   Birth Order and Multiple-Answer Problem Solving.   Five studies showed that those early in the birth order, especially eldest and onlyborn, do better on multiple-answer problem solving than those in other ordinal positions (see Table V), but three studies yielded no statistically significant effects regarding a child's position among its siblings. A unique study contrasting inventors who had a number of patents with those who had neither patents, grants, nor publications indicated no statistically significant effects of birth order.

   In summary, one finds a consistency between the results on birth order and single-answer and multiple-answer problem solving. Eldest, particularly from small families, do best followed by other earlierborn and onlyborn and that laterborn seem to do the most poorly in these types of problem solving. Consistent differences was shown by 13 of the 18 studies (see Table V). Possible reasons for other studies showing no differences in-

TABLE V

Relation of Creative Problem Solving to Sibship Characteristics

Investigators (date)	Measures of creativity	High-scoring sibship patterns
	Position in sibship	
Single-answer problems		
Aldous (1973)	Figural tasks of Minnesota Test of Creative Thinking	Eldest boys; only girls
Belmont & Marolla (1973)	Raven Progressive Matrices	Second and third born
Harris (1964)	Abstract or verbal creativity	Firstborn
Kellaghan & Newman, (1971)	Verbal reasoning	(None)[a]
Kellaghan & MacNamara, (1972)	Verbal reasoning	Earlier birth order
Lunneborg (1968)	Precollege test	Eldest men (onlyborn similar to laterborn)[a]
Lunneborg (1971)	Precollege test	Elder men
Marjoribanks & Walberg (1975)	Reasoning	(None)[a]
McCall (1973)	Mechanical reasoning	Earlier birth orders
Roberts & Engel (1974)	WISC Block Design	Firstborn
Stein (1964)	Miller's analogies	Firstborn chemists
Stewart (1967)	Embedded figures	Youngest men better than eldest men in otherwise sex-homogeneous sibships
Multiple-answer problems		
Cleland, Uno, Rago, Case, & McGavern (1975)	Number of patents by inventor	(None)[a]
Laosa & Brophy (1970)	Unusual uses, product improvement	Eldest and onlyborn
Lichtenwaller & Maxwell (1969)	Object-identification test	Eldest and onlyborn
Sellwood (1974)	Alternate uses, Remote Association Test (RAT)	(None)[a]
Wallbrown, Wallbrown, & Wherry (1975)	Wallach-Kogan (after RAT)	Earlier birth orders
Weisberg & Springer (1961)	Tin-can uses Ask-and guess test Circles test	(Eldest; lowest scores by middleborn in sibship of four to five)[a]
	Sibship size	
Single-answer problems		
Belmont & Marolla (1973)	Raven Progressive Matrices	Small
Cicirelli (1975)	Use of aid of sibling	(No difference)[a]
Claudy (1976)	Abstract reasoning	One to two sibs

(*continued*)

TABLE V (*continued*)

Investigators (date)	Measures of creativity	High-scoring sibship patterns
Kellaghan & MacNamara (1972)	Verbal reasoning	Small
McCall (1973)	Mechanical reasoning	Small
Nisbet & Endwistle (1967)	Verbal reasoning	Small
Multiple-answer problems Aldous (1973)	Figural tasks of Minnesota Test of Creativity Thinking	Small sibships ($r = -.29$)[a]
	Sex of adjacent sibs; sib spacing	
Belmont & Marolla (1973)	Raven Progressive Matrices	Wide spacing between sibs
Cicirelli (1967)	Minnesota Test of Creative Thinking	Like-sex sib close in age
Cicirelli (1975)	Accept aid better	Have older sister(s)
Eisenman & Foxman (1970)	Brick uses, pencil uses	More sisters

[a] Parentheses indicate statistical significance not reached.

clude type of test used, population samples, and size of age difference between siblings.

  c. Sibship Size and Single-Answer Problem Solving.   Again, there is consistency in that small families produce people better able to solve single-answer problems (Table V). In general, problem-solving ability decreases with increase in sibship size except that only children do less well than those with one or two siblings. Claudy (1976) has further specified that the child with one or two siblings does best in the abstract-reasoning type of problem solving in contrast to the only child or the child with three or more siblings. Belmont and Marolla (1973) also indicated that a progressive decline occurs with an increasing number of siblings beyond two. Onlyborn men do less well than men with one or two siblings, about equal to those with three, but better than those with four or more. Size of sibship does not seem to influence the use of a sibling to aid in problem solving. The six studies in this area are concordant and positive in concluding that small sibships produce better single-answer problem solvers. There are neither contradictory nor inconclusive studies.

  d. Sibship Size and Multiple-Answer Problem Solving.   There is a distinct dearth of studies relating multiple-answer problems to sibship size (Table V). Aldous (1973) showed a negative relationship between sibship size and scores on the Figural Tasks of the Minnesota Test of Creativity. Eisenman and Foxman (1970) found that a subject tended to do better in relation to the number of his sisters.

e.   Age Spacing, Sex of Adjacent Siblings, and Creative Problem Solving.   Belmont and her co-workers (1973, 1975) and Zajonc (1976) have demonstrated the pervasive and substantial interactive effects of sibling spacing, sibship size, and ordinal position. Zajonc and Markus (1975) have developed mathematical equations which can closely predict Belmont's data when birth interval, birth order, and sibship size are all specified. However, Zajonc and Markus did mention that birth interval tends to be a function of family size and birth order. The birth interval between the firstborn and secondborn tends to be smaller than later birth intervals (the smaller the family, the larger the birth interval); and the birth interval increases between successive children in families of any given size. Birth interval, then, is related to both family size and birth order, and should be taken into account when studying the relationship between family constellation and creativity measurements.

Both the sex of the sibling and the age spacing affect problem-solving ability. Cicirelli (1967) found that subjects with a like-sexed sibling close in age did better on the multiple-answer Minnesota Test of Creative Thinking.

B.   DISCUSSION

A question arising from the current review is "Why are firstborn better problem solvers?" Perhaps firstborn have a higher need to achieve. A number of studies indicate that more pressure to achieve is placed upon firstborn (Davis, 1959; McArthur, 1956; Rosen, 1961; Sampson, 1962; Sutton-Smith, Roberts, & Rosenberg, 1964). Of seven studies relating the need for achievement to birth order, five showed that firstborn have a higher need for achievement (Elder, 1962; Pierce, 1959; Rosen, 1961; Sampson, 1962; Sampson & Hancock, 1967), one (Moore, 1964) showed no difference, and one (Rosenfeld, 1966) showed that laterborn have higher achievement needs. Thus, consistent with the earlier cited studies, if more pressure is put on the firstborn to achieve, their reaction will result in higher scores on need for achievement measures. This higher need for achievement, in turn, will provide motivation for them to do better at problem solving. One way of validating this relationship further would be to find sibships, either subculturally or by individual variation, in which greater pressure to achieve is placed upon one or more of the laterborn than upon the firstborn and then to evaluate the school, creative, and other performance of each.

Additional areas of creativity and eminence need to be investigated to determine the strengths of other than firstborn. The present researchers, for instance, have preliminary evidence that, while actresses are over-represented among onlyborn and eldest, actors are more often youngest and onlyborn, and that those successful in body-contact and dangerous sports are largely middleborn. Further, do the subgroups within an area of creativity vary in sibship pattern as suggested by the finding that those who write autobiography only tend to be youngest while those who write autobiography in addition to other material do not. Is much of creativity mere persistence, as suggested by one researcher who found that younger girls persisted longer in a creative task. How much is due to being born into a family with special interests and knowledge of how to advance in a field, as suggested by the large percentage of actors, athletes, authors, and politicians who come from families with these respective interests and activities? Because the broken family often produces delinquents as well as eminent fiction writers and actresses, research is needed to determine the additional familiar factors that specifically produce each.

VII. Sibling-Constellation Effects on Health, Disease, and Physical Characteristics

Associative and causal relationships between intrafamilial and attitudinal factors and between these and bodily functioning have been topics, over the years, of a great deal of speculation and investigation. Here we are specifically concerned with the relation of sibship constellation variables to attitude with the subsequent effect of the latter on health, disease, and physical characteristics. Wolff (1953) described the sequence thus:

> The reactions of an individual to a life situation consist of an attitude and accompanying bodily changes. By attitude is meant the way in which he perceives his own position in the situation, and the action, if any, which he takes in dealing with it. . . . The accompanying bodily changes, if sufficiently intense and prolonged, give rise to experiences and sensations which are called symptoms. If these persist or recur . . . they become "disease." (p. 128)

The added thesis emphasized here is that differences in childhood experiences due to differences in sibship-constellation categories make for the acquisition of different attitudes which predispose an individual toward the diseases and physical characteristics later developed. Of course, physiologic and social factors also affect health. A mother's age, her number of previous pregnancies, and her general health affect the well-being of the child, as do nutrition, income, and social class.

Fortunately, in the area of sibship-constellation effects related to physical disease, reported findings are generally abundant and impressively consistent. For a few of the diseases discussed, conclusive results concerning the relationship of position among siblings and of sibship size to incidence of morbidity are not available. Such ambiguity may be due either to the collection of insufficient data, or to using broad categories, for example, for diseases, ulcer rather than peptic and duodenal ulcer, for sibships categories, firstborn rather than onlies and eldest, and for demographic measures, individuals rather than men and women.

A. SPECIFIC AILMENTS

1. Arthritis
Three studies (Cobb, Warren, Merchant, & Thompson, 1957; Rubin, Rosenbaum, & Cobb, 1956; Stecher, 1957) showed that arthritis is more frequent in large rather than in small families. This ailment also affected the parents of a large number of children (King & Cobb, 1958). In the studies reviewed, no ordinal position was identified as more prone to arthritis than another (Booth, 1937). Such a lack of positive findings for position among siblings may be due in part to the calculation of statistics on samples of combined men and women.

2. Asthma
Firstborn are more frequently asthmatic (Huet, 1955; Ikemi, Ago, Nakagawa, Mori, Takahashi, Sumatsu, & Sugita, 1973; Gessner, Lament, Long, Rollins, Whipple, & Prentice, 1955; McDermott & Cobb, 1939; Rubin & Moses, 1944; Schnyder, 1960; Schwartz, 1952). Of these studies, four distinguished onlyborn from eldest among firstborn; two studies (Huet, 1955; Ikemi *et al.,* 1974) showed that eldest are overrepresented among asthmatics; and two showed that onlyborn and eldest are more frequent. One study showed that youngest (Aaron, 1967) are at greater risk for developing asthma, and one (Rogerson, Hardcastle, & Duguid, 1935) showed that onlyborn, eldest, and youngest predominate over middleborn. Onlyborn and eldest, then, are most at risk for asthma, with youngest next, and middleborn relatively free from asthma.

3. Cardiovascular Disease
Two studies showed firstborn at greater risk of developing hypertension than other ordinals (Hau & Rueppel, 1966; Paffenbarger, Thorne, & Wing, 1968); one that onlyborn are the most frequently effected (Vincent, 1952); and one that eldest more frequently develop hypertension (Thomas & Duszynski, 1974). Benech (1968) found no significant birth-order effects. Overall, firstborn are most frequently hypertensive.

Parents of small families are more liable than those of larger ones to hypertension (Humerfeld & Wedervang, 1957; Miall, 1959). Miall and Oldham (1958) found no such relation, and Omran (1974) found parents of large families at greater risk of hypertension, with a decline in marital adjustment.

Coronary heart disease occurs more frequently among onlyborn medical doctors (Thomas & Duszynski, 1974) and other college male graduates (Paffenbarger, Notkin, Krueger, Wolf, Thorne, Lebaner, & Williams, 1966); cardiac arrhythmias occur more often among middle-class firstborn (Dunbar, 1943).

4. Obesity

Obesity is found most frequently in small families (Bruch & Touraine, 1940; Tanner, 1961, 1968; Tolstrup, 1953; Whitelaw, 1971); no study has shown it to be overrepresented in large families. Two studies showed onlyborn to be overrepresented (Atkinson & Ringuette, 1967; King & Cobb, 1958); another found no difference between onlyborn and nononlyborn (Witty, 1937); and one (Werkman & Greenberg, 1967) found no birth-order differences. Obesity is predominantly a disease of small families with overrepresentation of onlyborn, with eldest and younger appearing about equally.

5. Ulcers: Gastric (Peptic) and Duodenal

Illadvisedly, some researchers failed to report whether the ulcer was located within the stomach proper (gastric/peptic) or within the duodenum. Children from large families predominate among ulcer patients (Castelnuovo-Tedesco, Schwerfeger, & Janowski, 1970; Hamilton, 1950; Kellock, 1951; Ruesch, Christiansen, Harris, Devees, Jacobson, & Loeb, 1948). Laterborn, intermediates, and youngest are frequently overrepresented (Chen & Cobb, 1963; Castelnuovo-Tedesco, 1962; Hamilton, 1950; Hau & Rueppel, 1966; Kellock, 1951; Kezur, Kapp, & Rosenbaum, 1951; Ruesch et al., 1948). Onlyborn showed a tendency (that was statistically nonsignificant) to be ovrrepresented among peptic-ulcer patients in one investigation (Kezur et al., 1951) and eldest military men yielded similar results (Farber, 1945). One study indicated that the eldest have the highest pepsinogen level (Yessler, Reiser, & Rioch, 1959). Overall, ulcer (especially duodenal) patients seem predominantly the middleborn and youngest from large families. Eldest and onlyborn seem at some risk of peptic (gastric) ulcers. Ulcerative colitis is found more often in smaller families among onlyborn and younger (Castelnuovo-Tedesco, Schwerfeger, & Janowski, 1970; Monk, Mendeloff, Siegel, & Lilienfeld, 1970).

6. Cancer

Cancer is found more frequently in large families (Resnikoff, 1955; Thomas & Duszynski, 1974). Leukemic patients tend to be firstborn (MacMahon & Newill, 1962; Stewart, Webb, & Hewitt, 1958). There are no contradictory studies. LeShan (1966) showed that individuals followed by a sibling less than 2 years younger are at risk of cancer. Cancer, then, seems to occur more frequently in large families and among early displaced eldest.

7. Hyperthyroidism

Hyperthyroidism is found more frequently among firstborn (Bartels, 1941; Conrad, 1934; Lidz, 1955; Ruesch, Christiansen, Harris, Dewees, & Jacobson, 1947). There are no contradictory studies.

8. Miscellaneous Diseases

Tuberculosis (Pearson, 1914; Rivers, 1911; Still, 1927) occurs most frequently among firstborn. There are no contradictory data. Contagious diseases (Dingle, Badger, & Jordan, 1964; Spence, 1954) occur more frequently in large families. Pain and sensitivity or report of pain (Carman, 1899; Johnson, Dobbs, & Leventhal, 1970; MacDonald, 1901) appear most frequently among firstborn, but never more frequently in laterborn. Pain is reported more frequently by those from large families (Gonda, 1962; Mersky, 1965; Sweeney & Fine, 1970). Cobb (1950) found youngest more frequently among anorexia nervosa patients, but Rowland (1970) found an overrepresentation of first- and secondborn with this ailment. Pyke (1956) found that diabetics are overrepresented among parents with many children. Booth (1948) found youngest at more risk for Parkinsonism, Cover and Kerridge (1962) found secondborn more at risk for epilepsy, and Edgell (1953) found firstborn more at risk for eczema.

B. PHYSICAL CHARACTERISTICS

1. Diverse Ailments and Conditions

Although only a few studies, sometimes only one, are available for various health states and physical conditions, some interesting results have been obtained. Firstborn are likely to have abnormally high blood uric acid levels (Gordon & Gordon, 1967; Kasl, Brooks, & Cobb, 1966). Left-handedness is more frequent among twins (Bakan, 1971; Hubbard, 1971) and among laterborn and firstborn (Hubbard, 1971). Those from large families in low social classes are likely to play the sick role by presenting multiple physical symptoms (Petroni, 1969).

Two studies indicated that those from large families mature earlier (Douglas & Simpson, 1964; Tanner, 1968), but two other studies showed that those from small families mature earlier (Poppleton, 1968; Terhune, 1976). Parents with few children have better physical health than those with larger families (Hare & Shaw, 1965). Onlyborn were found to have better physical health than non-onlyborn children by one researcher (Terhune, 1976), but no differences were found between onlyborn and others by another researcher (Witty, 1937). A lack of separation by sex of index cases may confound the findings.

Laterborn have better vision than earlierborn (Becker, 1965), and middle born at middle age have the best prognosis for postoperative recovery (Boyd, Yeager, & McMillan, 1973).

2. Height

Those from smaller families are consistently found on average to have greater physical height than those from larger families (Belmont, Stein, & Susser, 1975; Douglas & Blomfield, 1958; Douglas & Simpson, 1964; Grant, 1964; Tanner, 1968; Tremolieres & Boulanger, 1950; Udjus, 1964). Peterson and Sharpe (1972) found that youngest tend to be taller, and Witty (1931) reported no differences between onlyborn and non-onlyborn in average height.

3. Longevity

Consistently, people who are followed by a relatively long interval to the next sibling experience a greater mean longevity than those followed by a short interval (Beeton & Pearson, 1901; Gordon, 1969; Morrison, Heady, & Morris, 1959; Spiers & Wang, 1976; Wyron & Gordon, 1962; Yerushalmy, 1945). Beeton and Pearson (1901) also found that longevity decreased with birth rank. Those from small families average greater mean longevity than those from larger families (Gordon, 1969; Morris & Heady, 1955; Wyron & Gordon, 1962; Yerushalmy, Bierman, Kemp, Connors, & French, 1956), with onlyborn averaging the greatest longevity (Terhune, 1976). Perinatal and postperinatal survival is greater for those with fewer older siblings (Elwood, MacKenzie, & Cran, 1974), becoming progressively poorer with each birth beyond the first.

C.   DISCUSSION

Considering the effects of size of the family: large families seem to produce greater risk of arthritis, peptic ulcer, and cancer, as well as greater neonatal and early childhood morbidity and higher mortality rates. Individuals from smaller sibships tend to be taller and more frequently obese, and to live longer, and perhaps to be at greater risk of having ulcerative colitis. Closer examination of the studies on ulcerative colitis by Castelnuovo-Tedesco (1970) and Monk *et al.* (1970) indicates that the ulcerative colitis sample shows significant difference only when compared to other clinical groups. No study shows that ulcerative colitis patients are from smaller sibships when compared with the general population. Therefore, the larger the sibship size, the greater the incidence of physical illness and the less longevity. The higher rate of illness is consistent with the study by Petroni (1969) showing that large families in most social classes tend to present multiple physical symptoms, which behavior Petroni describes as being more likely to play the sick role. People from small sibships tend to be larger physically in both height and weight. Since tall people have as a group a larger than expected proportion of obese members for their height than do shorter people, this relationship again shows a consistency.

Unfortunately, most relevant studies combine eldests and singletons into one category, firstborns, and middleborns and youngests into laterborns. As a result, the present summary is based largely on firstborns and laterborns. Firstborns then, combined eldests and onlyborns, predominate among those with asthma, eczema, high blood pressure, high uric acid level, gastric ulcer, hyperthyroidism, tuberculosis, and leukemia. They also have, on the average, greater sensitivity to pain and poorer vision. Onlyborns are at greater risk of obesity, colitis, and coronary heart disease.

Laterborns are at greater risk of duodenal ulcer, epilepsy, and neonatal and early childhood morbidity and mortality. These childhood misfortunes increase as the number of older siblings increases. The youngest (lastborn) tends to have better vision, to be taller, and to be at greater risk of colitis and of being injured in childhood accidents. Obviously, the studies with regard to ordinal position need replication with eldest and onlies and with middleborn and youngest separated. When grouped together, onlyborn, who represent a much smaller percentage of the population than eldests, are clearly eclipsed. Since the number of middleborns varies greatly with size of sibship, the relative frequency of middleborn and youngests is generally indeterminate. There is, then, need for studies on the effect of ordinal position for each of the four ordinal subgroups.

Finally, with regard to sibship spacing, the one repeated finding is that people with a relatively long interval to birth of the next sibling experience a greater mean longevity than those with a close younger sibling following. LeShan reported that those with a close younger sibling are more at risk of cancer. Sibship spacing deserves closer scrutiny with regard to other diseases as well as with regard to physical characteristics.

Although many of the numerous findings described above need cross-validation and refinement, there is considerable consistency, indicating the reliability of results. The overall conclusion is that sibship size, birth spacing, and ordinal position do have strong and lasting effects on disease and health, that are consistent with medical and psychological knowledge.

VIII. Overview and Implications

Because the retrospective family-constellation data are simple, objective, invariant, and usually overlearned, researchers using them have the advantage of working with a highly reliable independent variable. Each and all of the sibship variables have effects, from just demonstrable to uncommonly powerful, on intelligence, academic achievement, occupational success, creativity, emotional control, socialization, health, and longevity. Even though they are derived from variously oriented and designed investigations, the studies reviewed present overall amazingly consistent results. We concur with MacKinnon (1953) who stated "empirical investigator's findings which continue to hold up in repeated cross-validations may deserve more confidence than findings reported in researches much more elegant in design" (p. 144).

Intelligence and personality traits are powerfully influenced by parental behavior and sibling interaction especially during the child's first 3 years. However, both cognitive and conative characteristics lend themselves to improvement by positively altering parental behavior through psychotherapy, or, better yet, by widespread open recognition of the importance and the intricacies of child rearing which has been almost entirely left to parental whims and folklore. The available basic knowledge should be used as a foundation for high school and college courses aimed at upgrading child-rearing practices. This learning would make the next generation happier, more effective, creative, empathetic, and responsible individuals.

Research and clinical evidence strongly and definitely indicate that socially desirable personality traits result from small families in which the children are spaced 3 or more years apart. The goal in family planning and education in parenting would be to have each child wanted and welcomed and to have the parents devote sufficient time to the child to understand his or her needs.

More important than the need for energy research is research on how world-wide population growth may be most effectively and most immediately reduced. As the reviewed research indicates, widely spaced and fewer children are associated not only with upward mobility and an improved standard of living, but also with greater overall individual ability, well being, and creativity.

REFERENCES

Aaron, N. S. Some personality differences between asthmatic, allergic, and normal children. *Journal of Clinical Psychology,* 1967, **23,** 336–340.

Abernethy, E. M. Further data on personality and family position. *Journal of Psychology,* 1940, **10,** 303–307.

Adams, R. L., & Phillips, B. N. Motivational and achievement differences among children of various ordinal birth positions. *Child Development,* 1972, **43,** 155–164.

Adler, A. *The practice and theory of individual psychology* (P. Radin, trans.). New York: Harcourt, 1924.

Adler, A. Characteristics of the first, second, third child. *Parent's Magazine* (formerly *Children: The Magazine for Parents*), 1928, **3,** pp. 14, 52.

Adler, A. *The education of children.* (E. Jensen, trans.). London: Allen & Unwin, 1930.

Adler, A. *What life should mean to you.* Boston: Little, Brown, 1931.

Adler, A. *Understanding human nature* (W. B. Wolfe, trans.). Greenwich, Ct.: Fawcett, 1956. (Orginally published, 1927.)

Aldous, J. Family background factors and originality. *The Gifted Child Quarterly,* 1973, **17,** 183–192.

Alexander, C. N., Jr. Ordinal position and social mobility. *Sociometry,* 1968, **31,** 285–293.

Alexander, F. *Studies in psychosomatic medicine.* New York: Norton, 1948.

Alkaire, A. A., Brunse, A. J., & Houlihan, J. P. Avoidance of nuclear family relationships in schizophrenia. *Journal of Clinical Psychology,* 1974, **30,** 398–400.

Altus, W. D. Some birth-order parameters related to verbal and quantitative aptitude for 1,120 college students with one sibling. *American Psychologist,* 1963, **18,** 361. (Abstract)

Altus, W. D. Birth order and scholastic aptitude. *Journal of Consulting Psychology,* 1965, **29,** 202–205. (a)

Altus, W. D. Birth order and academic primogeniture. *Journal of Personality and Social Psychology,* 1965, **2,** 872–876. (b)

Altus, W. D. Birth order and its sequelae. *Science,* 1966, **151,** 44–49.

Angelini, H. B. Family structure and motivation to achieve. *Revista Interamericana de Psicologia,* 1967, **1,** 115–125.

Apperly, L. A study of relevant American Rhodes scholars. *Journal of Heredity,* 1939, **30,** 493–495.

Armstrong, C. P. Delinquency and primogeniture. *Psychology Clinic,* 1933, **22,** 48–52.

Arrowood, A. J., & Amoroso, D. M. Social comparison and ordinal position. *Journal of Personality and Social Psychology,* 1965, **2,** 101–104.

Arthur, G. The relation of IQ to position in family. *Journal of Educational Psychology,* 1926, **17,** 541–550.

Atkinson, R. M., & Ringuette, E. L. A survey of biographical and psychological features in extraordinary fatness. *Psychosomatic Medicine,* 1967, **29,** 121–133.

Bakan, D. The relationship between alcoholism and birth rank. *Quarterly Journal of Studies on Alcohol,* 1949, **10,** 434–440.

Bakan, D. *Duality of human existence.* Chicago: Rand McNally, 1966.

Bakan, P. Handedness and birth order. *Nature (London),* 1971, **229,** 195.

Baker, F., & O'Brien, G. M. Birth order and fraternity affiliation. *Journal of Social Psychology,* 1969, **78,** 41–43.

Barger, B., & Hall, E. The interrelationships of family size and socioeconomic status for parents of college students. *Journal of Marriage and the Family,* 1966, **28,** 186–187.

Barker, B., & Lewis, M. *A multidimensional analysis of the effect of birth order on mother-infant interaction.* Paper presented at the Eastern Psychological Association meeting, New York, April 1975.

Barry, H., III, & Barry, H., Jr. Birth order, family size, and schizophrenia. *Archives of General Psychiatry,* 1967, **17**, 435–440.

Barry, H., III, & Barry, H., Jr. Birth order of psychiatric patients. *Nature (London),* 1971, **231**, 57.

Bartels, E. *Heredity in Graves' Disease.* Copenhagen: Munksgaard, 1941.

Bartlett, E. W., & Smith, C. P. Child rearing practices, birth order, and the development of achievement-related motives. *Psychological Reports,* 1966, **19**, 1207–1216.

Bartlett, E. W., & Smith, C. P. Child-rearing practices, birth order, and the development of achievement-related motives. In E. Evans (Ed.), *Children: Readings in behavior and development.* New York: Holt, 1968. Pp. 58–68.

Bayer, A. E. Birth order and college attendance. *Journal of Marriage and the Family,* 1966, **28**, 480–484.

Bayer, A. E. Birth order and attainment of the doctorate: A test of economic hypotheses. *American Journal of Sociology,* 1967, **72**, 540–550.

Bayley, N. Comparisons of mental and motor test scores for ages 1–15 months by sex, birth order, race, geographical location, and education of parents. *Child Development,* 1965, **36**, 379–411.

Becker, G. Visual acuity, birth order, achievement versus affiliation, and other Edwards Personal Preference Schedule scores. *Journal of Psychosomatic Research,* 1965, **9**, 277–283.

Beeton, M., & Pearson, K. Inheritance of the duration of life and the intensity of natural selection in men. *Biometrika,* 1901, **1**, 50–89.

Belmont, L. Birth order, intellect, competence, and psychiatric status. *Journal of Individual Psychology,* 1977, **33**, 97–104.

Belmont, L., & Marolla, F. A. Birth order, family size, and intelligence. *Science,* 1973, **182**, 1096–1101.

Belmont, L., Stein, Z. A., & Susser, M. W. Comparison of associations of birth order with intelligence test score and height. *Nature (London),* 1975, **255**, 54–56.

Belmont, L., Stein, Z. A., & Wittes, J. T. Birth order, family size, and school failure. *Developmental Medicine and Child Neurology,* 1976, **18**, 421–430.

Benech, A. Stades pubertaires, tension arterielle, et pouls chez les garcons de 13 ans. *Biometrie Humane,* 1968, **3**, 53–68.

Berent, J. Fertility and social mobility. *Population Studies,* 1952, **5**, 244–260.

Berger, P. K., & Ivancevich, J. M. Birth order and managerial achievement. *Academy of Management Journal,* 1973, **16**, 515–519.

Bigner, J. J. The effects of sibling influence on sex-role development in young children (Doctoral dissertation, Florida State University, 1970). *Dissertation Abstracts International,* 1971, **31**, 6093–6094B. (University Microfilm No. 71-6964) 6 (a)

Bigner, J. J. Sibling position and definition of self. *Journal of Social Psychology,* 1971, **84**, 307–308. (b)

Bigner, J. J. Sibling influence of sex role preference of young children. *Journal of Genetic Psychology,* 1972, **121**, 271–282.

Bigner, J. J. Secondborns' discrimination of sibling role concepts. *Developmental Psychology,* 1974, **10**, 564–573.

Bigner, J. J. Personal communication, April 21, 1975.

Biles, D. Birth order and delinquency. *Australian Psychologist,* 1971, **6**, 189–193.

Birtchnell, J. Early parent death, in relation to size and constitution of sibship, in psychiatric patients and general population controls. *Acta Psychiatrica Scandinavia,* 1971, **47**, 250–270. (a)

Birtchnell, J. Mental illness in sibships of two and three. *British Journal of Psychiatry,* 1971, **119**, 481–487. (b)

Birtchnell, J. Birth order and mental illness: A control study. *Social Psychiatry,* 1972, **7**, 167–179.

Blane, H. T., & Barry, H., III. Birth order and alcoholism: A review. *Quarterly Journal of Studies on Alcohol,* 1973, **34,** 837–852.

Blatz, W. E., & Bott, E. A. Studies in mental hygiene of children: I. Behavior of public school children—A description of method. *Journal of Genetic Psychology,* 1927, **34,** 552–582.

Blau, P. M., & Duncan, O. D. *American Occupational Structure.* New York: Wiley, 1967.

Bliss, W. D. Birth order of creative writers. *Journal of Individual Psychology,* 1970, **26,** 200–202.

Bonney, M. E. Relationships between social success, family size, socioeconomic home background, and intelligence among school children in grades III to V. *Sociometry,* 1944, **7,** 26–39.

Booth, G. C. Personality and chronic arthritis. *Journal of Nervous and Mental Disease,* 1937, **85,** 637.

Booth, G. C. Psychodynamics of Parkinsonism. *Psychosomatic Medicine,* 1948, **10,** 1–14.

Bossard, J. H., & Boll, E. S. Personality rules in the large family. *Child Development,* 1955, **26,** 71–79.

Bossard, J. H., & Boll, E. S. *The large family system.* Philadelphia: University of Pennsylvania Press, 1956.

Bowerman, W. G. *Studies in genius.* New York: Philosophical Library, 1947.

Bowerman, C. E., & Elder, G. H., Jr. Training for independence. In *The adolescent and his family* (chap. 10). Unpublished manuscript, 1961. (Available from University of North Caroline, Chapel Hill, N.C.)

Boyd, I., Yeager, M., & McMillan, M. Personality styles in the postoperative course. *Psychosomatic Medicine,* 1973, **35,** 23–40.

Bradley, R. W. Birth order and school-related behavior: A heuristic review. *Psychological Bulletin,* 1968, **70,** 45–51.

Bradley, R. W., & Sanborn, M. P. Ordinal position of high school students identified by their teachers as superior. *Journal of Educational Psychology,* 1969, **60,** 41–45.

Bragg, B. W. Academic primogeniture and sex-role contrast of the second-born. *Journal of Individual Psychology,* 1970, **26,** 196–199.

Bragg, B. W., & Allen, V. L. Ordinal position and conformity: A role theory analysis. *Sociometry,* 1970, **33,** 371–381.

Breckenridge, S. P., & Abbott, E. *The delinquent child and the home.* New York: Russell Sage Foundation, 1912.

Breland, H. M. Birth order and intelligence (Doctoral dissertation, SUNYAB, 1972). *Dissertation Abstracts International,* 1972, **33,** 1536A. (University Microfilm No. 72-27238)

Breland, H. M. Birth order, family configuration, and verbal achievement. *Child Development,* 1974, **43,** 1011–1019.

Brim, O. G., Jr. Family structure and sex-role learning by children: A further analysis of Helen Koch's data. *Sociometry,* 1958, **21,** 1–16.

Brown, D. G. *Behavior modification in child and school mental health: An annotated bibliography on applications with parent and teachers* (U.S. Department of Health, Education, and Welfare Publication No. CHSM 71-9043). Washington, D.C.: U.S. Government Printing Office, 1971.

Brown, M., Bresnahan, T. J., Chalke, F. C. R., Peters, B., Poser, C. G., & Tougas, D. Personality factors in duodenal ulcer: A Rorschach study. *Psychosomatic Medicine,* 1950, **12,** 1–5.

Bruch, H., & Touraine, G. Obesity in childhood: V. The family frame of obese children. *Psychosomatic Medicine,* 1940, **2,** 141–182.

Bumpass, L., & Westoff, C. F. The "perfect contraceptive" population. *Science,* 1970, **169,** 1177–1182.

Burnand, G. Birth order and autobiography. *Journal of Individual Psychology,* 1973, **29,** 35–38.

Burt, C. *The young delinquent.* New York: Appleton, 1925.

Campbell, A. A. A study of the personality adjustments of only and intermediate children. *Journal of Genetic Psychology,* 1933, **43**, 197–206.

Campbell, A. A. The personality adjustments of only children. *Psychological Bulletin,* 1934, **31**, 193–203.

Carman, A. Pain and strength measurements of 1,507 school children in Saginaw, Michigan. *American Journal of Psychiatry,* 1899, **10**, 392–398.

Carson, R. C. Interpretative manual to the MMPI. In J. N. Butcher (Ed.), *MMPI: Research developments and clinical applications.* New York: McGraw-Hill, 1969.

Castelnuovo-Tedesco, P., Schwerfeger, H. D., & Janowski, D. S. Psychological characteristics of patients with ulcerative colitis and patients with peptic ulcer: A comparison. *Psychiatry in Medicine,* 1970, **1**, 69–75.

Castelnuovo-Tedesco, P. Emotional antecedents of perforation of ulcers of the stomach and duodenum. *Psychosomatic Medicine,* 1962, **24**, 398–416.

Cattell, J. M., & Brimhall, R. R. *American men of science* (3rd ed.). Garrison: N.Y.: Science, 1921.

Chauvin, R. Psychosomatic symptom development and family survival concepts. *Family Therapy,* 1972, **1**, 49–56.

Chen, E., & Cobb, S. *Family structure study.* Unpublished data, 1958 (University of Pittsburgh).

Chen, E., & Cobb, S. Family structure in relation to health and disease. *Journal of Chronic Diseases,* 1960, **12**, 544–567.

Chittenden, E. A., Foan, M. V., Zweil, D. M., & Smith, J. R. School achievement of first- and second-born siblings. *Child Development,* 1968, **39**, 1223–1228.

Cicirelli, V. G. Sibling constellation, creativity, IQ, and academic achievement. *Child Development,* 1967, **38**, 481–490.

Cicirelli, V. G. Effects of sibling structure and interaction on children's categorization style. *Developmental Psychology,* 1973, **9**, 132–139.

Cicirelli, V. G. Relationship of sibling structure and interaction to younger sib's conceptual style. *Journal of Genetic Psychology,* 1974, **125**, 37–49.

Cicirelli, V. G. Effects of mother and older sibling on the problem-solving behavior of the younger child. *Developmental Psychology,* 1975, **11**, 749–756.

Claudy, J. G. *Cognitive characteristics of the only child.* Paper presented at the 84th Annual Convention of the American Psychological Association, Washington, D.C., September 1976.

Clausen, J. A. Family structure, socialization, and personality. In M. L. Hoffman & L. W. Hoffman (Eds.), *Review of child development research* (Vol. 2). New York: Russell Sage Foundation, 1966. Pp. 1–53.

Cleland, C. C., Uno, T., Rago, W., Case, J. C., & McGavern, M. Ecology and ordinality in invention: An exploratory study. *Psychological Reports,* 1975, **37**, 815–818.

Cobb, S. *Emotions and clinical medicine.* New York: Norton, 1950.

Cobb, S., & French, J. R. P. Birth order among medical students. *Journal of the American Medical Association,* 1966, **195**, 312–313.

Cobb, S., Warren, J. E., Merchant, W. R., & Thompson, D. J. An estimate of the prevalence of rheumatoid arthritis. *Journal of Chronic Diseases,* 1957, **5**, 636–693.

Collard, R. R. Social and play responses of firstborn and laterborn infants in an unfamiliar situation. *Child Development,* 1968, **39**, 325–334.

Connors, C. K. Birth order and needs for affiliation. *Journal of Personality,* 1963, **31**, 408–416.

Conrad, A. The psychiatric study of hyperthyroid patients. *Journal of Nervous and Mental Disease,* 1934, **79**, 505–529.

Coopersmith, S. A. A method of determining types of self-esteem. *Journal of Abnormal and Social Psychology,* 1959, **59,** 87–94.

Coopersmith, S. A. *Antecedents of self-esteem.* San Francisco: Freeman, 1967.

Cornfield, V. K. The utilization of guidance clinic facilities in Alberta. *Alberta Psychologist,* 1968, **9,** 15–45.

Cover, T., & Kerridge, D. F. Birth order in epileptic children. *Journal of Neurology, Neurosurgery, and Psychiatry,* 1962, **25,** 59–62.

Cushna, B. Agency and birth order differences in very early childhood. *American Psychologist,* 1966, **21,** 638. (Abstract)

Cutts, N. E., & Moseley, N. *The only child: A guide for parents and only children of all ages.* New York: Putnam, 1954.

Dahlstrom, W. G., Welsh, G. S., & Dahlstrom, L. E. *An MMPI Handbook: Vol. I. Clinical Interpretation* (rev. ed.). Minneapolis: University of Minnesota Press, 1972. Pp. 257–266.

Dandes, H. M., & Dow, D. Relation of intelligence to family size and density. *Child Development,* 1969, **40,** 641–645.

Datta, L. Birth order and early scientific attainment. *Perceptual and Motor Skills,* 1967, **24,** 157–158. (Extended report available from author).

Datta, L. Birth order and potential scientific creativity. *Sociometry,* 1968, **31,** 76–88.

Davis, A. American status systems and the socialization of the child. In C. Kluckhohn and H. A. Murray (Eds.), *Personality in nature, society, and culture.* New York: Knopf, 1959. Pp. 567–576.

Dean, D. *Relation of ordinal position to personality in young children.* Unpublished Master's thesis, State University of Iowa, 1947.

Dimond, R. E., & Munz, D. C. Ordinal position of birth and self-disclosure in high school students. *Psychological Reports,* 1967, **21,** 829–833.

Dingle, J. H., Badger, G. F., & Jordan, W. S., Jr. *Illness in the Home: A Study of 25,000 Illnesses in a Group of Cleveland Families.* Cleveland: Western Reserve University Press, 1964.

Doren, M. P. Evaluation of studies on birth order and sibling position (Doctoral dissertation, University of Minnesota, 1972). *Dissertation Abstracts International,* 1973, **34,** 5542A. (University Microfilm No. 73-0543)

Douglas, J. W. B., & Blomfield, J. M. *Children under five.* London: Allen & Unwin, 1958.

Douglas, J. W. B., & Simpson, H. R. Height in relation to puberty, family size, and social class. *Milbank Memorial Fund Quarterly,* 1964, **40,** 20–34.

Dunbar, F. *Psychosomatic diagnosis.* New York: Hoeber, 1943.

Ebert, R. K. The reliability and validity of a mailed questionnaire for a sample of entering college freshmen (Doctoral dissertation, Temple University, 1973). *Dissertation Abstracts International,* 1974, **34,** 3462B. (University Microfilm No. 73-30,151)

Edgell, P. G. Eczema. In E. Wittkower & B. Russell (Eds.), *Emotional factors in skin disease.* New York: Hoeber, 1953.

Edwards, J. N., & Braunburger, M. B. Exchange and parent-youth conflict. *Journal of Marriage and the Family,* 1973, **35,** 101–107.

Eiduson, B. T. *Scientists, their psychological world.* New York: Basic Books, 1962. Pp. 44–66.

Eisenman, R., & Foxman, D. J. Creativity: Reported family patterns and scoring. *Psychological Reports,* 1970, **34,** 615–621.

Eisenman, R., & Taylor, R. Birth order and MMPI patterns. *Journal of Individual Psychology,* 1966, **22,** 208–211.

Elder, G. H., Jr. Family structure and the transmission of values and norms in the process of child rearing (Doctoral dissertation, University of North Carolina, 1961). *Dissertation Abstracts International,* 1962, **13,** 741–742. (University Microfilm No. 62-3120)

Elder, G. H., Jr. *Adolescent achievement and mobility aspirations.* Chapel Hill: Institute for Research in Social Science, University of North Carolina, 1962. (a)

Elder, G. H., Jr. Structural variations in the child rearing relationship. *Sociometry,* 1962, **25,** 241–262. (b)

Elliott, J. L., & Elliott, D. H. Effects of birth order and age gap on aspiration level. *Proceedings of the 78th Annual Convention of the American Psychological Association,* 1970, **5,** 369–370. (Summary)

Ellis, H. *A study of British genius.* Boston: Houghton, 1926. (Originally published, 1904)

Elwood, J. H., MacKenzie, G., & Cran, S. W. Observations on single births to women resident in Belfast, 1962–1966. *Journal of Chronic Diseases,* 1974, **27,** 517–562.

Exner, J. E., & Sutton-Smith, B. Birth order and hierarchical versus innovative role requirements. *Journal of Personality,* 1970, **38,** 581–587.

Eysenck, H. J., & Carlson, D. Personality in primary school children. III. Family background. *British Journal of Educational Psychology,* 1970, **40,** 117–131.

Fakouri, M. E. Relationship of birth order, dogmatism, and achievement motivation. *Journal of Individual Psychology,* 1974, **30,** 216–220.

Falbo, T. *Folklore and the only child: A reassessment.* Paper presented at the American Psychological Association meeting, Washington, D.C., 1976.

Falbo, T. The only child: A review. *Journal of Individual Psychology,* 1977, **33,** 47–61.

Farber, B., & Blackman, L. S., Marital role tension and number and sex of children. *American Sociological Review,* 1956, **21,** 596–601.

Farber, L. H., & Micon, L. Gastric neurosis in a military service. *Psychiatry,* 1945, **8,** 343–361.

Farina, A., Barry, H. III, & Garmezy, N. Birth order of recovered and nonrecovered schizophrenics. *Archives of General Psychiatry,* 1963, **9,** 224–228.

Farley, F. H. Birth order and a two-dimensional assessment of personality. *Journal of Personality Assessment,* 1975, **39,** 151–153.

Farley, F. H., Smart, K. L., & Brittain, V. Implications of birth order for motivational and achievement-related characteristics of adults enrolled in non-traditional instruction. *Journal of Experimental Education,* 1974, **42,** 21–24.

Feeney, F. E., Mindlin, D. F., Minear, V. H., & Short, E. E. The challenge of the skid row alcoholic. *Quarterly Journal Studies on Alcohol,* 1955, **16,** 643.

Fenton, N. The only child. *Journal of Genetic Psychology,* 1928, **35,** 546–556.

Finneran, M. P. Dependency and self concepts as functions of acceptance and rejection by others. *American Psychologist,* 1958, **13,** 332. (Abstract)

Fischer, E. H., & Winer, D. Participation in psychological research: Relation to birth order and demographic factors. *Journal of Consulting and Clinical Psychology,* 1969, **33,** 610–613.

Forbes, G. B. Fraternity or sorority membership and birth order: Sex differences and problems of reliability. *Journal of Social Psychology,* 1970, **82,** 277–278. (a)

Forbes, G. B. Smoking behavior and birth order. *Psychological Reports,* 1970, **26,** 766. (b)

Forbes, G. B. Birth order and political success: A study of the 1970 Illinois general elections. *Psychological Reports,* 1971, **29,** 1239–1242.

French, T. W., & Alexander, F. *Psychogenic effects in bronchial asthma.* Washington, D.C.: National Research Council, 1941.

Friedrichs, R. W. Alter versus ego: An exploratory assessment of altruism. *American Sociological Review,* 1960, **25,** 496–508.

Galton, F. *English men of science.* London: Macmillan, 1874.

Gandy, G. L. Birth order and vocational interest. *Developmental Psychology,* 1973, **9,** 406–410.

Gerstner, U. *Die Abhängigkeit der Beurteilung von Menschen auf dem "semantischen Differential" von der Familienkonstellation.* Unpublished doctoral dissertation, University of Erlangen-Nurnberg, 1967.

Gerwitz, J. L. *Dependent and aggressive interaction in young children.* Unpublished doctoral dissertation, University of Iowa, 1948.

Gilberstadt, H., & Duker, J. *A handbook for clinical and actuarial MMPI interpretation.* Philadelphia: W. B. Saunders, 1965.

Glueck, S., & Glueck, E. *Unraveling juvenile delinquency.* New York: Commonwealth Fund, 1960.

Goertzel, M. G., Goertzel, V., & Goertzel, T. G. *Three Hundred Eminent Personalities.* San Francisco: Jossey-Bass, 1978.

Gonda, T. A. The relation between complaints of persistent pain and family size. *Journal of Neurology, Neurosurgery, and Psychiatry,* 1962, **25**, 277–281.

Goodenough, F. L. The emotional behavior of young children during mental tests. *Journal of Juvenile Research,* 1929, **13**, 204–219.

Goodenough, F. L., & Leahy, A. M. The effect of certain family relationships upon the development of personality. *Journal of Genetic Psychology,* 1927, **34**, 45–71.

Gordon, J. E. Social implications of health and disease. *Archives of Environmental Health,* 1969, **18**, 216–234.

Gordon, K. K., & Gordon, R. E. Birth order, achievement, and blood chemistry levels among college nursing students. *Nursing Research,* 1967, **16**, 234–236.

Gormly, R. Birth order, family size, and psychological masculinity-femininity. *Proceedings of the 76th Annual Convention of the American Psychological Association,* 1968, **3**, 165–66. (Summary)

Grant, M. W. Rate of growth in relation to birth rank and family size. *British Journal of Preventive Social Medicine,* 1964, **18**, 35–42.

Granville-Grossman, K. L. Birth order and schizophrenia. *British Journal of Psychiatry,* 1966, **112**, 1119–1126.

Greene, W. A., Jr., & Miller, G. Psychological factors and reticuloendothelial disease. *Psychosomatic Medicine,* 1958, **20**, 124–144.

Gregory, I. An analysis of familial data on psychiatric patients: Parental age, family size, birth order, and ordinal position. *British Journal of Preventive Social Medicine,* 1958, **12**, 42–59.

Griffith, J. Social pressure on family size intentions. *Family Planning Pespectives,* 1973, **5**, 237–242.

Grinker, R. R., Sr., Grinker, R. R., Jr., & Timberlake, J. Mentally healthy young males (homoclites). *Archives of General Psychiatry,* 1962, **6**, 405–453.

Grosz, H. J. The depression-prone and the depression-resistant sibling: A study of 650 three-sibling families. *British Journal of Psychiatry,* 1968, **114**, 1555–1558.

Grosz, H. J., & Miller, I. Sibling patterns in schizophrenia. *Science,* 1958, **128**, 30

Guilford, J. P. *The nature of human intelligence.* New York: McGraw-Hill, 1967.

Guilford, R. B., & Worcester, D. A. A comparison study of the only and nononly child. *Journal of Genetic Psychology,* 1930, **38**, 411–425.

Gundlach, R. H. Data on the relation of birth order and sex of siblings of lesbians oppose the hypothesis that homosexuality is genetic. *Annals of New York Academy of Sciences,* 1972, **197**, 179–191.

Gundlach, R. H. Birth order among lesbians: New light on the only child. *Psychological Reports,* 1977, **40**, 250.

Gundlach, R. H., & Riess, B. F. Birth order and sex of siblings in a sample of lesbians and nonlesbians. *Psychological Reports,* 1967, **20**, 61–62.

Guthrie, G. N. *A study of the personality characteristics associated with the disorders encountered by an internist.* Unpublished doctoral dissertation, University of Minnesota, 1949.

Haeberle, A. W. *Interactions of sex, birth order, and dependency with behavior problems and symptoms in emotionally disturbed pre-school children.* Paper presented at the meeting of the Eastern Psychological Association, Philadelphia, 1958.

Hall, E., & Barger, B. Attitudinal structures of older and younger siblings. *Journal of Individual Psychology,* 1964, **20,** 59–68.

Hamilton, M. The personality of dyspeptics with special reference to gastric and duodenal ulcer. *British Journal of Medical Psychology,* 1950, **23,** 182–192.

Hancock, F. T. An empirical investigation of the relationship of ordinal position, sex, and sex of sibling to socialization, personality, and choice behavior among adolescents in one and two child families (Doctoral dissertation, University of California, Berkeley, 1965). *Doctoral Dissertation Abstracts,* 1966, **26,** 781–782A. (University Microfilm No. 66–3607)

Handlon, B. J., & Gross, P. The development of sharing behavior. *Journal of Abnormal and Social Psychology,* 1959, **59,** 425–428.

Hansson, R. O. The effects of test anxiety, birth order, and a confident or anxious role enactment on intellective task performance (Doctoral dissertation, University of Washington, 1973). *Dissertation Abstracts International,* 1974, **34,** 4019–4020. (University Microfilm No. 74–2212)

Hare, E. H., & Price, J. S. Birth order and family size: Bias caused by changes in birth rate. *British Journal of Psychiatry,* 1969, **115,** 647–657.

Hare, E. H., & Price, J. S. Birth rank in schizophrenia: With a consideration of the bias due to changes in birth rate. *British Journal of Psychiatry,* 1970, **116,** 409–420.

Hare, E. H., & Shaw, G. K. A study in family health: Health in relation to family size. *British Journal of Psychiatry,* 1965, **3,** 461–466.

Harris, I. D. *The promised seed.* New York: Free Press, 1964.

Harris, L. A. A study of altruism. *Elementary School Journal,* 1967, **68,** 135–141.

Hart, H. Personal communication to E. Chen & S. Cobb, 1960.

Hau, T. F., & Rueppel, A. Zur Familienkonstellation bei psychosomatisch Erkrankten. *Zeitschrift für Psychotherapie und Medizinische Psychologie,* 1966, **16,** 211–219.

Havighurst, R. L., & Wagner, M. E. *Sibship constellation of eminent educators and social scientists.* Unpublished manuscript, 1977.

Hawkes, G. R. Burchinal, L., & Gardner, B. Size of family and adjustment of children. *Marriage and Family Living,* 1958, **20,** 65–68.

Hayes, S. P., Jr. A note on personality and family position. *Journal of Applied Psychology,* 1938, **22,** 347–349.

Helmreich, R. Birth order effects. *Naval Research Reviews,* 1968, **21,** 1–16.

Helmreich, R., Kuiken, D., & Collins, B. Effects of stress and birth order on attitude change. *Journal of Personality,* 1968, **36,** 466–473.

Helson, R. Women mathematicians and the creative personality. *Journal of Counseling and Clinical Psychology,* 1971, **38,** 210–220.

Herbst, P. G. Family living—patterns of interaction. In D. A. Oeser & S. B. Hammond (Eds.), *Social structure and personality in a city.* New York: Macmillan, 1954.

Herrell, J. M. Birth order as a patient variable in combat-zone psychiatry. *USARV Medical Bulletin,* 1969, Nov.-Dec., 29–34.

Herrell, J. M. Birth order as a patient variable in military psychiatry. *Military Medicine,* 1970, **135,** 1001–1006.

Herrell, J. M. Birth order and the military: A review from an Adlerian perspective. *Journal of Individual Psychology,* 1972, **28,** 38–44.

Hilton, I. Differences in the behavior of mothers towards first and laterborn children. *Journal of Personality and Social Psychology,* 1967, **7**, 282–290.

Hollingshead, A. B., & Redlich, F. C. *Social class and mental illness: A community study.* New York: Wiley, 1958.

Horn, J. M., & Turner, R. G. Birth order effects among unwed mothers. *Journal of Individual Psychology,* 1975, **31**, 71–78.

Hough, E. Some factors in the etiology of maternal over-protection. *Smith College Studies of Social Work,* 1932, **2**, 188–208.

Howe, M. G., & Madgett, M. E. Mental health problems associated with the only child. *Canadian Psychiatric Association Journal,* 1975, **20**, 189–194.

Hoyt, M. F., & Raven, B. H. Birth order and the 1970 Los Angeles earthquake. *Journal of Personality and Social Psychology,* 1973, **28**, 123–128.

Hubbard, J. I. Handedness not a function of birth order. *Nature (London),* 1971, **232**, 276–277.

Huet, G. J. Asthma in relation to order of birth. *Nederlands Tydschrift voor Geneeskunde,* 1955, **994**, 3501.

Hug-Hellmuth, H. Vom "mittleren" Kinde. *Imago,* 1921, **7**, 84–94.

Humerfeld, S., & Wedervang, F. A study of the influence upon blood pressure of marital status, number of children, and occupation. *Acta Medica Scandanavia,* 1957, **159**, 489–497.

Ikemi, Y., Ago, Y., Nakagawa, S., Mori, S., Takahashi, N., Sumatsu, H., & Sugita, M. Psychosomatic mechanism under social changes in Japan. *Psychotherapy and Psychosomatics,* 1973, **23**, 240–250.

Ikemi, Y., et al. Psychosomatic mechanism under social changes in Japan. *Journal of Psychosomatic Research,* 1974, **18**, 15–24.

Jacobs, B. B., & Moss, H. A. *Birth order and sex of infant as determiners of mother-infant interaction.* Presented at the American Psychological Association 82nd Annual Convention, New Orleans, 1974.

Jacobs, B. B., & Moss, H. A. Birth order and sex of sibling as determinants of mother-infant interaction. *Child Development,* 1976, **47**, 315–322.

Jacobs, M. A. The addictive personality: Prediction of success in a smoking withdrawal program. *Psychosomatic Medicine,* 1972, **34**, 30–38.

Jamieson, B. D. The influences of birth order, family size, and sex differences on risk-taking behaviour. *British Journal of Social and Clinical Psychology,* 1969, **8**, 1–8.

Jan-Tausch, J. *Suicide of children 1960–1963.* Trenton, N.J.: Department of Education, 1963.

Johnson, J. E., Dobbs, J. M., Jr., & Leventhal, H. Psychosocial factors in the welfare of surgical patients. *Nursing Research,* 1970, **19**, 18–29.

Johnson, J. E., Leventhal, H., & Dobbs, J. M., Jr. Contribution of emotional and instrumental response processes in adaptation to surgery. *Journal of Personality and Social Psychology,* 1971, **20**, 55–64.

Johnson, P. B., & Johnson, H. L. Birth order and thumb sucking. *Psychological Reports,* 1975, **36**, 598.

Jones, H. E. Order of birth. In C. A. Murchison, P. Blanchard, & W. E. Blatz (Eds.). *A Handbook of Child Psychology.* Worchester, Mass.: Clark University Press, 1933. Pp. 204–241.

Jones, H. E. Environmental influence on mental development. In L. Carmichael (Ed.), *Manual of Child Psychology* (2nd ed.). New York: Wiley, 1954.

Judd, E., & Lewis, M. *Mother-infant dyads: Early sex differences.* Paper presented at the Eastern Psychological Association Meeting, New York City, April 1975.

Judd, E., & Lewis, M. *The effects of birth order and spacing on mother-infant relations.* Presented at the Eastern Psychological Association Meeting, New York, 1976.

Kammeyer, K. Birth order and the feminine sex role among college women. *American Sociological Review,* 1966, **31**, 508–515.

Kammeyer, K. Birth order as a research variable. *Social Forces,* 1967, **46**, 71–80.

Kaplan, H. B. Self-derogation and childhood family structure: Family size, birth order, and sex distribution. *Journal of Nervous and Mental Diseases,* 1970, **151**, 13–23.

Kasl, S. V., Brooks, G. W., & Cobb, S. Serum urate concentration in male high-school students. *Journal of American Medical Association,* 1966, **198**, 713–716.

Kay, D. W. K., & Roth, M. Environmental and hereditary factors in the schizophrenics of old age (late paraphrenia) and their bearing on the general problem of causation of schizophrenia. *Journal of Mental Science,* 1961, **107**, 649–686.

Kayton, L., & Borge, G. F. Birth order and the obsessive-compulisve character. *Archives of General Psychiatry,* 1967, **17**, 751–754.

Kellaghan, T., & MacNamara, J. Family correlates of verbal reasoning ability. *Developmental Psychology,* 1972, **7**, 49–53.

Kellaghan, T., & Newman, E. Background characteristics of children of high verbal ability. *Irish Journal of Education,* 1971, **5**, 5–14.

Kellock, T. D. Childhood factors in duodenal ulcer. *British Medical Journal,* 1951, **2**, 1117–1119.

Kennett, K. F. *A within cultural comparison: Intelligence, family size and socioeconomic status.* Paper presented at the XIVth Interamerican Congress of Psychology, Sao Paulo, Brazil, April 14–19, 1973.

Kennett, K. F., & Cropley, A. J. Intelligence, family size, and socioeconomic status. *Journal of Biosocial Science,* 1970, **2**, 227–236.

Kent, N., & Davis, D. R. Discipline in the home and intellectual development. *British Journal of Medical Psychology,* 1957, **30**, 27–33.

Kezur, E., Kapp, F. T., & Rosenbaum, M. Psychological factors in women with peptic ulcers. *American Journal of Psychiatry,* 1951, **108**, 368.

King, S. H., & Cobb, S. Psychosocial factors in the epidemiology of rheumatoid arthritis. *Journal of Chronic Diseases,* 1958, **7**, 466–475.

Klockars, A. J. Relationships between personality dimensions and the familial variables of birth order, sex of siblings, and family size (Doctoral dissertation, University of Washington, 1967). *Dissertation Abstracts,* 1968, **29**, 327A. (University Microfilm No. 68-09298)

Ko, Y. & Sun, L. Ordinal position and the behavior of visiting the child guidance clinic. *Acta Psychologica Taiwanica,* 1965, **7**, 10–16.

Koch, H. L. The relation of primary mental abilities in 5- and 6-yr. olds to sex of child and characteristics of his sibling. *Child Development,* 1954, **25**, 209–223.

Koch, H. L. Some personality correlates of sex, sibling position, and sex of sibling among five- and six-year-old children. *Genetic Psychology Monographs,* 1955, **52**, 3–50.

Koch, H. L. Children's work attitudes and sibling characteristics. *Child Development,* 1956, **27**, 289–310. (a)

Koch, H. L. Some emotional attitudes of the young child in relation to characteristics of his sibling. *Child Development,* 1956, **27**, 393–426. (b)

Koch, H. L. The relation of certain formal attributes of siblings to attitudes held toward each other and toward their parents. *Child Development Monograph,* 1960, **25**, 124 pp.

Koller, K. M., & Castanos, J. N. Parental deprivation and attempted suicide in prison populations. *Medical Journal of Australia,* 1969, **1**, 858–861.

Koller, K. M., & Castanos, J. N. Family background of prison groups: A comparative study of parental deprivation. *British Journal of Psychiatry,* 1970, **117**, 371–380.

Krall, V. Personality characteristics of accident repeating children. *Journal of Abnormal and Social Psychology,* 1953, **48**, 99–108.

Krebs, D. L. Altruism—an examination of the concept and a review of the literature. *Psychological Bulletin,* 1970, **73,** 258-302.

Krout, M. H. Typical behavior patterns in twenty-six ordinal positions. *Journal of Genetic Psychology,* 1939, **55,** 3-30.

Krumholtz, J. D., & Krumholtz, H. B. *Changing children's behavior.* New York: Prentice Hall, 1972.

Kurth, E., & Schmidt, E. Multidimensional examinations of stuttering children. *Probleme und Ergebnisse der Psychologie,* 1964, **12,** 49-58.

Landis, P. H. The families that produce adjusted adolescents. *Clearing House,* 1955, **29,** 537-540.

Langenmayr, A. *Der Einfluss der Familienkonstellation auf die Urteilbildung im sozialen Kraftfeld.* Unpublished dissertation, 1966. (University of Erlangen-Nurnberg)

Laosa, L. M., & Brophy, J. E. Sex X birth order interaction in measures of sex typing and affiliation in kindergarten children. *Proceedings of the 78th Annual Convention of the American Psychological Association,* 1970, **5,** 363-364. (Summary)

Lasko, J. K. Parent behavior toward first and second children. *Genetic Psychology Monograph,* 1954, **49,** 97-137.

LaVoie, J. C. Individual differences in resistance-to-temptation behavior in adolescents: An Eysenck analysis. *Journal of Clinical Psychology,* 1973, **29,** 20-22.

Lee-Painter, L. S., & Lewis, M. *Mother-infant interaction and cognitive development.* Paper presented at the Eastern Psychological Association Meeting, New York, 1976.

Lees, J. P. The social mobility of a group of eldest-born and intermediate adult males. *British Journal of Psychology,* 1952, **43,** 210-221.

Lees, J. P., & Newson, L. J. Family or sibship position of some aspects of juvenile delinquency. *British Journal of Delinquency,* 1954, **5,** 46-55.

Lees, J. P., & Stewart, A. H. Family or sibship position and scholastic ability: An interpretation. *Psychological Review,* 1957, **5,** 173-190.

LeShan, L. An emotional life-history pattern associated with neoplastic disease. *Annals of the New York Academy of Science,* 1966, **135,** 780-793.

Lessing, E. E., & Oberlander, M. Developmental study of ordinal position and personality adjustment of the child as evaluated by the California Test of Personality. *Journal of Personality,* 1967, **35,** 487-497.

Levinson, P. The relationship between birth order and reading ability (Doctoral dissertation, University of Pennsylvania, 1963). *Dissertation Abstracts International,* 1963, **24,** 2614. (University Microfilm No. 63-07064)

Levy, J. A quantitative study of behavior problems in relation to family constellation. *American Journal of Psychiatry,* 1931, **10,** 637-654.

Lewandowski, D., & Graham, J. R. Empirical correlates of frequently occurring two-point MMPI code types: A replicated study. *Journal of Consulting and Clinical Psychology,* 1972, **39,** 467-472.

Lewis, M., & Gallas, H. Cognitive performance in the 12-week-old infant; The effects of birth order, birth spacing, sex, and social class. *Research Bulletin,* Princeton, N.J., 1976.

Lichtenwaller, J. S., & Maxwell, J. W. The relationship of birth order and socioeconomic status to the creativity of preschool children. *Child Development,* 1969, **40,** 1241-1247.

Lidz, T. Emotional factors in the etiology of hyperthyroidism occurring in relation to pregnancy. *Psychosomatic Medicine,* 1955, **17,** 420-427.

Lieberman, E. J. Preventive psychiatry and family planning. *Journal of Marriage and the Family,* 1964, **26,** 471-477.

Lieberman, E. J. Reserving a womb: Case for the small family. *American Journal of Public Health,* 1970, **60,** 87-92.

Lilienfeld, A. M., & Pasamanick, B. The association of maternal and fetal factors with the development of mental deficiency, II. *American Journal of Mental Deficiency,* 1956, **60,** 557–569.

Linder, R. L., & Lerner, S. E. Self-medication and the only child. *Journal of Drug Education,* 1972, **2,** 361–370. (a)

Linder, R. L., & Lerner, S. E. Self-medication: An only child syndrome. *Journal of Psychedelic Drugs,* 1972, **5,** 62–66. (b)

Linder, R. L., & Lerner, S. E. Birth order and psychoactive drug use among students. *Drug Forum,* 1975–76, **5,** 1–5.

Lisansky, E. S. Alcoholism in women: Social and psychological concomitants. *Quarterly Journal of Studies on Alcohol,* 1957, **18,** 588.

Lompa, N. *Der Einfluss von Familienkonstellationen auf die Leistungsmotivation mit ihren Grundrichtungen "Hoffnung auf Erfolg" und "Furcht vor Misserfolg."* Unpublished dissertation, University of Erlangen-Nurnberg, 1967.

Lunneborg, P. W. Birth order, aptitude, and achievement. *Journal of Consulting and Clinical Psychology,* 1968, **32,** 101.

Lunneborg, P. W. *Birth order, family size, and sex and position of sibling effects on masculinity-femininity.* Seattle: Bureau of Testing, University of Washington, 1969.

Lunneborg, P. W. Birth order and sex of sibling effects on intellectual abilities. *Journal of Consulting and Clinical Psychology,* 1971, **37,** 445.

MacDonald, A. Measurements of girls in private schools and of university students. *Boston Medical and Surgical Journal,* 1901, **145,** 127–137.

MacDonald, A. P., Jr. Birth order and personality. *Journal of Consulting and Clinical Psychology,* 1971, **36,** 171–176.

MacKinnon, D. W. Fact and fancy in personality research. *American Psychologist,* 1953, **8,** 138–146.

MacMahon, B., & Newill, V. A. Birth characteristics of children dying of malignant neoplasms. *Journal of National Cancer Institute,* 1962, **28,** 231–244.

Maller, J. B. Size of family and personality of offspring. *Journal of Social Psychology,* 1931, **2,** 3–27.

Marjoribanks, K. Sibsize, family environment, cognitive performance, and affective characteristics. *Journal of Psychology,* 1976, **94,** 195–204.

Marjoribanks, K., & Walberg, H. J. Ordinal position, family environment, and mental abilities. *Journal of Social Psychology,* 1975, **95,** 77–84.

Marjoribanks, K. Walberg, H. J., & Borgen, M. Mental abilities: Sibling constellation and social class correlates. *British Journal of Social and Clinical Psychology,* 1975, **14,** 109–116.

Marks, P. A., & Seeman, W. *Actuarial description of abnormal personality.* Baltimore: Williams & Wilkins, 1963.

Martensen-Larsen, O. The family constellation analysis and alcoholism. *Acta Psychiatry* Supplement No. 100, 1956, 241–247.

Masterson, M. L. Family structure variables and need approval. *Journal of Consulting and Clinical Psychology,* 1971, **36,** 12–13.

Matejcek, Z., Dytrych, Z., & Schuller, V. A Prague study of children born from unwanted pregnancies: II. Girls and boys. *Psychologia a Patopsychologia Dietata,* 1975, **10,** 291–306.

Maxwell, A., & Huestis, R. R. Student test-score rank and family size. *Journal of Heredity,* 1930, **21,** 211–215.

Maxwell, J. Intelligence, fertility, and the future: A report on the 1947 Scottish Mental Survey. *Eugenics Quarterly,* 1954, **1,** 244–247.

McArthur, C. Personalities of first and second children. *Psychiatry: Journal for the Study of Interpersonal Processes,* 1956, **19**, 47–54.

McBride, W. E. Intrafamilial interaction analysis (Doctoral dissertation, Oklahoma State University, 1973). *Dissertation Abstracts International,* 1974, **34**, 6772. (University Microfilm No. 74–8070)

McCall, J. N. Birth-order differences in special ability: Fact or artifact? *Psychological Reports,* 1973, **33**, 947–952.

McClure, R. F. Birth order, income, sex, and school related attitudes. *Journal of Experimental Education,* 1971, **39**, 73–74.

McCurdy, H. G. The childhood pattern of genius. *Journal of Elisha Mitchell Scientific Annual Report of the Board of Regents of the Society,* 1957, **73**. (Also reprinted in Annual Report of Board of Regents of the *Smithsonian Institution,* Publication No. 4354. Washington, D.C.: U.S. Government Printing Office, 1959)

McDermott, N. T., & Cobb, S. A psychiatric survey of fifty cases of bronchial asthma. *Psychosomatic Medicine,* 1939, **1**, 203–244.

McGlynn, F. D. Academic performance among first-born students. *Journal of Individual Psychology,* 1969, **25**, 181–182.

McGurk, H., & Lewis, M. Birth order: A phenomenon in search of an explanation. *Developmental Psychology,* 1972, **7**, 336.

Mersky, H. Psychiatric patients with persistent pain. *Journal of Psychosomatic Research,* 1965, **9**, 299–309.

Miall, W. E. Follow-up study of arterial pressure in the population of a Welsh mining valley. *British Medical Journal,* 1959, **2**, 1204–1210.

Miall, W. E., & Oldham, P. D. Factors influencing arterial blood pressure in the general population. *Clinical Science,* 1958, **17**, 409–444.

Mikol, B. *Ego psychological aspects of the creative process in music.* Paper presented at the 83rd Annual Convention of the American Psychological Association, Chicago, 1975.

Miller, N., & Maruyama, G. Ordinal position and peer popularity. *Journal of Personality and Social Psychology,* 1976, **33**, 123–131.

Miller, N., & Zimbardo, P. G. Motives for fear-induced affiliation: Emotional comparison or interpersonal similarity? *Journal of Personality,* 1966, **34**, 481–503.

Mintz, S. B. Childhood schizophrenia: The factors of maternal identification, projection, and vicarious acting out as related to birth order, sibling spacing, and size of family (Doctoral dissertation, Brandeis University, 1965). *Dissertation Abstracts International,* 1967, **27**, 4564B. (University Microfilm No. 65–14433)

Mitchell, G., & Schroers, L. Birth order and parental experience in monkeys and men. In H. W. Reese (Ed.), *Advances in Child Development and Behavior* (Vol. 8). New York: Academic Press, 1973. Pp. 161–184.

Monk, M., Mendeloff, A. I., Siegel, C. I., & Lilienfeld, A. An epidemiological study: Ulcerative colitis and regional enteritis among adults in Baltimore. *Journal of Chronic Diseases,* 1970, **22**, 565–578.

Montgomery, R. L., Puetz, L., & Montgomery, S. M. Birth order, graduate school, and marriage. *Psychological Reports,* 1975, **37**, 746.

Moore, B., & Holtzman, W. H. *Tomorrow's parents: A study of youth and their families.* Austin: University of Texas Press, 1965.

Moore, R. K. Susceptibility to hypnosis and susceptibility to social influence. *Journal of Abnormal and Social Psychology,* 1964, **68**, 282–294.

Moran, G. Ordinal position and approval motivation. *Journal of Consulting Psychology,* 1967, **31**, 319–320.

Morris, J. N., & Heady, J. A. Social and biological factors in infant mortality, I. Objects and methods. *Lancet,* 1955, **268**, (1), 343–349.

Morrison, S. L., Heady, J. A., & Morris, J. N. Mortality in the postneonatal period. *Archives of Diseases of Children,* 1959, **34**, 101–114.

Munro, A. Some familial and social factors in depressive illness. *British Journal of Psychiatry,* 1966, **112**, 429–441.

Murrell, S. A. Relationships of ordinal position and family size to psychosocial measures of delinquents. *Journal of Abnormal Child Psychology,* 1974, **2**, 39–46.

Nagelbush, J. L. *Maternal behavior during bottle-feeding as a function of parity and sex of the neonate.* Paper presented at the 82nd Annual Convention of the American Psychological Asociation, New Orleans, 1974.

Navratil, L. Alcoholism and birth rank: Constitution of last child. *Wiener Klinische Wochenschrift,* 1956, **68**, 158.

Nichols, R. C. *Birth order and intelligence.* Unpublished manuscript, 1964. (Available from State University of New York, Buffalo, N.Y. 14214).

Nisbet, J. Family environment and intelligence. *Eugenics Review,* 1953, **45**, 31–42.

Nisbet, J. D., & Endwistle, N. J. Intelligence and family size, 1949–1965. *British Journal of Educational Psychology,* 1967, **37**, 188–193.

Nisbett, R. E. Birth order and participation in dangerous sports. *Journal of Personality and Social Psychology,* 1968, **8**, 351–353.

Norton, A. Incidence of neurosis related to maternal age and birth order. *British Journal of Social Medicine,* 1952, **6**, 253–258.

Norton, A. Unpublished data. Utica, N.Y.: State Hospitals Press, 1957. (For a reanalysis see Riess & Safer, 1973).

Nowicki, S., Jr. Birth order and personality: Some unexpected findings. *Psychological Reports,* 1967, **21**, 265–267.

Nowicki, S., Jr. Ordinal position, approval motivation, and interpersonal attraction. *Journal of Consulting and Clinical Psychology,* 1971, **36**, 265–267.

Nuttall, R. L., & Nuttall, E. V. *Family size and spacing in the United States and Puerto Rico.* Washington, D.C.: Center for Population Research, National Institute of Child Health and Development, U.S. Department of Health, Education, and Welfare, 1975.

Nye, I. Adolescent-parent adjustment: Age, sex, sibling number, broken homes, and employed mothers. *Marriage and Family Living,* 1952, **14**, 327–332.

Nye, I., Carlson, J., & Garrett, G. Family size, interaction, affect, and stress. *Journal of Marriage and the Family,* 1970, **32**, 216–226.

Oberlander, M. I., Frauenfelder, K.J., & Heath, H. The relationship of ordinal position and sex to interest patterns. *Journal of Genetic Psychology,* 1971, **119**, 29–36.

Oberlander, M., & Jenkin, N. Birth order and academic achievement. *Journal of Individual Psychology,* 1967, **23**, 103–109.

Oberlander, M. I., Jenkin, N., Houlihan, K., & Jackson, J. Family size and birth order as determinants of scholastic aptitude and achievement in a sample of eighth graders. *Journal of Consulting and Clinical Psychology,* 1970, **34**, 19–21.

Ogburn, W. F. The changing family with regard to the child. *Annals of the American Academy of Political and Social Science,* 1930, **151**, 20–24.

Ogden, E. J. D., De, L., & Horne, D. J. Birth order and delinquency: Findings from a youth training center. *Australian and New Zealand Journal of Criminology,* 1974, **7**, 179–183.

Ogden, E. J. D., De, L., & Horne, D. J. An Australian residential youth training centre: Population study. *Australian and New Zealand Journal of Criminology,* 1976, **9**, 49–54.

O'Hollaren, P., & Wellman, W. M. Alcoholism: Drinking pattern and birth order of 738 alcoholics. *Northwest Medicine,* 1957, **56**, 811–813.

Olson, R. E. Personal communication to E. Chen and S. Cobb, 1958.

Olson, T. D. Family constellation as related to personality and achievement (Doctoral dissertation, Florida State University, 1973). *Dissertation Abstracts International,* 1973, **33**, 5000–5001B. (University Microfilm No. 73-10,333)

Omran, A. R. Health benefits for mother and child. *World Health,* January, 1974, pp. 6–13.

Oswald, W. D. *Untersuchung der Abhängigkeit dominanten Verhaltens von speziellen prägenden Faktoren der kindlichen Umwelt.* Unpublished doctoral dissertation, University of Erlangen-Nurnberg, 1963.

Paffenbarger, R. S., Jr., Notkin, J., Krueger, D. E., Wolf, P. A., Thorne, M. C., LeBauer, E. J., & Williams, J. L. Chronic disease in former college students. II. Methods of study and observations on mortality from coronary heart disease. *American Journal of Public Health,* 1966, **56**, 962–971.

Paffenbarger, R. S., Jr., Thorne, M. C., & Wing, A. L. Chronic diseases in former college students, VIII. Characteristics of youth that predispose to hypertension in later years. *American Journal of Epidemiology,* 1968, **88**, 25–32.

Paffenbarger, R. S., Jr., Wolf, P. A., Notkin, J., & Thorne, M. C. Chronic disease in former college students, I. Early precursors of fatal coronary heart disease. *Americal Journal of Epidemiology,* 1966, **83**, 314–328.

Parsley, M. The delinquent girl in Chicago: The influence of ordinal position on size of family. *Smith College Studies in Social Work,* 1933, **3**, 274–283.

Patterson, R. M., & Zeigler, T. W. Ordinal position and schizophrenia. *American Journal of Psychiatry,* 1941, **98**, 455–458.

Payne, D. L. Birth-order, personality, and performance at the Air Force Academy. *Journal of Individual Psychology,* 1971, **27**, 185–187.

Pearson, K. *On the handicapping of the first born.* Lecture Series 10. London University, 1914.

Peck, E., & Senderowitz, J. (Eds.), *Pronatalism: The myth of mom and apple pie.* New York: Crowell, 1974.

Perry, C. J. G. Psychiatric selection of candidates for space missions. *Journal of the American Medical Association,* 1965, **194**, 841–844.

Peterson, R. A., & Sharpe, L. K. Effects of ordinal position: Tripartite analysis. *Psychological Reports,* 1972, **30**, 890–893.

Petroni, F. A. Social class, family size, and the sick role. *Journal of Marriage and the Family,* 1969, **31**, 728–735.

Pierce, J. V. *The educational motivation of superior students who do not achieve in high school* (U.S. Office of Education #20023, Project 208). Washington, D.C.: U.S. Government Printing Office, 1959.

Plank, R. The family constellation of a group of schizophrenic patients. *American Journal of Orthopsychiatry,* 1953, **23**, 817–829.

Poppleton, P. K. Puberty, family size, and the educational progress of girls. *British Journal of Educational Psychology,* 1968, **38**, 286–292.

Price, J. Personality differences within families: Comparison of adult brothers and sisters. *Journal of Biosocial Science,* 1969, **1**, 177–205.

Price, J. S., & Hare, E. H. Birth order studies: Some sources of bias *British Journal of Psychiatry,* 1969, **115**, 633–646.

Purpura, P. A. A study of the relations between birth-order, self-esteem, and conformity (Doctoral dissertation, Fordham University, 1970). *Dissertation Abstracts International,* 1971, **31**, 6266B. (University Microfilm No. 71-08737)

Pyke, D. A. Parity and the incidence of diabetes. *Lancet,* 1956, **270** (1), 818–820.

Quensel, C. T. E. The interrelations of marital status, fertility, family size, and intelligence test scores. *Population Studies,* 1958, **11**, 234–250.

Radloff, R., & Helmreich, R. *Groups under stress: Psychological research in Sealab.* New York: Irvington, 1968.

Rankin, E., & Bahnson, M. B. *Relation of birth order and sibling constellation to attitudes toward parents.* Paper presented at the 47th Annual Meeting of the Eastern Psychological Association, New York, 1976.

Raychaudhuri, M. Differential socialization and musical creativity: A comparison of Indian and American musicians. *Indian Journal of Psychology,* 1965, **40**, 51-59.

Raychaudhuri, M. *Studies in artistic creativity: Personality structure of the musician.* Calcutta: Rabindra Bharati, 1966.

Record, R. G., McKeown, T., & Edwards, J. H. An investigation of the difference in measured intelligence between twins and single births. *Annals of Human Genetics,* 1970, **34**, 11-20.

Reiss, A. J., Jr. Social correlates of psychological types of delinquency. *American Sociological Review,* 1952, **17**, 710-718.

Reznikoff, M. Psychological factors in breast cancer: A preliminary study of some personality trends in patients with cancer of the breast. *Psychosomatic Medicine,* 1955, 17, 96-108.

Ribal, J. E. Social character and meanings of selfishness and altruism. *Sociology and Social Research,* 1963, **47**, 311-321.

Richer, S. The economics of child rearing. *Journal of Marriage and the Family,* 1968, **30**, 462-466.

Riess, B. F. *Character disorder and sibling constellation.* Paper presented at the XVI Interamerican Congress of Psychology, Miami Beach, December 1976.

Riess, B. F., & Safer, J. Birth order and related variables in a large outpatient population. *Journal of Psychology,* 1973, **85**, 61-68.

Rivers, W. C. Consumption and order of birth. *Lancet,* 1911, **181** (2), 999-1004.

Roberts, J., & Engel, A. Family background, early development, and intelligence of children 6-11 years: United States. *Vital and Health Statistics, Series 11,* 1974 (142), 42.

Roe, A. A psychological study of eminent psychologists and anthropologists and a comparison with biological physical scientists. *Psychological Monographs,* 1953, **67**, 2 (Whole No. 352).

Rogerson, C. H., Hardcastle, D. H., & Duguid, K. A psychological approach to the problem of asthma and the asthma-eczema-pruritis syndrome. *Guys' Hospital Report,* 1935, **85**.

Rorvik, D. M., & Shettles, L. B. *Your baby's sex: Now you can choose.* New York: Dodd, Mead, 1970.

Rosen, B. C. Family structure and achievement motivation. *American Sociological Review,* 1961, **26**, 574-585.

Rosenberg, B. G., Goldman, R., & Sutton-Smith, B. Sibling age-spacing effects on cognitive activity in children. *Proceedings of the 77th Annual Convention of the American Psychological Association,* 1969, **4**, 261-262. (Summary)

Rosenberg, B. G., & Sutton-Smith, B. Ordinal position and sex-role identification. *Genetic Psychology Monographs,* 1964, **70**, 297-328.

Rosenberg, B. G., & Sutton-Smith, B. *Sibling association, family size, and cognitive abilities. Journal of Genetic Psychology,* 1966, **109**, 271-279.

Rosenberg, B. G., & Sutton-Smith, B. Family interaction effects on masculinity-femininity. *Journal of Personality and Social Psychology,* 1968, **8**, 117-120.

Rosenberg, B. G., & Sutton-Smith, B. Sibling age spacing effects upon cognition. *Developmental Psychology,* 1969, **1**, 661-668.

Rosenberg, B. G., & Sutton-Smith, B. Sex-role identity and sibling composition. *Journal of Genetic Psychology,* 1971, **118**, 29-32.

Rosenberg, B. G., & Sutton-Smith, B. Family structure and sex-role variations. In J. K. Cole and R. Dienstbier (Eds.), *Nebraska Symposium on Motivation* (Vol. 21). Lincoln: University of Nebraska Press, 1973. Pp. 195-220.

Rosenberg, B. G., Sutton-Smith, B., & Griffiths, J. Sibling differences in empathetic style. *Perceptual and Motor Skills,* 1965, **21**, 811-814.

Rosenberg, M. *Society and the adolescent self-image.* Princeton, N. J.: Princeton University Press, 1965.

Rosenfeld, H. M. Relationships of ordinal position to affiliation and achievement motives: Direction and generality. *Journal of Personality,* 1966, **34,** 467–480.

Rossi, A. S. Naming children in middle-class families. *American Sociological Review,* 1965, **30,** 499–513.

Rossiter, J. R., & Robertson, T. S. Children's TV commercials: Testing the defenses. *Journal of Communication,* 1974, **24,** 137–145.

Rothbart, M. K. Birth order and mother-child interaction in an achievement situation. *Journal of Personality and Social Psychology,* 1971, **17,** 113–120.

Rowland, C. V. Anorexia nervosa, A survey of the literature and a review of 30 cases. *International Psychiatric Clinics,* 1970, **7,** 37–137.

Rubin, R., Balow, B., & Dorle, J. *The relationship of maternal and infant variables to school readiness.* Paper presented at the 83rd Annual Meeting of the American Psychological Association, Chicago, August 1975.

Rubin, S., & Moses, L. Electrocephalographic studies in asthma with some personality correlates. *Psychosomatic Medicine,* 1944, **6,** 31–39.

Rubin, T., Rosenbaum, J., & Cobb, S. The use of interview data for the detection of associations in field studies. *Journal of Chronic Diseases,* 1956, **4,** 253–259.

Ruesch, J., Christiansen, C., Harris, R. E., Dewees, S., Jacobson, A., & Loeb, M. *Duodenal ulcer: Sociopsychological study of Naval enlisted personnel and civilians.* Berkeley: University of California Press, 1948.

Ruesch, J., Christiansen, C., Patterson, L. C., Dewees, S., & Jacobson, A. Psychological invalidism in thyroidectomized patients. *Psychosomatic Medicine,* 1947, **9,** 77–91.

Ruff, C. F., Ayers, J. L., & Templer, D. I. Birth order and hysterical versus obsessive-compulsive continuum. *JSAS Catalog of Selected Documents in Psychology,* 1975, **5,** 332.

Russo, N. F. The motherhood mandate. *Journal of Social Issues,* 1976, **32,** 143–154.

Rutter, M., & Graham, P. Social circumstances of children with psychiatric disorder. In M. Rutter, J. Tizard, & K. Whitmore (Eds.), *Education, health, and behaviour: Psychological and medical study of childhood development.* New York: Wiley, 1970.

Sampson, E. E. Birth order, need achievement, and conformity. *Journal of Abnormal and Social Psychology,* 1962, **64,** 155–159.

Sampson, E. E. Study of ordinal position. In B. A. Maher (Ed.), *Progress in experimental personality research* (Vol. 2). New York: Academic Press, 1965. Pp. 175–222.

Sampson, E. E., & Hancock, F. T. An examination of the relationship between ordinal position, personality, and conformity: An extension, replication, and partial verification. *Journal of Personality and Social Psychology,* 1967, **5,** 398–407.

Sandler, B. E., & Scalia, F. A. The relationship between birth order, sex, and leadership in a religious organization. *Journal of Social Psychology,* 1975, **95,** 279–280.

Saul, L. J. Hostility in cases of essential hypertension. *Psychosomatic Medicine,* 1939, **1,** 153–161.

Saul, L. J. Physiological effects of emotional tension. In J. McV. Hunt (Ed.), *Personality and behavior disorders.* New York: Ronald, 1944.

Schachter, S. *The psychology of affiliation.* Stanford, Calif.: Stanford University Press, 1959.

Schachter, S. Birth order, eminence, and higher education. *American Sociological Review,* 1963, **28,** 757–768.

Schachter, S. Birth order and sociometric choice. *Journal of Abnormal and Social Psychology,* 1964, **68,** 453–456.

Schaefer, J. M. A hologeistic study of family structure and sentiment, supernatural beliefs, and drunkenness (Doctoral dissertation, University of New York at Buffalo, 1972). *Dissertation Abstracts International,* 1973, **34,** 2434. (University Microfilm No. 73-29,131).

Schiller, D. *Untersuchung eines möglichen Zusammenhangs zwischen der Geschwisterposition und verschiedenen Daten zur Berufswahl.* Unpublished dissertation, Universat of Erlangen-Nurnberg, 1966.

Schindler, S. Family constellation and aggressive conduct. *Zeitschrift für Klinische Psychologie und Psychotherapie,* 1974, **22,** 180–182.

Schnyder, U. W. Neurodermitis asthma-rhinitis: Eine genetisch-allergologische Studie. *International Archives of Allergy* (Supplement), 1960, **17,** 1–106.

Schooler, C. Birth order and schizophrenia. *Archives of General Psychiatry,* 1961, **4,** 91–97.

Schooler, C. Childhood family structure and adult characteristics. *Sociometry,* 1972, **35,** 255–268.

Schooler, N. R., Boothe, H., Goldberg, S. C., & Chase, C. Life history and symptoms in schizophrenia: Severity at hospitalization and response to phenothiazines. *Archives of General Psychiatry,* 1971, **25,** 138–147.

Schooler, C., & Scarr, S. Affiliation among chronic schizophrenics: Relation to intrapersonal and birth order factors. *Journal of Personality,* 1962, **30,** 178–192.

Schoonover, S. M. The relationship of intelligence and achievement to birth order, sex of sibling, and age interval. *Journal of Educational Psychology,* 1959, **50,** 143–146.

Schubert, D. S. P. *Family structure of alcoholics.* Unpublished manuscript, 1966. (Available from the author, Cleveland Metropolitan General Hospital, Department of Psychiatry, 3395 Scranton Road, Cleveland, OH 44109.

Schubert, D. S. P. *Sibship constellation among nursing students.* Unpublished manuscript, 1976.

Schubert, D. S. P. Increase in creativity by prior response to a problem. *Journal of General Psychology,* 1977, **96,** 323–324.

Schubert, D. S. P., Wagner, M. E., & Schubert, H. J. P. One thousand references on sibling constellation variables: Ordinal position, sibship size, sibling agespacing, and sex of sibling. *JSAS Catalog of Selected Documents in Psychology,* 1976, **6,** 73. (Manuscript No. 1292)

Schubert, D. S. P., Wagner, M. E., & Schubert, H. J. P. Family constellation and creativity: Firstborn predominant among classical music composers. *Journal of Psychology,* 1977, **96,** 147–149. (a)

Schubert, D. S. P., Wagner, M. E., & Schubert, H. J. P. Interest in creativity training by birth order and sex. *Journal of Creative Behavior,* 1977, **11,** 144–145. (b)

Schubert, D. S. P., Wagner, M. E., & Schubert, H. J. P. *Family constellation and creativity: Persistence among the last-born.* Unpublished data, 1977. (c)

Schubert, D. S. P., Wagner, M. E., & Schubert, H. J. P. *Sibship cor. 'ellation of American and English women writers.* Unpublished data, 1979.

Schubert, D. S. P., Wagner, M. E., & Schubert, H. J. P. An additional 1,000 references on sibling-constellation variables: *Ordinal position, sibship size, sibling agespacing, and sex of sibling.* Unpublished data, 1980. (a)

Schubert, D. S. P., Wagner, M. E., & Schubert, H. J. P. *Sibship-constellation of artists.* Unpublished data, 1980. (b)

Schubert, H. J. P. *Twenty thousand transients.* Buffalo, N.Y.: Emergency Relief Bureau, 1935.

Schubert, H. J. P. *Sibship size and ordinal position of 968 VAH patients.* Buffalo, N.Y. 1970. (Available from the author at 500 Klein Rd., Buffalo, N.Y. 14221.)

Schubert, H. J. P. *Sibship constellation and personality of urban blacks and whites.* Paper presented at the XVI meeting of the Interamerican Congress of Psychology, Miami Beach, December 1976.

Schubert, H. J. P., & Wagner, M. E. The relation of individual personal data responses and transiency, place among siblings, and academic ability. *Journal of Abnormal and Social Psychology,* 1936, **30**, 474-483.

Schubert, H. J. P., & Wagner, M. E. *Ordinal position percentages in general-population and senior-citizen samples by race and sex.* Unpublished manuscript, 1976. (Available from author at 500 Klein Rd., Buffalo, N.Y. 14221.)

Schubert, H. J. P., Wagner, M. E., & Riess, B. F. Sibship size, sibsex, sibgap, and homosexuality among male outpatients. *Transnational Mental Health Research Newsletter,* 1976, **18**, 1-8.

Schutz, W. C. *FIRO: A three dimensional theory of interpersonal behavior.* New York: Holt, 1958.

Schwartz, M. *Heredity in bronchial asthma.* Copenhagen: Munksgaard, 1952.

The Scottish Council for Research in Education and the Population Investigation Committee. *The trend of Scottish intelligence.* London: University of London Press, 1949. Pp. 101-117.

Sears, R. R. Relation of early socialization experiences to self-concepts and gender role in middle childhood. *Child Development,* 1970, **41**, 267-289.

Sears, R. R., Maccoby, E., & Levin, H. *Patterns of child rearing.* Evanston, Ill.: Row-Peterson, 1957.

Sells, S. B., & Roff, M. Peer acceptance-rejection and birth order. *American Psychologist,* 1963, **18**, 355. (Abstract)

Sellwood, R. M., III. Birth order and creativity (Doctoral dissertation, Fordham University, 1974). *Dissertation Abstracts International,* 1974, **35**, 3598B. (University Microfilm No. 74-25084)

Sethi, B. B., & Gupta, S. C. Sibling position in India. *American Journal of Psychotherapy,* 1973, **27**, 61-69.

Sheldon, P. M. The families of highly gifted children. *Marriage and Family Living,* 1954, **16**, 59-67.

Shrader, W. K., & Leventhal, T. Birth order of children and parental report of problems. *Child Development,* 1968, **39**, 1165-1175.

Siegel, M. *Personality structure of children with reading disabilities versus children with other clinical problems.* Unpublished doctoral dissertation, New York University, 1951.

Simon, W. E. Ordinal position of birth in the family constellation and adult smoking behavior. *Journal of Social Psychology,* 1973, **90**, 157-158.

Simon, W. E., Sands, B., & Forman, M. R. Ordinal position of birth and perceived popularity for sixth graders. *Perceptual and Motor Skills,* 1971, **33**, 1097-1098.

Singer, E. Adult orientation of first and later children. *Sociometry,* 1971, **34**, 328-345.

Skipper, J. K., Jr., & McCaghy, C. H. Strip-teasers: The anatomy and career contingencies of a deviant occupation. *Social Problems,* 1970, **17**, 391-405.

Skovholt, T., Moore, E., & Wellman, F. Birth order and academic behavior in first grade. *Psychological Reports,* 1973, **32**, 395-398.

Slater, E. Birth order and maternal age of homosexuals. *The Lancet,* 1962, **282**, (1), 69-71.

Sletto, R. F. Sibling position and juvenile delinquency. *American Journal of Sociology,* 1934, **39**, 657-669.

Smart, R. G. Alcoholism, birth order, and family size. *Journal of Abnormal and Social Psychology,* 1963, **66**, 17-23.

Smelser, W. T., & Stewart, L. H. Where are the siblings? A re-evaluation of the relationship between birth order and college attendance. *Sociometry,* 1968, **31**, 294-303.

Smith, C. M., & McIntyre, S. Family size, birth rank, and ordinal position in psychiatric illness. *Canadian Psychiatric Association Journal,* 1963, **8**, 244-248.

Smith, E. E., & Goodchilds, J. P. Some personality and behavior factors related to birth order. *Journal of Applied Psychology,* 1963, **47,** 300–303.

Smith, W. D. Changing preference for a female child. *Journal of Individual Psychology,* 1976, **32,** 106–107.

Solomon, D., Hirsch, J. G., Scheinfeld, D. R., & Jackson, J. C. Family characteristics and elementary school achievement in an urban ghetto. *Journal of Consulting and Clinical Psychology,* 1972, **39,** 462–466.

Solomon, E. S., Clare, J. E., & Westoff, C. F. Fear of childlessness, desire to avoid an only child, and children's desires for siblings. *Milbank Memorial Fund Quarterly,* 1956, **34,** 160–177.

Spence, J. *A thousand families in Newcastle upon Tyne.* London: Oxford University Press, 1954.

Spiers, P. S. Previous fetal loss and risk of sudden infant death syndrome in subsequent offspring. *American Journal of Epidemiology,* 1976, **103,** 355–361.

Spiers, P. S., & Wang, L. Short pregnancy interval, low birthweight, and the sudden infant death syndrome. *American Journal of Epidemiology,* 1976, **104,** 15–21.

Spitz, R. A. Hospitalism. An inquiry into the genesis of psychiatric conditions in early childhood. *Psychoanalytic Study of the Child* (Vol. I). New York: International Universities Press, 1945.

Spitz, R. A. Hospitalism: A follow-up report on investigation described in Volume I, 1945. *Psychoanalytic Study of the Child* (Vol. 2). New York: International Universities Press, 1946.

Spitz, R. A. Reply to Dr. Pinneau. *Psychological Bulletin,* 1955, **52,** 453–459.

Spitz, R. A., & Wolf, K. Anaclytic depression. An inquiry into the genesis of psychiatric conditions in early childhood. *Psychoanalytic Study of the Child* (Vol. 2). New York: International Universities Press, 1946.

Srole, L., & Fischer, A. K. The social epidemiology of smoking behavior 1953 to 1970: The Midtown Manhattan study. *Social Science and Medicine,* 1973, **7,** 341–358.

Stagner, R. & Katzoff, E. T. Personality as related to birth order and family size. *Journal of Applied Psychology,* 1936, **20,** 340–346.

Start, A., & Start, K. B. The relation between birth order and effort or conscientiousness among primary school children. *Research in Education,* 1974, **12,** 1–8.

Stecher, R. M. *Documenta rheumatologica.* Cleveland: Western Reserve University Medical School, 1957.

Steckel, M. L. Intelligence and birth order in family. *Journal of Social Psychology,* 1930, **1,** 329–344.

Stein, M. Cited in Harris, I. D. *The Promised Seed.* New York: Free Press, 1964. p. 255.

Stendler, C. B. Possible causes of overdependency in young children. *Child Development,* 1964, **25,** 125–147.

Stewart, A., Webb, J., & Hewitt, I. A survey of childhood malignancies. *British Medical Journal,* January, 1958, pp. 1495–1508.

Stewart, L. The politics of birth order. *Proceedings of the 78th Annual Convention of the American Psychological Association,* 1970, **5,** 365–366. (Summary)

Stewart, R. H. Birth order and dependency. *Journal of Personality and Social Psychology,* 1967, **6,** 192–194.

Still, G. F. Place in family as a factor in disease. *Lancet,* 1927, **213** (2), 795–800.

Storer, N. W. Ordinal position and the Oedipus complex. *Laboratory of Social Relations of Harvard University Bulletin,* 1961, **10,** 18–21.

Stotland, E., & Dunn, R. E. Empathy, self-esteem, and birth order. *Journal of Abnormal and Social Psychology,* 1963, **66,** 532–540.

Stotland, E., Sherman, S. E., & Shaver, K. G. *Empathy and birth order*. Lincoln: University of Nebraska Press, 1971.

Stout, A. M. *Parent behaviour toward children of differing ordinal position and sibling status*. Unpublished doctoral dissertation, University of California, Berkeley, 1960.

Stunkard, A. J. *The pain of obesity*. Palo Alto: Bull Publ., 1976.

Sutker, P. B., & Moan, C. E. A psychosocial description of penitentiary inmates. *Archives of General Psychiatry*, 1973, **29**, 663-667.

Sutton-Smith, B. Modeling and reactive components of sibling interaction. In *Child Psychology*. Symposium at Institute for Child Development, Minneapolis, May, 1968.

Sutton-Smith, B., Roberts, J. M., & Rosenberg, B. G. Sibling associations and role involvement. *Merrill-Palmer Quarterly of Behavior and Development*, 1964, **10**, 25-38.

Sutton-Smith, B., & Rosenberg, B. G. Age changes in the effects of ordinal position on sex-role identification. *Journal of Genetic Psychology*, 1965, **107**, 61-73.

Sutton-Smith, B., & Rosenberg, B. G. Sibling consensus on power tactics. *Journal of Genetic Psychology*, 1968, **112**, 63-72.

Sutton-Smith, B., & Rosenberg, B. G. *The sibling*. New York: Holt, 1970.

Sutton-Smith, B., Rosenberg, B. G., & Landy, F. Father-absence effects in families of different sibling compositions. *Child Development*, 1968, **39**, 1213-1221.

Svalastoga, K. *Prestige, class, and mobility*. Copenhagen: Scandanavian University Books, 1959.

Sweeney, D. R., & Fine, B. J. Note on pain reactivity and family size. *Perceptual and Motor Skills*, 1970, **31**, 25-26.

Taintor, Z. Birth order and psychiatric problems in boot camp. *American Journal of Psychiatry*, 1970, **126**, 1604-1610.

Tanner, J. M. *Education and physical growth*. New York: International University Press, 1961.

Tanner, J. M. Earlier maturation in man. *Scientific American*, 1968, **218**, 21-27.

Tennent, T. G. Truancy and stealing. *British Journal of Psychiatry*, 1970, **116**, 587-592.

Terhune, K. W. *A review of actual and expected consequences of family size*. (U.S. Public Health Service Publications NIH 75-779.) Washington, D.C.: U.S. Government Printing Office, 1974.

Terhune, K. W. *Paradoxical status of the only child*. Paper presented at the 84th Annual Convention of the American Psychological Association, Washington, D.C., September 1976.

Terman, L. M. (Ed.) *Genetic studies of genius, Vol. I. Mental and physical traits of 1,000 gifted children*. Stanford, Calif.: Stanford University Press, 1925.

Thomas, E. B., Barnett, C. R., & Lieberman, P. H. Feeding behaviors of newborn infants as a function of parity of the mother. *Child Development*, 1971, **42**, 1471-1483.

Thoman, E. B., Lieberman, P. H., & Olson, J. P. Neonate-mother interaction during breast feeding. *Development Psychology*, 1972, **6**, 110-118.

Thoman, E. B., Turner, A. M., Lieberman, P. H., & Barnett, C. R. Neonate-mother interactions: Effects of feeding on behavior. *Child Development*, 1970, **41**, 1103-1111.

Thomas, C. B., & Duszynski, K. R. Closeness to parents and the family constellation in a prospective study of five disease states: Suicide, mental illness, malignant tumor, hypertension, and coronary heart disease. *The Johns Hopkins Medical Journal*, 1974, **134**, 251-270.

Thompson, V. D. Family size: Implicit policies and assumed psychological outcomes. *Journal of Social Issues*, 1974, **30**, 93-124.

Tizard, J., & Hemming, M. Social aspects of intellectual and educational retardation. In E. M. Rutter, J. Tizard, and K. Whitmore (Eds.), *Education, Health, and Behavior* (Chap. 8). New York: Wiley, 1970.

Tolman, R. S. Note of family position of certain delinquent boys. *American Journal of Orthopsychiatry,* 1939, **9,** 635-638.

Tolstrup, K. On psychogenic obesity in childhood. IV. *Acta Pediatrica,* 1953, **42,** 289-304.

Toman, W. Choices of marriage partners by men coming from monosexual sibling configurations. *British Journal of Medical Psychology,* 1964, **37,** 43-46.

Toman, W. *On the extent of sibling influence.* Paper presented at the conference of the Society for the Study of Behaviorial Development, Ann Arbor, Michigan, 1973.

Toman, W. *Family constellation: Its effects on personality and social behavior* (3rd ed.). New York: Springer, 1976.

Toman, W., & Preiser, S. *Familienkonstellationen und ihre Störungen: Ihre Wirkungen auf die Person, ihre sozialen Beziehungen und die folgende Generation.* Stuttgart: Enke, 1973.

Toman, W., Preiser, S., Gasch, B., & Plattig, G. *Die Wirkungen von Familienkonstellationen auf die Person, ihre sozialen Beziehungen und die nachfolgende Generation. Research project (1962-1966).* Bad Godesberg: Deutsche Forschungsgemeinschaft, 1967.

Toman, W., & Toman, E. Sibling positions of a sample of distinguished persons. *Perceptual and Motor Skills,* 1970, **31,** 825-826.

Tomasson, R. F. Social mobility and family size in two high-status populations. *Eugenics Quarterly,* 1966, **13** 113-121.

Tremolieres, J., & Boulanger, J. J. Contribution a l'étude du phenomène de croissance et de stature en France de 1940 à 1948. *Institut National d'Hygiene Recueil des Travaux,* 1950, **4,** 117-212.

Tuckman, J., & Regan, R. A. Ordinal position and behavior problems in children. *Journal of Health and Social Behavior,* 1967, **8,** 32-39.

Udjus, L. G. *Anthropometrical changes in Norwegian men in the twentieth century.* Oslo: Universitatsforlaget, 1964.

Very, P. S., & Prull, R. W. Birth order, personality development, and the choice of law as a profession. *Journal of Genetic Psychology,* 1970, **116,** 219-221.

Vincent, C. E. *Sociological factors in psychosomatic illness.* Unpublished doctoral dissertation, University of California, Berkeley, 1952.

Visher, S. S. Environmental backgrounds of leading American scientists. *American Sociological Review,* 1948, **13,** 65-72.

Vockell, E. L., & Bennett, B. Birth order, sex of siblings, and incidence of learning disabilities. *Exceptional Children,* 1972, **39,** 162-164.

Wagner, M. E. *Birth order variables among SUCB entrants.* Unpublished data, 1960. (Available from author, 500 Klein Road, Buffalo, N.Y. 14221.)

Wagner, M. E. *Ordinal position and MMPI scores among college freshmen.* Unpublished data, 1975. (Available from author, 500 Klein Road, Buffalo, N.Y. 14221).

Wagner, M. E. *Effect of size of family on its members.* Paper presented at the XVI meeting of the Interamerican Congress of Psychology, Miami Beach, December 1976.

Wagner, M. E., & Schubert, H. J. P. *Family size, sibling sex, sibling age-gap, and personality of middleborn college girls.* Paper presented at the 82nd Annual Convention of the American Psychological Association, New Orleans, September 1974.

Wagner, M. E., & Schubert, H. J. P. *The all-male sibship and the male without brothers.* Paper presented at the 24th Annual Convention of the American Society for Adlerian Psychology, Vancouver, B. C., May 1976.

Wagner, M. E., & Schubert, H. J. P. Sibship variables and the United States presidency. *Journal of Individual Psychology,* 1977, **33,** 78-85. (a)

Wagner, M. E., & Schubert, H. J. P. *Sibship patterns among United States military leaders.* Unpublished data, 1977. (b)

Wagner, M. E., Schubert, H. J. P., Zillich, M. M., & Schubert, D. S. P. *Athletes: Their siblings and parents.* Unpublished data, 1979.

Wagner, M. E., Zillich, M. M., & Schubert, H. J. P. *Actors and actresses: Their siblings and parents.* Unpublished data, 1979.

Wahl, C. W. Some antecedent factors in the family histories of 109 alcoholics. *Quarterly Journal of Studies on Alcohol,* 1956, **17,** 643–654. (a)

Wahl, C. W. Some antecedent factors in the family histories of 568 male schizophrenics of the United States Navy. *American Journal of Psychiatry,* 1956, **113,** 201–210. (b)

Walberg, H. J., & Marjoribanks, K. Family environment and cognitive development, twelve analytic models. *Review of Educational Research,* 1976, **46,** 527–551.

Waldrop, M. F., & Bell, R. Q. Effects of family size and density on newborn characteristics. *American Journal of Orthopsychiatry,* 1966, **36,** 544–550.

Walker, L. V., Johnson, D. L., & Goolishian, H. Ordinal position and psychopathology in two child families. *Texas Reports of Biology and Medicine,* 1973, **31,** 777–790.

Wallbrown, F. H., Wallbrown, J. D., & Wherry, R. J., Jr. The construct validity of the Wallach-Kogan creativity test for inner city children. *Journal of General Psychology,* 1975, **92,** 93–96.

Wark, D., & Swanson, E. *Birth order effects in a statewide testing program.* Minneapolis: University of Minnesota Student Counseling Bureau, 1971.

Warren, J. R. Birth order and social behavior. *Psychological Bulletin,* 1966, **65,** 39–49.

Weisberg, P. S., & Springer, R. J. Environmental factors in creative function. *Archives of General Psychiatry,* 1961, **5,** 554–564.

Werkman, S. L., & Greenberg, E. S. Personality and interest patterns in obese adolescent girls. *Psychosomatic Medicine,* 1967, **29,** 72–80.

West, S. S. Sibling configuration of scientists. *American Journal of Sociology,* 1960, **66,** 268–274.

Westoff, C. F., Potter, R. G., Jr., & Sagi, P. C. *The third child: A study in the prediction of fertility.* Princeton, N.J.: Princeton University Press, 1963.

White, B. L. *Reassessing our educational priorities.* Paper presented at the Education Commission of the State's Early Childhood Education Symposium, Boston, 1974.

White, B., Kaban, B., Shapiro, B., & Attanucci, J. Competence and experience. In I. C. Uzgiris and F. Weizmann (Eds.), *The structuring of experience.* New York: Plenum, 1976.

Whitelaw, G. L. The association of social class and sibling number with skinfold thickness in London school boys. *Human Biology,* 1971, **43,** 414–420.

Winterbottom, M. R. The relation of need for achievement to learning experiences in independence and mastery. In J. W. Atkinson (Ed.), *Motives in fantasy, action, and society.* Princeton, N. J.: Van Nostrand, 1958.

Wisdom, G., & Walsh, R. P. Dogmatism and birth order. *Journal of Individual Psychology,* 1975, **31,** 32–36.

Witkin, H. A., & Goodenough, D. R. Field dependence and interpersonal behavior. *Psychological Bulletin,* 1977, **84,** 661–689.

Witty, P. A. Only and intermediate children in the senior high school. *Journal of Experimental Education,* 1937, **6,** 180–186.

Wolff, H. *Stress and disease.* Springfield, Ill.: Thomas, 1953.

Wray, J. D. Population pressure on families: Family size and child spacing. In R. Revelle (Ed.), *Rapid population growth: Consequences and policy implications* (Vol. 2). Baltimore: Johns Hopkins Press, 1971. (Reprinted in *Reports on Population/Family Planning* (No. 9). New York: Population Council).

Wuebben, P. L. Honesty of subjects and birth order. *Journal of Personality and Social Psychology,* 1967, **5,** 350–352.

Wyron, J. B., & Gordon, J. E. A long-term prospective-type field study of population dynamics in the Punjab, India. In C. V. Kiser (Ed.), *Research in Family Planning.* Princeton, N.J.: Princeton University Press, 1962. Pp. 17–32.

Yerushalmy, J. On the interval between successive births and its effect on survival of the infant. *Human Biology,* 1945, **17,** 65–106.

Yerushalmy, J., Bierman, J. M., Kemp, D. H., Connors, A., & French, F. E. Longitudinal studies of pregnancy on the island of Kauai, Territory of Hawaii, I. Analysis of previous reproductive history. *American Journal of Obstetrics and Gynecology,* 1956, **71,** 80–96.

Yessler, P. G., Reiser, M. F., & Rioch, D. M. Etiology of duodenal ulcer. *Journal of the American Medical Association,* 1959, **169,** 99.

Zajonc, R. B. Family configuation and intelligence: Variations in scholastic aptitude scores parallel trends in family size and the spacing of children. *Science,* 1976, **192,** 227–236.

Zajonc, R. B., & Markus, G. B. Birth order and intellectual development. *Psychological Review,* 1975, **82,** 74–88.

Zimbardo, P., & Formica, R. Emotional comparison and self-esteem as determinants of affiliation. *Journal of Personality,* 1963, **31,** 141–162.

Zucker, R. A., & Van Horn, H. Sibling social structure and oral behavior: Drinking and smoking in adolescence. *Quarterly Journal of Studies on Alcohol,* 1972, **33,** 193–197.

Zweigenhaft, R. L. Birth order, approval-seeking, and membership in congress. *Journal of Individual Psychology,* 1975, **31,** 205–210.

THE DEVELOPMENT OF UNDERSTANDING OF THE SPATIAL TERMS *FRONT* AND *BACK*[1]

Lauren Julius Harris and Ellen A. Strommen

MICHIGAN STATE UNIVERSITY

[1] We are grateful to the principals, staffs, and children of the Sycamore and Midway Schools, Holt, Michigan, and the Red Cedar and Spartan Schools, East Lansing, Michigan, and to the undergraduates from Michigan State and McGill Universities for their participation in our studies. A number of other people helped us along the way. We especially want to thank Randolph Alexander, Catherine T. Best, John Konopa, Mark Lifland, Gail Nurmi, and Suzanne M. Seimerling for helping with the experiments and Mary Lee Nitschke, Roy Pea, and J. Kathryn Bock for comments on the manuscript. We also thank Mary Hyde and Jean Berko-Gleason for making new data analyses available to us. Finally, we thank those investigators who provided us with copies of dissertations and other unpublished reports. Some of our research was supported, in part, by NIH Grant MH 24 234-01, and by a Bio-Medical Grant and All-University Grants from Michigan State University.

Earlier reports of some of our experiments have been published or presented at scientific meetings, as indicated in footnote 2. Finally, the authors' contributions to the current paper were equal.

ADVANCES IN CHILD DEVELOPMENT
AND BEHAVIOR, VOL. 14

Copyright © 1979 by Academic Press, Inc.
All rights of reproduction in any form reserved.
ISBN 0-12-009714-1

I. Introduction

A. DELINEATION OF THE TOPIC

We want to discuss a very mundane skill: even quite young children can tell the difference between the front and back and sides of things, and they can say that something is in front of, in back of, or beside something else. How and when do children make these judgments?

Our interest in these questions began with a study not primarily of front-back but of left-right. It is well known that children frequently confuse left and right, and the purpose of this experiment (hereafter Experiment 1)[2], was to evaluate the influential explanation of this confusion proposed by Piaget (1928).

Piaget asked 4- to 12-year-old children several multipart questions about left and right. Only by 11 years could the children perform his most difficult task, which required that they grasp that the middle object of a three-object row was simultaneously to the right of one object and to the left of the other.

Piaget proposed that the children's confusion of left and right is logical—"egocentrism" prevents them from understanding relations or from grasping the relativity of notions or ideas—and the growing appreciation of left-right directionality therefore could be equated with growing ability to place themselves "at the point of view of others with regard to left and right" (p. 109).

However, if egocentrism is the key, then the particular spatial dimension being tested should be irrelevant. Young, still egocentric children thus

---

[2] To reduce redundancy we shall consecutively number all of our own experiments in the order of mention in this paper. Where no date is given, as in No. 4 below, the data are presented here for the first time. For the reader's convenience, a list of the experiments follows:

1. Relational understanding of front-back and left-right (children) (Harris, 1972)

2. Placements of featured objects in relation to themselves (children) (Harris & Strommen, 1972)

3. Placements of featured objects in relation to other featured objects (same children as Experiment 2) (Harris & Strommen, 1972)

4. Face vs. body cues as determinants of front (children)

5. Judgments of front and back of featureless and minimally featured geometric forms (adults) (Harris & Strommen, 1974)

6. Generalizability of front-back judgments across a range of minimally featured designs (adults) (Harris & Strommen, 1974)

7. Direction of imagined movement of minimally featured forms (adults) (Harris & Strommen, 1974)

8. Front-back placements of featureless objects (children) (Harris & Strommen, 1972)

9. Front-back judgments of a featureless form as seen from above (adults)

10. Replication of Experiment 9

11. Replication of Experiment 9 with a circle

12. Effects of immediately prior experience with featured objects on front placements of featureless objects (children)

13. Effects of repeated elicitations of front, back, or side placements of featureless objects (children)

14. Repeated beside placements of featureless objects (children)

15. Reversion of self-referential front-back judgments when referent is minimally featured (adults)

16. Influence of "social distance" on front, back, and beside placements of dolls (children) (Harris & Strommen, 1973)

ought to be equally stymied if questioned about the middle object of a three-object array whether the array is aligned right to left, front to back, or top to bottom. Experiment 1 showed that they were not. Twenty-seven kindergartners (5–6 years of age) and 12 second graders (7–8 years of age) first were tested using Piaget's procedures. When asked about a row of three objects, only three kindergartners and six second graders could describe the middle object as being simultaneously to the right of one object and to the left of the other. However, when the same children were asked about up and down (the same array arranged vertically) and front and back (a baby doll, chair, and mother doll, all facing in the same direction, with the chair in the middle), performance improved greatly and equally for these two spatial dimensions. The second graders all did perfectly, and the kindergartners were nearly as good.

The difference between the left–right and front–back tasks was still more evident in posttest questions. Children who correctly described the chair as behind one doll and in front of the other were challenged: "But how can that be? Can the chair be in front of something and behind something all at the same time?" (Most of the children now seemed puzzled. Five kindergartners shook their heads, No.) "Then let's try again: The chair is behind the baby, right?" (Every child agreed.) "Then if it's behind the baby, it must be behind the mother too." (However, each child either shook his head, or repeated "The chair is in front of the mother.") "But how can it be in front, when it's already behind something?" (Again, some children seemed puzzled but did not change their answer. Several children said, "Because it's in the middle," or "Because this [front] part of the chair is behind the baby and this [back] part is in front of the mother," or words to that effect.)

So the children simply knew front and back very well and could not be swayed. They were equally unshaken when pressed in the same way about up and down. On the left–right questions, however, the same challenge was more successful when posed to those children who had passed the three-object test. The children now readily changed their answers and said that the end objects were both either left or right of the middle object.

These results do not necessarily cast doubt on Piaget's (1928) emphasis on the role of egocentric thought in the development of logical thinking, but they do suggest that Piaget made an unfortunate choice of tests to assess his theory.

There are several reasons why the left-right dimension is so much more difficult than the front–back. First, left–right confusion may be an inevitable consequence of human bilateral symmetry (Mach, 1914; but see Bornstein *et al.,* 1978), and where mirror images can be discriminated at all, it may be only because the symmetry is imperfect. Certain asymmetrical features have evolved, most crucially, functional asymmetry of the two hemispheres of the brain (cf. Corballis & Beale, 1970, 1976), but such asymmetries do not provide salient perceptual cues. In contrast, the front and back are asymmetrical and are physically highly differentiated. In the case of the naked body, *front* designates that side having certain features, including the face and eyes, chest, throat, breast, abdomen, genitals, and knees, while *back* designates the back itself, the back of the head and neck, shoulder blades, buttocks, heels, and other features. When we have informally asked kindergarten-age children how they could tell their front from their back, some of these are the features they mentioned.

The front–back distinctiveness of the clothed body is at least as strong as that of the naked body, while left–right symmetry is maintained. Nearly all garments have pronounced bilateral symmetry but are clearly differentiated front from back by buttons, zippers, and the like. These were features of clothing that the children also frequently named in answer to our question about front–back differences. Sometimes, of course, the difference is subtle. One kindergartner, asked how he told the difference between the front and back of his turtleneck sweater, explained, "Well, you have to find this thing inside [the label]." "And if there's no label?" "Well, then you'll know it's on wrong 'cause it feels funny."

Besides the physical differences, the front–back orientation has far greater operational significance than the left–right orientation. Because of the design of the body and the location of its organs of perception, the front is the side of major action on the world and of social interaction with others, the side which the caretaker approaches and from which the child reaches out.

Another functional difference is direction of movement. Human beings and nearly all other animals are designed to move forward—in the direction of their front sides where their primary organs of perception are located. Very early we therefore may come to expect movement in any bilaterally symmetrical organism along the asymmetrical axis and in the direction of the front side.[3]

In the case of the human body and nearly all other animal bodies, all the

---

[3] This expectation regarding direction of movement is problematic in the case of animals with spherical or radial symmetry, such as many coelenterates, since their natural environment is water where environmental forces are as likely to act in one direction as another. From this observation the biologist-philosopher Herman Weyl (1953) suggests that spherical symmetry gave way to radial symmetry and then to bilateral symmetry as land organisms evolved and as they developed the capacity to move, since linear movement is accomplished most efficiently by a bilaterally symmetrical system. In such a system, the organs of locomotion—the arms and legs, or wings, or flippers—are arranged symmetrically so that movement is along the head–tail or front–back axis.

cues mentioned here work together, redundantly specifying, or "overdetermining," the front-back difference.

On the one hand, given these considerations, the mastery of front-back evidenced by the 5- or 6-year olds in Experiment 1 seems unremarkable. However, many other more complex uses of the terms *front* and *back* exist. For instance, certain objects embody different numbers and combinations of front and back cues. Vehicles incorporate both physical differentiation of front-back sides and forward movement, but buildings and pieces of furniture lack movement. For rooms where the public assembles, such as auditoriums or churches, the inside "front" is usually opposite the outside "front." Many other manufactured objects, however, lack front-back features altogether, as do nearly all plants and natural inorganic objects or bodies. Since the major force acting on, say, trees is gravity, trees have distinct tops and bottoms but grow horizontally in a nearly uniform fashion. Bodies of water likewise spread out more or less evenly, gravity acting equally at all points. Such objects or bodies therefore cannot be said to have either front or back or a left or right side, yet all can be—and are—said to exist in front-back relation to other objects. What principles govern these spatial relationships? Furthermore, how the terms *front* and *back* are used depends on other considerations, e.g., whether one intends an absolute meaning (my front, the object's front side) or a relative meaning (in front of me, in front of the object); whether one is speaking about oneself or some other object; whether the reference base for spatial placements is oneself or external to self; whether one is referring to one object's location in relation to a second object (in front or in back of the other object) or to the first object's orientation toward the second object (whether it is facing toward or away from the second object).

Of the many ways in which *front* and *back* may be understood, we have chosen to focus on several general categories of "knowing" front and back. A number of these categories of "knowing" front and back have been examined empirically by ourselves or by other investigators; these form the data base for this paper. To the extent that available data and theoretical considerations permit, we shall discuss these categories of knowing front and back in their probable order of acquisition.

B. SOME METHODOLOGICAL CONCERNS:
HOW CAN CHILDREN TELL US WHAT THEY KNOW?

In planning our research, we faced a problem familiar to all researchers studying children's understanding of word meanings—how to get children to tell us what they know. We face a similar problem in the analysis of language generally. All adult speakers regulate, for instance, the inflections on nouns and verbs, but few adults can state the underlying grammatical rules. Linguists therefore infer the underlying principles from examples of everyday speech. The "rules" governing uses of the terms *in front of, in back of,* and *beside* are undoubtedly simpler than those governing the construction of well-formed sentences, but the same plan of attack can be used to try to infer the "rules" from people's uses of these spatial terms.

Naturally occurring instances of behavior from which the psychological meanings of *in front of* and *in back of* and *beside* can be inferred are infrequent. The usual procedure has been to invent circumstances which elicit such behavior—circumstances which place as little demand as possible on speaking skill—and to confront subjects with them. The most general procedure used by us and by others has been to ask subjects to make in front, in back, and beside placements of ordinary objects, and then to see whether the placements change or stay the same according to the types of objects placed or the nature of the instructions.

II. Knowing the Intrinsic Front and Back of Self

If the major systems of spatial coordinates originate with one's own body, and "objective space" evolves from the "primitive" body orientation (e.g., Piaget, 1928; Werner, 1948), it follows that children's earliest front–back knowledge should be of front and back as intrinsic properties of their own bodies. Some evidence shows that this is so, and that this knowledge emerges very early. Virtually all 4-year-olds (Leehey, 1973) and 5-year-olds (Experiment 1) can already answer questions about their own fronts and backs perfectly. In fact, some childen already answer such questions correctly by age 3. Leehey and Carey (1978) asked a group of 36 children (ages 2 years 1 month [2:1] to 3:3, mean age 2:10) to point to the fronts and backs of themselves, of the experimenter, and of toy objects. Six children (passers, mean age 3:2) performed perfectly. Ten children (failers, mean age 2:9) responded randomly to the toys; but of these, three correctly pointed to their own backs, and one pointed to both his own back and his front. The remaining children (intermediates, mean age 2:11) were in between. No children made the opposite response pattern of responding correctly to other objects but not to their own bodies.

The discussion above deals with children's use of the words for front and back and not necessarily to the concepts to which the words are attached. Leehey (1973; Leehey & Carey, 1978) showed that even children unable to label intrinsic fronts and backs of objects, including their own bodies, were usually able to perform correctly on nonlinguistic tasks in which they were asked to "make a parade" of objects, and to orient objects so that they could "talk with" each other. Success on these tasks implies awareness of a front–back dimension according to which things can be aligned, and also awareness of typical front–back orientations of objects in two different types of situations. Evidently children have some functioning concept of front and back before they are able to use the words. It seems reasonable that development of the prelinguistic concepts of front and back should also begin with the front-back axis of one's own body, but data relevant to this question are not yet available.

The fact that in English and some other languages *back* names a body part as well as a spatial relation is a complicating feature which has as yet unexamined implications, not only for our analysis of the development of knowledge of the intrinsic front and back of self but for other manifestations of children's understanding of these terms. Studies comparing languages in which the term meaning "back" has both these meanings with languages in which it has only the spatial meaning should provide one source of information regarding this question.

III.   Self-referent System:
Relation of Other Objects to Self

Once children have learned where the fronts and backs of their own bodies are located, they should become able to follow an instruction to place an object in spatial relation to (*in front of* or *in back of*) their own bodies. In one sense, this chronology is logically required—something can be placed in front of oneself only if the self's front is known. Evidence for this proposed ordering of skills comes from a study by Kuczaj and Maratsos (1975), with additional data from our own work. Kuczaj and Maratsos tested 15 nursery-school children in each of three age groups, averaging 2 years 10 months (2:10), 3:5, and 3:11.

Each child was asked to place objects (doll, toy car) "in front of you," "in back of you," and "beside you." Performance on this self-relational task was compared with performance on four other tasks: a touch task (touching the fronts and backs of various featured toys); fronted objects placement task (placing a fronted object in spatial relation to another fronted object); a nonfronted object placement task (identical to the task just mentioned except that the object lacks intrinsic front–back features, e.g., drinking glass); and a generalization task (identifying the fronts and backs of novel objects with which the child has interacted).

The self-relational task was easiest. Even the youngest children (2:6–3:1) were correct on 83% of these placements; by 3:7 to 4:1, all were perfect.

TABLE I

Mean Percentage Correct (Showing Understanding of Concept)
Placements of Object in Relation to Own Body

	Age of child (years and months)	Front	Back	Beside
Kuczaj and Maratsos (1975)	2:6–3:1	83.3	83.3	16.7
	3:2–3:6	90	96.7	43.3
	3:7–4:1	100	100	76.7
Leehey (1973)	2:7–3:6	93.8	93.8	—[a]
Harris and Strommen (Experiment 2)	4:9–7:5	100	100	100

[a] Not tested.

The percentages for the three age groups are shown in Table I. Similar high percentages were obtained when Leehey (1973) asked 16 children ages 2:7–3:6 to place a button in front and in back of themselves.

Subjects in our Experiment 2 (the same children participated in Experiment 3; see footnote 2) were 80 kindergartners and first graders (4:9–7:5). The procedure in Experiment 2 was the same as Kuczaj and Maratsos' procedure, except that the children placed a greater variety of objects (dolls, toy bugs, toy trucks and cars, and dollhouse chairs). The results (Table I) were that all 80 children made all their placements in the appropriate location in relation to their own bodies. Table I also shows that beside placements lagged in Kuczaj and Maratsos' study at all ages, becoming completely accurate only for the older children in our experiment.

A.   ORIENTATION AND LOCATION

In developing a scoring system for our subjects' placements, we had to distinguish between where, in relation to themselves, the children placed (located) the object given to them and how they oriented it in that location. In our Experiment 2, the children's placements were completely uniform with respect to the location of their front, back, and beside placements. For the featured objects, however, there were variations in orientation within the same locations. Three major types of patterns emerged, accounting for 75% of the total number of placements (see Fig. 1 and Table II). In the facing pattern, the face side of the mobile object was toward the child in all three placements—in front, behind, and beside. In the lined-up pattern, the object faced the same way as the child. In the face-to-side pattern, the object was placed laterally so that its side was toward the child. (Beside placements could be to either right or left, but only right-side placements—the more frequently made—are shown.)

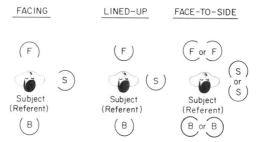

Fig. 1. *Placement patterns of featured objects on self-referent trials. (F, B, and S represent locations of front, back, and side placement.) The open part of each circle represents the featured, or front, side of the object.*

We suggest that each orientation reflects how the object ordinarily is held in play. Bugs and vehicles are grasped by the sides and pushed laterally, probably because small, wheeled toys are more comfortably played with this way. Dolls and chairs, however, more often are played with face to face. These characteristic orientations also may reflect the children's attempts to maximize information about the object, a possibility suggested by research on the orientation of objects in drawings. Rovet and Ives (1976) asked 273 children between nursery school (2–4 years) and eleventh grade, and 44 adults, to draw pictures of a man, house, owl, horse, boat, and car. The majority of 2- and 3-year-olds' drawings were nonrepresentational scribbles, though of the substantial minority who drew a recognizable man (45%) and owl (31%), all showed the facing orientation. By age 5 or 6, all the children made drawings with identifiable orientations, showing the man, house, and owl mainly in the facing view, and horse, boat, and car mainly in the face-to-side view. These orientations exactly parallel, for comparable objects, the characteristic orientations of our children's placements. (We expect the same would be true for a sculpturing task—that

TABLE II

Number of Children (N = 80) Showing Various Self-referent Placement
Patterns for Each Type of "Featured" Object[a]

Placement pattern	Dolls	Bugs	Vehicles	Chairs
Facing	48	11	10	38
Lined up	18	15	13	17
Face to side	0	24	32	6
Other	14	30	25	19

[a] From Harris and Strommen (1972, Experiment 2).

the horse or boat would be worked on from the side, the house or person from the front.)

Rovet and Ives suggested that these orientations are used because they provide maximum information about a referent in the static, two-dimensional graphic medium. Following Arnheim (1974, p. 117), they suggest that a horse is not easily recognizable if pictured from the front view because in this view the information about its tail and mane and its four legs cannot be easily represented. Rosch, Mervis, Gray, Johnson, and Boyes-Braem (1976) attribute similar findings about imagined orientations of objects to maximization of information relevant for assigning objects to categories.

It may be, then, that both the way an object is used and the way in which critical information about it is best represented influence its orientation in a front–back placement. Consequently, the very definitions of *front* and *back* become tied both to use and to effectiveness in conveying information for orientation in relation to other objects and perhaps for other components of these definitions as well. Indeed, we think use and information conveyed are closely linked because both are manifestations of fundamental attributes of the object, namely, whether the greater number of distinctive features lies along the vertical or the longitudinal planes. Thus people, owls, and houses are "vertical" figures, and our typical interactions with them are face to face. Horses, boats, and cars are "longitudinal" figures. When we relate to them (get information about them or get onto or into them) it is typically from the side.

B. THE ISSUE OF EGOCENTRIC RESPONDING

If the earliest use of front–back labels does begin with children's own bodies, it might be characterized as egocentric. Whether there are other ways in which children's understanding of front and back may reflect egocentrism has interested a number of researchers. Here, however, responses that are egocentric in Piaget's original sense of the term must be distinguished from responses that are deictically based. In linguistics, *deixis* refers to dependence of word meaning on situation—for example, the referent of the pronoun *I* depends upon who is speaking. Accordingly, Miller and Johnson-Laird (1976) call self-referential knowledge of spatial terms the "deictic system," i.e., the "space relative to a speaker's egocentric origin and coordinate axes . . . in the deictic system, spatial terms are interpreted relative to intrinsic parts of ego" (p. 396).

Miller and Johnson-Laird contrast the deictic system with the "intrinsic system" wherein spatial terms are "interpreted relative to coordinate axes derived fron intrinsic parts of the referent itself" (p. 396). Even 3-year-olds often can use either intrinsic or deictic cues for front and back appropriately in simple situations (Leehey & Carey, 1978).

We find the label *intrinsic* confusing here because it is also part of the definition of *deictic*; ego, like other objects, has intrinsic front–back parts. We therefore shall use the term *object-referent* to refer to the understanding of spatial relationships among objects external to ego or self. For consistency, we also shall use the term *self-referential* instead of *deictic*.

The ego-based responses described above are hardly egocentric in Piaget's original sense of the term, however. *Egocentrism* in this sense refers to failure to differentiate one's own experience of some object or event from the object or event itself. That even young children can shift appropriately from object-referent to self-referential cues indicates that self-referential responses, though based in the self, do not reflect lack of differentiation of experience but simply use of one of two available types of cues.

Are there any types of front–back judgments made by children which do reflect egocentrism in the sense of nondifferentiation? Children might define front, back, and beside egocentrically by placing an object on different sides of a featured object but always in the same location in relation to themselves regardless of the orientation of the other object: "in front" and "in back" on the near and far sides relative to themselves, "beside" to their own left or right of the object. Such responding occurs but only rarely, at least in children over 5 years of age. Of 304 children tested in our Experiments 3, 4, and 16, only two consistently made such placements.

We also have been impressed by the high regularity in the children's responses and have wondered whether this regularity may not also reflect egocentrism. We noted that there are at least two sets of cues (self- and other referent) to which children might respond in making judgments of front and back. Yet the children appear to fix unhesitatingly on one set, as though it never occurred to them to ask, "Front (or back, or side) from whose point of view?" As we shall see, object-referent cues, when present, dominate self-referent cues, which may account for the apparent lack of conflict between potentially competing sets of cues. However, inability to shift from a first-chosen basis for responding to other available bases for responding may be one manifestation of egocentric thinking. Our observations suggest that adults are much more likely than children to hesitate, ask questions, or otherwise show recognition that more than one response base is available. Leehey (1973) also noted that her 4-year-olds never showed such recognition, whereas her adult subjects frequently did so.

From these reports, egocentrism appears to have at most a minor influence on children's performance on tasks reflecting understanding of "in front," "in back," and "beside."

IV. Knowing the Intrinsic Front and Back of Featured Objects

If the body is the key to the major systems of spatial coordinates, then knowledge of the front-back planes of the body should be requisite to recognition of the front and back of other featured objects. Kuczaj and Maratsos (1975) applied a Guttman scaleogram analysis to their children's performance and it bore out this expectation. In their touch task, children were asked to touch the front and back of various featured objects. This task (see Table III) proved more difficult than placing objects in relation to self (compare Table I). Also relevant are Leehey and Carey's (1978) data, shown in Table III. Their subjects (2:1–3:3) made fewer errors pointing to their own fronts than to the fronts of other objects (they were not asked to place objects in relation to other objects). Because Kuczaj and Maratsos' data are reported for age groups, while Leehey and Carey's are reported for performance groups, they are not exactly comparable. However, performance improved with age in both studies and was already at high levels by 38 months.

At this point let us introduce a recurrent issue. How a researcher interprets children's knowledge of front and back depends upon how the question is asked. We mentioned that children who failed Leehey and Carey's linguistic task (intermediates and failers in Table III) could nonetheless use front-back axes to orient objects in a parade or to "talk to each other." Here, a functional use of front-back axes precedes ability to label these axes. In contrast, Golumb (1972) asked 125 children 2 to 6 years of age to make a series of objects from modeling clay. For human figures, pre-nursery-school children (2:4–3:4) made only undifferentiated blobs; no identifiable front-back dimension was represented. Less than half of

TABLE III

Mean Percentage Correct Responses in Tasks Requiring
Touching or Pointing to the Fronts and Backs[a] of Featured Objects

	Age of child (years and months)	Front	Back
Kuczaj and Maratsos (1975)	2:6–3:1	64.2	61.7
	3:2–3:6	75.0	78.3
	3:7–4:1	93.3	94.2
Leehey and Carey (1978)	Passers (mean 3:2)	93.0	100.0
	Intermediates (mean 2:11)	14.0	93.0
	Failers (mean 2:9)	12.0	9.0

[a] Note: Beside was not tested.

nursery-school children (3:3–4:5) showed this differentiation. Similarly, Rovet and Ives (1976) reported that from 55% to 100% of drawings by 2- and 3-year-olds, and up to 53% of drawings by 4- and 5-year-olds, were unrecognizable depending upon the object being drawn. Where drawings were recognizable, nearly all the preschoolers' drawings and the majority of the kindergartners' drawing showed face views. In comparison, more than half of the youngest children performing Kuczaj and Maratsos' touch task responded correctly, and the average ages of Leehey and Carey's passers and intermediates were 3:2 and 2:11, respectively. The age discrepancies in these studies very likely reflect the differences in task demands, since representation was required for the modeling and drawing tasks but not for the point and touching tasks.

V.   Object–Reference System: Relation of Objects to Each Other

The available data suggest that only after children know the intrinsic fronts of featured objects can they successfully place such objects in relation to each other. Relevant evidence comes from several laboratories (see Table IV). Most investigators have used quite similar tasks, requiring subjects to place a mobile object in front of, in back of, or beside another object.

A.   STUDIES WITH "STANDARD" TASKS

Kuczaj and Maratsos (1975) asked their children to place a doll in front of, in back of, and beside each of the same objects used in their touch task. There was regular improvement across the three age groups, with front and back at the same level and with beside trailing slightly.

Other investigations provide additional data on age differences in performance on relational tasks (Table IV). Hodun (1975) tested 24 children between ages 2:3 and 3:9. She gave her children various small objects to place in relation to six different featured objects, such as a toy desk. The results fit roughly with the chronology shown in Table IV. Though her children seemed to have had more difficulty than the children in the other studies listed, the older children were superior to the younger.

In experiment 3, we asked children older than those tested by Hodun (4:9–7.5) to place featured objects in relation to each other. The results indicate that this aspect of comprehension of in front of, in back of, and beside is well established at least by about 5 years of age.

Finally, Sinha and Walkerdine (1973) gave a similar placement task to

TABLE IV

Mean Percentage Correct Responses for Featured Objects
in Relation to Each Other

	Age of child (years and months)	N	Front	Back	Beside
Kuczaj and Maratsos (1975)	2:6–3:1	15	46.7	40.8	34.2
	3:2–3:6	15	55.8	57.5	40.8
	3:7–4:1	15	86.7	86.7	75.8
Hodun (1975)[a]	2:3–3:0	12	9	6.25	0
			(37.0)	(35.0)	(0)
	3:1–3:9	12	73.0	9.0	38.0
			(88.0)	(65.0)	(50.0)
Sinha and Walkerdine (1973)	3:6	16	22.0	21.0	46.0
	5:0	16	100	100	100
	Adults				
Harris and Strommen (Experiment 3)	4:9–6:1		100	100	100
	6:2–7:5		100	100	100
Goodglass *et al.* (1970)	3:4	30	63	67	77
	5:0	11	73	91	82
	6:0	11	100	100	100
	7:0	23	100	96	100
	8:0	19	100	100	100
	9:0	11	100	100	100

[a] The numbers in parenthesis are for a reinforced search procedure; see Section V, B.

children at both extremes of the age range we have been discussing. Children as young as 1:6 showed virtually no comprehension, while 5-year-olds' comprehension was perfect. Children of age 3:6, however, were correct only about 20% of the time for front and back, and near 50% for beside. These results are sufficiently different from those reported by other workers to raise the possibility of procedural or criterial differences among these studies.

Kuczaj and Maratsos' scaleogram analysis supports the hypothesis that development of the object-referent system depends on prior knowledge of the front and back of other objects, since their doll placement task was more difficult than their touch task. Another investigator, however, found no difference between knowing the intrinsic fronts and backs of objects and being able to place objects in spatial relationship to each other. Bialystock (1976) tested 48 children between ages 3:2 and 4:11. Her test of recognition of the front and back of a featured object seems roughly equivalent to Kuczaj and Maratsos' touch task—the children were told to place a self-adhesive dot "on the front" and "on the back" of a wood block, a bottle, and a toy car. The children also were asked to place a wood

star "in front of" and "behind" each of these same objects. Mean performance did not differ significantly between the two tasks for either front or
back; that is, the two kinds of skills appeared to have been acquired
simultaneously. Bialystock nevertheless argues that knowing the front actually came first, since something cannot be placed in front of something
else that has a front unless one knows where the front side is. Bialystock,
however, argued that the other-relational skill is acquired very soon after
the recognition skill, and that acquisition of the recognition skill immediately facilitates acquisition of the relational skill and creates the appearance of simultaneous acquisition. These results must be interpreted
with caution, because Bialystock did not separately analyze scores for the
car, which was featured, and the nonfeatured block and bottle. This distinction is important, as we shall see.

B.   ALTERNATIVE PROCEDURES

Bialystock's results, like Sinha and Walkerdine's, reinforce the notion
that procedural or criterial differences may be relevant to many questions
about understanding of front and back. The importance of procedure is
demonstrated in further experiments by Hodun (1975) and by Goodglass,
Gleason, and Hyde (1970). Hodun retested her children with a reinforced-
search task. Instead of having the child place an object in a given location,
the child had to locate an object that had been hidden in a given location;
the child was rewarded with candy for correct answers. This procedure is
analogous to an object-referent placement procedure in that the child now
must locate an object that has already been placed in relation to another
object. Performance clearly improved with this procedure (see Table IV,
scores in parenthesis).

Another procedure that depends more on recognition than on production is to have the child match a picture depicting objects in spatial relationship to each other to a verbal description. Goodglass *et al.* (1970; and J.
Berko-Gleason, personal communication, 1975) used this procedure to test
the understanding of directional prepositions in normal children from 3:4
to 9:0 years of age. The data for directional prepositions appropriate for
our interests are summarized in Table IV. Again, there is a rough fit with
the previous data, indicating complete mastery by about 6 years of age. The
one discrepant finding is the substantially higher score among the youngest
children for *in back* (93% correct) compared with *behind* (67%). One reason might be that *back* is the more common term for both children and
adults (Jones & Wepman, 1966; Lorge, 1949; Rinsland, 1945). In addition,
the fact that *back* is a homonym may facilitate its acquisition.

What is the significance of the different procedures? Presumably, the use of Hodun's reinforced-search procedure would show that the understanding of spatial locatives appears earlier. Thus, in the case of the self-referent system, which we have suggested develops before the object-referent system, children who fail to place an object in back of themselves may well succeed if instructed to find an object that is "in back of you."

Hodun's data do not imply that the acquisition order itself necessarily would change with procedural changes—rather, the absolute age of acquisition would change. If one's primary research goal is to discern the earliest appearance of the child's comprehension of spatial locatives, the reinforced-search procedure of Hodun and the recognition procedure of Goodglass *et al.* look to us like the methods of choice; for other research goals, other procedures might be equally good or even preferable.

VI. Does the Face or the Body Specify the Front?

We earlier remarked on the many cues distinguishing the front from the back of the body. This difference is more critically specified by some cues than others. Fillmore (1971) emphasized the eyes, arguing that for all animate beings except the least complex, the front is that portion containing the main organs of perception. Apparently, kindergarten-age children agree, for when we asked them, "How can you tell your front from your back?" they usually emphasized the eyes, nose, and mouth. For stationary objects, such as houses, Leech (1970) has made the further proposal that the front is "that part . . . usually exposed to observation" (p. 167). For the (nonstationary) human being, this seems to be so in the case of observation of self as well. Besides naming body features, our kindergartners in Experiments 2 and 3 frequently added that they could see the front but not the back. Some children helpfully demonstrated the difficulty of seeing the back by craning their necks. The results of the self-referent placements in our Experiment 2 also are consistent with both Fillmore's and Leech's proposals. Recall our speculation that the different placement patterns (see Fig. 1 and Table II) reflected characteristic play styles with toys as well as attempts to maximize information about the objects. The predominant pattern used for dolls—facing pattern—also represents the potential for social interaction. The greater salience of the face than the body in social interaction further supports the idea that the front, in the case of human figures, is specified by the face side.

An alternative view might be that it is the positions of the organs of locomotion, rather than the organs of perception, that are the most critical specifiers of front. The two kinds of cues nearly always are in harmony— for biologically practical reasons, animals are so designed with their main perceptual organs and organs of locomotion on the same side. Among other advantages, this design makes for greater efficiency in obtaining food. Fillmore (1971) saw an instructive exception in the crab, which we describe as moving sideways rather than having a head (or eyes) on the side of its body. Fillmore also speculated that a race of people who moved as people move in reverse motion pictures would be said to walk backward, not to have faces on the backs of their heads. Fillmore concluded from these examples that for animals, the location of the main perceptual organs outweighs the direction-of-motion criterion.

One way to determine which dimension—organs of perception as represented in the face, or organs of locomotion as represented in the body—is the more important cue for front would be to set the two dimensions into competition. The dolls we used in Experiments 2 and 3 always looked straight ahead, so from those experiments we cannot assume the primacy of the face as the defining feature of the spatial concept "in front." In Experiment 4, we therefore set face and body cues in competition with each other by using dolls with moveable heads.

The subjects were 80 5- to 10-year-olds (40 boys and 40 girls, average ages 6:8 and 6:9 years, respectively). Each child made a series of in front, in back, and beside placements with the dolls, following the procedure of our earlier experiment. For each subject, the stationary doll was presented in 12 different orientation/face–body alignment combinations: with the head facing in the same direction as, to the right of, and to the left of the doll's body; with the doll's body oriented toward, away from, to the right of, and to the left of the child. The order in which the child saw a given alignment/orientation of the stationary doll was randomized. The mobile doll's face–body alignment was constant for any given child, being in convergent alignment for half the subjects, looking to its right for one-fourth, and to its left for the remaining one-fourth. In this experiment, we chose not to include a biologically impossible condition wherein the doll's head is turned 180 degrees. We wanted to study children's judgments only of situations that have real-life counterparts.

The results were clear. At all ages, body cues of the stationary doll were the main basis for the locations of all placements. (Orientation of the mobile doll was also influenced by face cues of the mobile doll itself, as we shall see in Section XI, A.) Where, for example, the body of the stationary doll faced away (as shown in Fig. 2) the children uniformly located their in front placements on the far side of the stationary doll, their in back placements on the near side, and their beside placements to either the right or the left, regardless of the face–body alignment of either doll. (Figure 2 illustrates one orientation of the stationary doll and two of the possible combinations of head–body alignments of the stationary and mobile doll.)

Within these locations, children made the same types of patterns of orientations for objects placed in relation to each other as they did for objects placed in relation to themselves (compare Figs. 1 and 2). In both Experiments 3 and 4, children made both lined-up and facing patterns (see Fig. 2). The face-to-side pattern, which we supposed was peculiar to wheeled toys because of how they are used in play, was frequent in Experiment 3, where children placed cars and trucks in relation to each other, but was rare in Experiment 4. Instead, in Experiment 4, a new combined pattern appeared, in which the mobile doll faced the stationary doll in the front position but faced the same direction as the stationary doll in the back and side positions. The lined-up pattern accounted for a majority of the placements in both Experiments 3 and 4, though not so great a majority in Experiment 4 (61% vs. 86%). Of the remainder in Experiment 4, the combined pattern accounted for 14%, the facing pattern for 10%, and the rest took a variety of irregular forms.

Why the predominance of the lined-up pattern? This is how we see many things arranged, whether they are people seated in an auditorium, cars in traffic, or cans on a grocer's shelf. The lined-up pattern also constitutes the most symmetrical arrangement of the dolls, and symmetrical arrangements

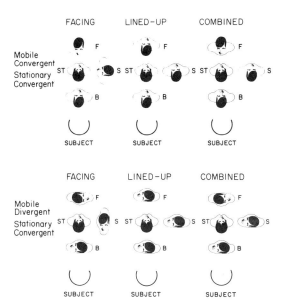

Fig. 2. *Examples of placement patterns on object-referent trials for two head–body alignment conditions of the mobile doll. (ST refers to stationary doll; F, B, and S represent front, back, and side locations of mobile doll. Subject faces in the direction of the open side of the circle.)*

are preferred in a variety of tasks (cf. Harris & Schaller, 1971; Paraskev-opoulos, 1968; Schaller & Harris, 1975).

The combined and facing patterns also reflect frequently occurring locations of bodies, though the front placements might instead represent locations for social interaction. For most kinds of social interaction, people stand with their bodies oriented toward each other rather than front to back. Indeed, some children, upon making their front placement, remarked that the dolls could see or talk with each other.

So the body of the stationary doll was the predominant cue, and where placements took account of the face, it was without violating the body's priority. For instance, because the stationary doll sometimes looked to its right or left, children could use any of the body-based patterns but shift their beside placements from right to left according to the direction of the stationary doll's face—and many children did this.

In Fig. 3, each set of beside placements shown would have been made by the same subject; judgment of use of face cue depended on comparing the placements within each set. In the examples shown, the stationary doll is looking to her left; the mobile doll is looking straight ahead. Where sets of placements were judged to reflect the use of face cues, the location of the mobile doll shifted from side to side, either to maintain face contact (top row) or to avoid face contact (middle row). Where the location of the

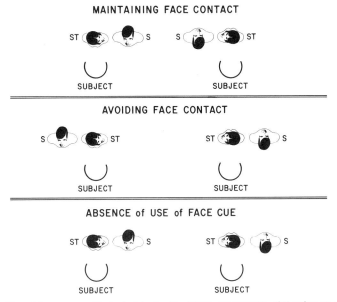

Fig. 3. Use of face cue as illustrated by beside ("S") placements. (ST refers to stationary doll.)

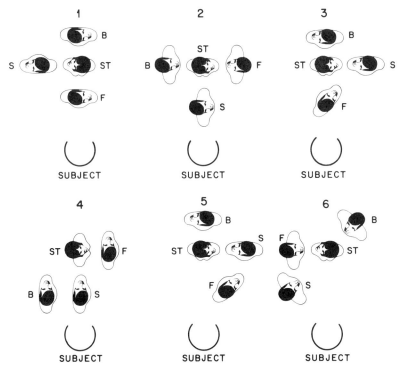

Fig. 4. Examples of irregular patterns reflecting use of face cues. (ST refers to stationary doll; F, front; B, back; S, side.)

mobile doll did not shift (bottom row), it was judged to reflect the absence of use of the face cue.

Other evidence of use of face cues came from the irregular patterns, some of which are illustrated in Fig. 4. Many of these patterns deviate from the regular patterns in ways that seem to stem from conflict between face and body as spatial cues resolved either in favor of face cues or in favor of some face–body combination. For example, in pattern 2, the locations of all three placements seem to have been determined by the head orientation of the stationary doll. Indeed, this pattern when categorized on the basis of face rather than body cues becomes the combined pattern. In pattern 6, the location of the front placement appears to be in response only to the face of the stationary doll, while the locations and orientations of the beside and behind placements appear to be attempts to effect a compromise between face and body cues. Of the total of 960 patterns, 150 were irregular. Of these, 80 clearly reflected use of face cues, and only 29 clearly failed to reflect such use. The remaining 41 patterns were ambiguous.

We found no age differences between the youngest and oldest children in this experiment. Whether among still younger children the same priority of the body holds is a question for further study.

We note that in this experiment, we did not actually have the dolls move, since we assumed (as Fillmore also would have to) that the position of the body would indicate the potential direction of movement. With this qualification, and the qualification that we did not include the biologically unnatural condition wherein head and body face in opposite directions, our results indicate—contrary to those of Fillmore (1971)—that the body, and by implication the organs of locomotion, primarily defines the front of an organism.

It seems likely that the body defines the front of a person because heads are mobile relative to bodies. This intrinsically greater mobility makes head movements more frequent and unpredictable than body movements. If the head were the basis for a labeling system that described spatial relations among persons, two people sitting beside each other would have to be said to change their spatial position with respect to each other each time their heads change orientation. The numerous and often momentary changes would result in a cumbersome and complex labeling system indeed.

VII. Generalization of Understanding of Front and Back to Novel Stimuli

In addition to learning the fronts and backs of familiar objects whose fronts and backs are richly and redundantly specified, children, and adults also, should be able to generalize these concepts to things they have never seen before to the extent that these novel objects possess the same kinds of differentiating front-back characteristics. So children may identify the fronts and backs of novel objects according to how they are used, the asymmetrical patternings of cues, or both, if we assume that children learn such principles through experience with familiar objects with front-back features. Because such generalization logically depends on identification of the fronts and backs of familiar objects, it should come later.

Kuczaj and Maratsos' (1975) developmental study provides data relevant to this question with respect to generalization based on functional cues. They designed two "nonsense" machines. For instance, the "gumdrop" machine had gadgets on two adjacent outside walls and nothing on the remaining two adjacent walls. Children manipulated the gadgets on one of the featured walls in order to "make a gumdrop." After using each machine, the children were asked on separate trials to "go touch the front" (or back) from a location several feet away. Even the youngest children frequently identified the side they had used as the front, and this tendency increased with age. As expected, these generalization tasks were harder than tasks that required locating the front, back, or side of familiar intrinsically featured objects or placing such objects in spatial relation to one another.

A. MINIMAL FEATURES SPECIFYING FRONT: ADULTS' RESPONSES

Kuczaj and Maratsos' children concluded that the side they used was the front. However, because physical and functional cues were confounded, the questions still remain: Can opposite, asymmetrical sides alone specify a front-back axis, and will children respond to such physical cues? We have made a first attempt to answer this question in two studies done in collaboration with Suzanne P. Marshall (Seimerling). The subjects were college students and the test stimuli were 3-in. squares printed on 8-in. square sheets of paper. In Experiment 5, appended to each square were either one or two ¼-in. circles, attached so as to generate four asymmetrical forms (numbers 1–4, Fig. 5), and two symmetrical forms (numbers 5 and 6, Fig. 6). Each subject judged only one form in only one orientation (location of feature relative to the subject). Since orientations had little effect on the subjects' judgments, data have been combined over orientations for each form.

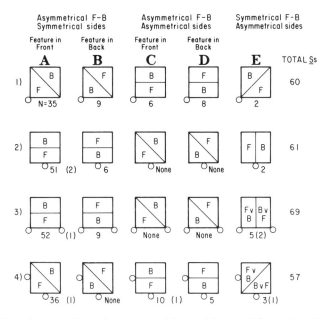

Fig. 5. *Front-back locations of asymmetrical featured forms, all four orientations for each form combined.* (N = 251: F, front; B, back; F v B, front for some subjects, back for others.) *Numbers in parentheses indicate subjects who drew a separating line but did not name the front and back sections.*

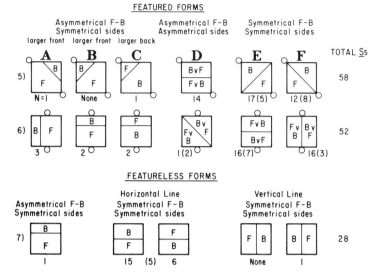

Fig. 6. *Front-back locations of symmetrical control forms for undergraduate subjects, both orientations combined, for forms 5 and 6. (See Fig. 5 for explanatory comments.)*

The subjects were instructed to look at the "geometric form" as though they were looking down on it from above, to draw a straight line to separate the front part of the form from the back part, and then to name the front and back. Ninety percent (324) of the 361 undergraduates complied with both parts of the instruction.

The different kinds of judgments made for the different forms are illustrated in Figs. 5 and 6. In Fig. 5, all dividing lines bisect the form. A few subjects drew their lines so as to create unequal areas, but in every case the divisions were of the same "family" as the ones shown here. In Fig. 6 all such unequal-area divisions are shown, since this represented the only way in which asymmetrical front-back sections could be produced for these forms.

First, did the subjects divide the forms so as to create asymmetrical front-back sections while preserving symmetry for these sections' sides? Second, did the subjects making this division then call the section containing the feature the "front," the section lacking the feature the "back"? In Table V, data pertaining to the first and second questions are summarized in columns 1 and 2, respectively. For forms 1–4, the answer to both questions is Yes. The subjects evidently used a symmetry principle both to identify the front-back axis and to differentiate front from back. For control forms 5 and 6 (Fig. 6) no bisecting line can make sections with only one section containing both circles. Asymmetrical front-back sections with symmetrical sides can be created only by drawing lines creating unequal-area front-back sections. Only 11 (10%) of the 110 subjects assigned forms 5

TABLE V

Summary of Distinction and Statistical Evaluations of Subjects' Judgments of Forms Shown in Figs. 5 and 6[a]

Form number	1. Did subjects divide forms into asymmetrical front-back sections with symmetrical sides? (Solutions A and B vs. solutions C, D, and E, Figs. 5 and 6.)				2. Given solutions A and B, is front on the featured side? (Solution A vs. solution B, Figs. 5 and 6.)[b]			
	Yes	No	χ^{2c}	p	Yes	No	χ^{2c}	p
1	44	16	23.07	.061	35	9	7.68	.01
2	59	2	53.26	.001	51	6	35.53	.001
3	62	7	43.84	.001	52	9	30.3	.001
4	37	20	2.77	>.05	36	1	33.11	.001
5	2	56	50.28	.001	1	1	<1	
6	7	45	27.77	.001	3	4	<1	

[a] From Harris and Strommen (1974).
[b] Subjects failing to label the sections are not included here.
[c] Note: all χ^2's have 1 df.

and 6 did so. Of the 11, front was the larger section in seven cases. Of the remaining subjects, 81 created symmetrical front–back sections with symmetrical sides (5E, 5F, 6E, and 6F), while 17 created sections with both asymmetrical front–back sections and sides (5D and 6D).[4]

Having established that for forms with one or two protruding features, front and back are asymmetric opposite sides with the featured side the front, we next asked, in Experiment 6, whether the asymmetric opposite sides will define the front–back axis for any design regardless of how its asymmetry is generated. Eleven different forms were used (Fig. 7). Each of 30 undergraduates made four judgments of each form, one judgment in each of the four cardinal orientations, for a total of 44 judgments.

The variety of designs assured that, from one judgment to another, the subject could not rely on a characteristic in any absolute way but instead had to use a common principle. Front is separated from back by drawing a line parallel to two opposing, different sides. The results are summarized in Fig. 7 and in Table VI. Over the 11 forms, in all but one instance (form 10—and for only one orientation of form 10), the students located front and back along the axis of asymmetry (solutions A and B; column 1, Table VI). The students evidently were using a principle of asymmetry regardless of how the asymmetry is produced or how the form is oriented.

Given solutions A or B, was the "odd" section designated the front? For forms 1, 2, 7, 9, 10, and 11, it was: A significant majority of students designated the odd side as front regardless of whether the "odd" side was generated by an external feature (forms 1 and 2) or the absence of a feature (forms 7 and 9). The results for forms 3, 4, 5, and 6 were equivocal, since the odd side was named the front only slightly more than half the time. In general, "front" appears to be the focal point of the form, the side toward which attention is drawn; and the focal point may or may not be on the odd side. Evidently, this focal point can be created through either the presence or the absence of a feature depending on the form's particular design. The results also suggest that an internal feature—forms 3, 4, and 5—is not so effective a focal point as an external feature.

B. MINIMAL FEATURES SPECIFYING FRONT: CHILDREN'S RESPONSES

We find that adults use a principle of asymmetry to identify front-back axes of unfamiliar forms and designate as front the odd section, particularly when it contains a focal point. Can children do the same? Some rele-

---

[4] Afterwards, we asked the students to explain their judgments. Those who judged forms 1–4 most often said that the nonsense form resembled a familiar object (27.6%) or mentioned the feature (31%). Evidently many more of the students were able to use the asymmetry principle than were able to articulate it: Only 5% of those judging forms 1–4, and 9% of those judging other forms, mentioned symmetry in their judgments.

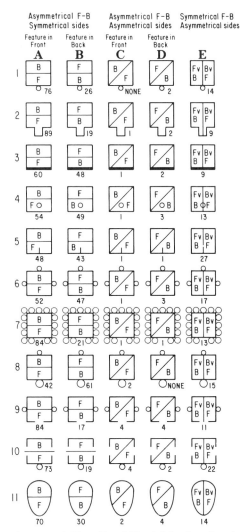

Fig. 7. Number of judgments of "front" and "back" in given locations for 11 different forms, 120 judgments per form except when subjects failed to make a judgment. (F, front; B, back; F v B, front for some subjects, back for others.)

vant data come from a study by Eiser (1975). The subjects were 22 first graders (mean age 6:9), 22 fourth graders (mean 9:7), and 22 seventh graders (mean 12:6). The children saw 10 abstract forms identical to forms used in our college studies. In Table VII, forms 1–7 and 9–10 refer to the same-numbered forms in Fig. 7. Form 8 is the same as form 3 in Fig. 5. The child judged each form once in only one of the four cardinal orientations. They were instructed to mark the "front" of each form. The first graders

TABLE VI

Summary of Distributions and Statistical Evaluations of Subjects' Judgment of Forms Shown in Fig. 7

Form number	1. Did subjects divide forms into asymmetrical front-back sections with symmetrical sides? (Solutions A and B vs. solutions C, D, and E.)				2. Given solutions A and B, is front on "odd" (usually featured) side? (Solution A vs. solution B.)			
	Yes	No	χ^2	p	Yes (solution A)	No (solution B)	χ^2	p
1	24–27	3–6	10.8–19.2	<.01	18–22[a]	2–9	3.0–16.7	>.05–<.01[b]
2	26–28	2–4	16.1–22.5	<.01	22–23	4–5	10.7–12.5	<.01
3	26–28	2–4	16.1–22.5	<.01	14–16	11–13	<1.0	NS[c]
4	24–27	3–6	10.8–19.2	<.01	13–14	11–14	<1.0	NS
5	21–24	6–9	4.8–10.8	<.05	11–13	10–12	<1–1.6	NS
6	23–26	4–7	8.5–16.1	<.01	11–12	12–14	<1	NS
7	25–28	2–5	13.3–22.5	<.01	20–22	4–6	7.5–12.5	<.01
8	25–27	3–5	13.3–19.2	<.01	7–14	13–18	<1–4.84	NS–.05[d]
9	24–27	3–6	10.8–19.2	>.01	19–22	3–5	8.2–14.4	<.01
10	20–26	4–10	3.3–16.3	<.05–.01[b]	16–22	3–8	3.2–12.5	>.05–<.01[b]
11	24–26	4–6	10.8–16.1	>.01	17–19	5–9	2.5–8.2	>.05–<.01[b]

[a] Separate groups of subjects saw each form in each of the four cardinal orientations. Data reported are the ranges of numbers of subjects over the four groups for each form who made the designated response (Yes column), who failed to make the designated response (No column), and the ranges of χ^2 comparing Yes vs. No over the four groups for the given form.

[b] One of the four contrasts was statistically nonsignificant.

[c] NS = Not significant.

[d] Only one of the four contrasts was statistically significant.

TABLE VII

Front–Back Judgments of Featured forms by First-, Fourth-, and Seventh-grade children[a,b]

		A Front	B Back	C Other			A Front	B Back	C Other
Form 1					Form 6				
Grade	1A	18.2	18.2	63.60	Grade	1A	36.4	31.8	31.8
	1	22.7	40.9	36.40		1	54.5	9.1	36.4
	4	81.8	4.5	13.7		4	54.5	18.2	27.3
	7	81.8	18.2	0.0		7	50.0	31.8	18.2
Form 2					Form 7				
Grade	1A	45.5	18.2	36.3	Grade	1A	31.8	27.3	40.9
	1	22.7	22.7	54.6		1	18.2	9.1	72.7
	4	27.3	4.5	68.2		4	6.36	13.6	22.8
	7	90.9	9.1	0.0		7	72.7	18.2	9.1
Form 3					Form 8				
Grade	1A	18.2	27.7	54.10	Grade	1A	9.1	22.7	68.2
	1	31.8	18.2	50.0		1	22.7	22.7	54.6
	4	59.1	22.7	18.2		4	45.5	13.6	40.9
	7	77.3	22.7	0.0		7	81.8	13.6	4.6
Form 4					Form 9				
Grade	1A	36.4	36.4	27.2	Grade	1A	18.2	36.4	45.4
	1	31.8	13.6	54.6		1	18.2	9.1	72.7
	4	54.5	22.7	22.8		4	45.5	13.6	40.9
	7	72.7	27.3	0.0		7	72.7	9.1	18.2
Form 5					Form 10				
Grade	1A	27.3	18.2	54.5	Grade	1A	40.9	36.4	22.7
	1	4.5	22.7	72.8		1	27.3	45.5	27.20
	4	54.5	13.6	31.9		4	63.6	22.7	13.70
	7	54.5	31.8	13.7		7	81.8	18.2	0.00

[a] Adapted from Eiser (1975).

[b] Note: Forms 1–7 and 9–10 refer to the same-numbered forms in Fig. 7. Form 8 is the same as form 3 in Fig. 5.

177

tended to select as the front the side occurring on the right-hand side of the page, possibly because demonstration examples used were blackboard pictures of real fronted objects facing to the subjects' right. As a control, a second group of first graders (1-A, mean age 6:6) was tested after seeing two examples, one oriented to the left and one to the top of the blackboard.

Columns A and B in Table VII include childen who placed front and back along the axis of asymmetry. Column C ("other") shows the proportion of children in each group who did not use the axis of asymmetry. The seventh graders chose the asymmetrical axis nearly all the time (over all forms, mean = 93.6%). First graders, in contrast, showed no consistent tendency to choose the axis of asymmetry (mean = 51.1%). Fourth graders were in between (mean = 70%).

As for whether children chose the odd side as front, Eiser (1975) reported analyses of variance showing that the number of children choosing the odd side as the front increased significantly with age. A similar analysis for choice of the odd side as back showed no change with age. Column A of Table VII shows the proportion of children in each grade who designated the odd side as front. First graders showed no systematic preference of choices within the axis of asymmetry, which is expected given that they did not respond consistently to the axis of asymmetry in the first place.

For fourth and seventh graders, the choice of the featured side as front is clear and consistent. For seventh graders, such choices were indeed made more consistently for nine of the 10 forms than had been true for the college students in our studies. One wonders whether Eiser's seventh graders were demonstrating overregularization of a perceptual principle in the same way that young children overregularize syntactic rules (e.g., Berko-Gleason, 1958). In the case of syntax, the responses of older individuals are more variable because of their greater familiarity (sophistication?) with irregular forms. With respect to front and back, the greater variability of adults' responses likewise may reflect more experience with objects whose fronts are located atypically. As for the first graders' failure to use the asymmetry principle, we should recall that the fronts and backs of realistic, familiar objects are usually multiply determined, in contrast to the minimal featured abstract forms used in these studies. Children may need more cue redundancy than adults do. If so, even first graders might respond to an axis of asymmetry in more richly featured novel objects.

VIII. Motion as Cue for Front–Back

We earlier have noted that direction of motion can specify the front-back axis, and we have suggested that human beings may be predisposed to expect movement in any bilaterally symmetrical object along the asymmetric axis. Consequently, if the geometric forms are perceived as having fronts and backs, we also might tend to see them move along the asymmetrical axis and in the direction of the featured, or face, side.

A. LOCATION OF FEATURE AND IMAGINED MOVEMENT

In Experiment 7, we tested this idea by showing forms 1 and 2 from Experiment 6 (Fig. 5) in all four cardinal orientations to 199 undergraduates, each of whom made one judgment for only one form in one orientation. Cover sheets initially hid the forms from view. The students were asked to imagine that the drawing was moving on the page and to mark, with an arrow, the apparent direction of movement "at the very moment you look at it."

A control group of 44 more undergraduates was shown a plain square. Presumably, reports of imagined movement by these students would reflect any predispositions to imagine movements in any particular direction in the absence of a feature that created asymmetry in the form.

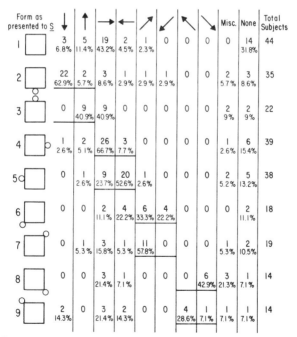

Fig. 8. *Number and percentage of subjects reporting direction of movement "seen" for a featureless form (form 1, judged by 44 subjects) and for two different featured forms, each in the four cardinal orientations (forms 2–5 and 6–9, judged by 199 undergraduates each making one judgment of one form). Underscored numbers are those cases in which direction of "seen" movement is congruent with the axis specified by the feature.*

The distribution of judgments is shown in Fig. 8. Of the 44 control subjects, only 14 (31.8%) reported no movement of the form compared with 22 (11.1%) of the 199 students shown the featured forms ($z = 3.51$, $p < .0005$). So movement is significantly easier to imagine with a feature than without. Nonetheless, 30 of the 44 control subjects (68.2%) reported movement without the feature. Of these, 19 reported rightward movement, suggesting a predisposition to see rightward movement in the absence of any explicit directional marker.

There also was some evidence of this tendency to perceive rightward movement in Experiment 6 in the case of form 11 (the oval). The tapered end failed to be named *front* by a significant majority of students only when oriented to the subject's left. This finding may be consistent with reports of laterality differences in perception favoring left-to-right processing (e.g., Braine, 1968). These results, in any event, provide a baseline against which to measure the effect of the feature in forms 2–9.

For the featured forms, significant proportions of the students who received forms 2, 4, and 5 reported imagined movement along the axis specified by the location of the feature (see columns underscored in Fig. 8). For example, of the 35 students assigned form 2, 24—a significant majority ($p < .05$)—reported imagined movement along the vertical axis.

For form 3, the tendency for rightward movement noted in the case of form 1 apparently weakened the effect so that as many students reported rightward movement as reported upward movement. Why rightward tendency was not also so strong as downward tendency for form 2 is unclear; obviously, location of feature in the up–down plane interacts with tendency to perceive rightward motion.

For forms 2–5, direction as well as axis was specified by the feature. For example, of the 24 students who reported vertical movement for form 2, 22 reported downward movement, and two reported upward movement ($p < .0001$). The effect was weaker for forms with features located on the diagonal (forms 6–9), though the diagonal location of the feature still was influential when compared with the featureless form (form 1).

A comparison of these distributions with the distribution of front–back judgments made by the subjects in Experiments 5 and 6 thus discloses a sizeable degree of overlap. The subjects in the current experiment imagined the forms most often as moving across the page in what, on the basis of the front–back judgments in Experiments 5 and 6 by different subjects, would be called a forward direction, i.e., in the direction of the featured side.

The question may be raised whether motion—this time real motion—would specify front and back for children. Apparently it can. Leehey (1973) allowed 14 children ages 2.7–4.9 years to play with a "truck," which was a block which could move only in one direction. The children then were asked to place a button either in front or in back of the "truck." For all children, placements were in the axis of movement and on the appropriate side. Of 11 adults, 10 responded the same way. The available data therefore suggest that motion is effective or criterial very early in specifying the front-back axis.

Whether direction of motion will be dominant in multiple-cue situations, particularly when cues conflict, is not yet known. Imagine, for example, sitting, or even walking, "backwards" on a forward-moving train. When would children distinguish their body-based from the train-based referent system?

B.   POSSIBLE ROLE OF MOTION IN LEARNING OF FIRST WORDS

Moveability, or potential for motion of objects, not only may be important in specifying the spatial planes of objects but, by drawing attention to the object itself, may enhance the learning of new words generally. Some evidence for this is provided in Nelson's study (1973) of children's initial language acquisition. Nelson reported that with very few exceptions, the words that children learn first are words that refer to manipulatable or moveable objects.

If children's first words are often those for objects having these dynamic properties, and if these early names reflect their concepts about the environment with its important spatial–locational features, then it is likely that children abstract cues, such as movement or asymmetry, from these early concepts to which they can apply new labels. This kind of argument helps to account for the early learning of the front–back dimension.

IX.   Do Objects Lacking Front–Back Features Have "Fronts" and "Backs"?

We can understand how children come to identify the fronts and backs of a great variety of objects having specifiable, distinct front–back features. However, we also put drinking glasses in front of boxes, beside plates, or behind bowls; we stand behind trees, in front of boulders, and so forth. How are spatial positions specified for these featureless objects?

A.   USE OF BODY COORDINATES: THE "CANONICAL ENCOUNTER"

One suggestion, by H. Clark (1973), is that the identification of the front and back of objects lacking intrinsic fronts and backs presupposes a "canonical encounter" between the person and object:

If the speaker is looking at a ball and a fly across the room, he can say: "The fly is in front of the ball." By this he means, "The fly is between the ball and me." Since the ball has no front or back, we are forced to the following conclusion on the application of these words: the speaker treats such an object *as if* it were the other person in a canonical encounter, a person facing directly towards the speaker. Once we assume this principle of application, all sentences like "The fly is in front of the ball," "The ball is in back of the tree," etc. become applicable. (pp. 45–56)

Clark thus defined the canonical encounter as the modal position for social interaction—face to face. In an object placement study, the implied location of placement would be as shown in Fig. 9. Using Clark's criterion for correct placement, Kuczaj and Maratsos (1975) found more errors among younger children for placements of featureless objects, such as drinking glasses, than for featured objects (compare Table VIII and Table IV). Bialystock (1976) likewise found lower accuracy, using Clark's criterion, for nonfeatured objects (block, bottle) than for a featured object (toy car). Finally, for 36 4-year-old children Leehey (1973) also found much more frequent choice of the near side as front when the instruction was to point to the front and back of cubes (see Table VIII). Kuczaj and Maratsos concluded from their analysis that of the skills they tested, responding to featureless referent objects is the latest to develop.

This conclusion presupposes that the canonical encounter placement is the only correct placement. However, it is just as reasonable to conceptualize featureless objects as lined up and facing in the same direction as oneself, in which case a far-side in front placement is correct. Recall that in our Experiment 2, in which we asked kindergartners and first graders to place featured objects in relation to themselves, between 13 and 17% of the children consistently lined the objects up with their own bodies rather than facing themselves (see Table II). In further research, we found that a minority of subjects, at all ages through adulthood, prefer the lined-up, far-side in front placement for featureless objects as well.

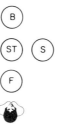

Fig. 9. Location of placement of featureless objects predicted by Clark's "canonical encounter" analysis. (See Fig. 2 for definitions of symbols.)

TABLE VIII

Percentage of Different Designations of Front, Back, and Side Nonfeatured Objects Reflected in Placements (Child Subjects) or Drawings (Adult Subjects)

	Front			Back			Beside		
	Near side	Far side	Lateral	Far side	Near side	Lateral	Lateral	Near side	Far side
Kuczaj and Maratsos (1975)[a]									
2:6–3:1 (N = 15)	21.7	?	?	22.5	?	?	22.5	?	?
3:2–3:6 (N = 15)	37.5	?	?	30.8	?	?	33.3	?	?
3:7–4:1 (N = 15)	68.3	?	?	72.5	?	?	76.7	?	?
Leehey (1973)									
4:0 (N = 36)	83	17	0	No data			No data		
Harris and Strommen (Experiment 8, children)[b]									
4:9–7:5 (N = 80)	67	26	7	67	26	7	67		33
Exp. 9, adults (N = 31)	52	19	3	52	19	1			
Exp. 10, adults (N = 30)	39	24	20	39	24	20			
Exp. 11, adults (N = 48)	25	58	17						

[a] Because only scores designated "correct" by Kuczaj and Maratsos (1975) are reported (i.e., near, far, and lateral placements for the front, back, and beside, respectively), incidence of other locations cannot be inferred, as indicated by ?.

[b] Percentages shown for Experiments 9, 10, and 11 do not sum to 100 because not all subjects completed the task.

Experiments 8-11

In Experiment 8, we had children ages 4:9-7:5 (the same children who participated in Experiments 2 and 3) make front, back, and beside placements of drinking glasses and wood cubes. As Table VIII shows, the proportions of near- and far-side front placements are about the same as those found by Kuczaj and Maratsos. We then devised paper and pencil tests for adults. In Experiment 9, we gave three groups of undergraduates a picture of a square printed in the middle of an 8 in. square page, told them to imagine that it was an object as seen from above (a "bird's-eye view"), and asked them to draw a line separating the front from back, and then to name the sides. Each subject made one judgment only. The procedure in Experiment 10 was the same except that the subjects (30 more undergraduates) each made judgments of four squares. Finally (Experiment 11), we showed 48 college students a "top view of a man wearing a black hat" (circle with a large black circle inside), and told them to draw his nose.

The results are summarized in Table VIII. In Experiment 9, 21 of the 31 subjects drew a horizontal line separating the front and back sections and named each side, as requested. Of these 21, 16 (or 52% of the total of 31) called the near side "front" and the far side "back," while the remaining six subjects (19%) did the exact reverse (χ^2 (1) = 3.86, p < .05). In Experiment 10, of the 30 subjects' 120 judgments, 76 dividing lines were horizontal. Of these, the bottom section was called "front" in 47 instances (39% of the 120 judgments), the top, in the remaining 29 instances (24% of 120). (The remaining subjects in both experiments either drew diagonal or vertical dividing lines or, regardless of orientation of line, failed to name the sections.) So in Experiments 9 and 10, the "front on near side" judgment was more frequent. Of the three experiments, the situation in Experiment 11 most resembles the "canonical encounter," inasmuch as the circle is identified as a person, and here, 40 of the 48 subjects (83%) drew the nose on the longitudinal axis, but most (58%) placed it on the top (far side).

Asked to explain their judgments, the subjects in all three experiments typically said, "I see it as facing me," or "I see it as facing in the same direction I'm facing" (or "facing to the side"), consistent with the judgments made.

Evidently, then, when the referent object lacks front-back features, most children and adults superimpose their own front-back orientation upon it, thereby giving it a front-back axis. They do place (or name) the nonfronted object as if it were fronted, but their model is not always the face-to-face canonical encounter. Instead they frequently see the nonfronted object as lined up in the same direction as their own body. As we have said, this latter view seems to us as correct as seeing the object as though facing oneself. If so, the results of our Experiment 8 and of Leehey's (1973) study indicate that in 4-year-olds, the total percent "correct" is at least 90. This means that ability to make front-back spatial placements of featureless objects is considerably easier than Kuczaj and Maratsos' scoring procedure indicates.

The data summarized here do show preference for the face-to-face model, and certainly researchers themselves prefer this model inasmuch as they have presumed it to be "correct." Why this preference with respect to featureless objects? There may be a social-cultural basis, as we shall see in Section XI.

We hasten to add that the strength of agreement among our subjects—whether for the face-to-face or the lined-up model—does not mean that all the children necessarily think that a featureless object really has a front in the same sense that a featured object has. If some of the younger children seemed to think so, most of the older children did not. This age difference is evident from further informal tests carried out with the 5- to 7½-year-olds in Experiment 8. We placed a block before the child, who was asked to point to its "front." Nearly all the older children pointed either to the side facing them or to the side opposite, though a few older children said that the block did not have a front ("See, it's the same all the way around," one girl said). These same children, however, unhesitatingly followed instructions to place another block "in front" of the first and used the longitudinal-axis locations exclusively.

For those children who designated a front, we said, "Now watch very carefully," slowly turned the block 90 or 180° and said again, "Now, point to the front." Our results might have been different had we asked the child to go around the block. With the test we used, however, the younger children nearly all pointed to the same side, now facing in a different direction as they named a moment before. For most of the older children, the rotation made no difference, and they now designated as front that new side that was now in the same orientation vis-à-vis their own bodies as they had designated before. As one girl explained, "It's always the one on this [near] side no matter how you turn it." The older children thus recognized that the "front" side of a featureless object is purely arbitrary, that it "belongs" to the object only in relation to another object. The younger children seemed to believe that the featureless object has a front absolutely.

B. OTHER CONTEXT CUES

Though the major cues designating the spatial position of featureless objects are the coordinates of one's own body, in certain cases these body-based cues can be replaced or augmented. One such instance is the immediate functional context in which the spatial placements are made.

For instance, imagine that the featureless object in Fig. 10 is a tree and

Fig. 10. Code for locations for placements of featureless objects.

that the child is told to place a doll "behind the tree." The available data indicate that the placement would be on the far side of the tree (location 1 in Fig. 10) with probability at least .65, and on the near side (location 3) with probability at most .30. However, if the child is given two dolls, is told they are playing hide and seek, and is instructed to place one "behind the tree," the probability of use of location 1 should increase, for now the context is a hiding game, and the definition of "behind" in the sense of "not accessible," "covered up," or "out of sight" should be enhanced.

C.   IMMEDIATELY PRIOR EXPERIENCE

Immediately prior experience with a featured referent also can "impose" features on a featureless object. We were first alerted to this point when we found an interaction between testing order and placements of featureless objects among children who participated in Experiments 2 (object-referent placements of featureless objects) and 3 (object-referent placements of featured objects). In both testing orders near-side in front placements were more frequent, but they were about four times more frequent than far-side in front placements when children had Experiment 2 first, and only about half again as frequent when children had Experiment 3 first. (The scores given in Table VIII are averages over the two testing orders.) Since the lined-up pattern (see Fig. 2) predominated in Experiment 3, we suggested in our original report (Harris and Strommen, 1972) that the prior experience with featured objects carried over to the object referent trials with featureless objects so that children, asked to place one featureless object in front of another, now behaved as though they had imposed the face orientation of the preceding objects onto the featureless object. Experiment 12 was designed to further test this suggestion. We had 22 kindergartners and 18 second graders first make eight consecutive placements of blocks or drinking glasses "in front" of a doll or toy chair placed before the child but always facing either toward or away from the child or to the side. The child then made six more "in front of" placements, now with a block or drinking glass replacing the doll or chair.

The results in trials 1–8 were straightforward. However the doll or chair was oriented, all second graders and all but three kindergartners made all their in front placements in the appropriate location, exactly what we expected on the basis of our previous experiments.

On the six transfer trials, we expected to be able to induce in front placements on the near side of the now featureless referent more easily than on the far side, since near-side placements were more frequent in Experiment 8 and, presumably, were the placements to which the children were predisposed. Lateral in front placements, so infrequent in the earlier study, therefore should have been still harder to induce. Here, our expectations were not borne out. All but one of the 40 children made all six in front placements in the same absolute location—whether near side, far side, or lateral—as they had used in the preceding trials. The exception was a second-grade girl. For her, the featured referent object, on trials 1–8, had faced to her right, and she made seven of eight "in front" placements in the appropriate lateral location. Then, when the featureless object replaced the featured object as referent, she paused for about 15 seconds, began to make her placement in the same location as before, abruptly stopped, and finally chose the far side of the referent object and did so for the five remaining trials. Afterwards, asked why she had hesitated, she explained that she had been looking to see whether the glass had a front—and finally saw that it did not.

No other children showed such hesitations on the featureless-object trials. Except for this one revealing instance, it appears that the primacy of both face-to-face and face-to-back patterns is easily overcome in young children by the child's immediately prior experience with featured objects. It remains to be seen how long lasting the effects are and over what age range they are functional.

D.   EFFECT OF ONE SPATIAL PLACEMENT ON OTHERS

Still another kind of "prior experience" also can create a context for the placements. In all our other studies, the children always made sets of in front–in back–beside placements (of featured as well as featureless objects). Did this procedure induce the consistent preference we found for longitudinal locations (relative to the child's body) for in front and in back and lateral locations for beside? In other words, were the placements independent, or did one placement "fix" the locations of the other two? To find out, we tested each spatial term by itself, in two further studies. In Experiment 13, we tested 38 kindergartners and 18 second graders, with individual subsets of children in each grade making five consecutive placements of the same featureless objects (blocks or drinking glasses) either in front of, in back of, or beside a featureless stationary object (block or drinking glass). Next (Experiment 14), to further clarify the effects of the "beside" instruction, we had 144 third and fourth graders make three consecutive beside placements only.

The code for the location of the children's placements is given in Fig. 10. The results, expressed as a percentage use of the various locations averaged across trials, are summarized in Table IX. They show that by kindergarten age, in front and in back are already recognized as lying along the longitudinal axis relative to the child's own body, and that this disposition is stronger by second grade.

Beside Placements

The results for "beside" present an interesting contrast. For neither kindergartners nor second graders does "beside" by itself occupy a privileged lateral location, even though for second graders given our standard test, front and back already had taken on distinct locations. Only by third and fourth grade does "beside" become assigned predominantly to the lateral axis relative to the body.

In earlier experiments (Tables I and IV), "side" and "beside" also were found to have been acquired consistently later than "front" and "back."

TABLE IX

Percentage Use Across Trials of Various Locations for Successive "in Front,"
"in Back," or "Beside" Placements when Objects are Featureless [a]

	Location used (see Fig. 10)	Placement instruction		
		In front	In back	Beside
Experiment 13		(N = 12)	(N = 14)	(N = 12)
kindergarten	1, 3	63	74	57
(five trials)	2, 4	27	18	27
	Other	10	7	17
Experiment 13		(N = 6)	(N = 6)	(N = 6)
Second grade	1, 3	100	77	48
(five trials)	2, 4	0	17	31
	Other	0	6	21
Experiment 14				(N = 144)
Third and fourth grades	1, 3			26
(three trials)	2, 4			62
	Other			

[a] Individual subjects received only one placement instruction.

This finding suggests that the consistent preference shown for the lateral location for side placements in previous studies with nonfeatured objects was a by-product of concurrent assignment of the front–back coordinate system. In other words, the rule for the location of "side" as a locational term in its own right appears to be less strong than for location of side in the context of front and back, or perhaps it is even based upon wholly different principles.

Inspection of the stability of individual children's placements across trials in both Experiments 13 and 14 further supports this conclusion. For 'in front" and "in back," nearly all the kindergartners and second graders were highly consistent (four out of five trials) in their choice of one axis, and nearly as consistent in choosing a location on that axis. (Additional testing of a small number of third graders has revealed complete consistency.) For "beside," there was much more shifting across trials both from one axis to another and within an axis. Furthermore, by third and fourth grade, there was an overall clear preference for the lateral axis (62%) over the longitudinal (26%) or any other (11%). However, the choice of location 2 or 4 changed sharply over trials from 74% to 54% to 52%. So even at third and fourth grade the notion that "beside" is the lateral location (relative to one's own body) is unfirm. Alternatively, the results could mean that the children are beginning to understand that *beside* can occupy any position where there is no front–back feature to stipulate a particular location, or more generally, that *beside* also means mere adjacency irrespective of feature, as in *next to*. We asked several children who had varied their locations whether, even so, there was one "best place" for "beside." One girl answered, matter of factly, that it would not make any difference—they were all "beside." The other children allowed for other possibilities but all chose a lateral location. It may be that lack of stability, for the older child, reflects understanding of the arbitrariness of a spatial term, but for the younger child, a lack of understanding of the term itself.

E.   REVERSION TO SELF-REFERENTIAL SYSTEM IN A RELATIONAL TASK
FOR MINIMALLY FEATURED FORMS

For both children and adults, even a single feature on an abstract form that creates an axis of asymmetry and marks one side as different from the rest will specify a front–back axis and mark front and back sides (Section VII, A). As we have just seen (Section IX, A), without the feature, both adults and children revert to the self-referential system. However, our method of assessing the effectiveness of the asymmetricizing feature may have been too easy. Since our adults subjects (Experiments 5 and 6), and Eiser's children, were told to name the front and back directly, it would not necessarily follow that the single asymmetricizing feature also would have specified "front" in a relational task, where the abstract form is referent and the subject places another object in relation to it. This relational skill, we earlier saw in the case of familiar, featured objects, appears to be achieved later than simple naming. In Experiment 15, to test this possibility, we showed undergraduate students the second form in Fig. 5 and asked them first to imagine seeing a bird's-eye view of a man standing either "in front of" or "beside" the form and then to mark his location with an X. The feature appeared in all four cardinal-point orientations. A total of 148 students participated, with roughly an equal number assigned to each spatial direction by feature orientation condition.

Most of the students responded self-referentially. In the front condition, of 26 students for whom the referent drawing was oriented along the front-back axis of their own bodies, 25 students drew the X along the asymmetrical axis (on the near or far side). Of 24 students for whom the referent was oriented laterally, however, only eight drew the X along the asymmetrical axis (i.e., laterally); the rest drew the X along the axis of symmetry (now in relation to their own bodies). The same weak response to the axis of asymmetry was evident for "in back" and "beside."

So most of these undergraduates used a self-referential system, making their placements on the near or far side. They thus ignored the feature which, in the direct naming task, other undergraduates as well as children could identify as the front. Because adults have overlearned *front* and *back,* the presumably greater difficulty of relational than absolute knowledge is difficult to assess. A possible test might be to request relational responding to a minimally featured object. Inasmuch as young adults responded self-referentially on this task, children would be expected to respond the same way.

X.   Front-Back as a Dimension of Time

The terms *front* and *back* and their variants not only describe parts of objects and their relative positions in space; they also can refer figuratively, or metaphorically, to the dimension of time (e.g., Leech, 1970). Imagine people waiting in line to buy tickets. Adults will agree that the first in line is "in front of," "ahead of," or "before" the second in line, and so on. However, "ahead of" and "before" have a temporal as well as a spatial meaning. The first person is "ahead" of the rest because he will buy his tickets before the rest. In other instances, spatial and temporal terms are less clearly interchangeable: One gets "ahead" of oneself, not "in front" of oneself; one arrives "ahead" of time, not "in front" of time. Hodun (1975) also has shown that adults judge *before* and *after* as more temporal than *ahead* and *behind,* though judgment of these terms depends in part on the extent to which the verb implies action (e.g., the truck *moves* ahead vs. the truck *is* ahead).

H. Clark (1973) has proposed a specific chronology in acquisition of the spatial and temporal meanings: "Since time is a spatial metaphor, the use of a term to denote time must have been preceded by the use of the comparable term to denote space" (p. 57).

This idea seems reasonable if it is true that spatial metaphors derive from the body and other physical referents (as Asch, 1958, has argued about metaphor generally). Nonspatial metaphors are indeed learned later than their physical referents, e.g., children know the physical meaning of such words as *hard, soft, blue,* and *sweet,* before they understand that people can have these same qualities (Asch & Nerlove, 1960; see also Gardner, Kircher, Winner, & Perkins, 1975).

Hodun (1975) has reported data showing earlier acquisition of spatial than temporal terms. She provided either spatial cues alone, spatial and temporal cues concurrently, or spatial and temporal cues in opposition. The subjects were 12 children who averaged 4:6 years and 12 children who averaged 5:1 years of age. Candy was placed in one of two small boxes located near or in toy vehicles, and the child was told to "wait for a clue where to look" before trying to "find the candy." At both 4:6 and 5:1 children were mostly correct when responding to spatial cues alone but mostly incorrect when responding to temporal cues in opposition to spatial cues. Responses when temporal and spatial cues coincided were in between. Evidently, introduction of the temporal cue, perhaps because it also involved movement, was disrupting even when it was congruent with the spatial cue. In all three conditions, the older children did better than the younger ones on all tasks and were more responsive to temporal cues, even though fewer than half of the older children themselves used the temporal cues.

Clark's prediction, however, was not supported in another study. Friedman and Seeley (1976) tested 15 3-year-olds, 12 4-year-olds, and 12 5-year-olds. Each child received seven test words (*before, after, first, last, ahead of, behind, together with*) in two tests of the spatial meanings of the terms and two tests of their temporal meanings. On one spatial test, for instance, a doll had to be placed in relation to a toy horse. On one of the temporal tasks, the children were asked to "make [two dolls placed in doll beds] get up the way I tell you."

Comprehension improved with age, but at each age, neither spatial nor temporal understanding had clear priority, each being better understood for some terms but not others. The authors interpreted their results as explicitly disconfirming Clark's prediction that the spatial meaning comes first.

Richards and Hawpe (1978) used yet a different procedure in which 5-and 6-year-olds and adults pressed buttons to indicate positions before and after those in which the experimenters had placed a cue. Their results showed that the children's responses were most "adultlike" on the temporal task and least on the spatial task, i.e., the temporal task was easier than the spatial task.

We are not sure we can explain the discrepancies among these studies, though we suspect that procedural differences were important. Friedman and Seeley's subjects expressed their understanding by manipulating the figures themselves; Hodun's subjects, though they had to find a candy, were judging the experimenter's manipulation. Richards and Hawpe's procedure required manipulation from their subjects but in response to arrays defined by the experimenter. Hodun's subjects also had to deal with temporal and spatial cues simultaneously in two of three conditions (possibly a disruptive element), but Friedman and Seeley's subjects were required to deal with only one kind of cue at a given time, as were Richards and Hawpe's subjects. Our intuition is to agree with Friedman and Seeley, noting as they do that both time and space, as categories of understanding, develop gradually and over the same developmental periods (Piaget, 1956; Piaget & Inhelder, 1956). Therefore, one concept is unlikely to depend on prior learning of the other. Understanding of metaphorical terms has usually been assumed to depend upon prior learning of referent terms. However, it is not clear that this sequence holds strongly, if at all, for locative words. (Perhaps it does not for the adjectives mentioned above either. Later acquisition of psychological than physical meanings might as reasonably be attributed to relative salience of psychological and physical cues as to any necessary dependence of psychological meanings upon physical meanings.) Even adults might use metaphors without knowing the physical referent. For instance, they might speak of a culturally deprived or stagnant area as a "backwater" without realizing, or without ever having learned, that *backwater* is water held or pushed back by (or as though by) a dam or current, especially water that is stagnant or still. Thus, though a metaphor has an original spatial–physical referent and in that sense depends on this referent, this dependence is etymological, but not necessarily psychological. We suspect this is the case with words that have both spatial and temporal meanings.

XI. Spatial Placement in Social Context

A. SPATIAL PLACEMENTS AND SOCIAL DISTANCE

In Experiment 4, we found that face cues, where used, appear to express a social as well as a spatial relation between the dolls. Studies of "personal space" show that the closer one's psychological relationship with someone, the closer (physically) that person is allowed to approach (e.g., Guardo, 1969). If children understood *front* and *back* as having social as well as spatial meanings, the physical distances at which placements of dolls are made might be expected to vary when the dolls were described as having different social relationships. There also may be behavioral expressions of social distance in forms such as seeking or avoiding eye contact or turning one's back, as in the case of the Scupins' 6-year-old who, when asked where he went during the school recess, said, "Wherever [the teacher's] back is" (Scupin & Scupin, 1931, Vol. 3, p. 22; cited in Werner, 1948, p. 174).

In Experiment 16 we tested these ideas by asking children to place dolls with movable heads. This time, a neutral placement instruction was followed by instructions to pretend the dolls either liked or disliked each other. Each child responded to all three instructions, with the order of "like" and "dislike" instructions counterbalanced over children. The subjects were 144 third and fourth graders (8–10 years old). Our procedure was similar to Experiment 4, except that the alignment of head and body of the mobile doll remained constant over trials for individual children. For 48 children the head and body were divergent for the mobile doll only, and for the remaining 48 children the head and body were divergent for the stationary doll only. The social instructions clearly influenced how far apart children placed the dolls. Mean distance was closest when the dolls "liked" each other (1.76 in., SD 1.47), next closest in the neutral condition (2.16 in., SD 1.99), and farthest when the dolls "disliked" each other (3.99 in., SD 1.32). These mean distance differences were all significantly different from each other.

We expected that both the "like" and "dislike" instructions would increase the influence of face cues. Examination of distributions of regular placement patterns showed that they were not responsive to the social manipulation. However, as in Experiment 4 the use of face cues was evident in beside shifts (see Fig. 3). On the "like" trials, as on control trials and as in Experiment 4, most shifts maintained face contact, whereas on "dislike" trials, nearly all shifts avoided face contact.

Irregular patterns yielded a similar result. After having been judged as in

Experiment 4 for presence or absence of use of face cues (see Fig. 4), those
irregular patterns judged as showing clear use of face cues were categorized
into those in which face contact was maintained and those in which face
contact was avoided. Only 5% of irregular patterns showed no use of face
cues, as compared with nearly 20% in Experiment 4. Further, of patterns
reflecting use of face cues, 65 occurred in the control condition (two looking away); 83 occurred in the "like" condition (one looking away); and 117
occurred in the "dislike" condition (94 looking away). The influence of
story condition on the frequency and orientation of these placements is
obvious.

  The greater use of face cues in the "dislike" story condition stems in part
from an ambiguity in our facing and combined placement patterns. In
these patterns, placements based on body orientation cannot be differentiated from placements based on face cues when the mobile doll is in convergent head–body alignment, since the two types of cues are redundant in
these circumstances. Whether the stationary doll is in convergent alignment
as illustrated in Fig. 11 or in divergent alignment (not shown in Fig. 11),
children will produce the facing or combined pattern if they place a doll in
convergent head–body alignment so that it can "look at" or "see" the

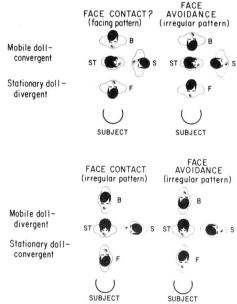

Fig. 11. *Illustration of the interaction of head–body alignment of the mobile doll and use of
face cues to make the dolls "see" or "look at" each other (left-hand side) or "not see" or
"look away from" each other (right-hand side). (See Fig. 2 for definitions of symbols.)*

referent doll (Fig. 11, top left). However, children placing a doll in divergent head–body alignment so that it can "see" the stationary doll will generate irregular patterns (Fig. 11, bottom left). In contrast, placing the doll so that it is "looking away from" or "can't see" the stationary doll will generate irregular patterns whether the doll is in convergent (Fig. 11, top right) or divergent (Fig. 11, bottom right) head–body alignment. For this reason, the true frequency of the use of the face cue in the "like" condition is underrepresented in this analysis of irregular patterns.

This discussion suggests a modification of our earlier conclusion (Experiment 4) that "front" is defined primarily by the body, not the face. It also suggests a qualification to our disagreement with Fillmore's (1971) emphasis on organs of perception as determinants of front. Now it looks as though the body of the stationary doll determines the location of the mobile doll, but the face—and presumably the direction of gaze—of the mobile doll determines how it is oriented in that location. There is a difference, then, in how the active (mobile) doll and the inactive (stationary) doll regulate the child's use of front, back, and beside.

B.   SPATIAL PLACEMENTS AND CULTURAL DIFFERENCES

The results of Experiment 16 show that working definitions of terms such as *in front* and *in back* do not depend solely upon spatial determinants. Given that such terms reflect nonspatial determinants, one might expect to observe the effects of such determinants not only in individual response patterns as documented in Experiment 16 but also in differences in how *front* and *back* have come to be construed by different cultural groups, and consequently in the meanings typically learned by children learning the language of these cultural groups.

Accepting this proposition, however, did not prepare us for the dramatic cultural contrasts reported by Hill (1975, 1978). Hill compared the responses of native speakers of Hausa, an African language, with the responses of native speakers of English. He also compared the responses of secondary-school-age bilingual subjects in Niger when examined in both Hausa, which was spoken at home, and French, which was the language of instruction at school. When he asked subjects to place one featureless object in front (or in back) of another, as we did in our featureless object study (Experiment 8), Hill found that the majority of speakers of Hausa, and more of the bilinguals examined in Hausa, placed the mobile object on the far side of the stationary object from themselves, but native speakers of English, or bilinguals examined in French, placed the mobile object between themselves and the stationary object. Hill showed that this performance difference between African and Western language speakers is so general that not only objects but events in time are conceptualized in different characteristic orientations in reference to the self. Hausa speakers conceptualize nonfeatured objects as facing the same direction as the self, with the self last in the queue. Thus, Hill reports that for Hausa speakers, *in front,* given no intrinsic cues, is first in the queue (on the far side of the stationary object), and today is the day *after* tomorrow! Western language speakers tend to conceptualize nonfronted objects as oriented toward themselves, so *in front,* given no intrinsic cues, is on the near side of the stationary object, and today is the day *before* tomorrow. As another example, we are confident that all Western readers of our article knew that when we used such expressions as, "The preceding experiment" or the one mentioned "before," we meant the one already discussed and not the one to come next; the native Hausa speaker, presented with a comparable sequencing in narrative form, might well have reversed these meanings.

Why this cultural difference? Hill proposed an explanation in something of the same spirit as our earlier discussion of the relation between mode of use and the way critical information about featured objects is best represented (see page 159). He suggested that in nontechnological societies, such as that in which his Hausa-speaking subjects were growing up, there are far fewer fronted objects with which individuals interact than is the case in technological societies with their machines, with which one typically interacts in a face-to-face mode. Consequently, persons from technological societies tend to conceptualize objects as facing toward themselves, whereas persons from nontechnological societies do not, and these divergent conceptualizations become embedded in the characteristic meanings of linguistic terms such as *front* and *back.*

Heinz Werner (1948, p. 168) anticipated this cultural difference. He cited an example from Baldus (1931, p. 114), who said: "If the Tumereha Indian sees an object he speaks of the side nearest to him as 'behind,' for the reason that this side is facing in the same direction as his own back. The reverse side he speaks of as 'forward,' because it corresponds to his own frontal aspect."

It is natural, Werner suggested, for the Tumereha Indian "to orient himself in a space with which he is identified corporeally and dynamically, which exhibits the spatial direction of his own body, and not in a space that stands out there, over against him as subject" (Werner, 1948, p. 168). Both of these examples suggest, for yet different reasons from those presented in Section III, A, that our very definitions of *front* and *back* are tied to characteristic modes of interaction with objects in the settings in which we grow up.

XII. Lexical Marking Hypothesis

So far our concern has been with the development of front–back as a dimension of space and time. A separate question is whether there are differences between the terms of the dimension itself. A body of psycholinguistic literature is addressed to this possibility. Our particular interest is in H. Clark's (1973) proposal that *front* and *back* (as relational prepositions, "in front of," "in back of") differ in their lexical marking, with one term unmarked, the other marked. In this respect they would be like other pairs of polar spatial terms, e.g., deep–shallow and long–short. This proposal can be tested in several ways.

A. NOMINAL–CONTRASTIVE DISTINCTION

First, unmarked and marked terms are said to be, respectively, "nominal" and "contrastive" (the criterion traditionally applied by linguists). Consider long and short. *Long* can be used in both senses in that it means both "of the dimension length" (nominal sense) and "longer than average" (contrastive sense, referring to comparisons between objects of different lengths). *Short,* however, can be used only in the latter, contrastive sense, and never means merely *length*. We usually say, "The board is ten feet long" but not "The board is ten feet short." *Long* therefore is unmarked because it can be used in either sense, and *short* is marked because it cannot be so used, since it always implies a comparative scale (see Donaldson and Wales, 1970).

With respect to English spatial adjectives, Clark points out that it is always the unmarked term that designates physical extension along a dimension, and that these spatial adjectives usually come in unmarked–marked pairs, for example, deep–shallow for depth, or long–short for length.

By the nominal–contrastive criterion, however, *front* and *back* do not clearly fit the unmarked and marked descriptions, respectively. Unlike other pairs of spatial terms, front–back does not clearly specify a dimension along which contrasts can be made. For instance, we can say "longer" or "shorter" for the dimension of "length" but there are no comparable terms "fronter" or "backer," and there is no such word as "frontness" that labels the front–back dimension as length labels the long–short dimension. Thus it is not obvious that *front* or *in front of* can be both nominal and constrastive, *back* or *in back of* only contrastive.

Clark, in fact, did not ever consider the nominal–contrastive criterion with respect to front–back, perhaps for the reasons we have noted above. He confined himself instead to two other criteria.

B. VALENCE

Another kind of asymmetry between marked and unmarked terms is in "valence"; the unmarked term is positive, the marked term negative. Compare *long* and *deep* with *short* and *shallow*. The same applies to *right* and *left*, metaphors for good and evil (cf. Needham, 1973), and *above* and *below*. *Front* and *back* are similarly distinguished, *front* generally being auspicious, like *right* and *above*, and *back, left,* and *below* being inauspicious.[5]

Like Asch, in his classic essay on metaphors (1958), H. Clark (1973) saw these valences, or metaphorical extensions, as rooted in the physical body itself. Thus, the senses are most sensitive to stimulation in front of the body, and least sensitive in back; everything in front is easily perceived, everything behind is not; forward direction is the positive perceptual direction, backward the negative, "where *positive* is taken in its natural sense to mean the presence of something, and *negative,* the absence" (H. Clark, 1973, p. 33). This is not always true. For instance, the scatalogical meaning of back obviously is traceable to the *presence* there of the anus.[6]

There are numerous nonscatalogical but still negative meanings too. Because of the smaller risk of detection and also perhaps because one's victim is depersonalized, a coward attacks from the back; thus to be betrayed is to be "stabbed in the back." Consider, too, such expressions as "backbite," "to go back on one's word," "backtalk," "backwater," and "back street," By contrast, news makes the "front page"; the good student goes "to the front of the class," the best musicians, scientists, writers, or actors move, figuratively, into the "front ranks" of their professions.

---

[5] A classical example, which characterizes all three dimensions of space at once, is Plato's myth of Er the Pamphylian. Plato describes the roads which the soul takes when it leaves the body and the place of the soul's arrival: "The judges sit between two openings; when they have pronounced their sentences, they order the just to take the right-hand road which leads to Heaven, after having attached to them, in front, a decree setting forth their judgment; but they order criminals to take the left-hand path leading downwards, they also carrying, but attached behind, a document on which is written all their deeds" (quoted by Hécaen & A-juriaguerra, 1964, p. 125).

[6] By no coincidence, H. L. Mencken once called a certain Southern state the bung-hole of the world. People, likewise, are obscenely named through this synecdochic reference. The scatalogical meaning is by no means peculiar to English. For example, in the language of the people of Roti, an island in Eastern Indonesia, *deak* has interrelated meanings of "in back of," "outside," and "behind" and is a basic coordinate of Rotinese classification. *Deak* also has scatalogical reference: one defecates *nai deak,* at some distance from the house, and a more polite expression for the verb "to defecate" (*tei*) is *nanga-deak* ("to make outside" or "to make backward"; Fox, 1973, p. 345).

C. TIME OF ACQUISITION

The second characteristic of the unmarked–marked dimension that Clark applies to front–back, and one which is more important than valence, is time of acquisition. The prediction is that the unmarked term is learned first, meaning that *front* (or *in front of*) will be acquired before *back* (in back of). The reason has to do with the greater complexity of the cognitive operations required to understand the negative term. The positive member—*front*—"specified the assumed normal direction or relation, and the negative member specifies its direction or relation by negating the assumed one." Negation of the assumed relation therefore "requires an extra rule of application" (H. Clark, 1973, p. 55), making the negative term more difficult to understand.

Another reason to suppose that *front* would be learned first is that it is perceptually more salient, more differentiated. For instance, we earlier described Golumb's (1972) study of children's modeling of human figures in clay. Once the front–back axis began to appear (by age 3:9), it was the front that was accented. Only after 5 years, and then only in the case of a few children, did the child turn the figure over and model the back. These results indicate an attention to frontal features long before attention to back features.[7]

Similarly, when we have asked kindergarten-age children to tell us the difference between front and back, the children typically named many more front features than back, often simply defining the back by exclusion, e.g., "The front has eyes, the back doesn't."

The complexity and saliency reasons notwithstanding, the evidence does not support the chronology predicted. Some relevant data have already been presented (see Tables III and IV). In nearly all cases, across the different tests of understanding of "front" and "back," any differences in accuracy scores are either insignificant or favor "back." When Leehey and Carey (1978; Section IV) asked children of ages 2:1 to 3:3 to point to fronts and backs of various objects, including self and the experimenter, back was identified significantly more often than front for intrinsic objects (see Table III) as well as for self and for experimenter. The difference for featureless objects was marginally significant. This priority of back has been confirmed in several more studies not previously cited. Johnston (1973, cited in Hodun, 1975) gave 3- to 5-year-olds an object placement task with featured objects (animal toys) and found that understanding of

[7] The back of the body may be so perceptually unsalient that the children either did not know how to model it or they merely left it out. Adult sculptors, too, often leave the back of their work undifferentiated if it will not be displayed. What would have happened had Golumb (1972) asked the children to copy a model of human figure whose back was as differentiated as its front? Would the back have been ignored?

"behind" significantly preceded understanding of "in front." Tanz (1976) found similar differences with children ages 2:6–5:3 on the directional preposition *in back of—in front of.* Johnston and Slobin (1977) found earlier production of *in back of* than *in front of* in a cross-linguistic study with 2- to 4-year-old speakers of English, Italian, Serbo-Croatian, or Turkish. In this instance, the measure was the children's verbal description of object positions. Finally, Friedman and Seeley (1976), in the experiment discussed earlier (Section X), found that when *ahead of* and *behind* were presented as spatial terms, *behind* was better understood.

We earlier (Section V, A) mentioned the study of Goodglass *et al.* (1970 and personal communication) of children's matching of verbal descriptions to pictured spatial relationships. Their youngest children did slightly better on *back* than *front* (see Table IV). They also tested five types of adult aphasic patients. The degree of linguistic deficit varied across groups but for every group, the deficit was greater, often substantially, for *front* than for either *back* or *behind.*

Word count data are congruent with the lexical priority of *back.* Whether in written work by first- to eighth-grade children (Rinsland, 1945), published materials by adults (Lorge, 1949), adults' verbal associations to Thematic Apperception Test cards (Jones & Wepman, 1966), or toddlers' and preschoolers' spontaneous verbalizations and answers to spatial questions (Ames & Learned, 1948), *back* is always substantially more frequent than *front.*

The lexical marking model also has been interpreted as making still another prediction—that the unmarked term, because it stands for both the nominal and the contrastive meaning, would be understood by very young children to mean both terms. Such a prediction has been made for *more* and *less* (Donaldson & Wales, 1970) as well as for other comparative terms (E. V. Clark, 1973), although research support for such predictions is equivocal (Glucksberg, Hay, and Danks, 1976; Holland and Palermo, 1975).

We earlier suggested that the nominal–contrastive distinction did not apply to front–back, but if it did, then *front* initially should be understood as meaning both front and back. What data are available however, suggest just the reverse. Leehey and Carey's (1978) "intermediate" subjects were so categorized because they used the front–back axis in response to the front–back instructions (which "failers" could not do) but did not differentiate front from back within the dimension. Instead, they used "back" when asked to point to either "front" or "back." Leehey and Carey argue that this preference for "back" was not simply a response bias, since the child tended to point to the top of an object when asked to point to its "wug." Also, the most frequent response of the linguistic "failers" was to point to the tops of toys when asked to point to their "fronts" and "backs"; 38% of their total responses were to point to the tops, only 4% to the backs, also suggesting a behavioral preference for top rather than back. We are not ready to conclude from these data that the nominal–contrastive distinction applies after all—and in the reverse of the expected direction—but we are not sure what alternative mechanism to suggest.

All the data reviewed in this section indicate that "back" is lexicalized earlier than, or is dominant over, "front." Why this advantage? An important reason may have to do with our question (Section II) about the status of *back* as both a nominal and relational term. Slobin (personal communication to Leehey & Carey, 1978) provides some evidence that when nominal and relational terms are the same, acquisition is facilitated. According to Slobin, the advantage of *back* is greater in children learning languages which use the same lexical item to refer to *back* as a part of the body and as a spatial relation. By contrast, we assume that in these same languages as in English, *front* rarely designates the front of the body per se. Therefore, the advantage for *back* would stem from its greater frequency. In this instance, then, the earlier acquisition of *back* may have little or nothing to do with its supposed lexical marking.

Back also may be more frequently used in all languages for other reasons. The child may have less reason to say *front* when he wants to localize an object. If an object is in front of something and the adult asks "Where is it?" the child may be more likely simply to point (gesture) or to say, "There," combined with a gesture. This is sensible, since both the adult and the child can see the object. If the object is behind the asker, however, then the child may be more likely to say, "In back of you," since pointing or saying "There" may be less efficient. Leehey and Carey make a similar point, as do Johnston and Slobin.

XIII. Possible Variations among Languages in Acquisition of Locative Terms

So far, we have discussed the acquisition of spatial-locative skills exclusively as reflections of changes in the child's cognitive complexity, with the assumption that such cognitive changes are similarly expressed in all naturally occurring languages. As many linguists (e.g., Slobin, 1971) have noted, however, formal linguistic complexity plays a role at some point in acquisition of certain terms, such as locatives, and certain types of meaningful contrasts may be learned earlier or more easily in some languages than in others because of differences in how these terms are coded.

Slobin (1971) gives examples of this possibility in the case of spatial locatives. In such languages as Turkish, Hungarian, and Finnish, spatial locatives are expressed through case endings on the nouns, while in English they are expressed only through prepositions. Because children universally learn nouns before prepositions, the implication is that children speaking Turkish, Hungarian, or Finnish would learn to express locative distinctions verbally more easily than children speaking English. The available evidence supports this idea. Slobin (1971) reported that children bilingual in Hungarian and in Serbo-Croatian (the latter being more like English than Hungarian with respect to the expression of locatives) used locative expressions in Hungarian well before they did in Serbo-Croatian.

We are reluctant to conclude that the same child has a concept when speaking one language that is lacking when speaking the other. We think the difference, instead, is in the ease with which the same concept can be articulated in one language compared with another. One factor that may affect children's ease of articulation is the readiness with which the construction of a concept embedded in a language maps onto the child's spontaneously developing concept. Front and back may be a case in point. We earlier cited Hill's (1975) work showing that front and back can be construed quite differently in different language families. It is possible, for instance, that because of the salience of early canonical encounters with other people, children tend to learn front-on-the-near-side (which matches the concept embedded in English and French) more readily than front-on-the-far-side (which matches the concept embedded in Hausa). If so, one might expect either that very young children learning English and French would have terms for "front" and "back" at earlier ages than young children learning Hausa, or that Hausa children younger than those tested by Hill might use *front* and *back* as English speakers do, only later being socialized into the conception characteristic of older speakers of Hausa. Recall that the preference for the near-side front location was sensitive to prior experience with featured objects for our young child subjects (Experiments 2, 3, and 12, Section IX, C). Entire cultures similarly might constitute appropriate "prior experiences" of this kind. These same considerations obviously also reinforce our view that verbal expression alone is an insufficient index of children's comprehension of spatial locatives.

If language differences in linguistic complexity can influence the rate of linguistic acquisition of spatial locatives, we wonder whether the same or other differences also lead to differences in the ultimate precision and richness with which the location of objects in space can be specified. Slobin draws no such inference about Serbo-Croatian and Hungarian, but Gagné (1968) has made such a suggestion about the Eskimo language. He argued that "Eskimos are able to specify, with more precision than is found in most languages, where things and places are located, how to reach them, their attributes in relation to their settings, and so on" (p. 38). The reason, he suggested, is understandable in terms of Eskimo ecology: "Their very lives depend on success in locating game and on travel over vast, uninhabited, and untracked reaches to develop cognitive maps adequate for these purposes" (p. 38). In view of the argued importance of spatial location in Eskimo life, the question may be raised whether Eskimos not only acquire the verbal expressions for spatial locatives earlier than other people but also acquire the underlying spatial concepts earlier. The question deserves a test.

XIV. Concluding Comments

We began our research with what we thought were straightforward questions about children's understanding of front and back. As we expected, such understanding begins very early in life with children's knowledge of the fronts and backs of their own bodies. This understanding quickly generalizes to other objects and relations between objects, although some difficult judgments may not be possible until the elementary school years.

We have already discussed our major conclusions and remaining questions, so there is no need to repeat them here. Instead we prefer to mention only a few issues that we consider particularly salient.

Something that impresses us especially strongly now is the necessity for cross-cultural and cross-linguistic research. The dramatic contrasts illustrated by Hill's (1975, 1978) work underscore the point that concepts which we consider fundamental or take for granted may be construed very differently by other cultural–linguistic groups. Only more such research can reveal where there are similarities and where differences between such psycholinguistic communities. Furthermore, only cross-cultural and cross-linguistic studies can resolve certain other issues, e.g., the universality/specificity of the sequence of acquisition of the different components of front and back identified in our paper; or the importance of attributes of the lexicon, such as whether or not a term (e.g., *back*) has both nominal and relational meanings or how it is expressed within the linguistic structure (e.g., with or without case endings).

We think the role of metaphor in development of understanding of *front* and *back* is a promising area for further study, given the metaphoric richness of spatial terms—*left* and *right* and others as well as *front* and *back*—and given that metaphor has been specifically implicated in acquisition of usage of these terms.

We spent little time in the text discussing the relationship between acquisition of front and back and performance on other cognitive tasks, but there may be many such links. For instance, there is reason to believe that the ease of labeling front and back features facilitates performance on perspective-taking tasks (e.g., Ives, 1976; Strommen, unpublished data, 1975). Identification of such stimulus conditions controlling children's responses should reduce our dependence on ambiguous constructs such as "egocentrism."

We are even more impressed now than we were at the outset of our work with the multidimensionality of the concepts "front" and "back." We have found that these "simple" terms are embedded in a complex network of perceptual, linguistic, cognitive, and even social–cultural processes. An explication of these or of any other locative terms must, therefore, lead in many directions. The concept is also multidimensional in the strictly perceptual sense, and more parametric studies would help to determine the relative importance of the cues we have discussed, such as movement and focal features.

Finally, our catalog of meanings of *front* and *back* is far from exhaustive, and more explication remains. For example, what of the phenomenon mentioned by Miller and Johnson-Laird (1976) that objects such as tables may acquire fronts by context from the room in which they are found? What happens when a barrier is imposed, as when a chair is facing oneself but is on the opposite side of a wall or screen? And what of circumstances such as size or distance that seem to limit the applicability of these spatial terms? For instance, in relation to an observer, one can stand in front or in back of a puddle, a boulder, or a patch of grass. But, it sounds odd to speak of standing "in front" or "in back" of Mount Whitney, the Atlantic Ocean, or the State of Michigan, even though we speak of "ocean fronts" and of going "beyond" the mountains." The more usual usage is "on the shore" of the ocean, or at "water's edge," and "on the other side" of the mountain. Oceans and puddles are both bodies of water, just as mountains and boulders are both masses of rock. The difference may have to do with the size or extent of the object relative (we would guess) to the human scale, whether larger or smaller. Whether and when children are sensitive to these limiting instances remains to be seen.

REFERENCES

Ames, L. B., & Learned, J. The development of verbalized space in the young child. *Journal of Genetic Psychology,* 1948, **72**, 63–84.

Arnheim, R. *Art and visual perception: The new version.* Berkeley, Calif.: University of California Press, 1974.

Asch, S. The metaphor: A psychological inquiry. In R. Taquiri & L. Petrullo (Eds.) *Person perception and interpersonal behavior.* Stanford, Calif.: Stanford University Press, 1958.

Asch, S. E., & Nerlove, H. The development of double function terms in children: An exploratory investigation. In B. Kaplan & S. Wapner (Eds.), *Perspectives in psychological theory: Essays in honor of Heinz Werner.* New York: International Universities Press, 1960.

Baldus, H. Indianerstudien im nordöstlichen Chiaco. *Forschungen zur Völkerpsychologie,* 1931, **XI.**

Berko-Gleason, J. The child's learning of English morphology. *Word,* 1958, **14,** 150–177.

Bialystock, E. *The development of spatial concepts in language and thought.* Unpublished doctoral dissertation, University of Toronto, 1976.

Bornstein, M. H., Gross, C. G., & Wolf, J. Z. Perceptual similarity of mirror images in infancy. *Cognition,* 1978, **6,** 89–116.

Braine, L. G. Asymmetries of pattern perception observed in Israelis. *Neuropsychologia,* 1968, **6,** 73–88.

Clark, E. V. What's in a word? On the child's acquisition of semantics in his first language. In T. E. Moore (Ed.), *Cognitive development and the acquisition of language.* New York: Academic Press, 1973.

Clark, H. H. Space, time, semantics, and the child. In T. E. Moore (Ed.), *Cognitive development and the acquisition of language.* New York: Academic Press, 1973.

Corballis, M. C., & Beale, I. L. Bilateral symmetry and behavior. *Psychological Review,* 1970, **77,** 451–464.

Corballis, M. C., & Beale, I. L. *The psychology of left and right.* Hillsdale, N.J.: Earlbaum, 1976.

Donaldson, M., & Wales, R. On the acquisition of some relational terms. In J. R. Hayes (Ed.), *Cognition and the development of language.* New York: Wiley, 1970.

Eiser, C. *Egocentrism and the child's concept of space.* Unpublished doctoral dissertation, University of Bristol, England, 1975.

Fillmore, C. J. *Toward a theory of deixis.* Paper presented at the Pacific Conference on Contrastive Linguistics and Language Universals. University of Hawaii, January 1971.

Fox, J. J. On bad death and the left hand: A study of Rotinese symbolic inversions. In R. Needham (Ed.), *Right and left: Essays on dual symbolic classification.* Chicago: The University of Chicago Press, 1973.

Friedman, W. J., & Seeley, P. B. The child's acquisition of spatial and temporal word meanings. *Child Development,* 1976, **47,** 1103–1108.

Gagné, R. C. Spatial concepts in the Eskimo language. In V. F. Valentine and F. G. Vallee (Eds.), *Eskimo of the Canadian arctic.* Toronto: McClelland & Steward, 1968.

Gardner, H., Kircher, M., Winner, E., & Perkins, D. Children's metaphoric productions and preferences. *Journal of Child Language,* 1975, **2,** 125–141.

Glucksberg, S., Hay, A., & Danks, J. H. Words in utterance contexts: Young children do not confuse the meanings of "same" and "different." *Child Development,* 1976, **47,** 737–741.

Golumb, C. Evolution of the human figure in a three-dimensional medium. *Developmental Psychology,* 1972, **6,** 385–391.

Goodglass, H., Gleason, J. B., & Hyde, M. R. Some dimensions of auditory language comprehension in aphasia. *Journal of Speech and Hearing Research,* 1970, **13,** 595–606.

Guardo, C. J. Personal space in children. *Child Development,* 1969, **40,** 143–151.

Harris, L. J. Discrimination of left and right, and development of the logic of relations. *Merrill-Palmer Quarterly of Behavior and Development,* 1972, **18,** 307–320.

Harris, L. J., & Schaller, M. J. Form and its orientation: Re-examination of a child's-eye view. *American Journal of Psychology,* 1971, **84,** 218–234.

Harris, L. J., & Strommen, E. A. The role of front-back features in children's "front," "back," and "beside" placements of objects. *Merrill-Palmer Quarterly of Behavior and Development,* 1972, **18**, 259–271.

Harris, L. J., & Strommen, E. A. *Children's spatial placements of dolls that "like" each other and of dolls that "dislike" each other: Role of eye contact and physical proximity in "personal space." Part 1: Physical proximity between the dolls. Part 2: Eye contact in spatial placements.* Papers presented at the Biennial Meeting of the Society for Research in Child Development, Philadelphia, Pa., March 30, 1973.

Harris, L. J., & Strommen, E. A. What is the "front" of a simple geometric form? *Perceptions & Psychophysics,* 1974, **15**, 517–580.

Hécaen, H., & Ajuriaguerra, J., de. *Left-handedness: Manual superiority and cerebral dominance.* New York: Grune & Stratton, 1964.

Hill, C. A. Sex-based differences in cognitive processing of spatial relations in bilingual students in Niger. In *Working papers in linguistics: Patterns of language, culture, and society: Sub-Saharan Africa.* Ohio State University, 1975, **19**, 185–198.

Hill, C. A. *Linguistic representations of spatial and temporal orientation.* Unpublished report, 1978, mimeo, 15 pp.

Hodun, A. *Comprehension and the development of spatial and temporal sequence terms.* Unpublished doctoral dissertation, University of Wisconsin—Madison, 1975.

Holland, V. M., & Palermo, D. S. On learning less: Language and cognitive development. *Child Development,* 1975, **46**, 437–443.

Ives, S. *Children's ability to coordinate spatial perspectives through rotational descriptions.* Unpublished doctoral dissertation, University of Toronto, 1976.

Johnston, J. *Early locatives and spatial notions.* Unpublished Master of Arts thesis, University of California, Berkeley, 1972.

Johnston, J. R., & Slobin, D. I. The development of locative expressions in English, Italian, Serbo-Croatian, and Turkish. *Progress in Research in Child Language Development,* 1977, **13**, 134–147.

Jones, L. V., & Wepman, J. M. *A spoken word count: Adults.* Chicago: Language Research Associates, 1966.

Kuczaj, S. A., & Maratsos, M. P. On the acquisition of "front," "back," and "side." *Child Development,* 1975, **46**, 202–210.

Leech, G. N. *Towards a semantic description of English.* Bloomington: Indiana University Press, 1970.

Leehey, S. C. *The child's lexical and conceptual knowledge of front and back.* Unpublished research, 1973.

Leehey, S. C., & Carey, S. *Up front: The acquisition of a concept and a word.* Paper presented at 10th Child Language Research Forum, Stanford, Calif., April 1978.

Lorge, I. *The semantic count of the 570 commonest English words.* New York: Teachers College, Columbia University, 1949.

Mach, Ernst. *The analysis of sensations and the relation of the physical to the psychical.* Chicago and London: Open Court Publ., 1914.

Miller, G. A., & Johnson-Laird, P. N. *Language and perception.* London and New York: Cambridge University Press, 1976.

Needham, R. (Ed.). *Right and left: Essays on dual symbolic classification.* Chicago: The University of Chicago Press, 1973.

Nelson, K. Structure and strategy in learning to talk. *Monographs of the Society for Research in Child Development,* 1973, **38** (Serial No. 149).

Paraskevopoulos, I. Symmetry, recall, and preference in relation to chronological age. *Journal of Experimental Child Psychology,* 1968, **6**, 254–264.

Piaget, J. *Judgment and reasoning in the child.* London: Routledge & Kegan Paul, 1928.

Piaget, J. *The child's conception of time.* London: Routledge & Kegan Paul, 1956.

Piaget, J., & Inhelder, B. *The child's conception of space.* London: Routledge & Kegan Paul, 1956.

Piaget, J., & Inhelder, B. *The psychology of the child.* New York: Basic Books, 1969.

Richards, M. M., & Hawpe, L. S. *Space, time and the acquisition of before and after.* Unpublished manuscript, 1978. (Available from authors at Performance Research Laboratory, University of Louisville, Louisville, Kentucky 40208.)

Rinsland, H. D. *A basic vocabulary of elementary school children.* New York: Macmillan, 1945.

Rosch, E., Mervis, C. B., Gray, W. D., Johnson, D. M., & Boyes-Braem, P. Basic objects in natural categories. *Cognitive Psychology,* 1976, **8**, 382–439.

Rovet, J., & Ives, S. W. *Graphic orientations of familiar and novel objects: A developmental and cross-cultural study.* Unpublished manuscript, 1976.

Schaller, M. J., & Harris, L. J. "Upright" orientations of forms change with subjects' age and with features of form. *Perception & Psychophysics,* 1975, **17**, 179–188.

Scupin, E., & Scupin, G. *III. Lebensbild eines deutschen Schuljungen.* Leipzig: Durr, 1931.

Sinha, C., & Walkerdine, V. Spatial and temporal relations in the linguistic and cognitive development of young children. *Progress Report of Research Project: Language development in pre-school children,* School of Education, University of Bristol, England, 1973 (mimeo, 47 pages plus appendices).

Slobin, D. I. Development psycholinguistics. In D. O. Dingwall (Ed.), *A survey of linguistic science.* College Park, Md.: University of Maryland Linguistics Program, 1971.

Tanz, C. M. Studies in the acquisition of deictic terms. (Doctoral dissertation, The University of Chicago, 1976). *Dissertation Abstracts International, Sciences and Engineering,* 1977, **37**, (9–10), 4657.

Werner, H. *Comparative psychology of mental development.* New York: International Universities Press, 1948.

Weyl, H. *Symmetry.* Princeton, N.J.: Princeton University Press, 1952.

THE ORGANIZATION AND CONTROL OF INFANT SUCKING[1]

C. K. Crook

DURHAM UNIVERSITY

DURHAM, ENGLAND

I. Introduction

As a topic for developmental psychololgy, the sucking response has a curious status. It is peculiarly characteristic of infancy; in many children it has apparently disappeared as an activity of any significance by the end of

[1] The author's research cited here was supported by funds from the W. T. Grant Foundation and the United States Public Health Service (Grant HD 03911) awarded to Professor L. P. Lipsitt. Professor Lipsitt's advice and encouragement have been invaluable to this project and to many others over a long period. Thanks are also due to the staffs of the Brown University Child Study Center and the Women and Infants Hospital of Rhode Island; their help and enthusiasm did much to foster my interest in child development.

ADVANCES IN CHILD DEVELOPMENT
AND BEHAVIOR, VOL. 14

the first year. Yet this transient behavior claims an important place in many familiar theories of development and has been the subject of a considerable volume of empirical research.

The interest it has provoked is organized around three broad areas of en-quiry. First there are those who see sucking as a potent manifestation of a more general orality in early childhood. Reasoning principally from clinical observations, the behavior is regarded as the focus of an important de-velopmental stage and as such is strongly implicated in the course of nor-mal personality development (Freud, 1930). Second, the sucking reflex has been identified as one of the earliest and most effective ways in which an infant has commerce with the environment. Insofar as the behavior is evidently put to use in such a wide range of circumstances, such as feeding and social interaction, the dynamics of those particular environmental transactions that sucking permits are likely to be of broad interest. Further-more, some have regarded sucking as one of a number of early "cognitive structures," and one whose adaptations provide a particularly clear il-lustration of certain general principles of cognitive growth (Piaget, 1953). Finally, because it is frequently occurring and readily recorded, the sucking response has recommended itself to those experimental psychologists who, confronted with the nonverbal infant, have sought a viable channel of com-munication with their subject. Its choice as a dependent variable in this area of research is made on pragmatic grounds only; it has allowed ques-tions regarding, say, the infant's perceptual or learning skills to be posed with comparative ease (Kaye, 1967).

The present review is inspired principally by recent advances made in the second of these three research orientations. It includes nothing regarding the psychodynamic theories of the first as, on the whole, long-term developmental consequences of infant sucking activity are outside of our scope. It calls extensively on material from the third; research performed in this tradition has rarely been directly concerned with sucking, but it has often incidentally made contributions to the literature that is.

The first aim of this paper is to assemble and evaluate recent studies con-cerning the organization and control of the infant's sucking reflex. The direction of research has been such that much of the discussion must focus upon factors determining the distribution of responses in time. Thus *organization* refers to the rhythm of the total activity rather than to the coordination of fine movements comprising a single response.

The literature review that defines our first goal is guided by the principle that sucking behavior is an activity of intrinsic interest and one whose organization can be analyzed and understood. What should emerge, therefore, is some feeling for how varied the rhythm of sucking may be and what the sources of this variability are. Special attention is focused upon the issue of whether the response is rigidly organized in the individual at birth, or whether it admits some degree of plasticity. *Plasticity of response* is taken here to mean alterations in topography or rhythm that are meeting changes in the immediate conditions of peripheral feedback: the capacity for adaptation. Such effects of course, may be quite transitory and are not limited to those special contingencies involved in conditioning procedures. The ability of infants to adjust their behavior in this manner has, on the whole, received less empirical study than has early perceptual competence. Thus the perspective of the first half of this paper may incidentally serve to redress a general imbalance within the literature.

Having analyzed the control of sucking per se and equipped with the conclusions that emerge, a second aim will be pursued; namely that of illustrating the functional significance of sucking rhythms and their plasticity. This is approached through a consideration of their relevance to three particular aspects of early development.

Before I proceed further, it is useful to consider how the sucking response is typically recorded and what parameters describe its organization. Kaye (1967) has considered this topic in greater detail. The interested reader is referred to this source for its discussion of measurement problems and for the full account it provides of earlier research into the organization of sucking rhythms.

In the course of executing a single sucking response, the infant will usually create within his mouth both positive pressure changes (expression) and negative pressure changes (suction). Ingenious modifications have been made to commercial nipples to permit both the recording of these pressures and the delivery of nutrient (Brenman, Pierce, Mackowiak, & Friedman, 1969; DeLucia, 1967; Kron, Stein, & Goddard, 1963; Sameroff, 1965; Nowlis, 1973). Despite the fact that most laboratories are thus equipped to quantify sucking amplitude, or vigor, this measure seldom has been reported. Usually, a pressure threshold is preset by the experimenter and whenever some oral activity causes it to be crossed a response is registered. The most popular sucking parameter to be extracted from this all-or-none record is rate of response.

Recently, crude measures of response frequency have given way to more detailed descriptions of sucking rhythms. In particular the episodic quality of the activity has been more fully documented and the sucking "burst" has been employed as a higher level unit of analysis. A *burst* is a group of responses bounded by a pause of some minimum duration, usually taken as about 2 or 3 seconds. Thus, within a given observation period we may ask not just how many responses have occurred but also whether and how the total output has been partitioned into bursts and pauses. This entails a report of the number of bursts, the average number of sucks within a burst, and the average pause duration or interburst interval. A still finer analysis of rhythms may be achieved by considering the temporal distribution of sucks within a burst, i.e., measuring within-burst interresponse times (IRTs). The average IRT is sometimes described as the "rate" of sucking. However, this is strictly a measure of within-burst rate only and should not be confused with absolute response frequency computed over longer periods that may include significant pausing. Within-burst rate, or the reciprocal of IRT, will be referred to here as *pace* of sucking. *Rate* will be reserved for frequency per unit time, inclusive of pauses.

In the following section the form of sucking rhythms is described in more detail and their susceptibility to modification by a variety of factors is discussed.

II. Some Factors That Modify the Sucking Rhythm

Two broad categories of experiments are discussed in this section: those concerned with the effects upon the sucking rhythm of discrete stimuli superimposed upon it, and those in which patterns of sucking are correlated with particular constitutional or biographical details of the individual.

Sucking provides a wealth of stimulation for the infant. We are perhaps inclined to think first of the intraoral feedback consequent upon the activity, but correlations with extraoral stimuli are also possible, and they have certainly been fabricated in the laboratory. Three methodological paradigms have emerged from research in which experimenters have control over the presentation of stimuli, and they each correspond to conditions that may occur in the normal sucking environment. They are illustrated in Fig. 1. In Fig. 1a and b, stimuli, usually of several seconds' duration or longer, are related to the burst and pause rhythms of the responses. They occur within a group of sucks (a), or within a pause (b). Given such correlations, the effects of stimuli upon parameters of the bursts and pauses with which they are associated may be studied. In Fig. 1c brief stimuli are contingent upon each sucking response. Changes in the total output of sucking have been the measure most often used under this condition.

The effects of discrete intraoral and extraoral stimuli are discussed in Section II, A and II, B. Attention is then turned to studies in which the investigator plays a less intrusive role, analyzing the effects upon sucking of variations in arousal, motivation, and prenatal or perinatal history.

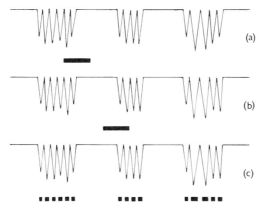

Fig. 1. *Three paradigms for superimposing stimuli upon the sucking rhythm. In (a) the stimulus onset occurs during a sucking burst, in (b) it occurs during a pause, and in (c) it occurs contingent upon individual sucks.*

A. INTRAORAL STIMULI

The stimuli in the intraoral category are the characteristics of the sucking object and of the fluid that it delivers. However, a comparison that must precede this discussion is the fundamental one between sucking with and sucking without any fluid feedback at all, or nutritive and nonnutritive sucking, respectively. Corresponding to these two conditions are two distinct ways of making the response: there is a nutritive and a nonnutritive mode of sucking. This distinction is widely recognized and has been discussed at greater length elsewhere (Dubignon & Campbell, 1968a, 1969b; Lipsitt, Reilly, Butcher, & Greenwood, 1976; Wolff, 1967, 1968a).

Wolff, who has written extensively on the difference, expressed it in these terms: "nutritive sucking is organized as a continuous stream rather than an alternation of bursts and rest periods; and, its mean rate per second [pace] is slower and usually about half that of non-nutritive mouthing" (1968a, p. 948). The human infant may be unique in possessing such distinct sucking patterns. In observation of many other species of mammal, none has been found that displays sucking in what we would refer to as the nonnutritive mode (Brown, 1973; Brown & Pieper, 1973; Wolff, 1968b, 1973). Of course, many are observed to suck on blind nipples and other objects, but they do so in the same slow and continuous rhythm that characterizes their response in feeding.

Thus there is a degree of plasticity in the human sucking pattern that is not typical of other species. Wolff attaches some significance to this observation and suggests that "differences between human and other mammals may represent a qualitative change in central nervous system control over the sucking reflex" (1968b, p. 363). He speculates that there exists distinct central oscillatory mechanisms determining the temporal organization of the behavior (Wolff, 1967, 1968a), and what emerges might be described as a "dual oscillator" theory; separate oscillatory centers control the rhythm of nutritive and nonnutritive sucking.

The terms of such a model imply that rhythms of sucking may be rather inflexible. That is, we may expect feedback from the act of sucking to be relatively unimportant in organizing and sustaining the behavior. In fact, Wolff is cautious not to discount the possible role of peripheral feedback in modulating the output of the oscillators, although he does himself present results from several kinds of study that generally suggest that the effects of such feedback are of minimal significance. For example, he examined the sucking rhythms of infants with congenital disorders of the relevant motor apparatus (e.g., with cleft palates or harelips) and found that, provided they were capable of nonnutritive sucking, they all did so in the normal manner (Wolff, 1967). Moreover, he has observed that if a pacifier is gently removed from the mouth of an infant who has initiated a burst of nonnutritive sucking, that infant will continue mouthing for approximately the length of time that would be expected if the pacifier had been kept in place (Wolff, 1972). Even more startling in this context are reports that, in quiet sleep, the normal burst and pause rhythm can be observed in the spontaneous mouthing of the infant equipped with no pacifier at all (Wolff, 1966, 1967).

All of these observations suggest that the hypothetical central oscillators are remarkably insensitive to feedback from the periphery and that sucking is rather rigidly organized. However, this has not inhibited parametric studies in which properties of the stimuli in Fig. 1c are manipulated. The sections that folow review some of these studies where the stimuli are intraoral.

1. Form of the Sucking Object
Some clinicians have claimed an ability to recognize individual anatomical differences pertinent to the ease with which a mother may be able to breast feed her child (Gunther, 1961; Ogden & MacKeith, 1955). It has been suggested that the female nipple may serve as a releasing stimulus, in the ethological sense, for the sucking act (Peiper, 1963). Surprisingly, there have been few studies in which physical properties of a nipple have been systematically varied in order to observe their influence on sucking rhythm.

Lipsitt and Kaye (1965) demonstrated differences in the total amount of sucking when "optimizing" and "nonoptimizing" stimuli were employed. A commercial nipple evoked almost twice as many responses as a piece of $\frac{1}{4}$-in. laboratory tubing. Dubignon and Campbell (1968a) varied the external diameter of such tubing and recorded less sucking given a tube of $\frac{11}{16}$-in. diameter than one of $\frac{1}{2}$- or $\frac{1}{4}$-in. diameter. In a second experiment "compressibility" was studied by comparing tubes whose walls were $\frac{1}{16}$- or $\frac{1}{8}$-in. thick. The softer tube evoked more sucking. Extending these findings to nutritive sucking, Christensen, Dubignon, and Campbell (1976) compared nipples of different sizes through which formula could be delivered. A large nipple, $\frac{11}{16}$-in. in diameter, was found to evoke fewer sucks at a slower pace than a medium, $\frac{1}{2}$-in. diameter, nipple. Thus, these differences in nipple size have a similar effect upon the rates of nutritive and nonnutritive sucking.

Brown (1972) has cited some unpublished studies in which almost twice as much sucking was evoked by a regular nipple as compared with a blunt nipple, i.e., one from which the elongated portion had been cut. In a further description of this work, Kaye (1972) reports that a regular nipple elicited more sucks per minute than a $\frac{5}{16}$-in. diameter tube, which in turn elicited more sucking than a blunted nipple.

In these studies the commercial pacifiers were dramatically more effective in promoting sucking than the laboratory stimuli. However, the differences between sucking on the laboratory stimuli themselves were rarely very great. These findings are puzzling and suggest that factors other than size and compressibility differences may be relevant to an interpretation of this work. A clue to the problems here may be found in some data reported by Kaye (1972). In his study, a blunt nipple and one cut halfway on the elongated portion elicited only a general agitation. However, two sizes of tubing did generate sucking and, most significant, its rhythm became more like that maintained by a normal nipple as the pressure threshold used to define a single suck was reduced. In fact when the response was simply defined as "observed jaw movements" there was little difference at all in the amount of sucking maintained by tubes and a normal pacifier. Perhaps the lesson in these observations is that while some objects will not elicit the behavior at all, if it does occur it will reliably display the familiar temporal organization of normal nonnutritive sucking; what is effected by "discrepant" sucking objects is the vigor or amplitude of the response. Thus, if the calibration of recording equipment is such that registering a response demands mouthing that exceeds a fairly conservative pressure threshold then laboratory substitutes may only appear to disturb the rhythm of the behavior.

2. *Amount of Fluid per Suck*

Fluid delivery was earlier identified as an important variable in determining sucking patterns, and nutritive and nonnutritive modes of sucking were distinguished. Just how rigidly should that distinction be drawn? Is slow continuous sucking a characteristic of all circumstances when a nutrient is delivered and is fast burst and pause sucking only observed on a blank nipple? One approach to these questions is to vary the amount of fluid delivered at each response.

Crook (1976) compared the sucking patterns of newborns who received either .01 or .04 ml of 5% sucrose solution contingent upon individual sucks. In 4-minute comparison periods, the number of sucks made did not differ, but the smaller amount of fluid caused an increase in the total pausing time. As would therefore be expected, the pace of sucking for the smaller amount was significantly faster. To summarize: The smaller amount of fluid evoked a pattern of responding comparable to the nonnutritive mode, while the larger amount evoked a pattern more typical of the nutritive sucking mode.

These results have been replicated by Burke (1977), who in addition recorded swallowing. Larger amounts of fluid at each suck led to more swallowing, and the interresponse times following a swallow tended to be longer. Interresponse times not associated with swallowing were unaffected by the amount of fluid variable. These findings suggest there are two populations of IRTs, one associated with swallowing and one independent of it. The slower pace of nutritive sucking reflects more swallowing and, thus, a relative increase in the size of the swallow-linked population of longer IRTs. This may account for the effects of amount of fluid upon pace of sucking. The changes in pausing time may represent incentive-motivational effects of manipulating the amount of fluid.

3. *Frequency of Fluid Delivery*

Nutrient need not be delivered after every suck that an infant makes. It can be presented intermittently. The rules governing the probability that any particular suck will be followed by nutrient delivery are comparable to the "schedules of reinforcement" employed in the study of operant conditioning (Ferster & Skinner, 1957).

Bosack (1973) compared groups of newborns who sucked nutritively or who were reinforced with dextrose solution after every third, fifth, or tenth suck made. Less frequent reinforcement increased the pace of responding and evoked shorter bursts. These contingencies of fluid delivery had no effect upon the total number of sucks emitted, although in a second study involving a longer observation period, the sparser schedules also evoked less overall sucking.

Hillman and Bruner (1972) have studied the effects of scheduling milk reinforcement during the normal feeds of two groups of infants, one aged between 1 and 2 months and the other between 3 and 4 months. Some infants experienced a fixed-ratio condition in which milk occurred after every response or after every second, third, or fourth response. Infants in a fixed-interval condition received milk for a response that occurred after a certain time had elapsed since the last reinforcement. The times employed ranged between .3 and 2.0 seconds. For both ratio and interval schedules, as reinforcement was made less frequent, sucking bursts became shorter and pauses became longer. Both effects were more marked for the older infants.

In discussing the fixed-interval results elsewhere, Bruner (1968) has suggested that they exemplify an early form of rule or strategy learning. The pattern of instrumental responding displayed by animal subjects exposed to fixed-interval schedules is a pause after reinforcement followed by positively accelerated responding (Ferster & Skinner, 1957). Bruner views the shorter sucking bursts and lengthened pauses on his longer interval schedules as reflecting a comparable attempt at solving the problem; the infant is learning that starting and stopping more may be efficient. However, in the absence of more detailed information regarding the relation between fluid deliveries and pausing, it is more parsimonious to regard the effects reported as reflecting changes in overall reinforcement frequency rather than changes in the specific distribution of reinforcements in time. If fact, the same changes in response rhythm were observed under the ratio conditions even though the two contingencies required different strategies for "solution."

4. Taste

The form of the nipple, the amount of fluid, and the frequency with which it is delivered all influence sucking. To some extent, the effects of manipulating each of these variables can be understood in terms of constraints associated with the mechanics and structure of the infant's feeding apparatus. The swallowing reflex has already been mentioned and the accommodation of sucking to different quantities of fluid may be an illustration of the interdependence of sucking and swallowing. However, variations in taste stimulation consequent upon sucking would not seem to require any comparable adjustment in the feeding mechanism. The effects of taste qualities are therefore of special interest, for they may reflect a movitational source of response plasticity. In several studies the effects of nutrient taste properties upon various aspects of sucking behavior have been reported; in others the dependent variable has simply been amount of nutrient ingested. In these cases we may assume that increased intake is correlated with an increase in the frequency of sucking, although changes in sucking amplitude may also be implicated.

Most available research concerns infants during the first days of life. Kron, Stein, Goddard, and Phoenix (1967) observed more sucking for milk formula than for 5% corn syrup. Dubignon and Campbell (1969b) report a similar finding in comparing formula with 5% dextrose and implicate the role of taste stimuli in this effect. The possibly confounding influences of texture and viscosity were controlled by Nisbett and Gurwitz (1970), who found greater intake of the sweeter of two formulas. Desor, Maller, and Turner (1973) compared various concentrations of sucrose, glucose, fructose, and lactose solutions. Infants ingested more as concentration increased. Also, the relative intakes of these sugars closely matched relative sweetnesses judged by adults. Finally, Kobre and Lipsitt (1972) found more sucking for a 15% sucrose solution than for distilled water.

The main conclusion to be drawn from these studies is that sweeter fluids increase the total amount of sucking within a feeding period. Crook (1977) has attempted to specify the exact changes in response rhythm that mediate this increase. Neonates sucked for either water or 5, 10, or 15% sucrose during a 12-minute period. Increasing concentration caused longer bursts and shorter pauses, and the pace of responding decreased with increasing concentration over the whole range studied. These effects were also observed in a within-subject comparison of sucking for 5 vs. 15% sucrose (Crook & Lipsitt, 1976). Variations in taste stimulation, therefore, can affect both the "coarse," burst and pause, structure of sucking as well as the "fine," within-burst, structure of the response.

One study of older children (5–11 and 20–28 weeks) by Desor, Maller, and Greene (1977) reveals comparable patterns of preferences to those reported for the newborn and thus implies that the effects of sweet taste upon sucking remain stable well into infancy.

Sweeter fluids evoke more sucking. However, if total intake of fluid reflects taste preference, finding that pace of sucking is actually slower for sweeter fluids seems paradoxical. However, Burke (1977) compared intake of 5 vs. 10% sucrose in Lipsitt's laboratory and found that swallowing occurred more often for the 10% solution. Given that a swallow lengthens the interresponse time with which it is associated, the mean IRT for 10% sucrose should be longer. This still does not account for all of the concentration effect, as Burke also found that not only swallowing but also nonswallowing IRTs were longer for the sweeter solution. A second factor that may be implicated is response amplitude. Slower sucking may conceal more vigorous sucking. If this is so, it would clarify the finding of higher heart rates accompanying the intake of sweeter solutions (Crook & Lipsitt, 1976). A report by Nowlis and Kessen (1976) also lends support to this suggestion. They found increased anterior tongue pressures associated with higher concentrations of glucose and sucrose. These various effects of sweet taste stimulation upon neonatal sucking have been described elsewhere in terms of "savoring" (Lipsitt *et al.,* 1976; Crook & Lipsitt, 1976). Whether there is an exact parallel with adult savoring maneuvers is unclear, but the research reviewed does force recognition of the hedonically positive properties of sweet taste for the newborn.

While the sucking rhythm may be modified by fluid sweetness, there is little information regarding the influence of other taste qualities. Maller and Desor (1973) have fed infants solutions of urea in various concentrations (.03–.18 M), also citric acid (.001–.012 M) and sodium chloride (.00312–.20 M). Intake of these solutions was not significantly different from that of water. Thus bitter, sour, and salt stimulation of moderate intensity do not appear to disturb the rhythm of sucking.

The reason for the sparse literature regarding effects of taste must be the risk associated with feeding many sapid solutions in all but the smallest amounts. Recently, an alternative method has been advanced that overcomes this problem while more adequately meeting the requirements of taste psychophysics (Crook, 1978). The effects of taste stimulation upon sucking have traditionally been studied within the paradigm described by Fig. 1c. However, intraoral stimuli may also be administered as in Fig. 1b. Thus, a .04-ml "pulse" of fluid was intermittently presented to newborns during the pauses in their nonnutritive sucking rhythms. A burst of (unreinforced) sucking reliably followed (Crook, 1978), and this burst was longer than recorded on randomly interspersed control trials. The potency of such stimulation initiating sucking is illustrated in Fig. 2. Response latency is the time between stimulus onset and the next recorded suck. Figure 2 shows the frequency distribution of such latencies when the stimulus was 5% sucrose solution and also for control trials upon which no stimulus was delivered but equivalent measures were taken. It is apparent that latencies are very short and that, often, a well-formed sucking response is initiated within 1 second of stimulus onset. This is noteworthy in view of the commonly expressed view that the newborn possesses a rather sluggish nervous system (e.g., Brackbill & Thompson, 1967, p. 17).

Is latency or burst length influenced by taste properties of the fluid stimulus? Latencies seem independent of taste stimulation. The immediacy of the sucking response presumably reflecting the potency of the stimulus fluid in the mouth. Burst lengths, however, are effected by the taste variable. The bursts potentiated become longer with increasing concentrations of sucrose solutions, at least to a moderate sweetness (about .4 M), after which there is a tendency for them to shorten. When sodium chloride solutions are the stimuli, increasing concentration results in a shortening of

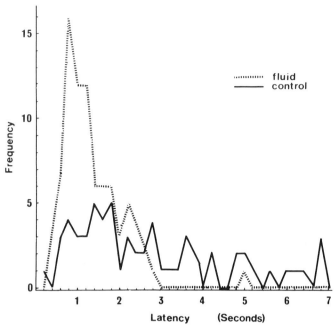

Fig. 2 Latencies to initiate nonnutritive sucking on trials in which a brief fluid stimulus occurs during a pause in the rhythm compared to latencies on unstimulated and interspersed control trials.

the bursts. Thus, brief intraoral fluid stimuli rapidly evoke a sucking burst,
the length of which is influenced by taste properties of that fluid.

5. Conclusions

The focus of research reviewed above has been upon neonates and our conclusions must therefore be limited to the behavior of very young infants. A
pacifier, or blind nipple, will evoke a pattern of sucking that has a marked
burst and pause character. Studies of infants born with gross central nervous system damage suggest that this rhythm is organized at a primitive
level within the brain (Peiper, 1963). Furthermore, observations of spontaneous mouthing, reactions to discrepant sucking objects, and the sucking
of infants with craniofacial abnormalities all lead to the conclusions that
once the behavior is initiated it displays a stereotyped temporal organization that is relatively independent of peripheral feedback. A more significant dimension of variability in nonnutritive sucking may be its vigor, but
as yet we have few data on that subject.

When fluid is made contingent upon sucking the plasticity inherent in the behavior becomes apparent. The basic change of rhythm that ensues has been widely acknowledged, but the results of recent experiments in which qualitative and quantitative properties of nutrients have been manipulated do argue against a strict dichotomy of nutritive and nonnutritive sucking modes. There appears to exist a continuum of response organization, from fast burst and pause responding to a slow continuous output. It is tempting to conclude that incentive variables control responding on this continuum, with reductions in the amount and quality of nutrients shifting the rhythm toward that typical of nonnutritive conditions. This may be broadly true, but close inspection of results from some of the studies cited above reveals a more complicated picture. These complexities deserve elaboration here, for they do make important points regarding the plasticity of nutritive sucking.

The quantity of fluid delivered within a feed can be manipulated by altering the amount delivered at each suck or by altering its frequency of delivery as described above. For example, we might halve the quantity available by halving the amount provided per individual suck or by delivering an unchanged amount after only every second suck. The relevant experiment has not been conducted but it can be inferred from data that are available that different response rhythms would be maintained by these two procedures. Although this asymmetry could be discussed with respect to measures of the continuity of sucking rhythms, the implications for control of the pace of responding are more interesting. Reducing the amount of fluid at each suck has dramatic effects on mean IRTs; however, intermittency of fluid presentation influences response pace hardly at all. Even when only every tenth response is reinforced (FR 10) mean IRTs remain considerably longer than those typical of nonnutritive conditions (Bosack, 1973; Dubignon & Campbell, 1968b, 1969a). Furthermore, given that fluid is delivered occasionally, the degree of intermittency exerts no strong effects. Thus, in Bosack's Experiment II, IRTs on FR 10 were actually slightly longer than those on FR 5 and while Dubignon and Campbell (1969a) found a large difference between nonnutritive sucking and FR 10 dextrose on this measure, the difference between FR 10 and a regular bottle feed was much smaller. Examination of a typical polygraph record describing FR 10 dextrose sucking (Dubignon & Campbell, 1968b, Fig. 2) suggests that after individual fluid deliveries, sucking slows down and is only just beginning to accelerate once more when another delivery occurs.

These results suggest that the effect of nutrient on a single sucking response is to "trigger" a slower and more typically nutritive mode of sucking. Direct support for this conclusion emerges from a study already described in which brief fluid presentation occurs in the pauses of nonnutritive sucking: the pace of the potentiated burst tends to be slow. In Fig. 3 the durations of successive IRTs at the beginning of stimulated and control bursts are compared. Group means for the first eight responses have been plotted. The common IRT lengthening effect is significant, $F(6,54) = 9.5$, $p < .01$, but so also is the difference between stimulated and control bursts, $F(1,9) = 7.7$, $p < .05$.

In conclusion, the effects of quantitative parameters of fluid delivery are not well illustrated by manipulating reinforcement frequency. The reason is that brief intraoral fluid stimulations, within a burst or prior to its onset, can effectively trigger a pattern of sucking—and one that is perhaps more appropriate to the condition in which that brief fluid stimulus continues to occur at each suck. Most important, these results indicate that the control of nutritive sucking, particularly with respect to response pace, is not solely accounted for in terms of the moment-to-moment feedback from nutrient delivery.

B.   EXTRAORAL STIMULI

The capacity of extraoral stimuli to modify the sucking rhythm has been examined with all three paradigms illustrated in Fig. 1. The intermittent presentation of stimuli lasting several seconds or longer whose effects are judged with respect to the organization of bursts and pauses, i.e., Fig. 1a and b, will be referred to as "The Bronshtein procedure." This

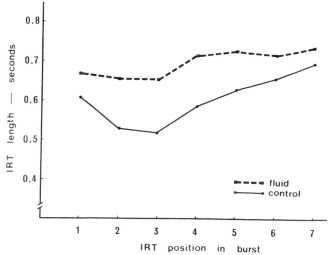

Fig. 3. Successive interresponse times at the start of nonnutritive sucking bursts that follow upon brief fluid stimulation and at the start of unstimulated control bursts.

acknowledges the early description of method (a) by Bronshtein, Antonova, Kamenetskaya, Luppova, and Sytova (1958). Stimulus presentation may be contingent upon some feature of the burst and pause rhythm
(response locked) or on a purely temporal basis (time locked).

Experiments that employ method (c), thus creating analogs to the feeding
situation with extraoral stimuli, will be termed "response-contingent procedures." Effects here are usually sought as changes in response rate.

1. The Bronshtein Procedure

In the experiment by Bronshtein *et al.* (1958), various stimuli were
presented within the sucking bursts of infants aged up to 1 week (Fig. 1a).
It was claimed that such stimulation shortened a burst. The effect was at-
tenuated on repeated stimulation. Subsequent experiments have attempted
to replicate and extend this finding; including some in which stimuli occur
during pauses (Fig. 1b). Kaye (1967) concluded that, in general, it has
proved very difficult to demonstrate any reliable disturbance of sucking
and, at best, the phenomenon was fragile. One difficulty in assessing Bronshtein's original studies is the wide range of ages represented in his sample.
The studies reviewed here are organized with respect to this variable.

Infants with a mean gestational age of 33.2 weeks were tested around the
third week of life by Barrett and Miller (1973) for effects of a 10-second
visual stimulus on nonnutritive sucking. They observed less sucking during
stimulus presentation than during 10-second control periods, a result most
marked in the chronologically older children. Miller (1975), however, was
unable to demonstrate any such effect with premature infants exposed to
10-second presentations of an auditory stimulus previously shown to elicit
an autonomic response. Brown (1973) superimposed two 30-second visual
stimuli upon the sucking of infants with a mean gestational age of 35.5
weeks. A 30-second intertrial interval separated the stimuli. The position of
the infant was then adjusted and a second test was begun involving a "loud
bell" of 5 seconds duration. Stimulations occurred within the initial bursts
of the second and fourth minutes. For both studies ratios were calculated
of response rate during stimulation to that rate plus response rate for a
period of the same duration immediately preceding. Ratios were below .5
on the first trial of both tests, indicating suppression, but increased
significantly on the second trials. This result is of interest, being the sole
claim to having replicated the attenuation of suppression reported by Bronshtein *et al.* (1958). Unfortunately, the experiment did not incorporate
unstimulated control subjects. If there were a gradual decrease in nonnutritive sucking rate from the time of pacifier insertion, then we would expect a suppression ratio to behave in the manner described, even in the total
absence of stimulation. Moreover, Levin and Kaye (1964) have reported that

such a change in response rate does typically occur across the initial few minutes of a sucking period.

Sameroff (1967) alternated 1-minute periods of visual or auditory stimulation with 1-minute control periods during the sucking of infants born at term. Although there was no effect of stimulation on a time-spent-sucking measure, there were more bursts during stimulation periods. *Post hoc* analysis of events at the points of stimulus change indicated that both bursts and pauses were lengthened if the change occurred within them. This finding is, of course, opposite to that typical of the Bronshtein effect. Wolff and Simmons (1967) administered a 2-second tactile stimulus to newborns in both pauses and bursts. In this study sucking was elicited by stimulation during a pause (they do not present within-burst data). A response-locked procedure with brief stimuli was also employed by Semb and Lipsitt (1968). A 1-second square-wave tone occurred either during pauses or during bursts; interspersed were unstimulated control trials. Both pauses and bursts were shortened by the stimuli that occurred within them. Sameroff (1971) considered both onset and offset of an auditory stimulus presented and terminated during the sucking bursts of newborns. A shortening of bursts was found at both onset and offset, although this effect was not stable across the four days on which subjects were observed.

With respect to the effects of stimulation occurring during bursts, these experiments involving newborns are in reasonable agreement: The bursts are shortened. An exception is the opposite effect reported by Sameroff (1967). Where stimuli have been presented during pauses the effect has been to shorten the pause or potentiate sucking. Again Sameroff (1967) found the opposite. These opposing results may be related to Sameroff's time-locked procedure or to the rather mild stimuli he employed. Thus, the intensity of his auditory stimulus was 60 db (background noise unspecified) while Semb and Lipsitt (1968), who obtained the complete reverse effect, used a 91-db tone (69-db background). All experimenters consistently failed to find any attenuation of the various effects reported.

Two experiments have extended these procedures to the study of older infants. Haith, Kessen, and Collins (1969) report a general suppression of sucking when visual movement of varying complexity was presented to infants aged between 2 and 4 months. Sameroff (1970) studied infants aged 1, 2, and 3 months in an attempt to see how far the wider age range employed by Bronshtein et al. (1958) might account for the more dramatic effects they report. He employed the same paradigm for auditory stimulus presentation as that later to be used in his study of newborns (Sameroff, 1971). Burst shortening effects did occur with the 3-month-old infants at stimulus onset; this supports the findings of Bronshtein et al. However, no such effects were found with the younger infants. These results are difficult to interpret, as Sameroff (1971) does subsequently find such effects, albeit weak ones, with newborns. Stimulus onset during a pause lengthened that pause for the 3-month-old group but had no effect in the other two age groups.

The rhythm of infant sucking is clearly susceptible to extraoral stimuli. Later we shall return to the question of how these results bear on the infant's capacity for orienting behavior. For the present it should be noted that the original Bronshtein burst suppression effect is well documented, although its habituation is not. Other effects are more controversial, but this is perhaps to be expected given that such a wide range of stimuli are represented in these experiments. It is likely that stimuli differing in intensity and quality will have different effects; parametric studies that consider this possibility would make a useful contribution to this problem.

2. Response-Contingent Stimulation

It is perhaps surprising that an exteroceptive analog of the brief delivery of fluid was not investigated until recently; moreover, when such studies did emerge they were not designed by analogy with nutritive sucking but were extensions of a conditioning procedure applied to the foot kicking response of infants and known as "conjugate reinforcement" (Lindsley, 1963). This involves a relationship between dynamic properties of responding and changes along prothetic dimensions of a stimulus, although an agreed formal definition of the procedure is hard to find. Some authors are consistent in providing a definition of conjugate reinforcement as a procedure in which contingent stimulus is made proportional to response pace (Lipsitt, Pederson, & DeLucia, 1966; Rovee & Rovee, 1969).

Siqueland and DeLucia (1969) report such an experiment. Groups of 4-and 12-month-old infants experienced conditions whereby faster sucking caused either an increase or a decrease in the illumination of certain visual patterns. A third group was permitted to suck normally but experienced no stimulus changes. For the increasing illumination groups, this contingency resulted in faster responding than both their own baseline levels and that of the control group. Removing the contingency was followed by a decline in response rate. Sucking was not suppressed in the group whose responding resulted in a decrease in stimulus illumination.

Increased sucking rate associated with conjugate reinforcement is not, of course, maintained indefinitely. An eventual decline toward baseline rates may, by analogy with studies of primary reinforcement, reflect stimulus satiation. If the infant is in fact "bored" with the stimulus his sucking exposes, it might be expected that were it to change suddenly, sucking rate would recover. Siqueland (1969) has reported that "satiation" does indeed occur and he also has demonstrated a recovery effect through the introduction of a novel stimulus. Milewski and Siqueland (1975) have been able with this habituation–dishabituation method to demonstrate a sensitivity to novel visual stimuli in infants as young as 3–5 weeks.

Kalnis and Bruner (1973) have adapted the procedure to demonstrate that infants between 5 and 12 weeks old increase their rate of sucking when this brings a motion picture into focus and maintains it thus as long as response rate remains high. However, sucking was not suppressed when the contingency required a low rate of response to focus the stimulus; it is interesting to note that Siqueland and DeLucia (1969) also failed to suppress sucking in their experiment. Nevertheless, both sets of results are clear in showing that by the fourth week of life sucking may be increased if it exposes the infant to certain visual stimuli.

Similar effects have been demonstrated with auditory stimuli. Wormith, Parkhurst, and Moffitt (1975) have utilized sucking habituation and dishabituation to demonstrate discrimination between 500- and 200- Hz pure tones by infants with an average age of 35 days. However, the bulk of research with auditory stimuli has involved speech sounds and originates from the work of Eimas, Siqueland, Juszyck, and Vigorito (1971). They were able to show that infants of 1 and 4 months could discriminate the acoustic cue (voice onset time) distinguishing stop consonants $|b|$ and $|p|$.

The original experiments on conjugate reinforcement were addressing the question of whether various stimuli could serve to reinforce the young infant. The emphasis of more recent research has been toward applying this plasticity of sucking to issues of developmental psychophysics. In the course of this enterprise the conjugate reinforcement aspect of the procedure has been gradually abandoned. Thus, simply using a fixed-duration stimulus contingent upon sucks above a preset amplitude, both Trehub and Rabinovitch (1972) and Eimas (1975) have successfully obtained evidence of discrimination between various natural and synthetic speech sounds. Regardless of such procedural details, the principles embodied in this method have allowed advances in our understanding of perceptual development that have been greeted with enthusiasm. The measure of this success seems to emphasize the practical gains to be made from studying the plasticity of infant sucking.

C.   CONDITIONING

Most of the modifications in sucking rhythm that have been discussed so far cannot be said to have exploited any capacity to learn that the infant may possess. Is there evidence for the kind of response plasticity associated with successful conditioning procedures? In this section, attempts to manipulate sucking through conditioning are considered. Earlier studies of the newborn judged successful by Kaye (1967) mainly concerned classical conditioning of the response. However, a more recent review of this literature (Sameroff, 1972) argues that the evidence for classical conditioning of sucking is not persuasive. Sameroff suggests the newborn is "prepared" for operant but not for classical contingencies (cf. Seligman, 1970).

Several experiments cited in Section II,B have been interpreted in terms of operant conditioning. These might well have been discussed here; however, many of them, being concerned more with perceptual than with learning skills, have neglected control groups necessary to demonstrate conditioning. In fact, the necessary controls are difficult to implement. Stimuli consequent upon each suck may modify the infant's general level of arousal and thus his sucking, or they may merely serve to elicit sucks rather than to reinforce preceding ones. However, Siqueland (1969) reports a crucial experiment in which sucking of a group of 1-month-old infants caused the presentation of a visual stimulus, while that of a second group caused its withdrawal. After several minutes the stimulus was changed and response rates after this change were compared with a no-shift control group. The presentation group sucked relatively more for the novel stimulus and the withdrawal group relatively less. The results provide strong support for interpreting the effects of response-contingent exteroceptive stimuli in terms of operant conditioning. Studies of this kind are often discussed in terms of the reinforcement of "high-amplitude" sucking; however, only rarely is it clear whether high-amplitude sucking increased disproportionately with any increase in the total sucking output. Such selective reinforcement of some property of an operant has elsewhere been termed *response differentiation* (Skinner, 1938). Siqueland and DeLucia (1969) provide evidence for the differentiation of sucking amplitude and several other conjugate reinforcement experiments may be viewed in terms of the differentiation of response rate through the selective reinforcement of interresponse times [these are conventionally considered a "property" of operant responses (Morse, 1966)]. These studies involve infants aged 1 month or over; recently, attempts have also been made to modify the sucking of newborns through response differentiation.

I did a study in which nutritive sucking interresponse times of newborns were selectively reinforced. Two groups of eight subjects were studied. Each subject's median IRT during a 2-minute period of sucking for 5% sucrose was calculated. One group was shifted immediately to a condition wherein only IRTs longer than their medians were reinforced, while the other group was reinforced for IRTs shorter than their medians. Neither group showed significant changes in response pace across a 20-minute period. For both groups, reinforcement frequency remained at approximately 50%. This result therefore suggests that the pace of sucking is not easily modified by selective reinforcement.

Sameroff (1968) reports more success in modifying topographical properties of sucking. During a 5-minute feed some subjects received nutrient on the suction component of sucking while others received it on expression. In the suction reinforcement group, suction amplitude was higher during the feed, although there was no reduction in the frequency of expression. Differential reinforcement of expression led to a diminution of suction frequency and amplitude. In a second study either a high or a low threshold of expression was set for reinforcement. Infants modified their amplitude of expression appropriate to the threshold in effect. Certain observations suggest these various changes do not result from operant conditioning. Infants were seen twice and the experience of the first session did not effect performance in the second. Moreover, the effects that were observed occurred very rapidly and disappeared during subsequent nonnutritive sucking. Sameroff concludes that his results probably illustrate the adaption of previously organized abilities rather than conditioning.

Differentiation of the duration of individual sucks has been attempted with newborns by Butterfield and Siperstein (1972). Durations were increased when complex auditory stimuli occurred during the sucking action but decreased when they occurred in the intervals between sucks. Thus, the infant effectively increased his exposure to the stimuli which, accordingly, are identified as reinforcers. No controls for differences in the effects of the two procedures upon general arousal or their differential eliciting properties were employed. However, in a later study (Siperstein, 1973) additional subjects were "yoked" to the experimental group such that they received comparable stimulation but independently of their sucking behavior. Modification of sucking duration was observed in the contingent but not in the yoked groups. The adequacy of the yoked control procedure in experiments of this kind has been questioned (Church, 1964); such considerations may be pertinent here, for if these findings do illustrate conditioning of neonatal sucking, they are in some ways rather puzzling. The changes in suck duration take place very rapidly after the contingencies are established and there is no satiation; response differentiation effects are maintained across a period including 800 sucks. Furthermore, when stimuli occurred between sucks the bursting character of sucking would ensure that subjects experienced the reinforcer around 75% of the session time. Slight decreases in the duration of individual sucks would make a small difference to this figure; a total suppression of the response would cause a more dramatic exposure to the "reinforcement" but it is not indicated whether such effects occurred.

The problems of interpretation characteristic of response differentiation procedures are overcome in a novel approach to neonatal conditioning described by Brown (1972). Following Premack's (1965) reinforcement principle, a contingency was established between two responses differing in their baseline probabilities of occurrence: sucking on a regular and on a blunt nipple. A given number of sucks on one nipple was followed by a reinforcement period of either continued access to the same nipple or access to the other. Rate of both regular and blunt nipple sucking was higher when followed by access to the regular nipple as opposed to access to the blunt. Response properties principally affected by reinforcement were the latency to initiate sucking following acceptance of the nipple and the length of sucking bursts. However, Brown does suggest that the less potent reinforcer does not inhibit the entire sucking response. Visual inspection of polygraph records indicated that subjects modified response rate by inhibiting the suction component of responses at the start of bursts. Results similar to those of Brown (1972) have also been reported by Brassell and Kaye (1974).

There is thus good evidence that the sucking response of the newborn may be modified by operant conditioning. Response rate within a given period of sucking opportunity may be increased by suitable reinforcement. The results of response differentiating procedures must be assessed with caution. Effects are clear for the infant 1 month and older but for the newborn, while sucking may be modified with such procedures, the interpretation of this plasticity as being due to operant conditioning is equivocal.

D.   AROUSAL AND HUNGER

In the preceding sections the plasticity of sucking has been illustrated by reference to the influence of what may be termed "peripheral factors." Two "central factors" that have effects on sucking are arousal, or state, and hunger. Neither of these is easily studied independently of the other and so it is perhaps appropriate to combine discussions of them here.

Both hunger and satiation may be operationally defined in terms of the time elapsed since a feed or the amount consumed at a feed. The definition of arousal is more complex.

In some studies, observational ratings of activity level are employed. These may be supplemented by polygraph recording of various autonomically controlled functions and the electroencephalogram (EEG) provides yet another basis for categorization. It must be realized for the present discussion that an infant's state of arousal is correlated with time since feeding (cf. Peiper, 1963, pp. 471–478) and although the exact pattern of state changes between feeds is not straightforward we may say that at least with the newborn, deep sleep is more likely immediately after a feed and awake states are more likely immediately before (e.g., Gaensbauer & Emde, 1973; Wolff, 1966).

One approach to understanding the relations of state and sucking is simply to observe those sucking movements which, as has been mentioned earlier, the neonate emits spontaneously in the absence of specific intraoral stimuli. Wolff (1966) has documented such mouthing in all arousal states except crying and certain epochs of regular or deep sleep. Korner (1969) observed them to be most frequent in regular sleep and Wenner, Douthitt, Burke, and Keenan (1970) observed them to some degree in all sleep–wake states. Where EEG criteria of sleep have been employed disagreement has arisen as to whether spontaneous sucking occurs in sleep characterized by rapid eye movements (REM). For example, Roffwarg, Muzio, and De-ment (1966) report that it does, but Goldie, Svedson-Rhodes, and Robertson (1970) observed sucking only in non-REM sleep.

It is clear that spontaneous sucking can occur during neonatal sleep. How its frequency of occurrence is distributed across the various phases of sleep is more controversial. However, it would seem that when such mouthing does occur it displays a temporal organization indistinguishable from that normally induced by a pacifier (Wolff, 1966). Wolff (1972) has also examined pacifier sucking itself during regular sleep, irregular sleep, and awake states. Variability in the various parameters of sucking rhythm tends to be greater in the more awake states and response amplitudes are higher. However, the temporal organization does in general remain fairly stable across changing states of arousal.

The relationship between state and sucking may also be explored by permitting infants only intermittent access to a pacifier and correlating measures of sucking with preceding arousal state; Levin and Kaye (1964) reported a positive correlation between the total number of sucks in 3-minute periods, each separated by 3-minute rests, and a degree of wakefulness score derived from ratings taken before each sucking period. However, neither Dubignon and Campbell (1968a) nor Bell and Haaf (1971) were able to find such correlations between nonnutritive sucking and immediately preceding state recordings. It is possible that in these two experiments there was a greater homogeneity of state among subjects. Dubignon and Campbell point out that their infants were all tested immediately before feeding. Infants in the Bell and Haaf (1971) study experienced a degree of handling in the course of another test preceding the sucking period; this may have reduced individual differences in state.

It was noted above that newborn infants commonly fall into regular sleep shortly after feeding. Kaye (1967) reports that nonnutritive sucking rate drops to a low around 30 minutes postfeeding, after which it begins to recover. He also noted closely parallel changes in state. These may be attributed to stomach loading, to oral fatigue, or to both of these factors. Although the nature of this relationship may be peripheral to our present concern, it is important to determine whether effects of a feed upon subsequent sucking are merely a consequence of the effects of feeding upon state, or whether some aspect of feeding per se is implicated.

Wolff (1972) has approached some of these issues and examined a group of infants with tracheoesophegeal fistulas during their recovery from surgical attention. Three treatments were compared: a normal oral feed administered as soon as it became tolerable, a direct gastronomy feeding with no sucking, and a sham feed in which oral consumption of fluid was accompanied by continuous aspiration of stomach contents. State readings were made before, during, and 30 minutes after a feed. There was no effect of sham feeding upon state but a full stomach was accompanied by greatly reduced arousal after the feed. This reduction was somewhat more marked if the stomach had been filled by a normal oral feed. Nonnutritive sucking was recorded in 5-minute probe tests before, during, and after feeding. It is known that the total amount of nutritive sucking declines across the course of a feed. It is not known whether fatigue plays a significant role in this decline. Wolff's results show that the organization of nonnutritive sucking was unaffected during or after any of these feeding experiences. After the gastric loading treatments there were cases of infants asleep and not sucking at all; however, if sucking did occur it manifested the same general rhythm.

The newborn infant's level of arousal will influence amount, if not organization, of nonnutritive sucking and a full or empty stomach is one correlate of arousal state. However, the activity of feeding and the consequent gastric loading do not seem to disturb nonnutritive sucking independently of their effects on states. Nutritive sucking, in contrast, is markedly reduced in the course of feeding. As for the periods between feeds, it would seem that state is a good predictor of how much an infant will suck, but time since feeding is only a moderate predictor of state.

E. PRENATAL AND PERINATAL FACTORS

There is relatively little research relating medical biography and sucking patterns. The literature that does exist suggests that normal sucking is little affected by nonoptimal conditions present before and during birth. Thus, Dubignon, Campbell, Curtis, and Partington (1969) related the sucking rates of neonates to a wide range of factors taken from their clinical records. Of the many correlations, few were statistically significant. They found less nutritive sucking in 2-minute test periods when labor had been short. They also found less sucking from infants delivered by mid forceps compared with low forceps or spontaneous delivery. None of the factors considered had any effect on nonnutritive sucking.

The nature of sucking by premature infants has received some study. Wolff (1968a) has succeeded in recording the response from infants of 33–34 weeks gestational age. However, only after the thirty-seventh week were sucking rhythms comparable to those of infants born at term. Other writers agree that prior to this time there can be seen a gradual increase in the pace and in the total amount of sucking (Cortial & Lezine, 1974; Dubignon, Campbell, & Partington, 1969).

Many drugs taken during pregnancy pass through the placental barrier and enter the fetal circulation. Several investigators have been concerned with the implications of this situation for neonatal behavior. Medication that is administered in the course of delivery has aroused special interest in this context and attempts have been made to measure its effect on aspects of infant behavior.

Unfortunately, it is often difficult to isolate causal relationships in such studies. A drug may influence a mother's postnatal behavior toward her infant and it may be this that affects the child rather than the direct influence of the drug. Moreover, the very reasons for applying medication may also be relevant. A study that was well controlled in these respects considered the effects of obstetric medication upon neonatal nutritive sucking (Kron, Stein, & Goddard, 1966). Two groups of women were randomly sampled from cases of uncomplicated pregnancies. Women in one group were administered 200 mg of secobarbital sodium during active labor and received no additional analgesia or anesthesia. Women in the other, control, group received no form of obstetric medication at all. Beginning at 24–36 hours after birth, sucking measures were taken from the infants with no maternal involvement. On three consecutive days, those infants born to mothers administered the barbiturate sucked significantly less during a 9-minute test. Sucking pressures were also reduced, although only on the first day.

The effects upon the baby of this routine dosage of barbiturate were described as "depressant." Kron and his colleagues have also investigated the influence upon sucking of drugs whose effects place infants at the other extreme of the arousal continuum. Such cases are provided by infants born to mothers suffering narcotic addictions during pregnancy. The neonate requires particularly sensitive care in these circumstances, as adjusting the level of postnatal drug therapy to the degree of narcotic withdrawal can be hazardous. Kron, Finnegan, Kaplan, Litt, and Phoenix (1975) have analyzed the sucking of infants born to addicted mothers. The response is much depressed in such cases and Kron et al. note that the high level of central nervous system (CNS) irritability associated with clinical withdrawal influences sucking in the same way as low level of arousal associated with obstetric sedation. It was suggested that sucking provides a convenient and useful measure of CNS excitation–depression. Subsequent research has shown nutritive sucking rate to be sensitive to different forms of pharmacotherapy employed for neonatal narcotic abstinence (Kron, Litt, Phoenix, & Finnegan, 1976).

It has been recognized for some time that neonatal feeding difficulties are correlated with obstetric medications (e.g., Brazelton, 1961). There is some, but still limited, evidence indicating that nutritive sucking can be directly affected by drug action; i.e., exclusively of the effects from associated factors in the mother's clinical condition or drug actions upon her own postnatal behavior. Nonnutritive sucking appears rather resistant to adverse prenatal and perinatal factors; although Dreier and Wolff (1972) found measures of response organization displayed greater variability in infants with a history of perinatal distress (but these effects are less compelling if two-tailed rather than one-tailed, statistical tests are applied to the data). The limited evidence available does encourage support of a conclusion Wolff (1968a) draws from examination of sucking patterns following various conditions of perinatal complication. It is more the diffuse insults to the nervous system that are associated with abnormal nonnutritive sucking patterns; even extensive damage to the "higher centers" alone may in no way be manifest in disturbed sucking activity.

F. CONCLUSIONS

Considering first the newborn period, nonnutritive sucking displays a distinct and very stable temporal organization. There are certain circumstances of extreme disturbance when it will not be emitted at all, for example, if grossly discrepant sucking objects are offered, or during generally depressed states such as occur during certain epochs of deep sleep or as a consequence of diffuse damage to the CNS. However, if the response does occur, its rhythm is remarkably resistant to modification, either from the intrusions of experimental procedure or as a consequence of particular medical biographies. The availability of a pacifier may not influence what is a basic rhythm of mouthing, merely its total output. Exteroceptive stimuli may disrupt the burst and pause rhythm, but these effects are transient and may well be mediated by state changes or even by a component of the general startle reaction. Some measures of success in modifying the response by conditioning procedures must be acknowledged; but even in these cases the underlying temporal organization of mouthing may remain stable with only particular topographical components of the response being affected (Brown, 1973, p. 78).

Changes in the amplitude of neontal nonnutritive sucking have been reported as a function of arousal and it is probably in the "vigor" of non-nutritive sucking that we find real variation in the behavior. In fact, it has been argued above that changes of this kind may well account for modifications in response rhythm consequent upon unusual forms of pacifiers.

There is less information on factors influencing the nonnutritive sucking pattern of older infants. However, the rhythm does become considerably more malleable to the influence of extraoral stimuli. Thus, by 3 or 4 weeks of age, an increase in response frequency can be achieved by making certain exteroceptive stimuli consequent upon its emission. By this time a plasticity of responding will serve an, evidently, more curious infant.

The plasticity of neonatal sucking becomes more apparent when nutrient is provided for the response. Sucking with differing degrees of pace and continuity can be evoked depending upon both quantitative and qualitative properties of the nutrient. Moreover, not all of these changes may be ascribed to the physical accommodations that must be made by other component activities in feeding. Hedonic properties of stimuli also exert an effect. Furthermore, it has been the rhythm of nutritive sucking that has shown variability as a function of medical biography.

In Section III, some of the results summarized and reviewed so far will be related to three aspects of development that concern psychologists. A degree of plasticity in the response, even at birth, has been highlighted in the discussion above. Its functional significance should now be considered.

III. The Significance of Sucking Rhythms for Early Development

A.   MOTIVATIONAL AND SOCIAL ASPECTS OF FEEDING

Much of the research reviewed so far was conducted in a laboratory environment. Can any of its findings be related to the circumstances of a normal feed? More specifically, can we draw any conclusions as to factors that promote the successful feeding of infants? "Success" in this context would usually refer to the satisfaction of those nutritional needs required for healthy growth and development. Thus, our main concern in this section is with summarizing the conditions found to elicit and maintain vigorous nutritive sucking—although a consideration of how sucking is terminated also becomes necessary.

The laboratory setting of most research on infant sucking often excludes the mother and it is worth stressing that feeding provides an occasion for social encounter and perhaps social interaction. It is reasonable to suppose that stimulation provided by the care giver in the course of a feed will effect the organization of an infant's sucking and this possibility must be assessed. However, evaluating social stimulation solely in terms of its effectiveness in promoting energetic sucking behavior may be too narrow a perspective. Although the physical wellbeing of a child is a primary criterion of "successful feeding," the role of the feeding situation in establishing a good emotional relationship between child and care giver should also be heeded when judging "success." The organization of sucking may usefully be considered in this context also.

1. Motivation

Level of arousal exerts a significant influence upon the newborn's sucking during a feed. Thus, the infant who is depressed or irritable as a result of prenatal circumstances displays poor nutritive sucking. A full stomach will also reduce arousal (Wolff, 1972), and it is therefore difficult to assess the direct effects of hunger upon willingness to suck.

The same problem arises in attempting to account for how an infant terminates feeding. Changes in arousal correlated with gastric load do occur within the feed (Wolff, 1972), but it is not possible to say whether this factor alone is the source of feedback that serves to regulate intake. Oral factors, such as fatigue or even cues from changing milk composition (Hall, 1975), may be implicated.

The actual change in sucking rhythm that occurs as feeding progresses is one toward a more episodic structure (Crook, 1977; K. Kaye, 1977; Luther, Arballo, Sala, & Cordero Funes, 1974), the principal effect being upon burst lengths rather than pause durations. Thus, bursting and pausing may occur during a feed, and while the pace of nutritive sucking is certainly slow, less emphasis should now be placed upon its overall continuity. The durations of these pauses at least in a breast feed do not correlate with preceding burst lengths and therefore do not result from momentary fatigue. Neither do they correlate with the lengths of bursts that follow, suggesting that the pause is not to allow the accumulation of milk. As the transfer of a baby from one breast to another often results in the resumption of vigorous sucking, it is unlikely that pausing results from specifically oral fatigue.

The determinants of pausing may well be different at the breast then at the bottle. There is likely to be much greater variation in quantitative and qualitative properties of milk both between and within breast feeds. When milk is flowing regularly but in small amounts we may expect a faster pace of sucking but more frequent rests. However, when milk is simply not flowing consistently, the effects may be less dramatic. Laboratory studies of intermittent nutrient feedback indicate that an isolated delivery of nutrient may potentiate a sucking pattern that resembles normal nutritive sucking and which may persist until the next delivery. There is thus a danger of inferring the regularity of milk flow from observations of the pace of sucking. In general the breast-fed infant is more likely to experience these variations in quantitative parameters of milk flow, not least because there are changes in milk viscosity and texture as feeding at a single breast progresses (Hall, 1975).

It is also reasonable to suppose the chemical senses to be more richly stimulated in breast-fed infants. It is apparent that sweetness is an important taste dimension regulating fluid intake. Furthermore, its effects are probably independent of the calorific value of nutrients (Desor *et al.,* 1977; Dubignon & Campbell, 1969b) and are not mediated by the postingestional consequences of sugar intake (Crook, 1978). There is rather little variation between individuals with respect to the concentration of lactose within human milk (Morrison, 1952) but changes in content within a feed may have some influence upon the infant's sucking.

Human milk could also be a source of variety in the more subtle chemical stimulation of flavor. Complex molecules associated with maternal ingesta can be passed into milk (Knowles, 1966) and those implicated in flavor perception may be among them. There is evidence that preferences within the olfactory system may be established shortly after birth (Macfarlane, 1975), but there is as yet no information as to whether flavor properties of early feeds exert any influence upon sucking. It is possible that they could have a more long-term influence and affect food acceptance at weaning; animal studies encourage this speculation (Capretta & Rawls, 1974; Galef & Sherry, 1973).

Our knowledge of intraoral variables that modulate sucking rhythms in the laboratory (Section II, B) suggests that the conditions of breast feeding are more likely to activate any appetitional control mechanisms that depend upon peripheral feedback from nutrient intake. It is possible that the homogeneous stimulation of intake from a bottle feed is indirectly related to the high incidence of overweight babies fed in this way.

An important question relating to qualitative properties of feeds remains: If some dimension of taste stimulation can enhance nutritive sucking, can others act to suppress it? Maller and Desor (1973) found no intake differences between water and salty, sour, or bitter solutions of moderate intensity. However, Crook (1978) has furnished evidence suggesting that salt solutions may be hedonically negative for the newborn. There need be no contradiction between these results. It is possible, as is widely believed (e.g., Gunther, 1972), that the effects of taste stimuli upon nutritive sucking are not such as to protect the neonate against the intake of potentially toxic fluids. The stimulation provided by fluid in the mouth may be so potent in evoking sucking that it overrides hedonically negative taste stimulation. In such cases we may speculate that nutritive sucking is maintained at a minimal level, while allowing the possibility that taste stimulation of greater intensity may elicit attempts at rejection of the nipple (cf. Nowlis, 1973). The study by Crook did not involve significant ingestion of the sapid solution and thus, although not bearing so directly on the control of intake, was a more appropriate test of hedonic aspects of taste. We must tentatively conclude that taste does not modulate sucking to provide reliable protection against the intake of harmful fluids.

The susceptibility of neonatal sucking to modification by incentive variables should encourage the wider study of motivational processes in very young infants. A lead in this direction has recently been given by the demonstration of one familiar phenomenon from the motivation literature: behavioral contrast. Kobre and Lipsitt (1972) have demonstrated that sucking for distilled water is suppressed if it occurs following experience with a solution of sucrose.

Most studies concerned with variables that promote nutritive sucking have considered only changes in its temporal organization. However, research by Pollitt, Gilmore, and Valcarcel (1978) indicates that a significant percentage of formula intake variance is accounted for by sucking amplitude. There is evidently a need to reconsider some of the variables discussed above in terms of their influence upon measures of response "vigor."

2. Social

Outside of the controlled conditions of the laboratory, can the rhythm of sucking be affected by the variety of stimuli the care giver provides during a feed? The stimuli involved would commonly be termed "social," but we may reasonably enquire whether their effects can be understood in terms of those described for other extraoral stimuli above (Section II, B).

Anecdote does suggest that, with experience, a mother will become more "efficient" in feeding. Thoman and her colleagues have considered this possibility by comparing the feeding styles of primaparous and multiparous mothers in the newborn period. They found that primaparous mothers devoted more time to feeding but with less success (Thoman, Turner, Leiderman, & Barnett, 1970). However, this difference may be a fragile one, for Dunn and Richards (1977) have indicated that it is short lived and in one later study (Thoman, Barnett, & Leiderman, 1971) it was only partially replicated. Brown, Bakeman, Snyder, Fredrickson, Morgan, and Hepler (1975) who also report a difference of this kind, speculate as to whether it may be attributable more to the infant's behavior than to the mother's. Moreover, Thoman *et al.* (1971) also present evidence for relevant infant differences by showing that the infants of primaparous and multiparous mothers behave differently at a first feed given by a nurse.

What might be the relevant stimuli in these situations? In their original study, Thoman *et al.* (1970) suggest that primaparous mothers are more passive, providing little tactile stimulation in the oral area and manipulating the nipple only infrequently. However, in a later study replicating the differences with breast-feeding mothers (Thoman, Leiderman, & Olson, 1972) it was suggested that primaparous mothers dominated or interfered with feeding more. These conclusions are difficult to interpret. However, it is clear that maternal experience must involve a more sensitive phasing of stimulation with those cues provided by the infant's behavior during the feed. The significance of such sensitivity should not be understated; some authors suggest it can help the growth of healthy attachment (Ainsworth & Wittig, 1969). Ainsworth and Bell (1969) actually discourage too much interference by the care giver during feeding, arguing that it may be preferable to allow the infant to pace the feed; experience in influencing its partner in this interaction may be important to developing feelings of "competence."

The studies discussed above identify the existence of a relation between patterns of maternal stimulation and amount of infant sucking. They do not specify the details of the relationship. These might best be explored by considering how social stimuli interact with the burst and pause pattern that we have indicated can characterize nutritive sucking. Observations of normal feeds reveal that care givers will usually reserve infant stimulation to the pauses in the sucking rhythm (Dunn & Richards, 1977; Field, 1977). For infants aged 4 months, this phasing of stimulation is found in both breast and bottle feeds (Field, 1977). However, Richards (1971) claims that in the newborn period at least, bottle-feeding mothers distribute their social stimulation more or less randomly within the feed.

Our discussion of how extraoral stimuli effect sucking that is non-nutritive (Section II, B) suggests that stimuli in the pauses of a feed are likely to recover the response. In fact, Crook, Burke, and Kittner (1977) have demonstrated such an effect when a brief auditory stimulus was superimposed on the pauses in the sucking of neonates receiving a sucrose solution. However, K. Kaye (1977) reports an observational study showing that when mothers "jiggled" their newborn infants during pauses in sucking at the breast, it was the end of the jiggle, not its onset, that increased the probability of resuming the feed. Such results are not necessarily in conflict with nursery common sense; they do not discourage jiggling to promote sucking, they merely recommend short jiggles. In fact evidence is also presented indicating mothers do gradually learn to shorten the duration of each jiggling intrusion they make.

These results suggest the burst and pause rhythm of sucking is involved in a very early form of social dialog based upon turn-taking routines between mother and infant. However, before stress is placed upon the "conversational" quality of early feeding, an experimental demonstration of the phenomenon would be valuable. The extent to which the disturbance during a jiggle is actually incompatible with sucking is unknown. Also, as the effect depends upon comparisons of the durations of pauses with and without jiggles, the possibility must be assessed that mothers could identify on the basis of some other cue which pauses would be longer than average and appropriately inserted their jiggles.

The few studies reviewed above provide some tantilizing findings and encourage further investigation of the role of social stimulation in evoking, maintaining, and terminating nutritive sucking. Students of social development could well consider dwelling more on the long-term effects of events that take place in this earliest of social encounters. The traditional view that the neonate comes to the world endowed with a sucking response well enough adapted to most conditions of feeding should not blind us to the range of stimulation that evidently can disturb the pattern of nutritive sucking: in so far as the care giver is a source of such stimuli, feeding may be considered a possible forum for the development of the social perceptions and competence of both infant and mother.

B. PERCEPTUAL PROCESSING

Results from experiments concerning the effects of exteroceptive stimuli upon sucking (Section II, B) have suggested to some that there may be important correlations between sucking rhythms and the processing of sensory information. Such notions have, therefore, provoked further experiments in which direct measures of the quality of processing are related to the availability of a sucking object, or, when one is available, the response rhythm it evokes.

The simplest question may be considered first: Are there aspects of perceptual activity that can be impaired or facilitated by the presence of a sucking object? Nonnutritive sucking does have a well-known pacification effect (Cohen, 1967; Kessen & Leutzendorff, 1963); this suggests that by reducing diffuse feedback to an active infant it may encourage more committed attention. Wolff and White (1965) made such a prediction and demonstrated that the newborn's visual pursuit is more effective when he has a pacifier than when he is in an active awake state without one. Gregg, Haffner, and Korner (1976) also implicate the pacification effect in their report of improved visual tracking from newborns permitted to suck. However, while it may facilitate active visual pursuit, sucking has been found to cause a reduction in size of the effective visual field of both newborns and of infants aged 1 month (Macfarlane, Harris, & Barnes, 1976). Subjects in that experiment were found to be less readily distracted by a stimulis introduced into the visual periphery. The effect of sucking upon thresholds for detection of such stimuli was not separated from any suppressive effects it might have upon overt scanning. However, the authors do report an impression that sucking may have disturbed scanning through an inhibition of head movements. This is probable, as a clear demonstration of such an effect has been provided elsewhere by Wolff and White (1965).

The calming effect of sucking upon the active infant appears to improve the quality of visual processing, perhaps through attenuating the total input of stimulation. A specific inhibitory effect upon head movements may serve to maintain more focused vision. The next question, and one more directly pertinent to this review, concerns the manner in which perceptual processing interacts with the specific organization of sucking into bursts and pauses. The relevant studies involve subjects whose perceptual activities are evaluated with a pacifier available, but who may not always be sucking upon it.

Bruner (1968) has described the relationship between sucking and looking as follows: during the period shortly after birth the infant sucks with his eyes closed; between 2 and 5 weeks of age eyes may be open during sucking, but the response typically ceases if visual fixation or tracking occurs; between 9 and 13 weeks most information processing still occurs during pauses, but by 4 months the infant may look and suck simultaneously. This account suggests that even though a pacifier may prepare an infant for more committed attention, significant perceptual activity will occur only in the pauses between sucking; perhaps it also implies that a particularly interesting stimulus will actively suppress the response.

With regard to the newborn, Bruner's account seems to be incorrect. Although the correlation between eye opening and sucking has not been studied directly, it can be inferred from experiments described above (Section II, B) and still others (e.g., Brown *et al.*, 1975) that for at least some of the time the newborn will suck with open eyes. Otherwise, the nature of stimulus effects upon the sucking rhythms of newborn and older children is confused by the existence of differing research methodologies. With one, a contingency is established such that sucking is actually necessary for exposure to the stimulus. But other studies follow the tradition of the Bronshtein procedure and employ intermittent stimuli of rather longer duration whose contingency with behavior is generally unlikely to promote learning effects. In work of this kind the investigator may focus either on the momentary consequences of stimulus change or the longer effects of sustained stimulation. Unfortunately, the kind of changes in behavior that result using these two methodologies may not be discussed together as easily as is sometimes assumed.

Stimulus onset during a sucking burst will generally suppress the response, if it has any effect at all. This might encourage the belief that sucking and perceiving are incompatible. Indeed some authors (e.g., Barrett & Miller, 1973; Bronshtein & Petrova, reprinted in Brackbill & Thompson, 1967) explicitly associate such effects with the information seeking of the so-called orienting response. However, such conclusions are hard to reconcile with Semb and Lipsitt's finding (1968) that the same stimulus that terminates sucking when it occurs during a burst will initiate the behavior when it occurs in a pause. Taking into account the physical characteristics of stimuli employed in many procedures of this kind, it is likely that some of the onset effects, especially those in which sucking is initiated, can be attributed to transient changes in arousal or even startle reactions. Thus, a clearer statement regarding the relation between sucking rhythms and active perceptual processing should be sought in studies in which the full effects of sustained stimulation are documented.

An earlier review (Kaye, 1967) finds no strong support for the proposition that sucking is suppressed during more prolonged stimulation, but recently Haith *et al.* (1969) have again claimed such suppression in 2- to 4-month-old infants exposed to complex visual movement. However, it is not clear whether sucking was suppressed on their stimulation trials or enhanced on the interspersed control trials against which the change was assessed. Continued exposure to alternation of the two kinds of trial could generate a frustration effect and their finding that the magnitude of difference in sucking rates becomes greater as the experiment proceeds does support this view.

Evidence that sucking and looking are at least not mutually exclusive is provided by procedures in which stimuli are not presented at all unless sucking also occurs. Infants as young as 3 or 4 weeks will dramatically increase their sucking output if certain stimuli are made contingent upon each response. However, the questions being raised here are probably best considered by procedures in which direct measures of the quality of perceptual activity are related to patterns of sucking.

Bruner (1973b) presented a motion picture to infants aged between 9 and 13 weeks and equipped with pacifiers. Regardless of whether they were oriented toward the stimulus, scanning saccadic eye movements were more frequent during bursts of sucking then during pauses. This result has been interpreted as evidence that sucking "facilitates" scanning

(Mendelson & Haith, 1975) and as evidence that sucking and perceptual processing are "mutually inhibitory" (Macfarlane et al., 1976). Bruner believes that sucking serves to buffer the rush of incoming stimuli and that this effect, rather than a maladaptive reaction to novelty, permits the infant to scan at a more optimal rate. While this conclusion may be true for the older infant, Mendelson and Haith (1975) have been unable to support it for the newborn; they found no correlation between an eye movement measure, independently shown to be valid index of processing, and the burst and pause structure of neonatal sucking.

The relationship between perceptual processing and sucking rhythms may be tentatively summarized. The availability of a pacifier will facilitate perceptual activities in the infant who is awake and active. In particular, it will focus vision by reducing the extent to which events in the periphery will distract. Stimulus change may then initiate sucking if it occurs in a pause, but during a burst it may temporarily inhibit the response. Sucking and perceiving are by no means mutually incompatible and there is little support for the notion that sustained information processing occurs principally in the pauses of the sucking rhythm; in fact the older infant may scan a visual stimulus more effectively during the bursts.

Whether or not sucking plays a significant role in perceptual processing, it is quite apparent that the effects of exteroceptive stimuli induced in the laboratory are a powerful tool for developmental psychophysics. While the Bronshtein procedure has not justified the great expectations held for it in this respect (e.g., Kessen, 1963), the response-contingent method of presenting stimuli has proved especially powerful, having dramatically contributed to our knowledge of sensory development, and incidentally has provided provocative data regarding early socialization (Watson, 1972).

C. INDIVIDUAL DIFFERENCES

Because many influential theories of development have attached great significance to infant orality we might anticipate a literature regarding individual differences in the organization of sucking at birth. Unfortunately, literature on this topic is actually fairly scarce. The empirical studies available have concentrated either on demonstrating short-term individual stability in the behavior or on relating particular response patterns to known clinical pathologies.

Day to day reliability in laboratory measures of nutritive sucking has been found with neonates. Kron et al. (1967) report that rate of sucking shows individual stability during feeding for milk, but not for a corn syrup solution. This finding was extended in a later study involving 18 testing sessions across the whole lying-in period (Kron et al., 1968). Now sucking pressure was found to show the greatest individual stability. Intersession correlations of the various sucking measures were lowest during the earliest testings and it was suggested that real individual differences may be confounded shortly after birth with the effects of obstetric medications. This is a cautionary observation; but if testing is delayed until the effects of medication have worn off, the problem then arises of accumulating maternal influence; individual consistencies in the sucking styles of infants may reflect, to an unknown degree, individual differences in the activities of mothers.

More recently, Pollitt *et al.* (1978) reported that measures of sucking rate, pace, amplitude, and burst length all remain stable across two adjacent feeds given on the second day. They also found more long-term effects, with significant stability in measures of time spent sucking and response amplitude taken on Day 2 and at 1 month.

With respect to neonatal nonnutritive sucking, Sameroff (1967, 1971) has examined individual stability over several sessions. He found consistencies in response pace, burst lengths, and pause durations and his results appear to confirm those cited above in finding stronger consistencies across later testing sessions. Lipsitt *et al.* (1976) also provide data on the stability of undisturbed nonnutritive sucking between the second and third days of life. They report stability in measures of the total number of sucks, interresponse times, burst lengths, and pause durations. However, when sucking delivered 15% sucrose solution, only IRTs displayed test–retest reliability.

These studies have involved normal, healthy infants; others reviewed above (Section II, E) demonstrate that adverse perinatal and prenatal conditions may also be a source of individual differences in sucking. Some authors (e.g., Dreier & Wolff, 1972; Kron, 1972; Wolff, 1968a) have raised the possibility that measures of sucking performance may prove valuable diagnostic and prognostic aids. They have supplemented this suggestion with evidence that such measures can discriminate groups of infants with known pathologies from normals and, in some cases, can identfy at-risk infants where a standard neurological test has failed. However, as Wolff (1968a) observed, although pathological and normal groups may be statistically distinguished, there is still much overlap between them, and absolute differences in sucking measures remain rather small. As the technology for recording sucking behavior becomes more sophisticated we may expect further advances in this area.

The clinical importance of identifying individual differences at birth are apparent. It is part of a general effort toward predicting the course of child development from very early behavior. Constitutional differences in behavior have attracted further interest following suggestions that the active role of the infant in determining the nature of social interaction has been underestimated (Bell, 1968). This view has encouraged the search for consistency in sucking styles; however, in exposing the infant's contribution to social interaction, the mother's role must not be forgotten, and any findings of infant differences after birth must be carefully evaluated with respect to the mother's influences, especially during feeding.

IV. Concluding Remarks

We began by laying emphasis upon the central place of the sucking response in very early childhood. Considerably more research than that cited here could have been summoned to elaborate this claim; its pacifying effects, its role in establishing and maintaining social attachments, and its long-term significance for personality development could all have been discussed. However, the present purpose has not been to make such a general evaluation of the behavior. We have tried first to view the response as an activity of intrinsic interest and reveal the factors that control its frequency and rhythm. It has then been argued that the actual structure of those rhythms and their malleability are of functional significance within early development. The important conclusions are highlighted in this section.

The recognition of two distinct styles of sucking, nutritive and nonnutritive, occurs throughout the literature. However, this distinction should not be made so strongly as to imply that they are both rigidly organized. Nonnutritive sucking, it is true, is very stereotyped in the newborn and is resistent to modification; but by even 3 or 4 weeks of age it will admit a degree of plasticity if contingencies are arranged with exteroceptive stimuli. Nutritive sucking is malleable from immediately after birth; research has revealed a range of circumstances that modify both its continuity and its pace. Obviously the distinction is of operational value, but a more fruitful perspective might be one recognizing a basic nonnutritive rhythm that displays orderly changes in organization as nutrient is introduced. One fact that nevertheless should not be lost sight of is the human infant's unique status among mammals in displaying such plasticity of sucking, and this may well reflect qualitative change in central nervous system organization.

Most obvious of the advantages to the baby provided by a malleable sucking response is the ability to regulate food intake. Thus the consequences of prolonged feeding are reflected in a more episodic sucking rhythm. The frequency of the response is also affected by stimulation of sweet taste. We may assume that there has been evolutionary value to a sweet tooth in the guidance of food selection; the same reasoning might lead us to expect that sucking frequency could be suppressed by potentially harmful foods if they had distinctive taste properties. Available evidence suggests that while the newborn may detect and even dislike salty, sour, and bitter tastes, in moderate strengths they are not able to inhibit sucking beneath a frequency maintained by pure water. Possibly it is more important for the altricial human neonate to have a labile feeding response readily elicited by fluid in the mouth rather than one prepared for somewhat improbable dangers. This is one of many topics that would benefit from study beyond the newborn period. Present research does encourage further study of how sucking is affected by the sensory properties of feeds.

Sucking rhythms do have importance aside from insuring healthy physical growth. Some authors have suggested that much of the neonate's time is occupied in dealing with internal stimuli and that it is principally during a feed that serious perception of the outside world occurs. There is evidence that the temporal organization of sucking is tuned to such perceptual activity. Students of perception have been understandably concerned with the resolving power of infant sensory systems. Possible relations between attention and sucking rhythms provide an important starting point for the growth of research into the early use of the senses.

Among the stimuli impinging upon the infant during a feed are those we would term "social." Sucking is the most tangible manifestation of the early social bond between child and care giver and there is some suggestion that its temporal structure may facilitate the development of social interaction.

The value of this labile sucking response to the psychologist as well as to infant himself must not be overlooked. The contingencies arranged between sucking and exteroceptive stimuli in the laboratory are often highly artifactual. However, the infant is evidently eager and able to manipulate the environment through his sucking activity and psychologists have not been slow to exploit this situaton in many impressive studies of perception and learning. In addition, both psychologist and pediatrician have a great interest in early behavior that may reflect different prenatal and perinatal histories or that may predict aspects of subsequent development. The sucking response has already proved of value in this context and with more refined techniques of measurement and analysis it has considerable potential.

One of two criticisms we may level at the course of research into sucking rhythms concerns the rather crude level of measurement that is applied to the behavior. There is sufficient evidence to indicate that the details of bursting and pausing are often more sensitive to external manipulation than the frequency of the response alone. Closer analysis of the rhythm would rarely represent a significant amount of extra labor. This may not be so true for measurements of response topography, such as peak amplitude or response duration. However, there is still reason to believe that more attention to these parameters would also be rewarded. The second criticism that is prompted by this review concerns the unfortunate concentration of research upon newborn infants. Obviously they are a rather accessible population of subjects and the newborn period must be one of special interest to psychology, but many of the effects upon sucking that have been discussed here do need to be viewed in a developmental context. The implementation of longitudinal studies of factors controlling the organization of sucking is an important task for the future.

REFERENCES

Ainsworth, M. D. S., & Bell, S. M. Some contemporary patterns of mother-infant interaction in the feeding situation. In A. Ambrose (Ed.), *Stimulation in early infancy.* New York: Academic Press, 1969. Pp. 133-163.

Ainsworth, M. D. S., & Wittig, R. A. Attachment and exploratory behavior of one-year-olds in a strange situation. In B. M. Foss (Ed.), *Determinants of infant behavior IV.* London: Methuen, 1969. Pp. 111-136.

Barrett, T. E., & Miller, L. K. The organisation of non-nutritive sucking in the premature infant. *Journal of Experimental Child Psychology,* 1973, **16**, 472-483.

Bell, R. Q. A reinterpretation of the direction of effects in studies of socialization. *Psychological Review,* 1968, **75**, 81-95.

Bell, R. Q. A congenital contribution to emotional response in early infancy and the preschool period. In *Parent-infant interaction.* Amsterdam: Ciba Foundation Symposium 33, New series, Asp., 1975. Pp. 201-208.

Bell, R. Q., & Haaf, R. A. Irrelevance of newborn waking states to some motor and appetitive responses. *Child Development,* 1971, **42**, 69-77.

Bosack, T. N. Effects of fluid delivery on the sucking response of the human newborn. *Journal of Experimental Child Psychology,* 1973, **15**, 77-85.

Brackbill, Y., & Thompson, G. C. *Behavior in infancy and early childhood.* New York: Free Press, 1967.

Brassell, W. R., & Kaye, H. Reinforcement from the sucking environment and subsequent modification of sucking behavior in the human neonate. *Journal of Experimental Child Psychology,* 1974, **18**, 448-463.

Brazelton, T. B. Psychophysiologic reaction in the neonate. II. Effect of maternal medication on the neonate and his behavior. *Journal of Pediatrics,* 1961, **58**, 513-518.

Brenman, H. S., Pierce, L., Mackowiak, R., & Friedman, M. H. F. Multisensor nipple for recording oral variables. *Journal of Applied Physiology,* 1969, **26**, 494-496.

Bronshtein, A. I., Antonova, T. G., Kamenetskaya, A. G., Luppova, M. N., & Sytova, V. A. On the development of the functions of analyzers in infants and some animals at the early stage of ontogenesis. *Problemy evolyutali fisiologicheskikh funktsii* (Problems of evolution of physiological functions.) Washington, D.C.: Office of Tech. Serv. Rep. No. 60-61066. 1960, pp. 106-116. Moscow-Leningrad: Akad. Nauk SSSR, 1958.

Brown, J. V. Instrumental control of the sucking response in human newborns. *Journal of Experimental Child Psychology,* 1972, **14**, 66-80.

Brown, J. V. Non-nutritive sucking in great ape and human newborns: Some pylogenetic and ontogenetic characteristics. In J. F. Bosma (Ed.), *Fourth Symposium of oral sensation and perception: Development in the fetus and infant.* Washington, D.C.: U.S. Government Printing Office, 1973. Pp. 118–131.

Brown, J. V., Bakeman, R., Snyder, P. A., Fredrickson, W. T., Morgan, S. T., & Hepler, R. Interactions of Black inner-city mothers with their newborn infants. *Child Development,* 1975, **46,** 677–686.

Brown, J. V., & Pieper, W. A. Non-nutritive sucking in great ape and human newborns. *American Journal of Physical Anthropology,* 1973, **38,** 549–554.

Bruner, J. S. *Processes of cognitive growth: Infancy* (Vol. 3). Heinz Werner Lecture series. Worcester, Mass.: Clark University Press with Barre Publ., 1968.

Bruner, J. S. Organization of early skilled action. *Child Development,* 1973, **44,** 1–11. (a)

Bruner, J. S. Pacifier-produced visual buffering in human infants. *Developmental Psychobiology,* 1973, **6,** 45–51. (b)

Burke, P. M. Swallowing and the organization of sucking in the human newborn. *Child Development,* 1977, **48,** 523–531.

Butterfield, E. C., & Siperstein, G. N. Influence of contingent auditory stimulation upon nonnutritional suckle. In J. F. Bosma (Ed.), *Oral sensation and perception: The mouth of the infant,* Springfield, Ill.: Thomas, 1972. Pp. 313–333.

Capretta, P. J., & Rawls, L. H. Establishment of a flavor preference in rats: Importance of nursing and weaning experience. *Journal of Comparative and Physiological Psychology,* 1974, **86,** 670–673.

Christensen, S., Dubignon, J., & Campbell, D. Variations in intra-oral stimulation and nutritive sucking. *Child Development,* 1976, **47,** 539–542.

Church, R. M. Systematic effect of random error in the yoked control design. *Psychological Bulletin,* 1964, **62,** 122–131.

Cohen, D. J. The crying newborn's accommodation to the nipple. *Child Development,* 1967, **38,** 89–100.

Cortial, C., & Lezine, I. Comparative study of nutritive sucking in the newborn (premature and full-term). *Early Child Development and Care,* 1974, **3,** 211–228.

Crook, C. K. Neonatal sucking: Effects of quantity of response-contingent fluid upon sucking rhythm and heart rate. *Journal of Experimental Child Psychology,* 1976, **21,** 539–548.

Crook, C. K. Taste stimulation and the temporal organization of neonatal sucking. In J. Weiffenbach (Ed.), *Taste and development: The ontogeny of sweet preference.* Washington, D.C.: U.S. Government Printing Office, 1977. Pp. 146–158.

Crook, C. K. Taste perception in the newborn infant. *Infant Behavior and Development,* 1978, **1,** 49–66.

Crook, C. K., Burke, P. M., & Kittner, S. Some effects of an exteroceptive stimulus upon the nutritive sucking of newborns. *Developmental Psychology,* 1977, **13,** 469–472.

Crook, C. K., & Lipsitt, L. P. Neonatal nutritive sucking: Effects of taste stimulation upon sucking rhythm and heart rate. *Child Development,* 1976, **47,** 518–522.

DeLucia, C. A. A system for response measurement and reinforcement delivery for infant sucking behavior research. *Journal of Experimental Child Psychology,* 1967, **5,** 581–521.

Desor, J. A., Maller, O., & Greene, L. S. Preference for sweet in humans: Infants, children and adults. In J. Weiffenbach (Ed.), *Taste and development: The ontogeny of sweet preference.* Washington, D.C.: U.S. Government Printing Office, 1977.

Desor, J. A., Maller, O., & Turner, R. Taste in acceptance of sugars by human infants. *Journal of Comparative and Physiological Psychology,* 1973, **84,** 496–501.

Dreier, T., & Wolff, P. H. Sucking, state and perinatal distress in newborns. *Biology of the Neonate,* 1972, **21,** 16–24.

Dubignon, J., & Campbell, D. Intraoral stimulation and sucking in the newborn. *Journal of Experimental Child Psychology,* 1968, **6,** 154–166. (a)

Dubignon, J., & Campbell, D. Sucking in the newborn in three conditions non-nutritive, nutritive, and a feed. *Journal of Experimental Child Psychology,* 1968, **6,** 335–350. (b)

Dubignon, J., & Campbell, D. Sucking in the newborn during a feed. *Journal of Experimental Child Psychology,* 1969, **7,** 282–298. (a)

Dubignon, J., & Campbell, D. Discrimination between nutriments by the human neonate, *Psychonomic Science,* 1969, **16,** 186–187. (b)

Dubignon, J., Campbell, D., Curtis, M., & Partington, M. W. The relation between laboratory measures of sucking, food intake, and perinatal factors during the newborn period. *Child Development,* 1969, **40,** 1107–1120.

Dubignon, J., Campbell, D., & Partington, M. W. The development of non-nutritive sucking in premature infants. *Biology of the Neonate,* 1969, **14,** 270–278.

Dunn, J. B., & Richards, M. P. M. Observations on the developing relationship between mother and baby in the neonatal period. In H. R. Schaffer (Ed.), *Studies in mother-infant interaction.* New York: Academic Press, 1977. Pp. 427–445.

Eimas, P. D. Auditory and phonetic coding of the cues for speech: Discrimination of the (r-1) distinction by young infants. *Perception and Psychophysics,* 1975, **18,** 341–347.

Eimas, P. D., Siqueland, E. R., Jusczyk, P., & Vigorito, J. Speech perception in infants. *Science,* 1971, **171,** 303–306.

Elder, M. S. The effects of temperature and position on the sucking pressure of newborn infants. *Child Development,* 1970, **41,** 95–102.

Engen, T., Lipsitt, L. P., & Peck, M. B. Ability of newborn infants to discriminate sapid substances. *Developmental Psychology,* 1974, **10,** 741–746.

Ferster, C. B., & Skinner, B. F. *Schedules of Reinforcement.* New York: Appleton, 1957.

Field, T. Maternal stimulation during infant feeding. *Developmental Psychology,* 1977, **13,** 539–540.

Freud, S. Three contributions to the theory of sex. *Nervous and Mental Disorders Monograph Series,* **7,** New York, 1930.

Gaensbauer, T. J., & Emde, R. N. Wakefulness and feeding in human newborns. *Archives of General Psychiatry,* 1973, **28,** 894–897.

Galef, B. G., & Sherry, D. F. Mother's milk: A medium for transmission of cues reflecting the flavor of mother's diet. *Journal of Comparative and Physiological Psychology,* 1973, **83,** 374–378.

Goldie, L., Svedsen-Rhodes, U., & Robertson, N. R. C. Sucking movements during sleep in newborn baby. *Journal of Child Psychology and Psychiatry,* 1970, **11,** 207–211.

Gregg, C. L., Haffner, M. E., & Korner, A. F. The relative efficacy of vestibular-proprioceptive stimulation and the upright position enhancing visual pursuit in neonates. *Child Development,* 1976, **47,** 309–314.

Gunther, M. Infant behaviour at the breast. In B. M. Foss (Ed.), *Determinants of infant behaviour,* London: Methuen, 1961. Pp. 37–39.

Gunther, M. *Infant feeding.* Harmondsworth: Penguin, 1972.

Haith, M. M. The response of the human newborn to visual movement. *Journal of Experimental Child Psychology,* 1966, **3,** 235–243.

Haith, M. M., Kessen, W., & Collins, D. Response of the human infant to level of complexity of intermittent visual movement. *Journal of Experimental Child Psychology,* 1969, **7,** 52–69.

Hall, B. Changing composition of human milk and early development of appetitional control. *Lancet,* 1975, 779–781.

Hillman, D., & Bruner, J. S. Infant sucking in response to variations in schedules of feeding reinforcement. *Journal of Experimental Child Psychology,* 1972, **13**, 240–247.

Johnson, P., & Salisbury, D. M. Breathing and sucking during feeding in the newborn. In *Parent-infant interaction.* Amsterdam: Ciba Foundation Symposium 33, New Series, Asp., 1975.

Kalnis, I. V., & Bruner, J. S. The coordination of visual observation and instrumental behavior in early infancy. *Perception,* 1973, **2**, 307–314.

Kaye, H. The effects of feeding and tonal stimulation on non-nutritive sucking in the human newborn. *Journal of Experimental Child Psychology,* 1966, **3**, 131–145.

Kaye, H. Infant sucking behavior and its modification. In L. P. Lipsitt & C. C. Spiker (Eds.), *Advances in child development and behaviour* (Vol. 3). New York: Academic Press, 1967. Pp. 2–50.

Kaye, H. Effects of variations of oral experience upon suckle. In J. F. Bosma (Ed.), *Third symposium on oral sensation and perception.* Springfield, Ill.: Thomas, 1972, Pp. 261–291.

Kaye, H., & Levin, G. R. Two attempts to demonstrate tonal suppression of non-nutritive sucking in neonates. *Perceptual and Motor Skills,* 1963, **17**, 521–522.

Kaye, K. Towards the origin of dialogue. In H. R. Schaffer (Ed.), *Studies in mother-infant interaction.* New York: Academic Press, 1977. Pp. 89–117.

Keen, R. Effects of auditory stimuli on sucking behavior in the human neonate. *Journal of Experimental Child Psychology,* 1964, **1**, 348–354.

Kessen, W. Research in the psychological development of infants: An overview. *Merrill-Palmer Quarterly of Behavior and Development,* 1963, **9**, 83–94.

Kessen, W., & Leutzendorff, A-M. The effect of non-nutritive sucking on movement in the human newborn. *Journal of Comparative and Physiological Psychology,* 1963, **56**, 69–72.

Kessen, W., Leutzendorff, A-M., & Stoutsenberger, K. Age, food deprivation, non-nutritive sucking and movement in human newborn. *Journal of Comparative and Physiological Psychology,* 1967, **63**, 82–86.

Kobre, K. R., & Lipsitt, L. P. A negative contrast effect in newborns. *Journal of Experimental Child Psychology,* 1972, **14**, 81–91.

Knowles, J. A. Excretion of drugs in milk: A review. *Journal of Pediatrics,* 1966, **66**, 1068–1082.

Korner, A. Neonatal startles, smiles, erections and reflex sucks as related to state, sex and individuality. *Child Development,* 1969, **40**, 1039–1053.

Korner, A. K., Chuck, B., & Donchtos, S. Organismic determinants of spontaneous oral behavior in neonates. *Child Development,* 1969, **39**, 1145–1157.

Korner, A. K., & Grobstein, R. Individual differences at birth. *Journal of the American Academy of Child Psychiatry,* 1967, **6**, 676–690.

Kron, R. E. The effect of arousal and of learning upon sucking behavior in the newborn. *Recent Advances in Biological Psychiatry,* 1968, **10**, 302–313.

Kron, R. E. Studies of sucking behavior in the human newborn: The predictive value of measures of earliest oral behavior. In J. F. Bosma (Ed.), *Second symposium on oral sensation and perception.* Springfield, Ill.: Thomas, 1970. Pp. 234–241.

Kron, R. E. Prognostic significance of sucking dysrhythmias. In J. F. Bosma (Ed.), *Third symposium on oral sensation and perception: The mouth of the infant.* Springfield, Ill.: Thomas, 1972. Pp. 362–374.

Kron, R. E., Finnegan, L. P., Kaplan, S. L., Litt, M., & Phoenix, M. D. The assessment of behavioral change in infants undergoing narcotic withdrawal: Comparative data from clinical and objective methods. *Addictive Diseases,* 1975, **2**, 257–275.

Kron, R. E., Ipsen, J., & Goddard, K. E. Consistent individual differences in the nutritive sucking behavior of the human newborn. *Psychosomatic Medicine,* 1968, **30,** 151–161.

Kron, R. E., Litt, M., Phoenix, M. D., & Finnegan, L. I. Neonatal narcotic abstinence: Effects of pharmacotherapeutic agents and maternal drug usage on nutritive sucking behavior. *Journal of Pediatrics,* 1976, **88,** 637–641.

Kron, R. E., Stein, M., & Goddard, K. E. A method of measuring sucking behavior of newborn infants. *Psychosomatic Medicine,* 1963, **25,** 181.

Kron, R. E., Stein, M., & Goddard, K. E. Newborn sucking behavior affected by obstetric sedation. *Pediatrics,* 1966, **37,** 1012–1016.

Kron, R. E., Stein, M., Goddard, K. E., & Phoenix, M. D. Effect of nutrient upon the sucking behavior of newborn infants. *Psychosomatic Medicine,* 1967, **29,** 24–32.

Levin, G. R., & Kaye, H. Non-nutritive sucking by human neonates. *Child Development,* 1964, **35.** 749–758.

Lindsley, O. R. Experimental analysis of social reinforcement: Terms and methods. *American Journal of Orthopsychiatry,* 1963, **33,** 624–633.

Lipsitt, L. P., & Kaye, H. Conditioned sucking in the human newborn. *Psychonomic Science,* 1964, **1,** 29–30.

Lipsitt, L. P., & Kaye, H. Change in neonatal response to optimizing and non-optimizing sucking stimulation. *Psychonomic Science,* 1965, **2,** 221–222.

Lipsitt, L. P., Pederson, L. J., & DeLucia, C. A. Conjugate reinforcement of operant responding in infants. *Psychonomic Science,* 1966, **4,** 67–68.

Lipsitt, L. P., Reilly, B. M., Butcher, M. J., & Greenwood, M. M. The stability and interrelationships of newborn sucking and heart rate. *Developmental Psychobiology,* 1976, **9,** 305–310.

Luther, E. C., Arballo, J. C., Sala, N. L., & Cordero Funes, J. C. Sucking pressure in humans: Relationship to oxytocin-produced reflex milk ejection. *Journal of Applied Physiology,* 1974, **36,** 350–353.

Macfarlane, A. Olfaction in the development of social preferences in the human neonate. In *Parent-infant interaction.* Amsterdam: Ciba Foundation Symposium 33, New Series, Asp., 1975. Pp. 103–113.

Macfarlane, A., Harris, P. L., & Barnes, I. Central and peripheral vision in early infancy. *Journal of Experimental Child Psychology,* 1976, **21,** 532–538.

Maller, O., & Desor, J. A. Effect of taste on ingestion by human newborns. In J. F. Bosma (Ed.), *Fourth symposium on oral sensation and perception: Development in the fetus and infant.* Washington, D.C.: U.S. Government Press, 1973. Pp. 279–303.

Mendelson, M. J., & Haith, M. M. The relation between non-nutritive sucking and visual information processing in the human newborn. *Child Development,* 1975, **46,** 1025–1029.

Milewski, A. E., & Siqueland, E. R. Discrimination of color and pattern novelty in one-month human infants. *Journal of Experimental Child Psychology,* 1975, **19,** 122–136.

Miller, L. K. Effects of auditory stimulation upon non-nutritive sucking by premature infants. *Perceptual and Motor Skills,* 1975, **40,** 879–885.

Morrison, S. D. *Human Milk.* Farnham Royal: Commonwealth Agricultural Bureaux, 1952.

Morse, P. A. The discrimination of speech and nonspeech stimuli in early infancy. *Journal of Experimental Child Psychology,* 1972, **14,** 477–492.

Morse, W. H. Intermittent reinforcement. In W. K. Honig (Ed.), *Operant behavior: Areas of research and application.* New York: Appleton, 1966. Pp. 52–108.

Nisbett, R. E., & Gurwitz, S. B. Weight, sex and the eating behavior of human newborns. *Journal of Comparative and Physiological Psychology,* 1970, **73,** 245–253.

Nowlis, G. H. Taste-elicited tongue movements in human newborn infants: An approach to palatability. In J. F. Bosma (Ed.), *Fourth symposium on oral sensation and perception.* Washington, D.C.: Government Printing Office, 1973. Pp. 292–303.

Nowlis, G. H., & Kessen, W. Human newborns differentiate differing concentrations of sucrose and glucose. *Science,* 1976, **191**, 865–866.

Ogden, K. M., & MacKeith, R. Good nipples promote successful breast feeding. *Journal of Pediatrics,* 1955, **46**, 210–214.

Peiper, A. *Cerebral function in infancy and childhood.* New York: Consultants Bureau, 1963.

Piaget, J. *The origins of intelligence in the child.* London: Routledge & Kegan Paul, 1953.

Pollitt, E., Gilmore, M., & Valcarcel, M. The stability of sucking behavior and its relationship to intake during the first month of life. *Infant Behavior and Development,* 1978, **1**, 347–357.

Premack, D. Reinforcement Theory. In D. Levine (Ed.), *Nebraska Symposium on Motivation.* Lincoln: University of Nebraska Press, 1965, Pp. 123–180.

Richards, M. P. M. Social interaction in the first weeks of life. *Psychiatria, Neurologia, Neurochirurgia,* 1971, **74**, 35–42.

Roffwarg, H. P., Muzio, J. N., & Dement, W. C. Ontogenetic development of the human sleep-dream cycle. *Science,* 1966, **152**, 606–619.

Rovee, C. K., & Rovee, D. T. Conjugate Reinforcement of infant exploratory behavior. *Journal of Experimental Child Psychology,* 1969, **8**, 35–39.

Sameroff, A. J. An apparatus for recording sucking and controlling feeding in the first days of life. *Psychonomic Science,* 1965, **2**, 355–356.

Sameroff, A. Non-nutritive sucking in newborns under visual and auditory stimulation. *Child Development,* 1967, **38**, 443–452.

Sameroff, A. J. The components of sucking in the human newborn. *Journal of Experimental Child Psychology,* 1968, **6**, 607–623.

Sameroff, A. J. Changes in the non-nutritive sucking response to stimulation during infancy. *Journal of Experimental Child Psychology,* 1970, **10**, 112–119.

Sameroff, A. J. Respiration and sucking as components of the orienting reaction in newborns. *Psychophysiology,* 1971, **7**, 213–222.

Sameroff, A. J. Learning and adaption in infancy. In H. W. Reese (Ed.), *Advances in child development and behavior* (Vol. 7). New York: Academic Press, 1972. Pp. 169–214.

Seligman, M. E. P. On the generality of the laws of learning. *Psychological Review,* 1970, **77**, 406–418.

Semb, G., & Lipsitt, L. P. The effects of acoustic stimulation on cessation and initiation of non-nutritive sucking in neonates. *Journal of Experimental Child Psychology,* 1968, **6**, 585–597.

Siperstein, G. N. *Differential modification of neonatal behavior.* Paper presented at meeting of society for Research in Child Development, Philadelphia, Penn., 1973.

Siqueland, E. R. *The development of instrumental exploratory behavior during the first year of human life.* Paper presented at meeting of Society for Research in Child Development, Santa Monica, Calif.: 1969.

Siqueland, E. R., & DeLucia, C. A. Visual reinforcement of non-nutritive sucking in human infants. *Sciences,* 1969, **165**, 1144–1146.

Skinner, B. F. *The behavior of organisms.* New York: Appleton, 1938.

Thoman, E. B., Barnett, C. R., & Leiderman, P. H. Feeding behaviors of newborn infants as a function of parity of the mother. *Child Development,* 1971, **42**, 1471–1483.

Thoman, E. B., Leiderman, P. H., & Olsen, J. P. Neonate-mother interaction during breast-feeding. *Developmental Psychology,* 1972, **6**, 110–118.

Thoman, E. B., Turner, A. M., Leiderman, P. H., & Barnett, C. R. Neonate-mother interaction: Effects of parity on feeding behavior. *Child Development,* 1970, **41**, 1103–1111.

Trehub, S. E., Rabinovitch, M. S. Auditory-linguistic sensitivity in early infancy. *Developmental Psychology,* 1972, **6**, 74–77.

Watson, J. S. Smiling, cooing and "the game." *Merrill-Palmer Quarterly,* 1972, **18**, 323–339.

Wenner, W. H., Douthitt, T. C., Burke, M. E., & Keenan, P. A. Observations on the regular recurrence of groups of spontaneous rhythmic oral activity in infants. In J. F. Bosma (Ed.), *Second symposium on oral sensation and perception.* Springfield, Ill.: Thomas, 1970. Pp. 291–305.

Wolff, P. H. The causes, controls and organization of behavior in the neonate. *Psychological Issues,* 1966, **5,** (1, Whole No. 17).

Wolff, P. H. The role of biological rhythms in early psychological development. *Bulletin of the Menninger Clinic,* 1967, **31,** 197–218.

Wolff, P. H. The serial organization of sucking in the young infant. *Pediatrics,* 1968, **42,** 943–956. (a)

Wolff, P. H. Sucking patterns in infant mammals. *Brain, Behavior and Evolution,* 1968, **1,** 354–367. (b)

Wolff, P. H. The interaction of state and non-nutritive sucking. In J. F. Bosma (Ed.), *Third symposium on oral sensation and perception,* Springfield, Ill.: Thomas, 1972. Pp. 293–310.

Wolff, P. H. Natural history of sucking patterns in infant goats: A comparative study. *Journal of Comparative and Physiological Psychology,* 1973, **81,** 252–257.

Wolff, P. H., & Simmons, M. A. Non-nutritive sucking and response thresholds in young infants. *Child Development,* 1967, **38,** 631–638.

Wolff, P. H., & White, B. L. Visual pursuit and attention in young infants. *Journal of Child Psychiatry,* 1965, **4,** 473–484.

Wormith, S. J., Pankhurst, D., & Moffitt, A. R. Frequency discrimination by young infants. *Child Development,* 1975, **46,** 272–275.

NEUROLOGICAL PLASTICITY, RECOVERY FROM BRAIN INSULT, AND CHILD DEVELOPMENT

Ian St. James-Roberts

UNIVERSITY OF LONDON, LONDON, ENGLAND

ADVANCES IN CHILD DEVELOPMENT
AND BEHAVIOR, VOL. 14

I. Introduction

One of the outstanding paradoxes of neuropsychology is that of differential completeness of recovery from cerebral injury. Why is it that one individual who experiences central nervous system (CNS) trauma will regain almost all faculties, while another with apparently identical injury will not? One variable traditionally assigned considerable influence is age: A young nervous system will recover more quickly and more completely than an old. Indeed, the view that the young nervous system is somehow more "plastic" than the mature one is so embedded in the folklore of psychology that it is now part of the unquestioned dogma. Blundell (1975), for example, writes of the "general principle in which lesions in young animals have less deleterious effects on behavior than similar lesions in adults of the same species" (p. 55) and Lenneberg similarly writes that "It is generally known and is beyond dispute, that focal lesions in young children carry a prognosis different from that of similar lesions in adults" (Lenneberg & Lenneberg, 1975, p. 13).

The impetus for a state-of-the-art review of the research in this area derives from two sources. First, the authority with which the plasticity view is endowed stands in marked contrast to the equivocality of the evidence on which it is based. Hence, by undertaking a critical evaluation of human and animal findings it is hoped to put the view that the young brain is preferentially plastic into perspective. It will be argued that the phenomenon is neither as universal nor as important as is currently supposed. Second, this is an area of extraordinary complexity and contradictions. Data linking cerebral palsy and retardation (Drillien, 1967; McDonald, 1967; Douglas, 1960) to low birth weight or anoxia, for example, are difficult to reconcile with the failure of prospective studies to isolate effective risk criteria (Parmelee, Sigman, Kopp, & Haber, 1975) or with the importance of social class as a determinant of trauma outcome (Sameroff & Chandler, 1975). Equally, the continuum of reproductive casualty (Pasamanick & Knobloch, 1961) demands different research emphases and different intervention strategies from the theory of developmental discontinuity (Sameroff, 1975) or the continuum of caretaker casualty (Sameroff & Chandler, 1975). Consequently, there is currently a pressing need to take stock of research and therapeutic priorities in this area. The nature and extent of CNS recuperative potential is of obvious importance to these issues.

As always when investigation of brain–behavior relationships is undertaken, two strategies are possible. Either human subjects are employed, in which case the experiments are natural and so confounded, or animals are used, in which case the effects are relatively clear-cut, but their relevance to human situations is dubious. Since both strategies have generated data widely supposed to support CNS plasticity, they are each considered separately below. However, it is first appropriate to consider general principles which apply to both approaches.

II. Models of Recovery Processes

The "recovery" paradigm concerns any situation where CNS insult is followed by a period of aberrant behavior which, in turn, is succeeded by a return to a more normal level of performance. In any such situation, the explanations included in Sections II, A–F may each be applied (see discussions, and slightly different use of terminology, by Goldberger, 1974; Greenough, Foss, & DeVoogt, 1976; Rosner, 1970; and Walsh & Cummins, 1976).

A. VICARIOUS FUNCTIONING

The vicarious functioning explanation, originally formulated by Munk (1881), proposes that resumption of normal behavior follows "takeover" of the function concerned by a separate brain area, which has been either unemployed or functionally dormant previously, or whose function may be sacrificed to fulfill the role of the damaged area. This is perhaps the most common view of how recovery from brain damage occurs and is also frequently the view underlying the hypothesis of preferential immature plasticity. The neurological substrates of young brains are presumed to be less committed in respect of function, and consequently takeover is achieved more readily. This view implies that experience may play some part in specifying and respecifying the functional characteristics of CNS tissue and, in extreme environmentalist form, it sees the CNS as functionally equivocal until experience occurs, whereupon psychological determination of function ensues. We may note, however, that the vicarious model of transfer need not imply environmental intervention, since endogenous neurological systems may relocate function to a new neural substrate independently (Greenough *et al.,* 1976).

B. EQUIPOTENTIALITY

The equipotentiality view, originally proposed by Lashley (1938), also assumes considerable redundancy within the CNS. However, it differs from vicariation in two respects. First, the functional aspects of any neural system are genetically predetermined, so no redistribution of function— with or without experiential intervention—is possible. Second, diffusely organized neural systems, consisting of many equipotential units, are hypothesized rather than specialized individual "centers." Hence recovery in this case reflects the mass action of the remaining parts of the system, which are able to maintain function because of inherent redundancy in the makeup of the original system. The extent of recovery here will presumably reflect the topography of the system damaged as well as the site and, particularly, the size of the lesion.

The term equipotential is much abused. The cerebral asymmetry literature, for instance, makes frequent references to the possible equipotentiality of the two hemispheres for language. In such cases, the implication is not that the two hemispheres normally contribute equally to language, but that if the hemisphere which normally subserves language becomes damaged, the other is able to take over. This might be viewed as vicariation or substitution.

C. SUBSTITUTION

So far, the term *function* has been used to refer to neurophysiological processes, but it is apparent that equivalent mental and behavioral functions are being assumed. Recovery via substitution rejects this formulation. Recovery may follow the employment of analogous neurophysiological processes, which are able to achieve the original end by different means.

Animal experiments do not typically concern themselves with mental events, and consequently empirical interest has centered on whether different neural processes may obtain the same behavior. Even here, considerable confusion exists. Goldberger (1974), for example, assigns the term *behavioral substitution* to the use of different processes to achieve the same behavior. In principle, there is no reason that neurophysiological, mental, and behavioral processes should not each vary independently. In practice, however, equivalence of physiological and mental function is normally assumed by the model. Behavioral substitution proper—i.e., the use of new neurophysiological and behavioral processes to achieve the same goal—is also normally neglected. This may be appropriate in gross cases as, for example, when the foot substitutes for the hand in making a response. In other cases, however, substitution of motor behavior may be more subtle.

The substitution model of recovery supposes that CNS damage often spares neural substrates whose topography and characteristics are both invariate and different from those of the damaged area but which can be redeployed to achieve the original behavior. An obvious example exists in the human literature in the use of iconic codes to assist memory when verbal ones are disrupted and Gazzaniga (1974, 1975) has written extensively about redeployment of this sort. Similar compensation processes have been hypothesized in animal lesion work. Meyer (1974), for example, reviews experiments suggesting that animals with occipital cortical lesions are eventually able to solve disrupted pattern discriminations by using edge, contour, and flux cues.

D.   REGROWTH AND SUPERSENSITIVITY

It has long been known that mature neurons are incapable of mitosis (Cajal, 1928) and, unlike in some species (e.g., cats and rats), neural proliferation in humans seems to be completed some time before birth (Dobbing, 1974). Although neural regeneration is, consequently, ruled out, recent evidence suggests that some types of regrowth following injury are possible within the CNS. Two main types are distinguished: collateral and regenerative sprouting. For convenience, denervation supersensitivity is also considered here, although growth per se is not strictly involved.

Collateral sprouting. Following neuronal ablation, an undamaged neuronal process in the vicinity of the damaged area appears sometimes to be able to invade the damaged tissue and to make synaptic contact with neurons beyond the lesion. This work is reviewed by Moore (1974). Such collateral sprouting could result in reestablishment of damaged connections, leading to restoration of original function, or it could underlie the development of substitute or vicarious systems. At present, no uncontroversial data exist concerning which of these processes occurs. Indeed Isaacson (1976) has emphasised that in some cases regrowth may be detrimental to recovery, since inappropriate tracts may be formed.

Regenerative sprouting. In this case, contact is reestablished by regeneration of the damaged axon; that is, recovery involves the original damaged neuron(s) rather than alternatives. The implications of such resprouting are again unclear (Moore, 1974).

Denervation supersensitivity. Following denervation, remaining postsynaptic processes may become supersensitive to residual neurotransmitter. Hence, small quantities of neurotransmitter leaking from prelesion neurons may activate postlesion pathways. Normal pathway activity and restoration of original function would thus be achieved (Glick, 1974). However, the status of the supersensitivity phenomenon is again unclear.

The importance of regrowth in the CNS is thus ambiguous at present (Kerr, 1975; Mathers, 1977). Although some evidence exists that regrowth may sometimes be more extensive in the young brain, resulting in some instances in aberrant tract formation (Schneider, 1969), whether the additional pathways contribute effectively to the system or disrupt its function is undecided (Kerr, 1975). Isaacson (1976) has demonstrated that in some instances animals whose sprouting is chemically inhibited recover better than those in whom sprouting occurs naturally. It may be noted, too, that much of the evidence concerning collateral sprouting has been obtained in adult animals (Moore, Bjorklund, & Stenevi, 1971; Raisman, 1969), while Stenevi, Bjorklund, and Moore (1972) have demonstrated that, in some cases at least, sprouting is a temporary phenomenon and has no chronic significance.

E. DIASCHISIS

The tendency so far has been to regard the period of posttraumatic behavior as indicative of damage to the area responsible for the normal version of the aberrant behavior obtained, while recovery results either from restoration of the system or assumption of control by other systems. Diaschisis (originally formulated by von Monakow, 1914) sets this on its head, proposing that the aberrant period tells us nothing specific about the nature of damage. It reflects only general disruption of the CNS. Recovery results from the freeing of the original neural systems from the disruptive influences.

Isaacson (1975, 1976) has recently reformulated this explanation of recovery in some detail. He lists some 16 consequences of CNS trauma, of which destruction of cells at the location of damage is only one. Others include changes in cerebrospinal fluid pressure and composition, hematoma, edema, and changes in vascular supply. Many of these indirect consequences of lesion are of a temporary nature and their dispersion results in recovery.

Except insofar as any young body system recuperates more effectively than an old, diaschisis does not prescribe important age differences in recovery. However, it does draw attention to the duration of the recovery period as a significant and underrated variable. Where immature neural systems are being compared with mature, particularly, care must be exercised to separate effects attributable to chronicity and maturation from those due to recovery or impairment. This important distinction is reconsidered in Section III, A, 1.

F. EMERGENCE TRAUMA

The notion of emergence trauma may be linked with diaschisis but the mechanism envisaged is rather different (Fuller, 1967; Melzack, 1969). The important consideration here is the (typically) lesioned animal's bewildered reaction to the postinsult situation, where the bewilderment presumably reflects both the direct effects of diaschisis and the animal's negative affective response to its disorientation. The latter may also reflect the broadness of experience of the individual and the complexity of the postinsult situation it encounters. The assumption made by this model is that the animal is capable of making an appropriate response if only it can "find its bearings." Disentanglement of such an effect from the consequences of recovery presents obvious methodological difficulties. However, we may note that the model prescribes some mature CNS advantages in some cases, since experience may help to reduce emotional reactivity to disorientation.

G. SUMMARY OF MODELS

The distinction between diaschisis, vicariation, substitution, and equipotential models is best summarized in terms of the relationship between the identity and functional characteristics of the preinsult system to the identity and characteristics of the postinsult system, as follows:

1. If both pre- and postinsult system and characteristics are the same, recovery reflects diaschisis.
2. If part of the original system, retaining its original characteristics, mediates the recovered behavior, equipotentiality is involved.
3. If a new system, employing inherent characteristics which are different from (but analogous to) the original ones is responsible for the recovered behavior, substitution is implicated.
4. If a new system, employing identical characteristics to the original system, is involved, vicarious transfer has taken place. In this case, an issue of some importance is whether the postinsult function of the area concerned is the same as its preinsult function. If these are identical, the structures may be said to be homologous (Denenberg, 1972). Alternatively, the postinsult system may have been devoid of functional characteristics prior to insult, or its function may have been sacrificed in favor of the new one.

It may be apparent that these models are neither completely independent nor mutually exclusive and that the distinctions drawn in logical terms need not apply at the CNS level. Suppression of function for some period of time (diaschisis), for example, is incorporated in all models in the difference between acute and chronic effects, and whether recovery is attributed to the original system or to a separate one depends on how parochial a view of CNS "systems" is adopted. Similar obfuscation accompanies the notion of function, which lacks definitional or observable referents. Hence, the conceptually precise distinction between functional reorganization (substitution or vicariation) and functional potentiation (learning) becomes obscured at the empirical level. Parallel difficulties also confuse differentiation of analogous from homologous systems. Nonetheless, the models serve a heuristic purpose in directing thinking and as reminders of the diversity of recovery explanations available.

Of the models, environmentalist vicariation theory alone implies that superior recovery should occur in the damaged young CNS, principally because it views the immature brain as largely unspecified, with experience gradually determining the functional role of each brain area. As noted, however, one version of vicariation theory emphasizes intrinsic rather than experiential specification of the function of CNS areas, and it is not clear how age would reduce plasticity in this case. For the other models, age is not seen as a crucial variable, except insofar as it covaries with experience. Prior experience may facilitate substitution or equipotential recovery by increasing the functional interaction—and hence the overlap of different CNS areas—and thus supplement overall redundancy. However, if postinsult neural systems retain partial repertoires, the latter may presumably transfer negatively to some learning situations and so interfere with recovery processes. Thus, either the naive or the mature brain could be advantaged, depending on the sort of system in which damage occurs and on what sort of pre- and postinsult situation is used in assessment. This formulation has the obvious advantage that age differences in recovery effects may be readily explained by existing neurological and psychological wisdom: That is, no additional processes, such as respecification or plasticity, need be hypothesized. Its disadvantage is that it is difficult to test, although some relevant data are reviewed presently.

Although age per se is not, then, of primary importance for most of the models, its significance may be increased if additional mechanisms are hypothesized. Two such mechanisms are currently proposed in the literature: depletion tuning and the critical period.

That active depletion of superfluous neuronal material may facilitate functional validation of systems being used has been proposed by Hirsch and Jacobson (1975), on the basis of Jacobson's finding (1970, 1973) that considerable discarding of neurons occurs in some CNS areas during ontogenesis. Although this is a plausible hypothesis and one which predicts reduction in CNS flexibility with age, it need not imply functional equivocality in the young brain. Rather, it seems to suggest a degree of fine tuning and of decreasing imprecision with age. Unfortunately, whether neuronal deterioration actively contributes to function has not yet been tested, so that functional depletion remains only an interesting speculation at the present time. It should also be noted that the Russian neuropsychologist Luria (Luria, Naydin, Tsvetkova, & Vinarskaya, 1969) has argued that neglected CNS pathways are often inhibited, rather than destroyed, and so may be restored to function throughout life.

The critical period hypothesis, which has been widely applied, proposes that the functional contribution of each CNS area remains equivocal until some critical point in ontogenesis, whereafter it is irrevocably fixed. Its emphasis on early plasticity suits it most readily to an environmentalist vicariation model but, in combination with functional depletion, it may be applied also to substitution and intrinsic vicariation (though not to equipotential) models. Such an application is typified by Lenneberg's (1967) hypothesis of hemisphere equivalence for language, which proposes that a critical period exists during which language function may be transferred from the left to the right cerebral hemisphere. Whether transfer involves analogous or homologous systems and why one hemisphere should normally be dominant prior to the end of the critical period are, of course, questions begged by models of this sort.

Although they are not explicit on this point, it is believed that dynamic models of ontogenetic recovery processes, such as that of Sameroff and Chandler (1975), are essentially vicarious models which incorporate a critical period element. Thus Sameroff and Chandler (1975) view CNS ontogenesis as a succession of qualitative reorganizations, each of which may incorporate adjustments to function which overcome the effects of insult and redirect development toward a normal level. Because of the importance of such models for human developmental and recovery processes, their validity and relationship to vicarious and other models are given particular attention in this review.

III. Animal Experiments

In principle, a clear-cut distinction may be drawn between experiments which employ direct CNS lesion and those which employ "environmental surgery" (Hirsch & Jacobson, 1975) via enrichment or deprivation of experience. In practice, the latter experiments tend to merge unobtusively into investigations of the effect of particular types of learning, while pre- and postoperative learning as a mediator of lesion effects had recently attracted considerable research attention. This trend alone reveals much about the erosion of the traditional dichotomy of damaged vs. normal function in animal experimentation. Not surprisingly, the increasing sophistication of the questions has been matched by increasingly complex answers and the idiosyncrasy of the behavior of traumatized animals now often threatens to equal that of humans. This blending of designs presents obvious problems when subclassification is to be attempted. Consequently, the three categories used below, according to whether (1) lesion, (2) environmental deprivation and enrichment, or (3) remedial learning might be considered the prime independent variable, must be accepted as somewhat arbitrary.

A.   LESION EXPERIMENTS

Much of the early lesion work serving to show both the significance of lesion site and the differential effects of age was confounded by inadequate control of lesion size and location. More sophisticated lesion techniques and routine use of autopsy have overcome most of these problems and reevaluation of work in some areas has resulted. Considerable qualification of early neurological plasticity findings has also been achieved in two separate ways. Either adult animals have been shown to be less handicapped than previously thought, or to recover; or animals lesioned when immature have been shown to have handicaps not previously detected when more extensive or prolonged testing is undertaken. These two approaches are considered according to the site of lesion. Much of the work to follow has been reviewed by Isaacson (1975, 1976) and in Stein, Rosen, and Butters (1974).

1. Frontal Lobe Lesions

Early work by Kennard (1936, 1938) demonstrating reduction in some debilitating effects of frontal lobe lesions if the lesions were performed in infancy provided much of the fuel for the plasticity argument. Subsequently, Kennard's findings were replicated and extended to other frontal lobe areas by Akert, Orth, Harlow, and Schiltz (1960), Harlow, Blomquist, Thompson, Schiltz, and Harlow (1968), Goldman (1971), and others. Doubts as to the ubiquity of the findings were revealed when Thompson, Harlow, Blomquist, and Schiltz (1971) showed that the effect was task dependent—that is, that the infant-lesioned monkeys who (unlike adult-lesioned ones) were unhampered on the classic delayed-response task were markedly inferior to controls on discrimination-learning tasks. The work of Goldman (1971, 1974, 1976), however, has prompted the most radical reevaluation of research in this area.

Prefrontal lobe cortical lesions may be subdivided into dorsalateral and orbitofrontal lesion sites. It is dorsolateral lesions which classically are related to delayed-response deficits (Jacobson, 1935) and where infant sparing has been most clearly observed. Goldman (1974) showed that the sparing phenomenon was correct in animals lesioned at 50 days and tested at the usual adult age of about 18 months. However, if testing was postponed until 2 years of age, some delayed response deficits could be detected, and by 2½–3 years of age the full deficit syndrome was apparent. The animals had actually grown into the syndrome—a peculiar notion from the plasticity point of view. The finding may be supplemented, too, by the Thompson *et al.* (1971) demonstration that young monkeys not showing delayed-response deficits (presumably because too young) do have detectable deficits if the testing is broadened to include discrimination-learning tasks. Goldman (1974) has also investigated the consequences of infantile orbitofrontal lesions and, in this case, the effects on delayed response are the reverse of dorsolateral ones—the animals are impaired at 15 months but normal by 24 months of age. For discrimination tasks, the effects are reversed again, with normal performance being obtained until 12 months of age and impaired performance thereafter. Interestingly, Goldman also emphasizes the importance of individual animal variations in the ages at which impairments appear and disappear, even in identically lesioned and aged animals. She attributes these to individual differences in maturation rates.

Goldman's experiments clearly cause difficulties for the plasticity viewpoint. They suggest that function—at least in the frontal lobes—is directly linked to structure and that the consequences of damage are irreversible. It is particularly significant that frontal lobe function should be circumscribed in this way, since their freedom from direct afferent and efferent pathways suits them admirably to the sort of plasticity which many writers have assumed association cortex to possess (e.g., Tizard, 1974). Goldman's findings show, too, that age does have a limited role to play, in that maturational variables change the neural systems which are employed to deal with a particular type of problem at different ages. Cognitive restructuring of this sort has long had a respectable pedigree in human developmental theorizing (Piaget, 1954; Sameroff, 1975), but it is relatively new to animal work. Satz, Friel, and Rudegear (1974) have observed analogous age-related alterations in the deficits of reading-retarded children.

One interesting implication of Goldman's work is that lesion recovery and CNS maturational effects are sometimes difficult to unravel. Indeed the work emphasizes an underestimated aspect of all animal work comparing lesioned mature with immature animals: that it is impossible to have different lesion ages, the same test ages, and identical recovery periods. If age differences at lesion are preserved when adult testing is undertaken, the results may be attributed to an age-at-test effect as readily as to an age-at-lesion one. If age at testing is equated, the infant-lesioned animals inevitably have a considerably longer recovery period. This variable might not matter so much if a stable mature level of function could be prescribed or if testing were characteristically undertaken well into adulthood. However, as Thompson, Bergland, and Towfighi (1977) emphasize, this is still seldom the case.

Goldman's (1974) data provide little information on the importance of experience. Addressing this issue for orbitofrontal lesions, Goldman (1976) and Goldman and Mendelson (1977) found recovery to occur only if training was provided. The effect however, was, a puzzling one since it occurred only after a subsequent "incubation" period of a year. Interpretation of this finding, and of a possible age effect for some tasks, must await more detailed investigation, since the design included successive training on a number of tasks and allowed different age groups different experience/incubation period combinations. Of particular interest from the present viewpoint is Goldman's (1976) suggestion that recovery from the orbitofrontal lesions resulted specifically from use of dorsolateral function—recovery did not occur, even with training, if dorsolateral areas were also ablated. Hence it is interesting to speculate whether a maturational 'crossover' from orbitofrontal to dorsolateral mediation of delayed response skill occurs with the assistance of appropriate experience. If so, different types of cognitive strategy might be used by the two systems. Although no direct support for this view exists, Pribram, Plotkin, Anderson, and Demetria (1977) have recently demonstrated that delayed alternation skills in adult monkeys may be subdivided according to whether temporal or spatial cues are used. Recovery in even adult frontal-lesioned animals can be improved to normal control levels by arranging experimental conditions to foster the use of one or other of these skills. Pribram *et al.* (1977) specifically note the development by their monkeys of substitute mnemonic skills with which to overcome lesion deficits. These data are very suggestive that different frontal lobe areas function in different ways and that their employment on a particular type of task reflects maturational, experiential, and task variables.

2. Occipital Cortex Lesions

Tsang's data (1937a,b) established that sparing effects similar to Kennard's were obtained if lesions of the occipital cortex were undertaken in infant rats, and the effect was confirmed in cats by Doty (1961). More recently, however, Doty (1971) has reported that the original effects were due to the more extensive distribution of the adult lesions, which impinged upon adjacent areas not damaged by the lesions in infants. Other experimenters have also questioned Tsang's findings. Both Bland and Cooper (1969) and Murphy and Stewart (1974), for example, found visual discrimination tasks to be as disrupted in infant-lesioned as in adult-lesioned animals.

The permanence of cortical lesion effects in adult animals has also been questioned, most notably by Meyer (1974) and Le Vere (1975). Meyer, Isaac, and Maher (1958) found that the loss of an avoidance response conditioned to a visual stimulus could be avoided if the lesion was undertaken in two stages and if the animal was kept in the light in between lesions—the sparing did not occur if the animals were kept in the dark. The implied importance of interlesion experience was confirmed by Thompson (1960). Interlesion training is considered further in Section III, C, 3.

Although these adult sparing effects could be interpreted according to vicariation, substitution, equipotentiality, or diaschisis, subsequent experimentation has tended to favor the two latter models. First, demonstration that some, but not all, of the original visual skills remained intact influenced Dalby, Meyer, and Meyer (1970) to interpret the effect in terms of vestigial mechanisms. Remaining visual skills were regarded as compatible with subsidiary visual mechanisms, located either subcortically or in other cortical areas. Presumably, this is equipotentiality of a sort, although ambiguity remains as to whether these vestigial systems were actively used in original intact visual function. An alternative explanation, however, is possible. This follows from demonstrations by Braun, Meyer, and Meyer (1966) and Meyer, Horel, and Meyer (1963) that some visual skills may be reinstated by administration of amphetamine for as long as the effects of the drug last. A parsimonious interpretation is that the original visual function has not been obliterated at all, but has been somehow suppressed by the lesion—i.e., diaschisis. This interpretation has also received support in demonstrations by LeVere and Morlock (1973, 1974) that cats trained prior to lesion on black/white discrimination tasks are less able to learn tasks requiring reversed skills after the lesion than are cats without the pretraining—i.e., that negative transfer effects are obtained. This implies that not only general visual abilities but particular visual skills may remain intact and it is difficult to see how the effect can be explained unless at least part of the original engram has survived.

Data at present do not allow selection of either diaschisis or equipotentiality models to explain these effects, if indeed both are not involved. However, the results are all strongly suggestive that the original visual system, or some aspect of it, continues to be employed after the lesion, rather than a novel system being substituted.

It may be noted that some, albeit limited, evidence exists to support the view that infant occipital cortex lesions may be less deleterious than adult ones in some circumstances. Wetzel, Thompson, Horel, and Meyer (1965) have shown that cats lesioned in infancy can solve tasks with reduced flux and contour cues not solved by adult-lesioned animals. Stewart and Riesen (1972) and Tees (1976) have demonstrated infant-lesioned superiority on visual cliff, placing, and object-avoidance tasks. It is interesting to speculate whether, since these effects appear to be task specific, they reflect the characteristics of the immature systems at the time of testing. Perhaps the advantage would disappear in time as frontal lobe lesion effects do (Goldman, 1974). Unfortunately, extensive follow-up retesting has not been undertaken. Hicks and D'Amato (1970), however, have shown that at least one of these responses, the placing response, does deteriorate over time, while Braun, Lundy, and McCarthy (1970) have also demonstrated some depth discrimination in adult-lesioned animals with intensive training and motivational remediation.

3. Efferent System Lesions

The motor system appears to be the one area in which consistent infant lesion sparing effects occur, although it should be noted that, here too, the advantages are specific both to particular types of task (Lawrence & Hopkins, 1970) and to particular lesion locations. Taub, Perrella, and Barro (1973), for instance, have demonstrated permanent debilitating effects following deafferentation of the motor system at any age, and cerebellar lesions are similarly inflexible (Brunner & Altman, 1974). Lawrence and Hopkins (1970), in an experiment analogous to Goldman's (1974) work considered earlier, have shown increasing deficiency in fine motor control with age in monkeys with infantile pyramidal lesions. An additional consideration is that although adult lesions have, in general, more severe consequences, the effects of lesion are equally heterogenous. Goldberger (1974) draws a distinction, for example, between loosely coupled (i.e., topographically diffuse) and somatotopically (tightly) coupled systems. An example of the former is the reticulospinal system, where the extent of recovery reflects simply the size of the lesion, whereas a lesion limited to the hand area of the primary motor cortex produces a complete and irreversible loss of tactile placing response. Equally diverse effects are revealed by training, undertaken either pre- or postlesion, which appears to have remediating consequences where the adult lesion is cortical, but not where it is cerebellar (Goldberger, 1974).

Explanations for the apparently unique resistance of the motor system to lesion tend to emphasize its considerable redundancy and the presence of twin efferent (pyramidal and extrapyramidal) and bilateral (primary contralateral and secondary ipsilateral) systems (Geschwind, 1974; Brinkman & Kuypers, 1973). It is not clear why these systems should recover more effectively following infant damage. In general, motor recovery effects suggest that the systems implicated in the recovery exist and have motor capacities prior to insult—i.e., that recovery is best explained in equipotential terms.

4. Subcortical Lesions

The vast majority of subcortical lesion work has found no lessened effect of early lesions. Brunner and Altman (1974) showed no early lesion sparing effects from cerebellar or hippocampal lesions. Similarly negative findings have been obtained for septal lesions (Johnson, 1972) and thalamic lesions (Goldman, 1974). Some experimenters, however, have found some early lesion advantages on some tasks. Schneider and Jhaveri (1974) reported that when infant- and adult-lesioned hampsters were compared, each group was better on some types of task and worse on others. Isaacson (1975) has also noted the variability of early lesion effects, which he believes to be both task specific and subject to considerable interanimal differences, even between identically aged lesioned and tested animals. In explaining these, Isaacson emphasized both genotypic and experiential variables. Thompson *et al.* (1977) recently found amygdalectomy to produce identical behavior deficits in both infant an adult rhesus monkeys, but in the infant group effects became more pronounced with age. These findings are remarkable for their similarity to Goldman's (1974, 1976) frontal lobe and Lawrence and Hopkins' (1970) pyramidal lesion results, cited earlier.

5. *Summary of Lesion Work*
The work supports three main conclusions:

1. Neither recovery nor deficit are general properties but are specific both to the size and location of the lesion made and to the task used to assess postlesion performance.

2. Although some age effects exist, these may prove advantageous or disadvantageous, depending on the lesion location and task used. They may also subsequently reverse their effects. Sparing effects seem more likely in some neural systems than others. Hence, age must be considered a relevant but not overwhelming variable.

3. Although many questions are unresolved, the data do not support respecification models. In general, some aspects of the original neural system, or of a substitute system, seem to be involved in mediating postlesion behavior. Doubt as to the prelesion contribution of these systems to the behavior observed prevents more definitive conclusions.

B.   ENVIRONMENTAL DEPRIVATION AND ENRICHMENT EXPERIMENTS

Three types of environmental manipulation experiment are distinguished here: (a) general experiential enrichment and deprivation studies: (b) sensory deprivation studies, and (c) malnutrition studies.

1. *General Experiential Enrichment and/or Deprivation Studies*
This sort of experiment, originated by Rosenweig and colleagues (Rosenzweig, Bennett, & Diamond, 1967; Rosenzweig & Bennett, 1972; Rosenzweig, 1971) involves rearing animals in generally enriched or de-

prived environments, following which they are sacrificed and brain bio-chemical and morphological characteristics assayed. In the main, enriched experience produces increases in CNS structural and physiological param-eters, deprivation produces the converse.

Where the experiments are to be viewed in the context of plasticity, the results must be qualified in three respects. First, it is well established that the changes are achieved in adult animals as readily as in immature ones (Rosenzweig, 1976). Second, the relationship of the tissue alterations to changes in function is not clear-cut. Although deprived animals achieve less than controls, whether the enriched animals are truly intellectually "brighter" (in the sense of performing better on tasks not closely related to enrichment tasks) is unresolved (Greenough *et al.,* 1976). Finally, the status of enrichment has recently come in for some reevaluation. This is due to the finding of Rosenzweig, Bennett, and Diamond (1972) that laboratory animals allowed to exist in natural, wild environments are more advantaged in measures of brain microstructure and chemistry than the erstwhile "enriched" laboratory animals. Consequently, the latter may not be truly enriched at all.

The importance of generalized enrichment and deprivation studies, then, is not so much to show adaptation of CNS in response to experience, but to emphasize that experience is essential if optimal brain composition and behavior are to result. These experiments have also provided the founda-tion material for more detailed investigations of experiential-brain-behavior relationships to be examined in Section III, C.

2. Sensory Deprivation Studies

Since the early pathfinding work of Hubel and Wiesel (1962, 1965), sensory deprivation experiments have undergone considerable refinement and it is now clear that both species differences and deprivation techniques are im-portant variables. Rabbits, for example, are not disadvantaged by early visual deprivation to anything like the extent of the habitually used kitten (Mize & Murphy, 1973), a result normally attributed to species differences in visual pathway anatomy and topography (Rosenzweig, 1976). Equally, the effects of monocular deprivation are far more severe than those of binocular deprivation (Wiesel & Hubel, 1965), where considerable recovery appears to occur in time. Explanations of this difference tend to favor the idea that visual pathways compete for cortical sites during early "wiring up" of the CNS. However, exact morphological and anatomical substrates for this phenomenon have not yet been confidently identified (Hubel, Wiesel, & LeVay, 1977), and some researchers have recently demonstrated partial recovery even from monocular deprivation effects (Olson & Free-man, 1978). At present, the following general principles are widely accepted:

1. Both retinas and visual cortex have some degree of "tuning" prior to use in visual function. That is, they operate with some degree of selectivity concerning the type of stimuli which will cause them to respond prior to any experience. However, this tuning is sharpened up by experience (Blakemore, 1977).

2. A sensitive period exists during which appropriate experience must occur if the functional attributes of the visual system are to be normal. Visual deprivation outside this period does not have as severe or enduring effects (Blakemore, 1974), although some reports of prolonged deprivation in the adult cat suggest it may have some similar, but less severe, effects (Chow & Stewart, 1972). Unfortunately, the exact features of visual pathway maturation which constitute the sensitivity remain ambiguous. This is an important issue since the time tabling of CNS maturation varies in different species. In humans, neurogenesis is largely completed before birth (Dobbing, 1974), whereas in kittens neural proliferation continues postnatally and it may be significant that eye opening and the onset of the critical period for deprivation effects are delayed until the second week postnatally (Blakemore, 1975). Similar deleterious human visual deprivation effects have, however, been reported by Freeman and Thibos (1973).

3. Partial behavioral recovery can take place in the absence of detectable changes in physiological parameters. For example, deprived kittens become more adept at avoiding objects and visual orienting generally as they become older, in spite of the absence of improvement in visual acuity or cortical electrical activity (Spinelli, Hirsch, Phelps, & Metzler, 1972; Muir & Mitchell, 1973). The mechanism here remains obscure, although a parsimonious suggestion would be that the kittens have got better at using the limited acuity available to them.

4. More controversially, and of more central importance for the plasticity hypothesis, it can be claimed that transfer of functional properties, rather than just deterioration of them, has been identified (Blakemore & Cooper, 1970).

This difference is both a vital and a subtle one. All binocular and monocular experiments so far mentioned demonstrate only that early insult effects are more, rather than less, debilitating than late ones. That functional plasticity is greater in the young brain requires evidence that function can be exchanged, not just lost. Three experiments bear on this question. First, both Blakemore and Cooper (1970) and Hirsch and Spinelli (1970) found that raising kittens in a visual environment containing only vertically oriented stimulation (stripes) produces a visual cortex sensitive only to these orientations. The animals are "blind" to horizontal stimuli. Recent doubts as to these findings (Stryker & Sherk, 1975) have subsequently been

satisfactorily resolved (Blakemore, 1977). However, differences of interpretation remain. Blakemore and Cooper (1970) interpreted their results as
showing that cortical cells which would have selected for horizontal orientations had been adjusted by the experience to verticality. Hirsch and
Spinelli's (1970) interpretation is that unstimulated horizontal cells have
merely died off, leaving only the stimulated vertical ones. The issue re-
volves around the question of whether silent "gaps" are found when cells
are successively sampled across the striate cortex. Blakemore and Cooper
(1970) found no such silent regions. However, Stryker and Sherk (1975) did
report that about half the cells they sampled were unresponsive, sluggish,
or nonspecific in their response. Final resolution of this disagreement must
presumably await further replication work, although it may be noted that
Blakemore (1977) has recently concluded "It seems unlikely that the early
visual environment does much more than validate and make more selective
the preferred orientations genetically pre-specified" (p. 432).

The second experiment involves raising the kittens in environments consisting entirely of discrete small patches of light (spots). Cats raised under
these circumstances have cortical cells selective for spotty stimuli (Pettigrew
& Freeman, 1973; Van Sluyters & Blakemore, 1973) which are rare in the
normal cortex. This experiment does not appear to have been replicated or
extended, although the relationship between spots and short lines might
well be called into question.

The third, very recent, experiment by Spinelli and Jensen (1979) uses a
novel technique to train kittens to discriminate safe from unsafe visual
stimuli in an otherwise normal environment. Microelectrode recordings
showed revision of functional properties toward the relevant stimulus
qualities in younger, but not older, animals. This experiment does suggest
some degree of respecification, in that the number of cells responding to,
for example, vertically oriented visual stimuli was increased above the normal level in the younger kittens. However, the functional significance of
the changes remains unclear, since the (single) older animal learned the task
without needing this augmentation; while the permanence of the changes
also remains to be demonstrated—it may be, for example, that the super-
fluity of cells responsive to vertical lines will diminish with time. In addition, some rather perplexing findings, such as respecification of cells to
stimulus orientations opposite to those used in training, require explanation. Nonetheless, if replicated, the results would go some way toward
demonstrating plasticity, albeit of a circumscribed kind, limited to a single
sensory system and species and of equivocal value to function.

3. Malnutrition Studies

Several investigators have suggested that a critical period, or periods,
analogous to the sensory deprivation one exists for malnutrition effects

(Dobbing & Sands, 1971; Winick & Noble, 1965; Winick, Rosso, & Brasel, 1972). Hence malnutrition at this time produces irreversible deficits of CNS components which cannot be remedied by subsequent normalization of diet. Equivalent malnutrition at later periods does not have the same catastrophic effects. This view has also been augmented in some instances by the concept of growth spurts, that is, periods during which particular CNS areas are undergoing maximum growth. Knowledge of when each CNS area has its growth spurt(s) enables accurate prediction of particular neurological and behavioral sequelae of malnutrition to be made (Dobbing & Sands, 1971; Dobbing, Hopewell, & Lynch, 1971).

Although the evidence for CNS tissue deficits following early malnutrition appears convincing, there are two reasons for concern about the significance of the findings. First, the lack of information defining minimum tissue characteristics necessary for "normal" function makes interpretation of tissue deficit evidence difficult. Effects of malnutrition are normally sweeping, including reduction in brain size and weight, cortex thickness, cell processes, myelination, and other variables (Chase, 1976). Yet these measures all vary considerably both between brains and within the same brain ontologically—Jacobson (1973) has reported that active revision of CNS components, including drastic reduction in neuron numbers, is one process whereby the brain increases its efficiency. This criticism would not be so important if the behavioral consequences of tissue deficit and, particularly, the remediability of these consequences were better understood. Unfortunately, the second caveat to the work in this area concerns the inadequacy of the research directed at these issues.

In a recent review, Levine and Wiener (1976) have drawn attention to three separate problems in animal experiments concerned with recuperation from malnutrition:

1. An important distinction must be drawn between experiments employing chronic malnutrition and those employing acute malnutrition followed by a recovery period. Experiments of the former type, including those where testing is done in infancy, confound the direct effects of malnutrition at test with those of the consequences of acute malnutrition they aim to investigate.

2. All experiments which have used postnatal malnutrition as the independent variable have confounded this with the effects of psychosocial deprivation. In experiments where social variables were controlled (Frankova, 1974; Slob, Snow, & Natris-Mathot, 1973) no adult consequences of early malnutrition were found. Since social manipulations of the same kind are capable of producing the sort of changes in adult behavior obtained independently (Denenberg, Rosenberg, Paschke, Hess, Zarrow, & Levine, 1968; Levine & Thoman, 1969) the contribution of

malnutrition remains dubious. Consequently it may readily be argued that no significant brain insult effects were obtained in these experiments.

3. Studies using both open-field behavior and learning as dependent variables contain many contradictory findings and replication failures. Use of differing designs and methodology by the different researchers precludes resolution of these discrepancies at present. Levine and Wiener (1976) conclude:

> The studies which examine the behavior of rehabilitated animals do not present any clear or consistent set of results which would support a generalization that there are profound and permanent behavioral deficits as a consequence of early malnutrition. (p. 62)

4. Summary of Environmental Enrichment and Deprivation Studies

Studies in this area may be usefully subdivided into those concerned only with debilitating consequences of inadequate early experience (deprivation) and those which have attempted to manipulate the quality of experience.

Deprivation experiments employing general environmental, sensory, and nutritive deprivation have been considered. Although some doubt as to both the significance and the permanence of deprivation effects exists, particularly with malnutrition studies, in general the measures both of CNS and of behavioral variables support the view that the young CNS is particularly sensitive to the effects of environmental deprivation.

Studies attempting to show transfer or change in qualitative aspects of CNS function as a result of environmental manipulation appear, for the most part, to have failed to do so. At present, little or no convincing evidence that the function of CNS areas may be advantageously altered according to the characteristics of stimulation exists in this area of research.

C. EXPERIMENTS EMPLOYING LEARNING TO REMEDIATE CENTRAL NERVOUS SYSTEM INSULT

Following early demonstrations that handling (Levine, Haltmeyer, Karas, & Denenberg, 1967) and the postoperative environment (Ahmad & Harvey, 1968) altered the consequences of brain lesion, research concerned explicitly with use of experience to offset the effects of brain damage has evolved in several directions. These may be conveniently trisected, according to whether learning is implemented (a) before, (b) after, or (c) between CNS insults. When scrutinizing any of these experiments particular attention must be paid to the nature of control or comparison groups used. In many cases, "enriched" and deprived groups only are being compared, so that the extent to which differences are due to deprivation effects alone is unclear. Some experiments which have employed three groups, such that one experiences a normal social (but not especially enriched) environment, have shown this group to be spared by lesions every bit as much as the enriched group (Hughes, 1965).

1. Preinsult "Immunization"

The issue of general vs. specific enrichment of experience, already encountered in Section II, B, is also of importance for lesion "Immunization" work. However, although the issue of general vs. task-specific brightness is of interest, distinctions between task-related skills, overall intellectual gain, and augmented motivation which are clear at the theoretical level have proved less so in practice. For the most part, it appears that those experiments which have achieved the most impressive postlesion performance have done so on tasks very similar to those used in prelesion enrichment (Greenough, 1975; Rosenzweig, 1976). Correspondingly, studies which have tested performance on a wide variety of postlesion tasks have found even enriched animals to be deficient on some types of task. If general vs. specific carryover effects are to be identified in lesioned animals, it seems essential that generalization gradients be established for the tasks in question in nonlesioned animals. Data reported should also include measures of the rate of postlesion acquisition of task skills, so that recovery and relearning effects can be separated. These data have not been reported. Consequently, the status of general prelesion enrichment must be regarded as equivocal at the present time. Bearing in mind the confusion which surrounds the similar issue of IQ in humans, it may be supposed that this will remain the case for some time to come.

The optimum experiment in this area would seem to be one where prelesion experience is related in some way to the postlesion deficit anticipated. One study of this sort, by LeVere and Morlock (1974), showing negative transfer has already been described and several others demonstrating facilitation also exist. Bauer and Cooper (1964) tried to accustom their adult animals to the consequences of visual cortical lesions anticipated by making them wear translucent goggles during preoperative brightness discrimination training. They found this obviated the extensive postlesion training normally needed to reestablish brightness discrimination. Later, Cooper, Blochert, Gillespie, and Miller (1972) qualified this result as attributable only to small lesions—recovery from large lesions was much more protracted irrespective of prelesion experience.

Studies concerned with more vegetative responses have shown similar results. Lateral hypothalamic lesions, for instance, normally cause adipsia and aphagia so severe that immature or adult animals lesioned in this way will die if left to their own devices. Teitelbaum and Epstein (1962), however, have shown that remediative postlesion forced feeding and drinking will eventually reestablish normal appetitive function. This seems clear evidence for plasticity, albeit at any age. Subsequently, however, Powley and Keesey (1970) demonstrated that if the experimental animal is starved to 80% body weight prior to ablation, there is no postoperative aphagia or adipsia. If starved beyong 80% body weight, the immediate post operative behavior is hyperphagic—a complete reversal of the original symptoms. As do LeVere and Morlock's experiments (1974), this clearly suggests that the original skill is not really lost at all, but the hypothalamic experiment does not allow conclusions as to whether motivational or prior learning variables underlie the recovered behavior. That the latter are at least partly responsible is indicated by Dicara's (1970) demonstration that prelesion experience with milk facilitates postlesion milk drinking behavior. Along the same lines, Chase and Wyrwicka (1973) found that rats pretrained to drink liquid to obtain pleasurable septal electric stimulation retained the drinking behavior postoperatively. Greenough et al. (1976) interpret both these and analogous ventromedial hypothalamic recovery effects in terms of Hebb's (1949) model, suggesting that the CNS has learned preoperatively to regulate over a broader range of experience and consequently compensation for loss of one component of the multiply organized function is more easily achieved. That prelesion experience may increase the redundancy of a function in this way is a hypothesis of obvious importance.

2. Postinsult Remediation

Since, as outlined earlier, most animals recover to some extent from most lesions if left for long enough, care has to be taken to isolate those results attributable specifically to experiential manipulation. Ideally, three groups are again needed, with deprived, normal, and enriched postlesion experience, respectively. Unfortunately, few studies in this area have included all three.

Postlesion handling and social variables have frequently been shown to affect recovery from limbic lesions in quite specific fashions. For example, Gotsick and Marshall (1972) found that rage behavior typically produced by septal lesions was exacerbated by frequent handling immediately after the lesion, but diminished if gradual gentling was used. Equally, the consequences of septal and amygdaloid lesion are both affected by specific social variables. Rage in septal-lesioned rats, for instance, subsides in 17 days if the rats are kept in groups but takes 45 if they are kept in isolation (Ahmad & Harvey, 1968). The classic timid amygdalectomied animal can be made every bit as aggressive as normals if repeatedly annoyed (Fuller, Rosvold, & Pribram, 1957), and the drop in social hierarchical status associated with amygdalectomy in monkeys (Rosvold, Mirsky, & Pribram, 1954) may be prevented if the lesioned animal is allowed to recuperate in a group of submissive younger monkeys (Mirsky & Harman, 1974).

Although there appears to be a consensus that both ordinary experience and specific training elicit improvement in function following cortical as well as subcortical lesions, specific principles which govern the improvement, if these exist, have remained elusive. The work of Meyer and colleagues (reviewed by Meyer, 1974) on visual systems and of Goldman (1974, 1976) and Pribram *et al.* (1977) on frontal lobe lesions has already been mentioned. Both Bland and Cooper (1970) and Tees (1975, 1976) have reported that dark rearing after visual cortical lesions inhibits recovery of some visual behaviors, but the researchers differ on the nature of behaviors recovered. Schwartz (1964) and Will *et al.* (1977) have shown postoperative enriched environments to improve maze performance in animals with cortical lesions. Dru, Walker, and Walker (1975) have emphasized the importance of active postlesion experience for recovery and attribute some of the failures to obtain improvement to the use of passive enrichment, that is, to use of exposure to tasks only instead of training.

A few demonstrations of training-mediated recovery following more generalized CNS insult are also available. The difficulties associated with malnutrition studies have already been noted. Davenport and colleagues in a series of papers (summarized by Davenport, 1976) have reported considerable reduction in the deficits produced by hypothyroidism in rats. The beneficial effects were found to be long lived, but in common with lesion workers, Davenport found the effects to be task specific and his rats were as handicapped as unremediated controls on some tasks. Interestingly, the beneficial enrichment effects were not obtained in unlesioned animals in this study, causing Davenport to speculate that some enrichment effects may be specific to particular types of deficit. However, it should be noted that most other studies of general enrichment in normal animals have obtained improvement effects (Rosenzweig, 1976). Finally, it should be observed that postlesion remediation may sometimes exacerbate the effects of insult rather than alleviate them (Bauer, 1974; Schmaltz & Isaacson, 1966).

3. Interlesion Remediation

Extensive literature now exists to show that lesions performed in stages, and particularly two successive unilateral lesions where structures are represented bilaterally, produce less severe deficits than single complete lesions. Although any of the models of recovery outlined earlier could be used to explain these effects, interest has centered mostly on the question of whether the effects can be attributed exclusively to lessened diaschisis, because small lesions are used (Isaacson, 1975), or to interlesion experience (Greenough *et al.,* 1976). It could also be argued that these are not independent; that is, that experiential variables may help to dissipate diaschisic effects.

One frequent finding is that a critical minimum interlesion period must be employed if sparing effects are to be obtained (Stein, 1974; Finger, Walbran, & Stein, 1973). The period, however, may vary in different animals and CNS areas (Stein, 1974). Isaacson (1975) believes that this is clear evidence for viewing the results as due to decreased surgical stress. He points out that in cases where extended recovery periods are allowed (Greene, Stauff, & Walters, 1972; Tanaka, 1974) animals with single bilateral lesions do recover, it just takes longer. Consequently the recovery period used prior to assessment of function becomes a significant variable and Isaacson believes that this has been insufficiently evaluated.

Evidence exists to link eventual advantaged level of function following sequential lesions both to normal experience (Meyer *et al.,* 1958) and to specific practice effects (Thompson, 1960) and in general the latter are superior when the two groups are compared on the enriched task (Petrinovich & Bliss, 1966). However, both overall lesion size (Petrinovich & Carew, 1969) and task variables, (Kirchner, Braun, Meyer, & Meyer, 1970) again appear important. Some experimenters (Dawson, Conrad, & Lynch, 1973; Isaacson and Schmaltz, 1968) have been unable to obtain less severe consequences of staged, compared with equivalent unilateral lesions.

4. Summary of Studies Attempting Immunization against or Remediation of CNS Insult

Those studies which have employed extensive postinsult testing of function appear, without exception, to have found deficits of some sort and, in general, the recovery behaviors appear to reflect the behavior used in remediation quite faithfully. Indeed, it might be considered that this effect exists too for studies which have used normal (rather than particularly enriched) posttrauma experience, since the range of behaviors on which these animals have recovered are the ones experienced in their normal environment. It also appears that the extent of recovery is always limited according to the size and location of lesion and the task used, and it is interesting that Stein (1974) concludes that even the most carefully nurtured two-stage lesioned animals are never quite normal in their abilities. Few, if any, age differences have been reported in the recent literature in this area.

Bearing in mind the complex dynamic and transactional models currently being used to explain experiential recovery effects in humans (e.g., Sameroff & Chandler, 1975) it is interesting to note that the animal recovery effects in the contemporary literature may be plausibly and parsimoniously explained by three general principles. First, the extent of recovery of any function will depend on whether structures capable of subserving it are damaged and in what degree. Second, the recovered behaviors will reflect the kind of learning the animal has in a fairly direct and circumscribed fashion. Third, in consequence, whether or not recovery is obtained will depend on how recovery assessment reflects these two considerations. These principles are able to explain recovery effects in ordinary as well as in enriched environments, since the performance of lesioned animals with normal environmental experience is appropriate to that experience. Differences between normal and enriched experience will only be obtained if testing selects in favor of the characteristics of the latter.

D. OVERVIEW OF ANIMAL STUDIES

It is clear from this review of the animal literature concerned with recovery from cerebral insult that the emphasis of the research in this area has changed during the last few years. Increasing use of multivariate testing and protracted postinsult assessment, particularly, have played an important part. It now appears that, given sufficient convalescent time, a remarkable degree of recovery will follow most brain insult at any age. In general, age has ceased to be a dominant consideration in this work. Bearing in mind the need to generalize to the recovery process in humans, the following tentative conclusions appear justified.

1. Although some reservations apply, most studies of both brain constituents and behavior suggest that the infant CNS is particularly susceptible to all kinds of insult. However, this critical period phenomenon concerns sensitivity to deficit rather than plasticity. It is impossible to say whether the infant CNS recovers better or worse than the adult one in this respect, since the adult brain is not disadvantaged in an equivalent fashion. Although Jacobson's (1970) suggestion that depletion of superfluous neuronal material (tuning) may reduce CNS redundancy, and so recovery potential, with age has not been rejected, no firm supportive evidence has been found. In addition, it appears likely that such tuning would produce relatively small and system-specific variations.

2. In other respects age has not proved an overriding consideration. There seems to be little or no evidence to support the general view that the young CNS is less committed in respect of function, or recovers from insult more readily, than the old one. In some cases, the opposite has proved to be the case, with deficit incrementing with maturation. Age has come to be regarded as a variable of the same magnitude of importance as others which mediate recovery effects, viz.: individual differences in the genetic characteristics and experience of animals, their sex, the location and extent of the lesion or other insult, the topography and redundancy of the neural system affected, the time tabling of lesions, the recovery period, and the particular tasks used in assessment.

It is noteworthy that at least two series of animal experiments (Goldman, 1971, 1974; Thompson *et al.,* 1977) have demonstrated maturational reorganizations of CNS function analogous to those posited for humans by the theory of developmental discontinuity (Sameroff, 1975). Since evidence at present concerns one species (rhesus monkey) and only two lesions sites (frontal lobe and amygdala) the generality of the finding is not yet known. Nonetheless the data support two comments. First, it is remarkable that the effects apply to frontal cortical lobes, whose lack of direct afferent and efferent innervation seems to make them a likely CNS site for functional plasticity. Hence the failure to obtain such plasticity is all the more impressive. Second, the effect of age does not seem to be to nullify early brain trauma, as the discontinuity theory suggests. Rather, the consequence of maturation is to alter the characteristics of the deficit observed at each age, but the animal continues to perform inadequately throughout the protracted assessment period.

3. Although data currently available do not allow final selection from among the six models outlined earlier, some progress has been made. Several pieces of research have produced evidence favoring diaschisis and in all cases the function regained following lesion seems to resemble that of the original system, its parts, or the normal properties of substitute systems. Rather than attempting a conclusion on the basis of inadequate evidence it may be more useful to formulate a working hypothesis for future research. In these terms, the overriding impression given by the evidence is that redundancy and overlap between neural systems surviving trauma will obey the existing laws of psychology and neurology for undamaged systems. That is, in neurological terms, redundancy and consequent compensation will be greatest when neurological systems are duplicated or overlap. In psychological terms, redundant compensation will be possible only when the systems remaining are normally capable of interacting effectively in learning in the undamaged individual. Parsimony alone suggests that this formulation should be tested before the dubious concept of functional specification is adhered to.

4. Experience prior to CNS insult, between successive insults, and following insult are all capable to offsetting the consequences of the insult. In all cases so far investigated, the relationship between the type of environment experienced and the type of recovery obtained appears to be fairly specific. In all cases, too, recovery has been found to be limited by the (typically) lesion used, although this ceiling effect is itself governed by the site and extent of lesion.

The finding that prior experience may offset lesion consequences is an interesting one and suggests a mechanism whereby the redundancy of a system may be effectively increased without its original characteristics being altered. This view sees loss of behavioral function resulting in many case not from loss of the entire mechanism underlying the behavior, but from damage to the access system. Correspondingly, probability of post-traumatic recovery will be increased according to the number of access systems linked together through learning pretraumatically.

5. The general tenor of the data in this area has been to confirm that structure–function relationships in the CNS are tightly specified throughout life. Recovery results not from redefinition of remaining CNS areas, but from the normal functional characteristics of remaining systems and/or from normal learning processes. An additional and related implication of the data is that "active" or dynamic models of ontogenetic recovery processes are not needed to explain experimental findings and do not increase explanatory power. Maturational processes appear to occur independently of recovery effects and interactions between them are likely to be coincidental rather than directional or purposive. Intrinsic CNS contributions to direction in recovery processes appears to be limited to diaschisis, which obeys physiological rather than psychological laws and operates only to restore normal functional properties.

6. Finally, it is appropriate to mention the importance of terminological confusion in this area. Throughout this review the ambiguity of such terms as *damage, trauma,* and *insult* has caused difficulties. Presumably, overall reductions in CNS components below some critical level may cause deficits at least as serious as discrete physical damage, which is itself varied in its effects in relation to factors identified here. Since any CNS parameter will vary between individuals and even within an individual over time, progress is especially hampered by lack of normal-range criteria. Data on sequelae of malnutrition in infant animals, for example, suggest that although considerable morphological and biochemical CNS deterioration follows such insult, behavior appears little affected by malnutrition per se in the long run, if at all. Whether this reflects the insignificance of the changes or the inadequacy of monitoring techniques, however, is not known. Equally, the point at which Hirsch and Jacobson's (1975) concept of functionally advantageous neuronal depletion gives way to the morphological deficits typically found in retarded animals and humans (Huttenlocher, 1974; Purpura, 1974, 1976) is a matter of conjecture. One consistent result in the animal literature has been that if the search for consequences of insult is widened, some effect will be found and will be more complex than first thought. Thus, perhaps the greatest problem in this area at the moment is to develop measurement instruments which are valid and sensitive enough to account both for individual differences in the normal range and for deviance. This problem seems likely to be considerably exacerbated when the increased heterogeneity of human behaviors is considered.

IV. Human Studies

Like animal work so far reviewed, human research concerned with the consequences of early brain insult has undergone a considerable change of emphasis during the last few years. Following early retrospective research (Pasamanick & Knobloch, 1961) it appeared clear that a number of early-risk factors could be identified which were associated with cerebral insult and subsequent psychopathology. Indeed, the view that such eventualities as perinatal anoxia, prematurity, and malnutrition could cause cerebral deficit seemed so plausible that a continuum of reproductive casualty (Pasamanick & Knobloch, 1961) was envisaged to accommodate different degrees of cerebral injury, with severe handicaps ranged at one end and the ubiquitous minimal brain damage at the other. Recently, the environmentalist emphasis in research as a whole and, particularly, the failure of prospective studies (Campbell, Cheseman, & Kilpatrick, 1950; Corah, Anthony, Painter, Stern, & Thurston, 1965) to confirm retrospective effects has caused complete reversal of this trend. In place of a continuum of reproductive casualty, we now have the concept of "developmental discontinuity" (Sameroff, 1975) which proposed that:

transition from one stage of functioning to another with qualitatively different levels of organization may make many of the maladaptations of the earlier stage obsolete (p. 268)

together with the "continuum of caretaking casualty" (Sameroff & Chandler, 1975) which argues that:

Early factors which have enduring consequences are assumed to do so because of persistent influences acting throughout the life span, rather than at discrete points in development. Self-righting influences are powerful forces toward normal human development, so that protracted developmental disorders are typically found only in the presence of equally protracted distorting influences. (p. 189)

Hence the contemporary model completely rejects the older view that such events as anoxia permanently damage the brain at all. Instead the young brain is allotted an intrinsic homeostatic mechanism which both undertakes recuperation and, in the process, steers the CNS continuously toward a normal psychological level. Plasticity indeed.

In contrast to the infant literature, the adult is distinctly pessimistic. Even the use of concerted therapy seems unable to overcome the effects of cerebral stroke, which are both severely debilitating and more or less permanent in their action (Sarno, Sarno, & Levita, 1971; Stern, McDowell, Miller, & Robinson, 1971).

How, then, are differences in the effects of early and late CNS insult in humans and the discrepancy between these findings and those of the animal literature, reviewed earlier, to be explained? In attempting an answer, research studies will be subdivided according to whether brain damage is verified (for example, in cases of cerebral trauma and hemiplegia) or is presumed to occur on the basis of behavioral measures, but where no other validatory evidence is available. The latter include, particularly, malnutrition studies and investigations of pre- and perinatal risk factors. It is believed that confounding of these different etiologies and of quantitative and qualitative differences in brain damage contributes to conceptual confusion in this area. Subsequently, the implication of the nonplasticity view for contemporary transactional models of maturation-linked recovery processes is considered, since it is believed that these models misconceive brain-damage and recovery processes.

As with animal research, two main points will be made. First, where testing of individuals brain damaged as infants or children has been broadened, deficits contrary to the plasticity view have been found. Second, age and other individual differences in recovery phenomena can be explained satisfactorily in terms of existing neurophysiological and psychological processes. Although space considerations and the concern with the plasticity principle preclude detailed examination of adult data, it is emphasized that the alternative strategem employed with animal studies, of demonstrating adult recovery superior to that assumed by the plasticity model, may also be used here. Geschwind (1974), for example, speaks of the "widespread unawareness of the rates of significant recovery in adult aphasics" (p. 479). Other adult studies have obtained complete recovery in 50% of cases (Kertesz & McCabe, 1977), adult recovery comparable with child cases (Gott, 1973; Messerli, Tissot, & Rodriguez, 1976; Smith, 1974), or task-dependent effects such that either child or adult patients appear advantaged, depending on test circumstances (Teuber & Rudel, 1962).

A.   LOCALIZED CEREBRAL TRAUMA

As Isaacson (1975) has emphasized, comparison of the consequences of intrinsic and extrinsic CNS injury across age groups presents a number of methodological problems. First, the sort of events most likely to traumatize the young brain—for example, perinatal anoxia—do not occur in adults. Hence not only the brains at the two ages but the "experimental procedure" are different. Second, the inability to localize tissue damage means that the origins of remaining function cannot be specified. In a right hemiplegic, for example, we cannot be confident the left hemisphere is not contributing to language function. Fortunately, one exception to this rule exists in hemispherectomy studies, that is, studies where one complete hemisphere (or at least the cortical mantle) has been surgically excised, normally because of its epileptogenic effect. The preeminence of hemispherectomy studies as evidence for the plasticity argument in humans is emphasized by the importance assigned them by Lenneberg (1967), Chase (1973), and others. Consequently, they are examined first. Subsequently, other trauma studies are briefly reviewed.

1. Hemispherectomy Studies

Hemispherectomy evidence for plasticity of brain function depends on the observation that in some individuals surgical removal of the complete left hemisphere some time after it has been damaged has no deleterious effect on language function as long as the original damage occurred early in life. A critical period is often assigned for this transfer of language function to the right hemisphere. Lenneberg (1967) thought hemispheric transfer was possible up to 12 years of age, although his data were reanalyzed by Krashen (1973) and the critical period was reduced to 5 years of age. McFie (1961) concluded that optimal recovery only followed if brain damage occurred in the first year of life.

Hemispherectomy evidence for plasticity of CNS function depends, then, on evidence concerning functional asymmetry of the two cerebral hemispheres for language: Language normally resides in the left hemisphere but, if this is damaged, the right hemisphere is capable of supporting language function. Consequently, hemispherectomy data may be attacked on two fronts. Either the contemporary view that the hemispheres are asymmetric for language function may be questioned, or the hemispherectomy data themselves may be reinterpreted. Both strategies will be employed here.

Use of hemispherectomy to treat infantile hemiplegia achieved respectability when Krynauw (1950) reported results for 12 individuals ranging in age from 8 months to 21 years at operation. In general, remarkable improvement in overall function seemed to result, although no specific measures were attempted. In 1961, White reviewed 150 cases, in the majority of whom overall improvement and, particularly, reduction in antisocial behavior seemed to occur. Again, few formal measures had been obtained. In 1961, McFie's important study was undertaken. McFie criticized previous studies for their failure to obtain pre- and posthemispherectomy indexes of ability and reported repeated IQ measures for his own patients. In 1962, Basser's extensive series of operations was reported. Since Basser's study is widely cited, it, together with McFie's study, which is the only early one reporting pre- and postoperative measures, is reviewed here in some detail. By 1970, when Wilson reported follow-up data on McFie's patients, and on others operated by the same group, hemispherectomy had lost favor, partly because the acute improvement obtained in many patients was not matched by good chronic results. Many patients deteriorated markedly, and some died. Wilson again did not report formal follow-up measures. However, he did note that, whereas many of the original 50 patients had proved educable and employable, many were grossly mentally defective and 16 of the 47 patients traced had died. Except for the work of Dennis *et al.* (Dennis & Kohn, 1975; Dennis & Whitaker, 1976, 1977; Kohn & Dennis, 1974), which will also be considered below, few recent hemispherectomy studies have been reported. A more comprehensive analysis of posthemispherectomy intellectual and sensory–motor function is included in St. James-Roberts (submitted-a, b).

a. McFie's Study (1961). McFie's data concern 34 hemispherectomied hemiplegic patients, ranging in age from birth to 5 years at hemiplegia onset and from 1 to 31 years at hemispherectomy. In 21 cases the right hemisphere was removed and in 13, the left. An attempt was made to define the status of the remaining hemisphere via postoperative electroencephalogram (EEG) and even this gross measure suggested that only 13 patients had normal remaining hemispheres after hemispherectomy. The aberrant status of both pre- and posthemispherectomied hemispheres is also represented in the IQ measures which were obtained both before and after surgery for 28 subjects. Only six patients were of an intellectual level sufficient to be tested on an accredited IQ test (the Weschler–Bellevue) and most patients were clearly severely mentally handicapped both before and after surgery. McFie attributes the postoperative deficiencies to "overloading" of the remaining hemisphere as it attempted the normal function of two hemispheres. However, the findings of Dennis and Whitaker (1976), Smith (1974), and others have shown that normal or superior IQ levels can be achieved by a single hemisphere. Consequently, it seems probable that the majority of McFie's patients had damaged residual hemispheres. Elsewhere (St. James-Roberts, submitted-a, b) it has been concluded that the status of the residual hemisphere is an important source of error affecting all comparisons of hemispherectomied patients, but particularly interage comparisons. Although, as McFie's findings and Wilson's (1970) follow-up data imply, both mortality and residual-hemisphere damage are common sequelae in infant-brain-damaged cases, the relatively large number of such patients and the tendency of authors to concentrate on optimum cases has given the impression of favorable recovery of function. In contrast, the small number of adult cases and typical etiology, tumor–often recurring in the remaining hemisphere—have contributed to an impression of poor recovery in such patients. So, for example, Gardner, Karnosh, McClure, and Gardner (1955), in a widely cited study, concluded recovery in their adult cases to be inferior to infantile cases; but closer examination reveals their infant baseline to be an unrepresentatively favorable one abstracted from other studes rather than derived from infant matches to their adult subjects. Moreover, of their eight adult cases, four died within a year or remained decerebrate, with an additional patient also dying from intracranial pathology 3½ years postoperatively. Hence, the inference that the adverse postoperative state of many of their patients contributed to their poor recovery seems a plausible one. Fortunately, recent studies have shown that adult-brain-damaged hemispherectomied patients are capable of levels of function comparable with those of optimum infant cases (Gott, 1973; Smith, 1974), although no adult-damaged left hemispherectomy cases have survived without tumor recurrence for long enough for possible interhemispheric transfer of language skills to be investigated.

McFie's major finding concerns existance of a critical period for advantageous recovery from hemispherectomy where brain-damage onset occurred prior to 1 year of age. Unfortunately, this conclusion does not withstand close scrutiny. Several shortcomings exist in the study, including dependence on IQ scores taken from young children (13 patients were 7 years old or younger when first tested), which are unreliable (Lewis & McGurk, 1972); unequal distribution of three different psychometric tests across age groups; and inadequate control of recovery period characteristics. However, the study's principal deficiency is its failure to allow for the effects of arbitrary IQ fluctuations in small subject samples.

Since IQs of even normal children fluctuate over time (Hindley & Owen, 1978) and since the process of compiling IQ difference measures exacerbates existing score error variance, it is of importance that reliability estimates be obtained to identify arbitrary IQ fluctuations. This is especially the case if small, or unequal-sized, groups are compared, and McFie's early brain-damaged group has 21 patients, the late one, seven. Since no standardized estimates exist for the tests in question when used with hemiplegic subjects of either age group, the stratagem of choice is to obtain reliability scores from matched retested hemiplegic individuals without hemispherectomy. Since McFie did not obtain these, it is difficult to know what sort of reliability criterion to impose. Fortunately, a quick look at the data suggests that the question may remain academic, since even a conservative threshold of plus or minus half a standard deviation (7.5 IQ points) negates the suggested age-group differences. Distribution of improved: unchanged: deteriorated posthemispherectomy IQ for the two groups becomes 12:8:1 (early group) and 1:5:1 (late group). With a criterion of ± 8 IQ points, the early group distribution is 10:10:1 and the late one, unchanged. Hence, contrary to McFie's conclusion, neither group shows much evidence of IQ deterioration, while the likelihood that the retested IQ will be the same versus improved does not differ in the age groups.

Although these statistical arguments are considered sufficient grounds for scepticism about McFie's proposed critical period for preferential recovery, the superiority of criticism based on replication evidence is acknowledged. Griffith and Davidson's (1966) study, which involves successive posthemispherectomy retesting of patients, provides suitable material. Their data are shown, subdivided accordingly to McFie's age criteria, in Table I.

As can be seen, these data are inconsistent with McFie's conclusion, with small posthemispherectomy increases being obtained in both age groups and, indeed, in all patients tested; while both pre- and posthemispherectomy mean IQs of late-onset brain-damage patients are higher than those of early-onset patients. In addition, although only two matched pairs of their most intelligent patients were tested, Griffith and Davidson did notice cerebral asymmetry effects. Patients with left-hemisphere damage were deficient on verbal comprehension subtests and those with right-hemisphere damage, on block design subtests, irrespective of age at brain damage. The severe mental handicap of most of McFie's patients prevented him from investigating qualitative IQ differences.

It is emphasized that Griffith and Davidson's data are not considered

TABLE I

Data of Griffith and Davidson (1966) Study Subdivided According to McFie's (1961) Age Criteria

	Mean prehemispherectomy IQ (Stanford–Binet test)	Mean early[a] posthemispherectomy IQ (Stanford–Binet test)	Mean late[b] posthemispherectomy IQ (WISC and WAIS tests)
Early (onset < 1 year old) brain damage ($N = 4$)	55[c]	59	64[d]
Late (onset > 1 year old) brain damage ($N = 7$)	75	79	77[d]

[a] Recovery period within range 2–12 months.

[b] Recovery period within range 4–15 years.

[c] Based on test results of three patients only.

[d] Full IQ scores derived from Wechsler Adult Intelligence Scale (WAIS) and Wechsler Intelligence Scale for Children (WISC) verbal and performance IQs provided by Griffith and Davidson using test manuals.

evidence for preferential late-brain-damage recovery effects. Rather, in conjunction with McFie's, they illustrate how use of small samples and poor control procedures has led to misinterpretations of findings in this area. In a systematic analysis, St. James-Roberts (submitted-a) has failed to find any significant age-dependent differences in posthemispherectomy IQs. Finally, it is noteworthy that McFie's (1975) own later nonhemispherectomied cerebral trauma data are inconsistent with the critical period hypothesis.

  b. Basser's (1962) Study. Like McFie's, Basser's conclusions have been widely cited and form a major component of Lenneberg's (1967) thesis concerning a language acquisition critical period. The study's importance derives from its large sample and from its findings concerning both IQ and language recovery after hemispherectomy. A closer analysis, however, reveals some important discrepancies between Basser's data and their usual interpretation.

One of Basser's most cited conclusions is that the verbal IQ of his patients is the same, irrespective of the hemisphere removed. However, although data are reported for 102 hemiplegics, only 35 of these received hemispherectomy and only 20 hemispherectomies are reported in any detail. Hence, we have no information as to the verbal IQ's of patients with one functioning hemisphere and so this result reveals little about hemisphere equivalence for verbal skills. Further, the IQs reported are generally very low: the modal group, which contains nearly twice the subjects of any other group, has the lowest score measured by Basser's tests—"less than 67." Consequently, it appears these are mostly severely mentally handicapped individuals, probably with damaged residual hemispheres. Studies which have reported qualitative differences in hemisphere intellect (Dennis & Whitaker, 1976; Griffith & Davidson, 1966; Smith, 1974) have obtained them only in patients with relatively high IQ scores; the inference being that the existance of general retardation obscures, or prevents development of, more complex skills.

For the 20 hemispherectomy cases, age at brain damage ranges from birth to 5 years; while follow-up periods and age at hemispherectomy and at test (where reported) show considerable diversity. Although Basser reports postoperative language findings, no formal tests are used and data are limited to short descriptive phrases, such as "speech improved" or "simple speech," which are difficult to interpret. Since experiments in both normal (Gordon, 1974) and commissurotomied (Gazzaniga & Sperry, 1967) adults have shown the right cerebral hemisphere to have some language abilities, Basser's failure to report detailed language measures is of obvious importance. Such measures as he does provide suggest heterogeneity of speech recovery to be characteristic of his patients. Thus, of the six patients with left-hemisphere damage prior to 3 months of age, none recovered normal speech abilities; whereas three of the five patients with left-hemisphere damage after speech acquisition had begun (15–20 months of age) do appear to have done so. However, even in the latter group one dysphasic patient was found, and patients with right-hemisphere damage at different ages present an equally diverse recovery picture, suggesting that neither age nor hemisphere per se is a major contributing factor in these cases.

   c.   *Studies by Dennis et al.* The inadequacy of Basser's language assessment becomes particularly pertinent when the detailed analyses of Dennis and colleagues (Dennis & Kohn, 1975; Dennis & Whitaker, 1976, 1977; Kohn & Dennis, 1974) are reviewed. Like other researchers, Dennis *et al.* do not believe that right- and left-hemisphere processing differences can be explained in gross language terms. Geschwind (1974), for example, proposes that the difference lies not in the hemispheres' capacity to process linguistic information as such, but in dominance of reponse systems. Unfortunately, space constraints preclude consideration of this controversy, although a few relevant findings are presented below.

   The strategy adopted by Dennis *et al.* is to use a number of psychometric instruments to explore differences in the information-processing skills of left- and right-hemispherectomied infant hemiplegics in considerable detail. In all cases, subjects have been carefully matched for age at hemiplegia and hemispherectomy, and verbal IQ. That such matching is possible and that the verbal IQs of these patients are normal, or near normal, emphasizes the inadequacy of earlier studies employing general or verbal IQ measures as dependent variables.

   When tested in some detail, subtle, but consistent, differences in the language capacity of right and left hemiplegics emerge. Understanding of syntax is significantly better developed in individuals retaining only the left hemisphere, while those with the right hemisphere not only have poorer syntax but develop syntax later than intact-left-hemisphered individuals. This difference is most noted when stimulus material is most complex and when task times are short. Conversely, if visuospatial skills are measured (sense of direction and orientation and route finding) individuals with only right hemispheres intact are markedly superior in their performance. The Dennis *et al.* finding of qualitative differences in right- and left-hemisphere function has also been reported by other hemispherectomy studies (Damasio, Lima, & Damasio, 1975; Gott, 1973; Griffiths & Davidson, 1966; Smith, 1974; Zaidel, 1977) as well as in hemiplegic studies, to be reviewed in Section IV, A, 2.

   One interesting implication of the data of Dennis *et al.* and others, is that neither IQ tests nor gross verbal and performance scores provide acceptable measures of cerebral asymmetry effects. A similar argument may be advanced for language, in that there is no reason for assuming discrete unilateral representation of all language capacities and, indeed, good reason in both neuropsychological and psychophysical literatures for assuming the existance of some language capacities in both hemispheres. Hence, confusion seems likely to result from the presumption that language is a single-process function, subsumed by the left hemisphere. Several alternative formulations are possible. A hypothesis compatible with existing literature is that the two hemispheres correspond in many of their functional properties, the specialization of each being a relative and subtle one which is emphasized by experience. In such a case, there is no reason to assume total domination of communication systems by the left hemisphere, and right-hemisphere skills, or a combination, would be employed, depending on stimulus properties and previous stimulus experience. This hypothesis has the advantage that developmental data, such as Bakker, Teunison, and Bosch's (1976) and Sadick and Ginsburg's (1978) suggested age trends from slow-wholistic right-hemisphere reading skills to rapid-sequential left-hemisphere ones can be accommodated, while Hardyck's (1977) finding that left-hemisphere superiority exists only for familiar verbal material would also be explained. Moreover, if the left hemisphere is damaged, substantial language recovery by an intact and unhampered right hemisphere should be possible, even in an adult, with appropriate experience. Unfortunately, as previously noted, no adult left-hemispherectomy cases have survived for long enough for the hypothesis to be tested. Although further speculation is therefore unwarranted, the existence of such a hypothesis is of some relevance, since it provides a nonplasticity interpretation of hemispherectomy and other data which is more parsimonious than the alternative plasticity hypothesis.

Before I leave hemispherectomy studies, brief mention should be made of an argument which implies that such studies are inappropriate for investigation of general brain-damage recovery effects. The argument proposes that once a suitable neural system has acquired responsibility for a function it will retain it, even though damaged and in spite of the existence of alternative systems able to undertake the function more effectively. Hence, it is the restraining influence of a damaged brain area which is its dominant property and, in removing this, hemispherectomy studies provide an unrepresentative model. This argument is compatible with the finding that functions in unilaterally damaged individuals without hemispherectomy remain in the original area in spite of the damage (Fedio & Mirsky, 1969; Milner, 1967).

This argument may take two forms. In the first, the influence of the damaged area is primarily diaschisic and predicts no age-difference effects. Alternatively, domination of sensory or response systems by the damaged area may be implicated, in which case learning may contribute to this domination. In the latter case, age effects may occur, since in immature systems learning-related domination should be less established than in mature ones. At present, however, no convincing evidence for this phenomenon exists and some aspects of hemispherectomy studies argue against it. Moreover, if it does occur, the effect seems likely to be a relatively subtle one, to increment gradually with age rather than via discrete critical periods, and should be reversible through learning.

2. *Localized Cerebral Trauma without Hemispherectomy*

Since patients with cerebral trauma retain the use, for better or worse, of the damaged brain area and since differences in etiologies, recovery periods, and recovery circumstances of patients hamper comparisons, it might be expected that studies of trauma outcomes would take these sources of variance into account. However, as Sarno (1976) has emphasized, this has seldom happened, so that patients with a wide variety of trauma circumstances have typically been grouped together to accommodate statistical priorities. Whether such heterogeneity has contributed not only to variance within groupings, but also to the impression of recovery age differences, is a question of obvious importance. Unfortunately, neither differences in the quality and degree of brain damage nor the effects of experiential variables has received systematic analysis, although suggestive findings exist in all three areas.

Recently, provisional attempts to develop independent criteria to quantify severity of brain damage have suggested the existence of posttraumatic coma, amnesia, or seizures to have prognostic significance (Field, 1976). Thus, Shaffer, Chadwick and Rutter (1975) found that although the majority of their traumatized children did not have persisting intellectual deficits, those with coma of 3 days or longer did do so. These authors also found a positive, but nonsignificant, relationship between posttraumatic epilepsy and psychiatric referral. Heiskanen and Kaste (1974) and Van Dongen and Loonen (1977), similarly, have concluded that prolonged coma is prognostic of poor recovery, while Teasedale and Jennett (1974) have developed a standardized coma scale. Unfortunately, the failure of most studies to report any measures of injury severity precludes any present attempt to establish whether age differences in the degree of brain damage bias recovery findings. Moreover, it is doubtful whether distinctions emphasizing quantitative parameters alone would have much validity since, for example, the tendency for older children to have more severe head injury (Field, 1976) is linked to differing damage circumstances and hence, presumably, to differing pathological syndromes. Equally, it seems that such variables as amnesia will be related to the nature of damage as well as to its degree.

It is for qualitative differences that the clearest case for age biases exists, although here too the picture is obscured by lack of appropriate epidemiological data. Such findings as are available come either from particular syndromes, such as hemispherectomy, which may not be representative; or from general clinic and hospital attendance, admission, and morbidity data, which are at best very gross measures. With this provision in mind, however, it does appear that age differences in predominant brain-damage etiology exist. Thus, both hemispherectomy studies (Smith, 1974) and the British Hospitals In-Patient Enquiry (HIPE, 1974) confirm the commonest infant etiology to involve pre- or perinatal insult or early encephalic or meningeal infection, which is much less common at older ages. Hospital admission for brain damage in midchildhood is more likely to involve extracerebral trauma, so that Craft, Shaw, and Cartlidge (1972) reported it to be the commonest single cause of hospital admission at this age. Field (1976), reviewing epidemiological studies of head injury in general, reported a trend for cranial injuries to be more substantial in older children, particularly boys, such that although the phenomenon was common in young children, it was typically due to a fall and not severe in its effects. In the 15- to 19-year age group, however, damage was more likely to be due to a traffic accident and to be correspondingly more serious and long lasting. Klonoff (1971) reported similar findings for a Canadian sample. The significance of extracerebral trauma for child brain-damage findings is also reflected in the high proportion of such cases included in samples used in follow-up studies (Boll, 1974; McFie, 1975). Etiologies involving brain tumor, thrombosis, or hemorrhage rarely occur in childhood, whereas measures of incidence, hospital stay, morbidity, and death confirm the increasing influence of these intracerebral pathologies with age (HIPE, 1974). Adult hemispherectomy cases show a similar pattern (St. James-Roberts, submitted-b). Interestingly, the distribution for brain neoplasm peaks at a younger age (45–65 years) than that for vascular disorder (> 65 years) and in each case is more than twice as common at that age range than any other.

Although of importance, it is not aparent that such etiological age variations contribute directly to age-difference recovery effects. That they do so is strongly implied by research concerned with recovery in aphasic patients. Sarno (1976), summarizing early studies, concluded that although quantification was difficult, the impression gained was that recovery from aphasia due to exogenous trauma (missiles or blows to the head) was better than for endogenous cases (vascular or disease etiologies). Confirming this impression, Kertesz and McCabe (1977) reported clear differences in recovery outcomes, more than half the exogenous adult trauma cases in their study recovering completely. In a remarkably parallel study involving children with acquired aphasia, Van Dongen and Loonen (1977), too, concluded that complete or near-total recovery occurred only in children with exogenous trauma causation. The latter authors also suggested that many reports have overrepresented the recovery potential of brain-damaged children, while both groups of researchers emphasized the prognostic significance of individual etiological circumstances.

In spite of the extensive literature linking child brain-damage effects with psychosocial variables (Rutter, 1977; Rutter, Graham, & Yule, 1970), the third source of recovery variability identified by animal studies, experiential differences, has also been neglected in most human studies. In this respect, a variable assigned importance by Geschwind (1974) and Isaacson (1975) is that of acuteness of injury. Since, for example, a perinatal hemiplegia must be followed by a recovery period of at least 7 years before reliable psychometric testing is possible, infant hemiplegics are by definition chronic when tested. Adult recovery periods are typically much shorter. The importance of the recovery period variable even for adults is clear from Fitzhugh, Fitzhugh, and Reitan's (1962) demonstration that gross verbal:performance differences in IQ scores are observable in left:right hemiplegic adults only if the damage is acute. With long recovery periods the differences disappear, suggesting that diaschisis, or post-traumatic experience, influence scores obtained. That the quality, as well as quantity, of experience matters is shown by later research by Finlayson, Johnson, and Reitan (1977). In this study, a direct relationship was found between superior educational experience and enhanced posttraumatic performance on some tests. Interestingly, the measure on which most pronounced educational influence was observed, verbal IQ, is among the most widely used in brain-damage studies and has often provided the basis for demonstrations of superior recovery in child brain-damaged patients (Basser, 1962). The implication, that adult:child recovery differences often reflect the partiality of tests used to the experience of one group (particularly schooling) is of obvious importance. Among other experiential variables found to influence recovery outcomes are initial intelligence (Panting & Merry, 1970), occupational status (Rusk, 1969), and family supportativeness (Fahy, Irving, & Millac, 1967).

Unfortunately, few longitudinal studies of children with cerebral damage have been published and none which has looked in detail at the effects of experiential variables. Hjern and Nylander (1963) found that if parents of head-injured children were given encouraging rehabilitative counseling at the time of hospital discharge the children were less maladjusted at follow-up than comparison groups without counseling. Klonoff and Paris (1974) obtained different sequelae and complaints at 1 and 2 years after trauma, with a particular tendency for girls to complain less than boys with increasing convalescence. Posttraumatic improvement in language skills in aphasic children reported by Van Dongen and Loonen (1977) has already been mentioned. Fuld and Fisher's (1977) two child cases were continuing to improve on psychometric tests, including IQs, 14 months after injury. Cummulating improvements in hemispherectomy cases many years after trauma and surgery have also been observed by Griffith and Davidson (1966) and Smith and Sugar (1975).

Although, then, there are good grounds for supposing experiential and recovery variables to be of considerable importance, few data exist to support more detailed hypotheses. Moreover, it cannot be assumed that prolonged recovery periods will necessarily prove advantageous since, in other cases, existence of more severe damage, damage to different neural systems, postinsult complications, or poor rehabilitation may lead to an accumulating psychopathology. As previously noted, ample evidence for such effects exists in the hemispherectomy literature, with initial improvement frequently being followed by long-term deterioration (Mensh, Schwartz, Matarazzo, & Matarazzo, 1952; Wilson, 1970).

Given these sources of confusion, it is perhaps surprising that any consensus has emerged in the child cerebral trauma literature. However, a number of recent studies have obtained findings consistent with each other and with conclusions derived earlier from hemispherectomy data. Annett (1973) found that although groups overlapped, left-sided cerebral lesions produced speech impairments more frequently (in 41% of subjects) than right lesions (15% of subjects). Kershner and King (1974) concluded that although their left and right hemiplegics were all progressing satisfactorily at school, both Wechsler Intelligence Scale for Children (WISC) IQ subtests and neuropsychological tests showed that left hemisphere damage was accompanied by language skill deficits and right hemisphere by visuospatial ones. McFie (1975), in a study involving 250 child or juvenile cases with circumscribed lesions of mixed etiology, found no age-related overall recovery effect. McFie (1975) noted the relatively consistent effect of left-hemisphere damage at any age on verbal long-term memory and span of apprehension and drew attention to qualitatively different language subprocesses, which he labeled language intelligence and language memory. Warrington (1975) also interpreted McFie's (1975) data in nonplasticity terms. In studies involving both child and adult brain-damaged patients, Rudel, Teuber, and Twitchell (1974) and Teuber and Rudel (1962) observed task-dependent age differences in both groups, such that either child or adult patients appeared advantaged, depending on test circumstances.

Their 1974 results were interpreted as indicating the adult pattern of hemispheric specialization to antedate birth, and the extent of lesion was considered of primary importance. Wedell (1960) observed visual–spatial deficits to be characteristic of right-hemisphere-damaged hemiplegic children. In what is probably the best controlled study to date, involving 98 children with exogenous trauma and visible cortical damage, Shaffer *et al.* (1975) found no relationship between age and follow-up intellectual or psychiatric measures, although intellectual deficits were found in children with more severe damage, as indexed by period of coma. Nine of the children had mild or moderate aphasia and four had hemiplegia, although the etiologies in these cases are not provided. One surprising aspect of this study is its failure to find any site of lesion effect. However, this may be attributed, as Rutter (1977) suggests, to the relative mildness of the brain damage concerned, or to the design used, since a recovery period of at least 2 years was allowed. As Van Dongen and Loonen (1977) have shown, children with extracerebral etiology do tend to recover well if allowed adequate recovery periods. An alternative explanation, drawing on doubts expressed earlier about the efficacy of IQ tests as brain-damage measures, is that Shaffer *et al.* failed to find intellectual sequelae because of the insensitivity of measures used. In this respect it is interesting that subsequent analyses (Chadwick & Shaffer; cited by Rutter, 1977) have found approximately one-third of the sample to be at least 2 years reading retarded.

3. Summary of Localized Cerebral Trauma Studies

Although human data are more scarce and equivocal than animal findings, they appear to be along similar lines. Thus, etiological variables, resulting in differences of type and degree of brain damage, and recovery period and experiential variables have been identified as important confounding influences. Some systematic age biases in the contribution of such influences have been identified and it has been suggested that these may sometimes give the impression of preferential age-related recovery, although age itself is not the causative factor. The use of insensitive or inappropriate assessment techniques has also been implicated in this respect.

For hemispherectomy studies, primary sources of error are the status of the residual hemisphere, the recovery circumstances, and the use of inadequate tests. For nonhemispherectomy cases, these are supplemented by the facilitative or handicapping influence of residual damaged systems. Recent studies of adult-brain-damaged cases have shown greater recovery than previously obtained, while those of early-onset brain damage have identified deficits which conform to the adult pattern.

As with animal data, then, there appears to be no evidence to support a general rule that the young brain recovers from brain injury better than the adult or that radically different recuperative processes are involved. Unfortunately, findings do not allow selection from among the models of recovery processes outlined earlier.

Although several types of putative insult may be identified, including the consequences of infection, clinical and nonclinical use of drugs and chemicals, stress, malnutrition, and obstetric complications of various kinds, research has tended to concentrate on the two latter areas. Consequently, although it is appropriate to note that research in other areas is growing (Berry, 1976; Sameroff & Chandler, 1975), attention here also is confined to research on malnutrition and pre- and perinatal phenomena.

1. Malnutrition Studies
The design problems affecting research in this area have recently been reviewed by Lloyd-Still (1976) and Richardson (1976) so that only a brief summary is attempted here. Two main sources of error may be identified. First, in almost all cases, subjects are malnourished prenatally, postnatally, and at the time of test. Consequently, separation of the immediate effects of malnutrition from those causing deficient CNS development is impossible. Second, control of psychosocial variables has proved extraordinarily difficult, to the extent that Chase (1976) has recommended adoption of the term *environutritional deprivation* in preference to use of categories isolating particular effects unrealistically. This is largely because psychosocial factors interact with sample selection factors as well as with postnatal experiential variables: Lower socioeconomic class mothers tend to produce babies with lower birth weights, dietary deficiencies, and lower IQs in the first place (Drillien, 1967; Smithells, 1977). The obvious solution—to match within social groups, and often within families—may be criticized in that children similar in social terms are also more likely to be similarly malnourished. These problems are examined in detail by Stein *et al.* (Stein, Susser, Sanger, & Marolla, 1975; Stein & Susser, 1976).

Fortunately, a number of partial solutions to these problems offer themselves. Although psychological variables are difficult to control, manipulation of nutritive ones is practicable. Consequently, a method whereby psychosocial effects may be minimized exists in studies undertaking nutritive intervention, such that calorific or qualitative aspects of diet are systematically varied, during pregnancy or subsequently. Two such intervention studies, each involving approximately 1000 mothers and children, have been reported recently. The Guatamalan study (Habicht, Yarbrough, Lechtig, & Klein, 1974; Klein, Irwin, Engle, Townsend, Lechtig,

Martorell, & Delgado, 1977) added various protein and calorific supplements to the basic diet of their mothers. They found the amount of calorie intake to be inversely related to the incidence of low-birth-weight children, to continuing growth retardation at 3 years of age, and to depressed IQ scores at 3–5 years of age. The effect was calorie, rather than protein, related. Although this finding seems plausible, it requires confirmation, since the design used allowed mothers to select the quantity of their own intake. Consequently, regression analyses, instead of design parameters, were used to exclude effects attributable to maternal differences rather than dietary ones. In contrast, the Harlem study (Rush, Stein, Christakis, & Susser, 1974; Susser, Stein, & Rush, 1977), using a randomized design, found no overall supplement effect on birth weight, although 1 year postnatally the supplemented babies demonstrated superior attentional capacities. Two surprising effects were an increased incidence of prematurity and stillbirths in mothers with greatest dietary supplement, and increased birth weight in subsamples of supplemented mothers who were of low initial physical weight or who were heavy cigarette smokers.

A second way to control psychosocial variables is to isolate a socially heterogeneous population which has suffered a short period of famine and to compare measures of the malnourished individuals with those in the population before and after the famine. One such study exists, in the series of reports of the consequences of the famine in Holland during the winter of 1944/1945 (Smith, 1947; Stein *et al.*, 1975; Stein & Susser, 1976). The only objection to this study concerns its dependence on retrospective data and the lack of detailed information on dietary intake. However, its comprehensiveness and control of social variables make it uniquely important. The study found no association between either pre- or early-postnatal malnourishment and intelligence, although some correlations with physical measures (such as birth weight and head size) were obtained. The familiar relationship between social class and IQ was also found but was not influenced by malnutrition.

Together, these three studies suggest that consequences of early malnutrition are complex in their effects and cannot be considered in isolation. Differences in the findings of the Guatamalan and Harlem projects, for instance, may be attributed to population or environmental differences (such as disease), to differences in baseline diet, to psychosocial effects, or to design variables. Stein and Susser's demonstration of the importance of psychosocial variables is supported by recent carefully controlled small-sample studies elsewhere (Richardson, 1976). Hence, these findings parallel animal malnutrition data in a remarkable way. In view of the subtlety of such situational effects, a question of some importance is whether the contribution of interacting variables is to negate the effects of starvation or to camoflage them. This question may be rephrased in quite specific terms, since in almost all studies the measures used to assess malnourishment effects are psychometric and, particularly, IQ tests. Consequently, whether such tests are sensitive enough, or appropriate, to measure effects of CNS insult of this sort is an issue of considerable relevance. This question is taken up again in Section IV, B, 2.

2. Studies of the Consequence of Perinatal Complications

Since excellent reviews of research in this area again exist (Sameroff & Chandler, 1975; Stewart & Reynolds, 1975) only a summary of the issues and findings is attempted here.

Use of peri- and postnatal intensive care offers an informative intervention strategy in this area, since present mortality and handicap incidences may readily be compared with those obtained in the same obstetric units prior to use of intensive care techniques. This approach has been adopted by Hagberg, Olov, and Hagberg (1973), Davies and Tizard (1975), and Davies and Stewart (1975). The most dramatic reductions are in overall mortality rate and in the incidence of cerebral palsy—particularly spastic diplegia. Stewart and Reynolds (1975) have reported a gradually improving survival rate for infants weighing less than 1000 gm at birth from 50% in the years before intensive care, to 69% in 1966–1970, and to 75% in 1968–1972, and other centers have obtained similar or better results. Culliton (1975) reports a 68% improvement in recent survival rates for one New York unit. Hagberg et al. (1973) have obtained a reduction in spastic diplegia of nearly 50% in their Swedish unit, and Davies and Tizard (1975) report a reduction in spasticity from 10% of 58 children in 1961–1964 to 0% of 107 children in 1965–1970. Whether similar improvement has been obtained in other areas of handicap is less certain, although reductions in the incidence of deafness have been reported by Davies and Tizard (1975). However, it seems safe to attribute some cases, at least, of spastic diplegia occurring in the past solely to perinatal CNS insult. This finding confirms the view of retrospective researchers (Pasamanick & Knobloch, 1961) that birth complications are capable of producing permanent brain damage, rather than their being merely the consequence of preexisting pathology.

As Davies and Stewart (1975) note, an area of concern where intensive care is used is whether more children with subtle CNS damage are being introduced into society in consequence. The similar issue of whether peri- and postnatal complicating factors, such as anoxia and low birth weight, cause mental handicap is central to Sameroff and Chandler's (1975) extensive review of this area.

Although retrospective studies (Pasamanick & Knobloch, 1966) link most childhood psychopathology syndromes to peri- and postnatal risk factors, prospective studies have shown that the majority of children experiencing such supposed insult are not handicapped in later life (Graham, Pennoyer, Caldwell, Greenman, & Hartman, 1957; Keith & Gage, 1960; Ucko, 1965). In general, too, the longer the follow-up period has continued for, the less the risk group differs from controls (Graham, Ernhart, Thurston, & Craft, 1962; Corah *et al.,* 1965). In contrast, the importance of socioeconomic variables as predictors of follow-up intellectual levels has been confirmed by all (Birch & Gussow, 1970; Drillien, 1964; McDonald, 1964). Sameroff and Chandler (1975) interpret this evidence in terms of a continuum of caretaking casualty, whereby inadequate upbringing potentiates the effects of early insult, whereas a stimulating and supportive environment is able to dissipate them.

Although the importance of psychosocial variables in this area is undeniable, several qualifications of their therapeutic omnipotence are necessary. First, although the data concerning consequences of perinatal anoxia (Campbell *et al.,* 1950; Fraser & Wilks, 1959; Usdin & Weil, 1952) have mostly revealed no long-term deleterious consequences, some studies have obtained clear relationships between anoxia, particularly in association with other risk factors, and both mortality and handicap (Stewart & Reynolds, 1975). Second, a number of studies which have followed up premature babies have revealed consistent and enduring, albeit small, intellectual deficits (McDonald, 1964; Taub, Goldstein, & Capito, 1977; Wiener, Rider, Oppel, & Harper, 1968). This is particularly the case if prematures followed were of very low birth weight or small for gestational age (Drillien, 1964; McDonald, 1964; Neligan, Kolvin, Scott, & Garside, 1977). Finally, the potency of psychosocial variables must be qualified according to the efficacy of the follow-up methods used and, particularly, the universal dependence on IQ measures.

Whether IQ tests are appropriate for use in detecting CNS insult effects has been questioned before (Graham *et al.,* 1957; Haywood, 1969, 1971; Spreen, 1976). The following objections are pertinent to the use of IQ measures as indexes of brain damage in this area:

1. Hemispherectomy and hemiplegia data, reviewed earlier, have shown that an individual may have both severe brain damage and normal IQ. In such cases, more detailed testing has revealed specific functional deficits. Hence, the sensitivity of IQ measures may be questioned, particularly since deficits in this area are expected to be relatively subtle. One example of such a specific relationship between etiology and pathological syndrome exists in this area in data linking perinatal anoxia to spastic diplegia (Davies & Tizard, 1975). Although causality cannot be assumed even in this case, evidence linking the syndrome to perinatal cerebeller growth spurts (Dobb-

ing, 1974), is strongly suggestive of such a relationship. For other risk factors, such as low birth weight or hyperbilirubinemia, where no such secondary evidence is available, failure to differentiate different types and severities of etiology, which is common in the literature, seems likely to hamper the search for sequelae. The possibility that if tests other than IQ are used such sequelae will be found is suggested by findings linking obstetric risk factors to problems of temperament (Thomas, Chess, & Birch, 1968), sociability (Douglas, 1960) and attentional or emotional difficulties (Parmelee & Michaelis, 1971; Prechtl & Beintema, 1964).

2. The principal reason for the dependence on IQ tests is the assumption that they provide standardized measures of recovery which are unaffected by situational variables. The invalidity of this assumption has already been emphasized in demonstrations that recovery period and experiential variables both before and after brain damage affect IQ scores obtained. The effect of environmental influences on IQ scores in adverse circumstances has also recently been demonstrated by intervention projects aimed both at infancy (Garber & Heber, 1977) and at later childhood (Clarke & Clarke, 1976), which have commonly obtained IQ changes at least as great as those at issue here.

3. As previously noted, psychosocial variables relate both to recovery outcomes and to criteria used in selecting risk samples. Hence, for example, low-socioeconomic-class mothers are more likely to have babies of low birth weights which have low IQs at school age, and they are more likely to have children with depressed IQs in general. Middle-class mothers, in contrast, are less likely to have such babies and, where they do so, the babies are less likely to have low IQs at school age (Sameroff & Chandler, 1975). This finding both mitigates against the use of IQ tests and provides two non-brain-damage interpretations of recovery data.

One interpretation is that the low follow-up IQs reflect only the congenital characteristics of the sample in question—the obstetric risk factor has had no effect. A second, and more plausible, interpretation is that the measures reflect differences in the experience of the two groups. Hence, the high-socioeconomic-status group is viewed as receiving experience appropriate to the follow-up measures to be used, whereas the experience of the low-socioeconomic group is less directed toward intellectual priorities. Considered in these terms, recovery measures in this area currently reveal more about biases inherent in IQ testing than about either brain damage or whether the deficits of one group have been remedied and the other not. This view is compatible with both animal and human brain-damage and intervention findings, reviewed earlier, showing that optimum improvement occurs on tasks which reflect the characteristics of experience.

In principle, the validity, or otherwise, of these arguments can be tested by using matched, noninsulted, control groups. In practice, as other writers have emphasized (Graham, Matarazzo, & Caldwell, 1956; Richardson, 1976), the problems involved in matching and the relatively subtle nature of the deficits in question make this goal difficult to achieve. A particular problem is to identify appropriate factors on which to match. For example, in their exhaustive follow-up analysis of children with gestational and birth-weight anomalies, Neligen *et al.* (1977) identified both gestational and socioeconomic effects. However, the latter could be attributed to maternal variables which the researchers labeled "neighborliness." Not surprisingly, neighborliness has not been used in control matching in other studies.

At present, then, the primary impression in this area is one of heterogeneity and it is apparent that more detailed analyses of interactions between obstetric and situational variables are needed. Some models which can be fitted to existing findings are considered in Section IV, C. For present purposes, the conclusion of primary importance is that tests currently used in assessing CNS insult effects are subject to unestimated false-positive and false-negative distortions. Consequently, the existence and nature of recovery mechanisms are not amenable to analysis.

3. Overview of Studies where Insult Is Presumed

Not surprisingly, in crossing the boundary between observable trauma and presumed insult, the relationships between CNS deficits and behavioral anomalies have again increased in complexity. In general, it seems reasonable to conclude that effects of CNS insult in this area are more subtle and less enduring than in cases where tissue damage is confirmed. With this decrease in magnitude of effects and the relatively long time scale intrinsic to the area, psychosocial variables have increased in importance, to the point where it is difficult to disagree with Sameroff and Chandler's (1975) view that:

> Even if one continues to believe that a "continuum of reproductive casualty" exists, its importance pales in comparison to the massive influence of socio-economic factors on pre-natal and post-natal development. (p. 192)

The implication of this view is that research priorities in this area lie outside the brain-damage arena. Rather than speculative statements about insult, detailed normative information is needed about upbringing differences which cummulatively influence developmental processes. That this research is underway is clear from the explosion of literature in this area, reviewed by Beckwith (1976) and Bronfenbrenner (1974) and in Mittler (1977) and Tjossem (1976).

Although a strong argument can, therefore, be made against use of brain-damage rationales in this area, it must be borne in mind that this conclusion reflects the clinical rule of thumb that an effect must be robust enough to withstand intervening variables, rather than an adequate data base. In this respect, the lesson of animal research that effects of early brain damage were overlooked until more extensive testing was undertaken is of obvious pertinence. In this area, the insensitivity of testing used has preempted understanding of whether putatively insulting variables have no effect, a transient effect, a small effect which is remediable by good caretaking, or an enduring effect sometimes camoflaged by psychosocial variables. A significant source of obfuscation has been the tacit assumption that psychometric, and primarily IQ, tests provide direct measures of normal CNS function and are unaffected by experiential variables. This is an exaggeration of the properties of these tests.

Shortcomings of psychometric tests in this area present obvious problems for prospective screening and are one reason that neuropsychologists have attempted to devise tests which tap neural, in preference to psychological, processes. An alternative approach, which is again of a more pragmatic nature, is to select test objectives on the basis of social priorities rather than conceptual ones. As Senf (1976) has pointed out, many types and degrees of individual difference are tolerated by society such that, for example, being a singing disordered person has none of the pernicious implications of being a reading disordered one. Considered in these terms, the idea of a normal CNS becomes an oversimplification and no attempt is made to devise tests to measure CNS attributes directly. Instead, the goals of testing derive from cultural values and the aim of research is not to isolate direct effects of CNS insult, so much as to question whether early insults limit the function so identified to a significant degree relative to other exigencies. Researchers employing psychiatric referral (Rutter *et al.,* 1970), reading retardation (Satz *et al.,* 1974), or psychosocial problems (Klonoff & Paris, 1974) as dependent variables reflect this philosophy. Where it is adopted, an important consideration both for this area and for intervention work is to make overt, and agree on, the goals in question.

For individuals concerned with neurological plasticity and brain-damage recovery processes, contemporary data in this area currently provide few insights. Consequently, three priorities exist. First, we need to identify which CNS parameters are depleted by insult and to relate this knowledge to existing data concerning ontogenetic time tabling and recuperative potential. Buchwald (1975) and Purpura (1974, 1976) have begun this work. Whether damage occurs to myelination, which is capable of catchup, to redundant neurons due to be discarded, or to vital and irreplacable neurons is of obvious significance. Second, we need to know how much a given CNS parameter may be distorted, and in what combinations with other parameters, before function limiting occurs. Third, we need to develop infant assessment techniques with greater reliability and predictive validity for both normal and abnormal function than those currently available. Lipsitt (1977) and Lipsitt, Mustaine, and Zeigler (1977) have documented the current state of the art in this area and have pointed to the promise of techniques employing psychophysiological and neurobehavioral parameters for this work.

Finally, it is emphasized that these separate directions for research need not be mutually exclusive and should be complementary. The intention here has been to acknowledge the existence of alternative priorities and the need to make research goals explicit. Otherwise, confusion seems likely to occur between concepts of normality derived from cultural, and those which reflect empirical, baselines.

C. DYNAMIC MODELS OF CENTRAL NERVOUS SYSTEM RECUPERATION

A number of writers (Escalona, 1968; Reese & Overton, 1970; Sameroff & Chandler, 1975) have contrasted the complexity of child development with the crassness of linear, organic, main effect, or medical models frequently used to explain it. Instead, interactive, synergistic, transactional, or dynamic models have been proposed, such that development is viewed as a succession of qualitative reorganizations of function, each of which may impose a radically new direction on development. Although this change of emphasis has assisted research by discouraging those who would otherwise have fitted simple explanations to complex problems, it is important that the complexity of the models be evaluated against the data they generate. In particular, it is currently relevant to question whether data concerned with "reciprocity" and the active contribution of infants to their early interactions have implications for our understanding of brain-damage recovery processes.

In the general area of developmental psychopathology, Sameroff and Chandler (1975) have recently produced an important and influential review of the prospective and retrospective screening literature which exemplifies the contemporary view. Linear and main effect models are criticized for their inability to accommodate the low predictive validity of infant casualty measures, and interactive ones as too passive to match the dynamic nature of child development. A transactional model which emphasizes the directionality and "self-righting" nature of development is proposed. Children who remain handicapped do so either because of their continuing negative transactions with caretakers or because their original reproductive casualty has been "extreme." For convenience, criticisms are confined here to Sameroff and Chandler's model, but they may be generalized to other similar conceptions of recovery processes. Three points must be made. First, although Sameroff and Chandler's model makes an important contribution by emphasizing the significance of caretaker and psychosocial variables, it does not generate testable hypotheses. Calling those reproductive risk factors which lead to continuing deficit "extreme" does not improve identification or understanding of the processes involved and is tautological. Second, in being based primarily on negative evidence—our inability to identify deficits in many high-risk infants at follow-up—the argument is of a weak kind. A stronger argument would identify those factors which restore function to normal. It is believed that Sameroff and Chandler's conception of the normalization process misconstrues it. Third, and most important, the transactional model confuses direction, and implied purpose in psychosocial terms, with CNS maturational processes, which are neither directional nor purposive in the same sense.

The distinction between transactional and interactional models of recovery effects may readily be seen if Sameroff and Chandler's explanation of recovery following early insult is contrasted with an interactionist explanation. According to their view, the CNS's intrinsic regulating capacity is able to actively respecify CNS function in order to overcome insult effects. This process occurs in successive qualitative reorganizations, which undertake dynamic adjustment of functional systems as part of the "self-righting and self-organizing tendency" (p. 235) which characterizes maturation. The alternative, interactionist, explanation does not view maturational reorganizations as susceptible to experiential modification, although experience may be necessary to maintain intrinsic maturation processes. Consequently, recovery cannot depend on environmental reorganization of CNS functional characteristics and, indeed, the model implies that in some instances maturational reorganizations may result in equal, though sometimes altered or even exacerbated, handicap effects, as obtained by Satz *et al.* (1974) for reading retardation and by Goldman (1974, 1976) and Thompson *et al.* (1977) following lesions in monkeys.

For the interactionist model, recovery can depend only on normal learning processes and on changes in function brought about by maturational reorganizations. The nature of these reorganizations cannot be advantaged by experiential variables or by an intrinsic self-righting mechanism of the sort proposed by Sameroff and Chandler. Hence, when recovery occurs, one of two explanations may apply. Either the CNS has not been damaged in the first place—in which case any transitory behavior deficits are due either to diaschisis or to related maturational delays—or the behavior recovered simply reflects remaining systems plus the sort of improvement which normal learning can be expected to produce.

A further sense in which the models differ is in respect of the range of behaviors over which recovery occurs. For the transactional model, experience serves as the basic material used by the CNS to achieve its self-righting reorganization. Consequently, the tendency for high-socioeconomic-group children to improve their IQs after early insult more than low-socioeconomic children is attributed to their general normalization of function and to the inadequacy of the latters' experience. The interactionist model, in contrast, sees the IQ effects as reflecting the relationship between the different experience of the two groups and the assessment measure (IQ) used. The CNS itself is neutral in this situation and maturational reorganizations, being common to both groups, are equally impartial. That the change in performance (IQ) achieved by the high-socioeconomic group is afforded such emphasis as evidence for "improvement" reflects cultural priorities more obviously than CNS ones.

Although these two models make different predictions is some respects, selecting one or the other is unlikely to be a straightforward matter. In any event, choice is precluded at present by the lack of available data. However, a number of points which detract from the transactional model may be made.

First, the direction and, by implication, purpose implied by the model is not specified and it is difficult to see what it comprises. At present, normalization has been measured mostly in IQ terms, but presumably CNS self-righting is not aimed toward IQ tests. Rather, IQ tests are assumed to measure the sort of abilities a normalized CNS displays. As already noted, this proposition overstates the comprehensiveness of IQ tests. While the capacity of IQ tests to measure a comparative level of intellectual function is not disputed, the appropriateness of the measure, its ubiquity, and its freedom from bias in this situation all require qualification. In this respect, it is also relevant that some authorities have argued against interpreting socioeconomic differences in IQ in terms of a deprivation model. Instead, a "difference" model is used to explain data obtained (see, too, Beckwith, 1976; Bricker & Bricker, 1976; Kagan & Tulkin, 1971; Lewis & Wilson, 1972) such that qualitative differences in upbringing techniques are seen as producing different types of competence in different socioeconomic groups and consequently, in the present circumstances, different types of recovery. That socioeconomic differences in parent–child interactions should be viewed as qualitatively rather than quantitatively different is supported by data from Lewis and Wilson (1972), Wachs, Uzgiris, and Hunt (1971), and others, and the view that lower socioeconomic environments may sometimes disadvantage intellectual progress because of excess (rather than deficit) of stimulation has also been expressed (Hunt, 1976).

Second, the transactional model tends to imply that unless it is severely damaged, the CNS will invariably tend to self-heal if it is given adequate general experience. This proposal is only saved from being disquieting in its implications by the impreciseness with which "severe" damage and "adequate" experience are defined.

Finally, the principal objection to the transactional model is that, like the concept of neurological plasticity itself, it is unnecessary. The more parsimonious interaction model can account for all experimental data so far obtained and has the additional advantage of making specific predictions concerning the relationship between experience and recovery. It is therefore proposed that research be confined to this model until such time as it proves inadequate to account for recovery effects obtained.

V. General Summary and Conclusions

On the basis of the literature reviewed in this area, two kinds of "plasticity" may be proposed for the CNS. The first is its capacity to generate adaptive behavior. This property, most notable in the human brain, concerns the CNS's propensity to alter behavior to facilitate interactions with the environments it encounters. Adaptability in this sense is characteristic of the normal brain and is influenced both by CNS intrinsic characteristics and by experience. Consequently, it will differ between brains and within any brain over time as both CNS and experiential variables alter. Recovery effects due to this mechanism seem likely to obey existing psychological laws, and it appears that the importance of some well-researched learning phenomena, such as proactive interference and facilitation effects, have been overlooked. Second, the brain may also be said to be plastic in that, in common with other body organs, it tends to recuperate following damage. Two sorts of neurophysiological recuperation mechanism have been identified. First, diaschisis has frequently emerged as an underrated phenomenon. In this respect, this review has been unable to find major age differences in the way in which diaschisic recuperation occurs. Second, recuperation may take place where vestigial systems remain, where neurological systems are duplicated, or where functional overlap between systems occurs. Some ways in which learning may add to this redundancy have been tentatively proposed. No evidence to support disadvantage in the older brain for this type of recuperation has been unambiguously obtained, although a "tuning" mechanism which predicts such disadvantage has been noted. Throughout, the impression gained is that although age may contribute to neurophysiological recovery phenomena to some extent in some cases, no overriding age effects exist. Instead, age has to be considered as one of a considerable array of individual difference phenomena, each of which interacts with others in influencing recovery effects. In some cases, age has emerged as a covariate of other phenomena, such as nature and severity of injury and recovery circumstance variables. The overall confounding influence of these has been acknowledged and it has been proposed that it is often the effects of such influences which have been measured when age-related recovery effects have been reported. Except in that the young brain is prone to some types of insult, no biological or critical period age effects have been found. It is noteworthy that others have recently reached an analogous conclusion in respect of the importance of early experience generally in non-brain-damaged children (Clarke & Clarke, 1976).

Throughout this review, parallels between animal and human literatures have emerged. In both areas, situational variables related to the nature of damage, to experience and recovery period variables, and to how these are represented by assessments used to index recovery have proved of dominant and underrated importance. For human brain damage, particularly where the damage is mild or unconfirmed, psychosocial criteria appear to be good predictors of outcome, although the nature of the relationship is not clear. Some evidence suggesting that psychosocial criteria are merely convenient, if blunt, descriptors of experiential variables has been noted. Isaacson's (1975) suggestion that in many cases secondary effects of brain damage are more important than the lesion itself has received some support, although data are susceptible to alternative interpretations. Rutter *et al.* (1970) have also argued that the effects of physiological disturbance are sometimes of greater importance than those attributable to ablation of neural tissue. If this phenomenon is confirmed, etiological age trends related to it seem likely to prove of dominant concern in the future.

The view which emerges from this analysis of the developmental brain-damage literature is that of direct concordance of CNS physiological and behavioral processes. Each CNS area makes a precise contribution to overall function which is specified in the young brain as much as the old, albeit sometimes in a different, provisional, form only. No functional equivocality in the young brain need be assumed and no special respecification processes are required to explain its performance after damage has occurred. However, considerable detail of information concerning both neurological and psychological data is required before prognoses can be offered.

The importance of experience as a mediator of CNS insult effects has been recognized throughout this review. However, the impression gained is that experience affects maturation only in a synergistic or interactive fashion and not in a dynamic or transactional one. Maturational changes in CNS function appear to occur autonomously and are not directed by experience, except insofar as interactions occur between capacities at each age and learning. Maturation may, however, be delayed by diaschisis and this is one mechanism whereby developmental delays (Satz, 1976) might be explained, although no direct supportive evidence exists. It has been suggested that the proposal of dynamic recovery effects results from confusion of neurological with psychosocial conceptions of normality.

Unfortunately, other than to reject environmental vicariation, it has not proved possible to choose from among the models of recovery processes outlined in the introduction. The existence of chronic recovery effects in animal and human research suggests that diaschisis alone is insufficient to explain all recovery phenomena, while lack of precise criteria for diaschisic processes imposes its own limitations on this model. In many cases, equipotentiality, emergence trauma, functional substitution, and homologous vicariation models are all capable of explaining the findings obtained, and it is clear that detailed information is urgently needed concerning relationships between the functional properties of postinsult neural systems and those of preinsult ones. The suggestion of Fuld and Fisher (1977) that individuals with cerebral trauma benefit if allowed long convalescent periods before being reintroduced to taxing situations suggests that diaschisis and emergence trauma may sometimes sum to influence recovery. It is likely that other interactions also occur.

Finally, it is believed that the "myth of recovery from early brain damage" (Isaacson, 1975) in this area has impeded advances in both adult and immature CNS remedial research. In the adult areas, as Walsh and Cummins (1976) have noted, the view that the mature brain is "set in its ways" has led to a remedial nihilism which has precluded attempts to develop therapies. In the developmental area, the view that the young brain is plastic has sanctioned use of imprecise intervention techniques. It is proposed that precise identification of concomitants of CNS insult and application of therapeutic techniques appropriate to remaining functions will lead to conceptual and remedial advances in both areas.

REFERENCES

Ahmad, S. S., & Harvey, J. A. Long term effects of septal lesions and social experience on shock-elicited fighting in rats. *Journal of Comparative and Physiological Psychology,* 1968, **66**, 595–602.

Akert, K., Orth, O. S., Harlow, H. F., & Schiltz, K. A. Learned behaviour of rhesus monkeys following neonatal bilateral prefrontal lobotomy. *Science,* 1960, **132**, 1944–1945.

Annett, M. Laterality of childhood hemiplegia and the growth of speech and intelligence. *Cortex,* 1973, **9**, 4–33.

Bakker, D. J., Teunissen, J., & Bosch, J. Development of laterality—reading patterns. In R. M. Knights & D. J. Bakker (Eds.), *The neuropsychology of learning disorders.* London: University Park Press, 1976.

Basser, L. S. Hemiplegia of early onset and the faculty of speech with special reference to the effects of hemispherectomy. *Brain,* 1962, **85,** 427–460.

Bauer, J. H., & Cooper, R. M. Effects of posterior cortical lesions on performance of a brightness-discrimination task. *Journal of Comparative and Physiological Psychology,* 1964, **58,** 84–92.

Bauer, R. H. Brightness discrimination of pretrained and non-pretrained hippocampal rats reinforced for choosing brighter or dimmer alternatives. *Journal of Comparative and Physiological Psychology,* 1974, **87,** 987–996.

Beckwith, L. Caretaker-infant interaction and the development of the high risk infant. In T. D. Tjossem (Ed.), *Intervention strategies for high risk infants and young children.* London: University Park Press, 1976.

Bell, R. Q. A reinterpretation of the direction of effects in studies of socialisation. *Psychological Review,* 1968, **75,** 81–95.

Berry, C. L. (Ed.). Human malformations. *British Medical Bulletin,* 1976, **32**(1), 1–97.

Birch, H., & Gussow, G. D. *Disadvantaged children.* New York: Grune & Stratton, 1970.

Blakemore, C. Development of functional connections in the mammalian visual system. In R. M. Gaze & M. J. Keating (Eds.), Development and regeneration in the nervous system. *British Medical Bulletin,* 1974, **30**(2), 152–157.

Blakemore, C. Central visual processing. In M. S. Gazzaniga & C. Blakemore (Eds.), *Handbook of psychobiology,* New York: Academic Press, 1975.

Blakemore, C. Genetic instructions on developmental plasticity in the kittens visual cortex. In H. B. Barlow & R. M. Gaze (Eds.), *A discussion on structural and functional aspects of plasticity in the nervous system.* London: Philosophical Transactions of the Royal Society, 1977.

Blakemore, C., & Cooper, G. F. Development of the brain depends on the visual environment. *Nature (London),* 1970, **228,** 467–468.

Bland, B. H., & Cooper, R. M. Posterior neodecortication in the rat: Age at operation and experience. *Journal of Comparative and Physiological Psychology,* 1969, **69,** 345–254.

Bland, B. H., & Cooper, R. N. Experience and vision of the posterior neodecorticate rat. *Physiology and Behavior,* 1970, **5,** 211–214.

Blundell, J. *Physiological psychology.* London: Methuen, 1975.

Boll, T. L. Behavioral correlates of cerebral damage in children aged 9 through 14. In R. M. Reitan & L. A. Davison (Eds.), *Clinical neuropsychology: Current status and applications.* London: Wiley, 1974.

Braun, J. J., Lundy, E. G., & McCarthy, F. Depth discrimination in rats following removal of visual cortex. *Brain Research,* 1970, **20,** 283–291.

Braun, J. J., Meyer, P. M., & Meyer, D. R. Sparing of a brightness habit in rats following visual decortication. *Journal of Comparative and Physiological Psychology,* 1966, **61,** 79–82.

Bricker, W. A., & Bricker, D. D. The infant, toddler, and preschool research and intervention project. In T. D. Tjossem (Ed.), *Intervention strategies for high risk infants and young children.* London: University Park Press, 1976.

Brinkman, J., & Kuypers, H. G. Cerebral control of contralateral and ipsilateral arm, hand, and finger movements in the split brain rhesus monkey. *Brain,* 1973, **96,** 653–674.

Bronfenbrenner, U. Is early intervention effective? *A report on longitudinal evaluations of preschool programs* (vol. II). U.S. Department of Health, Education, and Welfare, Publication No. (OHD) 76–30025. Washington, D.C.: U.S. Government Printing Office, 1974.

Brunner, R. L., & Altman, J. The effects of interference with the maturation of the cerebellum and hippocampus on the development of adult behavior. In D. G. Stein, J. J. Rosen, & N. Butters (Eds.), *Plasticity and recovery of function in the central nervous system.* New York: Academic Press, 1974.

Buchwald, J. S. Brainstem substrates of sensory information processing and adaptive behavior. In N. A. Buchwald & M. A. Brazier (Eds.), *Brain mechanisms in mental retardation.* New York: Academic Press, 1975.

Cajal, S. R. *Degeneration and regeneration of the nervous system.* London and New York: Oxford University Press, 1928.

Campbell, W., Cheseman, E., & Kilpatrick, A. The effects of neonatal asphyxia on physical and mental development. *Archives of Diseases in Childhood,* 1950, **25,** 351–359.

Chase, H. P. Undernutrition and growth and development of the human brain. In J. D. Lloyd-Still (Ed.), *Malnutrition and intellectual development.* Lancaster: MIT Press, 1976.

Chase, M. H., & Wyrwicka, W. Electrical stimulation of the brain as reinforcement of food consumption in aphagic rats. *Experimental Neurology,* 1973, **40,** 153–160.

Chase, R. A. Neurological aspects of language disorders in children. In J. V. Irwin & M. Marge (Eds.), *Principles of childhood language disabilities.* New York: Appleton, 1973.

Chow, K. L., & Stewart, D. L. Reversal of structural and functional effects of long-term visual deprivation. *Experimental Neurology,* 1972, **34,** 409–433.

Churchill, J. A. The relationship between intelligence and birth weight in twins. *Neurology,* 1965, **15,** 341–343.

Clarke, A. M., & Clarke, A. D. B. (Eds.). *Early experience: Myth and evidence.* London: Open Books, 1976.

Cooper, R. M., Blochert, K. P., Gillespie, L. A., & Miller, L. G. Translucent occluders and lesions of posterior neocortex in the rat. *Physiology and Behavior,* 1972, **8,** 693–697.

Corah, N. L., Anthony, E. J., Painter, P., Stern, J. A., & Thurston, D. L. Effects of perinatal anoxia after seven years. *Psychological Monographs,* 1965, **79** (3, Whole No. 596).

Craft, A. W., Shaw, D. A., & Cartlidge, N. E. Head injuries in children. *British Medical Journal,* 1972, **4,** 200–203.

Culliton, B. J. Intensive care for newborns: Are there times to pull the plug? *Science,* 1975, **188,** 133–134.

Dalby, D. A., Meyer, D. R., & Meyer, P. M. Effects of occipital neocortical lesions upon visual discrimination in the cat. *Physiology and Behavior,* 1970, **5,** 727–734.

Damasio, A. R., Lima, A., & Damasio, H. Nervous function after right hemispherectomy. *Neurology,* 1975, **25,** 89–93.

Davenport, J. W. Environmental therapy in hypothyroid and other disadvantaged animal populations. In R. N. Walsh & W. T. Greenough (Eds.), *Environments as therapy for brain dysfunction.* New York: Plenum, 1976.

Davies, P. A., & Steward, A. L. Low-birth-weight infants: Neurological sequelae and later intelligence. *British Medical Bulletin,* 1975, **31**(1), 85–91.

Davies, P. A., & Tizard, J. P. M. Very low birthweight and subsequent neurological defect (with special reference to spastic diplegia). *Developmental Medicine and Child Neurology,* 1975, **17,** 3–17.

Dawson, R. G., Conrad, L., & Lynch, G. Single and two-stage hippocampal lesions: A similar syndrome. *Experimental Neurology,* 1973, **40,** 263–277.

Denenberg, V. H. (Ed.). *The development of behavior.* Stamford: Sinauer, 1972.

Denenberg, V. H., Rosenberg, K. M., Paschke, R., Hess, J. L., Zarrow, M. X., & Levine, S. Plasma corticosterone levels as a function of cross-species fostering and species differences. *Endocrinology,* 1968, **83,** 900–902.

Dennis, M., & Kohn, B. Comprehension of syntax in infantile hemiplegics after cerebral hemidecortication: Left hemisphere superiority. *Brain and Language,* 1975, **2,** 472–482.

Dennis, M., & Whitaker, H. A. Language acquisition following hemidecortication: Linguistic superiority of the left over the right hemisphere. *Brain and Language,* 1976, **3,** 404–433.

Dennis, M., & Whitaker, H. A. Hemispheric equipotentiality and language acquisition. In S. Segalowitz & F. Gruber (Eds.), *Language development and neurological theory.* New York: Academic Press, 1977.

Dicara, L. V. Role of post-operative feeding experience in recovery from lateral hypothalamic damage. *Journal of Comparative and Physiological Psychology,* 1970, **72**, 60–65.

Dieckman, W. J., Adain, F. L., Michel, H., Kiamen, S., Dunkle, F., Arthur, B., Costin, M., Campbell, A., Wensley, A. C., & Lorang, E. Calcium, phosphorous, iron and nitrogen balance in pregnant women. *American Journal of Obstetrics and Gynecology,* 1944, **47**, 3–11.

Dobbing, J. Prenatal development and neurological development. In J. Cravioto, L. Hambraeus, & B. Vahlquist (Eds.), *Early malnutrition and mental development.* Stockholm: Almquist & Wiksell, 1974.

Dobbing, J., & Sands, J. Vulnerability of developing brain: IX. The effect of nutritional growth retardation of the timing of the brain growth-spurt. *Biologic Neonatorum,* 1971, **19**, 363–378.

Dobbing, J., Hopewell, J. W., & Lynch, A. Vulnerability of the developing brain: VII. Permanent deficits of neurons in cerebral and cerebellar cortex following early mild undernutrition. *Experimental Neurology,* 1971, **32**, 439–447.

Doty, R. W. Functional significance of the topographical aspects of the retinocortical projection. In R. Jung & H. Kornhuber (Eds.), *The visual system: Neurophysiology and psychophysics.* Berlin and New York: Springer-Verlag, 1961.

Doty, R. W. Survival of pattern vision after removal of striate cortex in the adult cat. *Journal of Comparative and Physiological Psychology,* 1971, **143**, 341–369.

Douglas, J. W. B. "Premature" children at primary schools. *British Medical Journal,* 1960, **1**, 1008–1013.

Drillien, C. M. *The growth and development of the prematurely born infant.* Baltimore: Williams & Wilkins, 1964.

Drillien, C. M. The long-term prospects of handicap in babies of low birth weight. *British Journal of Hospital Medicine,* 1967, **1**, 937–944.

Dru, D., Walker, J. P., & Walker, J. B. Self produced locomotion restores visual capacity after striate lesions. *Science,* 1975, **187**, 265–266.

Escalona, S. K. *The roots of individuality.* Chicago: Aldine, 1968.

Fahy, T. J., Irving, M. H., & Millac, P. Severe head injuries. *Lancet,* 1967, **2**, 475–479.

Fedio, P., & Mirsky, A. F. Selective intellectual deficits in children with temporal lobe or centrencephalic epilepsy. *Neuropsychologia,* 1969, **7**, 287–300.

Field, J. H. *Epidemiology of head injuries in England and Wales.* Research Division, Department of Health and Social Security. London: H.M.S.O, 1976.

Finger, S., Walbran, B., & Stein, D. G. Brain damage and behavioural recovery: Serial lesion phenomena. *Brain Research,* 1973, **63**, 1–18.

Finlayson, M. A. J., Johnson, K. A., & Reitan, R. M. Relationship of level of education to neuropsychological measures in brain damaged and non-brain damaged adults. *Journal of Consulting and Clinical Psychology,* 1977, **45**, 536–542.

Fitzhugh, K. B., Fitzhugh, L. C., & Reitan, R. M. Weschler-Bellevue comparisons in groups with "chronic" and "current" lateralised and diffuse brain lesions. *Journal of Consulting and Clinical Psychology,* 1962, **26**, 306–310.

Frankova, S. Interaction between early malnutrition and stimulation in animals. In J. Cravioto, L. Hambraeus, & B. Vahlquist (Eds.), *Malnutrition and mental development.* Stockholm: Almqvist & Wiksell, 1974.

Fraser, M. S., & Wilks, J. The residual effects of neonatal asphyxia. *Journal of Obstetrics and Gynecology of the British Commonwealth,* 1959, **66**, 748–752.

Freeman, R. D., & Thobos, L. N. Electrophysiological evidence that abnormal early visual experience can modify the human brain. *Science,* 1973, **180**, 876–878.

Fuld, P. A., & Fisher, P. Recovery of intellectual ability after closed head injury. *Developmental Medicine and Child Neurology,* 1977, **19**, 495–502.

Fuller, J. L. Experiential deprivation and later behavior. *Science,* 1967, **158**, 1645–1652.

Fuller, J. L., Rosvold, H. E., & Pribram, K. H. The effect on affective and cognitive behavior in the dog of lesions in the pyriform-amygdala-hippocampal complex. *Journal of Comparative and Physiological Psychology,* 1957, **50**, 89–96.

Garber, H., & Heber, F. R. Indications of the effectiveness of early intervention in preventing mental retardation. In P. Mittler (Ed.), *Research to practice in mental retardation* (Vol. I). London: University Park Press, 1977.

Gardner, W. J., Karnosh, L. J., McClure, D. C., & Gardner, A. K. Residual function following hemispherectomy for tumour and for infantile hemiplegia. *Brain,* 1955, **78**, 487–502.

Gazzaniga, M. S. Determinants of cerebral recovery. In D. G. Stein, J. J. Rosen, & N. Butters (Eds.), *Plasticity and recovery of function in the central nervous system.* New York: Academic Press, 1974.

Gazzaniga, M. S. Brain mechanisms and behavior. In M. S. Gazzaniga & C. Blakemore (Eds.), *Handbook of Psychobiology.* New York: Academic Press, 1975.

Gazzaniga, M. S., & Sperry, R. W. Language after section of the cerebral commisures. *Brain,* 1967, **90**, 131–148.

Geschwind, N. Late changes in the nervous system: An overview. In D. G. Stein, J. J. Rosen, & N. Butters (Eds.), *Plasticity and recovery of function in the central nervous system.* New York: Academic Press, 1974.

Gil, D. *Violence against children.* Cambridge, Mass.: Harvard University Press, 1970.

Glick, S. D. Changes in drug sensitivity of mechanisms of functional recovery following brain damage. In D. G. Stein, J. J. Rosen, & N. Butters (Eds.), *Plasticity and recovery of function in the central nervous system.* New York: Academic Press, 1974.

Goldberger, M. E. Recovery of movement after CNS lesions in monkeys. In D. G. Stein, J. J. Rosen, & N. Butters (Eds.), *Plasticity and recovery of function in the central nervous system.* New York: Academic Press, 1974.

Goldman, P. S. Functional development of the pre-frontal cortex in early life and the problem of neuronal plasticity. *Experimental Neurology,* 1971, **32**, 366–387.

Goldman, P. S. Plasticity of function in the CNS. In D. G. Stein, J. J. Rosen, & N. Butters (Eds.), *Plasticity and recovery of function in the central nervous system.* New York: Academic Press, 1974.

Goldman, P. S. The role of experience in recovery of function following orbital prefrontal lesions in infant monkeys. *Neuropsychologia,* 1976, **14**, 401–412.

Goldman, P. S., & Mendelson, M. J. Salutatory effects of early experience on deficits caused by lesions of frontal association cortex in developing rhesus monkeys. *Experimental Neurology,* 1977, **57**, 588–602.

Gordon, H. W. Auditory specialisation of the right and left hemispheres. In D. M. Kinsbourne & W. L. Smith (Eds.), *Hemispheric disconnection and cerebral function.* Springfield, Ill.: Thomas, 1974.

Gotsick, J. E., & Marshall, R. C. Time course of the septal rage syndrome. *Physiology and Behaviour,* 1972, **9**, 685–687.

Gott, P. S. Cognitive abilities following right and left hemispherectomy. *Cortex,* 1973, **9**, 266–274.

Graham, F. K., Ernhart, C. B., Thurston, D. L., & Craft, M. Development three years after perinatal anoxia and other potentially damaging newborn experiences. *Psychological Monographs,* 1962, **76** (3, Whole No. 522).

Graham, F. K., Matarazzo, R. G., & Caldwell, B. M. Behavioural differences between normal and traumatised newborns: II. Standardisation reliability and validity. *Psychological Monographs,* 1956, **70** (21, Whole No. 428).

Graham, F. K., Pennoyer, M. M., Caldwell, B. M., Greenman, M., & Hartman, A. F. Relationship between clinical status and behaviour test performance in a newborn group with histories suggesting anoxia. *Journal of Paediatrics,* 1957, **50,** 177–189.

Greene, E., Stauff, C., & Walters, J. Recovery of function with two-stage lesions of the formix. *Experimental Neurology,* 1972, **37,** 14–22.

Greenough, W. T. Experiential modification of the developing brain. *American Scientist,* 1975, **63,** 37–46.

Greenough, W. T., Fass, B., & DeVoogd, T. J. The influence of experience on recovery following brain damage in rodents: Hypotheses based on developmental research. In R. N. Walsh & W. T. Greenough (Eds.), *Environments as therapy for brain dysfunction.* New York: Plenum, 1976.

Griffiths, H., & Davidson, M. Long-term changes in intellect and behaviour after hemispherectomy. *Journal of Neurology, Neurosurgery and Psychiatry,* 1966, **29,** 571–572.

Habicht, J. P., Yarbrough, C., Lechtig, A., & Klein, R. E. Relation of maternal supplementary feeding during pregnancy to birth weight and other sociobiological factors. In M. Winick (Ed.), *Nutrition and foetal development* (Vol. 2): *Current concepts in nutrition.* New York: Wiley, 1974.

Hagberg, B., Olow, I., & Hagberg, G. Decreasing incidence of low birth weight diplegia—An achievement of modern neonatal care? *Acta Paediatrica Scandinavia,* 1973, **62,** 199–200.

Hardyck, C. *Are ongoing cognitive processes lateralised?* Paper given at European Conference, International Neuropsychology Society, Oxford, U.K., 1977.

Harlow, H. F., Blomquist, A. J., Thompson, C. I., Schiltz, K. A., & Harlow, M. K. Effects of induction age and size of frontal lobe lesions on learning in rhesus monkeys. In R. L. Isaacson (Ed.), *The neuropsychology of development.* New York: Wiley, 1968.

Harrington, J. A., & Letermendia, F. J. J. Persistent psychiatric disorders after head injuries in children. *Journal of Mental Science,* 1958, **104,** 1205–1207.

Haywood, H. C., Behavioural research in mental retardation: Goals of a new decade. *Alabama Journal of Medical Science,* 1969, **6,** 378–381.

Haywood, H. C. *Labeling: Efficacy, evils and caveats.* Paper presented at Joseph P. Kennedy Jr. Foundation International Symposium on Human Rights, Retardation and Research. Washington, D.C. 1971.

Hebb, D. O. *The organisation of behaviour.* New York: Wiley, 1949.

Heiskanen, O., & Kaste, M. Late prognosis of severe brain injury in children. *Developmental Medicine and Child Neurology,* 1974, **16,** 11–14.

Hicks, S. P., & D'Amato, C. J. Motor-sensory behaviour after hemispherectomy in newborn and mature rats. *Experimental Neurology,* 1970, **29,** 416–438.

Hindley, C. B., & Owen, C. F. The extent of individual changes in I.Q. for ages between six months and seventeen years, in a British longitudinal sample. *Journal of Child Psychology and Psychiatry,* 1978, **19,** 329–350.

Hirsch, H. V. B., & Jacobson, M. The perfectible brain: Principles of neuronal development. In M. S. Gazzaniga & C. Blakemore (Eds.), *Handbook of psychobiology.* New York: Academic Press, 1975.

Hirsch, H. V. B., & Spinelli, D. N. Visual experience modifies distribution of horizontally and vertically oriented receptive fields in cats. *Science,* 1970, **168,** 869–871.

Hjern, B., & Nylander, I. Acute head injuries in children: traumatology, therapy and prognosis. *Acta Paediatrica,* 1963 Supplement 152.

Hubel, D. H., & Wiesel, T. N. Receptive fields binocular interaction and functional architecture in the cat's visual cortex. *Journal of Physiology,* 1962, **160,** 106–154.

Hubel, D. H., & Wiesel, T. N. Receptive fields and functional architecture in two non-striate visual areas (18 and 19) of the cat. *Journal of Neurophysiology,* 1965, **28,** 229–289.

Hubel, D. H., Wiesel, T. N., & LeVay, S., Plasticity of occular dominance columns in monkey striate cortex. In H. B. Barlow & R. N. Gaze (Eds.), *A discussion on structure and functional aspects of plasticity in the nervous system.* London: Philosophical Transactions of the Royal Society, 1977.

Hughes, K. R. Dorsal and ventral hippocampus lesions and maze learning: Influence of preoperative environment. *Canadian Journal of Psychology,* 1965, **19,** 325–332.

Hunt, J. McV. Environmental programming to foster competence and prevent mental retardation in infancy. In R. N. Walsh & W. T. Greenough (Eds.), *Environments as therapy for brain dysfunction.* New York: Plenum, 1976.

Huttenlocher, P. R. Dendritic development in neocortex of children with mental defect and infantile spasms. *Neurology,* 1974, **24,** 203–210.

Isaacson, R. L. The myth of recovery from early brain damage. In N. E. Ellis (Ed.), *Aberrant development in infancy.* London: Wiley, 1975.

Isaacson, R. L. Recovery "(?)" from early brain damage. In T. D. Tjossem (Ed.), *Intervention strategies for high risk infants and young children.* London: University Park Press, 1976.

Isaacson, R. L., & Schmaltz, L. W. Failure to find savings from spaced, two-stage destruction of hippocampus. *Communications in Behavioral Biology,* 1968, **1,** 353–359.

Jacobsen, C. F. Functions of the frontal association areas in primates. *Archives of Neurology and Psychiatry,* 1935, **33,** 588–569.

Jacobson, M. Development specification and diversification of neural circuits. In F. O. Schmidt (Ed.), *The neurosciences second study program.* New York: Rockerfeller University Press, 1970.

Jacobson, M. A plentitude of neurons. In G. Gottlieb (Ed.), *Studies on the development of behavior and the nervous system* (Vol. 2). New York: Academic Press, 1973.

Johnson, D. A. Developmental aspects of recovery of function following septal lesions in the infant rat. *Journal of Comparative and Physiological Psychology,* 1972, **78,** 331–348.

Kaelber, C. T., & Pugh, T. F. Influence of intrauterine relations of the intelligence of twins. *New England Journal of Medicine,* 1969, **280,** 1030–1034.

Kagan, J., & Tulkin, S. R. Social class differences in child rearing during the first year. In H. R. Schaffer (Ed.), *The origins of human social relations.* New York: Academic Press, 1971.

Keith, H. M., & Gage, R. P. Neurologic lesions in relation to asphyxia of the newborn and factors of pregnancy: Long-term follow-up. *Paediatrics,* 1960, **26,** 616–622.

Kennard, M. A. Age and other factors in motor recovery from precentral lesions in monkeys. *American Journal of Physiology,* 1936, **115,** 138–146.

Kennard, M. A. Reorganisation of motor function in the cerebral cortex of monkeys deprived of motor and premotor areas in infancy. *Journal of Neurophysiology,* 1938, **1,** 477–496.

Kerr, F. W. L. Structural and functional evidence of plasticity in the central nervous system. *Experimental Neurology,* 1975, **48,** 16–31.

Kershner, J. R., & King, A. J. Laterality of cognitive functions in achieving hemiplegic children. *Perceptual and Motor Skills,* 1974, **39,** 1283–1289.

Kertesz, A., & McCabe, P. Recovery patterns and prognosis in aphasia. *Brain,* 1977, **100,** 1–18.

Kirchner, K. A., Braun, J. J., Meyer, D. R., & Meyer, P. M. Equivalence of simultaneous and successive neocortical ablations in production of impairments of retention of black-white habits in rats. *Journal of Comparative and Physiological Psychology,* 1970, **71,** 420–425.

Klaus, M., & Kennell, J. *Maternal-infant bonding.* St. Louis: Mosby, 1976.

Klein, R. E., Irwin, M., Engle, P. L., Townsend, J., Lechtig, A., Martorell, R., & Delgado, H. Malnutrition, child health, and behavioral development. In P. Mittler (Ed.), *Research to practice in mental retardation* (Vol. 3): *Medical aspects.* London: University Park Press, 1977.

Klonoff, H. Head injuries in children: Predisposing factors, accident conditions, accident proneness, and sequelae. *American Journal of Public Health,* 1971, **61** (12), 2405-2417.

Klonoff, H., & Paris, R. Immediate, short term, and residual effects of acute head injuries in children: Neuropsychological and neurological correlates. In R. M. Reitan & L. A. Davison (Eds.), *Clinical Neuropsychology: Current status and applications.* London: Wiley, 1974.

Kohn, B., & Dennis, M. Selective impairments of visuo-spatial abilities in infantile hemiplegics after right cerebral hemidecortication. *Neuropsychologia,* 1974, **12**, 505-512.

Krashen, S. Lateralisation, language learning, and the critical period: Some new evidence. *Language and Learning,* 1973, **23**, 63-74.

Krynauw, R. A. Infantile hemiplegia treated by removing one cerebral hemisphere. *Journal of Neurology, Neurosurgery and Psychiatry,* 1950, **13**, 243-267.

Lashley, K. S. Factors limiting recovery after central nervous system lesions. *Journal of Nervous and Mental Disorders,* 1938, **88**, 733-755.

Lawrence, D. G., & Hopkins, D. A. Bilateral pyramidal lesions in infant rhesus monkeys. *Brain Research,* 1970, **24**, 543-544.

Lenneberg, E. H. *Biological foundations of language.* New York: Wiley, 1967.

Lenneberg, E. H., & Lenneberg, E. *Foundations of language development: A multidisciplinary approach.* New York: Academic Press, 1975.

LeVere, T. E. Neural stability, sparing and behavioral recovery following brain damage. *Psychological Review,* 1975, **82**, 344-358.

LeVere, T. E., & Morlock, G. W. The nature of visual recovery following posterior neodecortication in the hooded rat. *Journal of Comparative and Physiological Psychology,* 1973, **83**, 62-67.

LeVere, T. E., & Morlock, G. W. The influence of pre-operative learning on the recovery of a successive brightness discrimination following posterior neodecortication in the hooded rat. *Bulletin of the Psychonomic Society,* 1974, **4**, 507-509.

Levine, S., & Thoman, E. B. Physiological and behavioral consequences of postnatal maternal stress in rats. *Physiology and Behavior,* 1969, **4**, 139-142.

Levine, S., & Wiener, S. Malnutrition and early environmental experience. In R. N. Walsh & W. T. Greenough (Eds.), *Environments as therapy for brain dysfunction,* London: Plenum, 1976.

Levine, S., Haltmeyer, G. C., Karas, G. G., & Denenberg, V. H. Physiological and behavioral effects of infantile stimulation. *Physiology and Behavior,* 1967, **2**, 55-59.

Lewis, M., & McGurk, H. The evaluation of infant intelligence: Infant intelligence scores— true or false? *Science,* 1972, **178**, 1174-1177.

Lewis, M., & Wilson, C. D. Infant development in lower-class American families. *Human Development,* 1972, **15**, 112-127.

Lipsitt, L. P. The study of sensory and learning processes of the newborn. *Clinical Perinatology,* 1977, **4**, 163-185.

Lipsitt, L. P., Mustaine, M. G., & Zeigler, B. Effects of experience on the behavior of the young infant. *Neuropadiatrie,* 1977, **8**, 107-133.

Lloyd-Still, J. D. *Malnutrition and intellectual development.* Lancaster: MTP Press, 1976.

Luria, A. R. *Traumatic aphasia.* The Hague: Mouton, 1970.

Luria, A. R., Naydin, V. L., Tsvetkova, L. S., & Vinarskaya, E. N. Restoration of higher cortical function following local brain damage. In P. J. Vinken & G. W. Bruyer (Eds.), *Handbook of clinical neurology* (Vol. 3). Amsterdam: North-Holland, 1969.

McDonald, A. D. Intelligence in children of very low birth weight. *British Journal of Preventive and Social Medicine,* 1964, **18**, 59–74.

McDonald, A. D. *Children of very low birth weight.* London: Medical Education and Information Unit of the Spastics Society, 1967. (Research Monograph No. 1).

McFie, J. The effects of hemispherectomy on intellectual functioning in cases of infantile hemiplegia. *Journal of Neurology, Neurosurgery and Psychiatry,* 1961, **23**, 240–249.

McFie, J. Brain injury in childhood and language development. In N. O'Connor (Ed.), *Language, cognitive deficits and retardation.* London: Butterworth, 1975.

Melzack, R. The role of early experience in emotional arousal. *Annals of the New York Academy of Science,* 1969, **159**, 721–730.

Mensh, I. N., Schwartz, H. G., Matarazzo, R. R., & Matarazzo, J. D., Psychological functioning following cerebral hemispherectomy in man. *Archives of Neurology and Psychiatry,* 1952, **67**, 787–796.

Messerli, P., Tissot, A., & Rodriguez, J. Recovery from aphasia: Some factors of prognosis. In Y. Lebrun & R. Hoops (Eds.), *Recovery in aphasics.* Amsterdam: Swets & Zeitlinger, 1976.

Meyer, D. R., Isaac, W., & Maher, B. The role of stimulation in spontaneous reorganisation of visual habits. *Journal of Comparative and Physiological Psychology,* 1958, **51**, 546–548.

Meyer, P. M. Recovery of function following lesions of the subcortex and neocortex. In D. G. Stein, J. J. Rosen, & N. Butters (Eds.), *Plasticity and recovery of function in the central nervous system.* New York: Academic Press, 1974.

Meyer, P. M., Horel, J. A., & Meyer, D. R. Effects of *d l*-amphetamine upon placing responses in neodecorticate cats. *Journal of Comparative and Physiological Psychology,* 1963, **56**, 402–404.

Milner, B. Brain mechanisms suggested by studies of the temporal lobes. In C. H. Millikan & F. L. Darley (Eds.), *Brain mechanism underlying speech and language.* New York: Grune & Stratton, 1967.

Mirsky, A. F., & Harman, N. On aggressive behavior and brain disease—Some questions and possible relationships derived from the study of men and monkeys. In R. E. Whalen (Ed.), *The neuropsychology of aggression.* New York: Plenum, 1974.

Mittler, P. (Ed.). *Research to practice in mental retardation.* London: University Park Press, 1977.

Mize, R. R., & Murphy, E. H. Selective visual experience fails to modify receptive field properties of rabbit striate cortex neurons. *Science,* 1973, **180**, 320–323.

Moore, R. Y. Central regeneration and recovery of function: The problem of collateral reinnervation. In D. G. Stein, J. J. Rosen, & N. Butters, (Eds.), *Plasticity and recovery of function in the central nervous system.* New York: Academic Press, 1974.

Moore, R.Y., Bjorklund, A., & Stenevi, U. Plastic changes in the adrenergic innervation of the rate septal area in response to denervation. *Brain Research,* 1971, **33**, 13–35.

Muir, D. W., & Mitchell, D. E. Visual resolution and experience: Acuity deficits in cats following early selective visual deprivation. *Science,* 1973, **180**, 420–422.

Munk, H. *Ueber die Funktionen der Grosshirnrinde. Gesammelte Mitteilungen aus den Jahren 1877–1880.* Berlin: August Hirschwald, 1881.

Murphy, E. H., & Stewart, D. L. Effects of neonatal and adult striate lesions on visual discrimination in the rabbit. *Experimental Neurology,* 1974, **42**, 89–96.

Neligan, G. A., Kolvin, I., Scott, D. M., & Garside, R. F. *Born too soon or born too small.* Spastics International Medical Publications. London: Heinemann, 1976.

Olson, C. R., & Freeman, R. D. Monocular deprivation and recovery during sensitive period in kittens. *Journal of Neuropsychology,* 1978, **41,** 65–74.

Panting, A., & Merry P. H. Long term rehabilitation of severe head injuries—Social and medical support for the patient's family. *Injury,* 1970, **2** (1), 33–37.

Parmelee, A. N., & Michaelis, R. Neurological examination of the newborn. In Helmuth, J. (Ed.), *Exceptional infants: Studies in abnormalities* (Vol. 2). New York: Brunner/Mazel, 1971.

Parmelee, A. H., Sigman, M., Kopp, C. B., & Haber, A. The concept of a cumulative risk score for infants. In N. E. Ellis (Ed.), *Aberrant development in infancy.* London: Wiley, 1975.

Pasamanick, B., & Knobloch, H. Epidemiologic studies on the complications of pregnancy and the birth process. In G. Caplan (Ed.), *Prevention of mental disorders in children.* New York: Basic Books, 1961.

Pasamanick, B., & Knobloch, H. Retrospective studies on the epidemiology of reproductive casualty: Old and new. *Merrill-Palmer Quarterly,* 1966, **12,** 7–26.

Petrinovitch, L., & Bliss, D. Retention of a learned brightness discrimination following ablations of the occipital cortex in the rat. *Journal of Comparative and Physiological Psychology,* 1966, **61,** 136–138.

Petrinovich, L., & Carew, T. J. Interaction of neocortical lesion size and interoperative experience in retention of a learned brightness discrimination. *Journal of Comparative and Physiological Psychology,* 1969, **68,** 451–454.

Pettigrew, J. D., & Freeman, R. D. Visual experience without lines: Effect on developing cortical neurons. *Science,* 1973, **182,** 599–601.

Piaget, J. *The construction of reality in the child.* New York: Basic Books, 1954.

Powley, T. L., & Keesey, R. E. Relationship of body weight to the lateral hypothalmic feeding syndrome. *Journal of Comparative and Physiological Psychology,* 1970, **70,** 25–36.

Prechtl, H. F. R. Prognostic value of neurological signs in the newborn infant. *Proceedings of the Royal Society of Medicine,* 1965, **58,** 1.

Prechtl, H. F. R., & Beintema, D. J. The neurological examination of the newborn full term infant. *Little club clinics in developmental medicine, No. 12.* London: National Spastics Society, 1964.

Prechtl, H. F. R., & Stemmer, C. J. The choreiform syndrome in children. *Developmental Medicine and Child Neurology,* 1962, **4,** 119–127.

Pribram, K. H., Plotkin, H. C., Anderson, R. M., & Demetria, L. Information sources in the delayed alternation task for normal and "frontal" monkeys. *Neuropsychologia,* 1977, **15,** 329–340.

Purpura, D. P. Dendritic spine "dysgenesis" and mental retardation. *Science,* 1974, **186,** 1126–1128.

Purpura, D. P. Discussants comments. In T. D. Tjossem (Ed.), *Intervention strategies for high risk infants and young children.* London: University Park Press, 1976.

Raisman, G. Neuronal plasticity in the septal nuclei of the adult rat. *Brain Research,* 1969, **14,** 25–48.

Reese, H. W., & Overton, W. F. Models of development and theories of development. In L. R. Goulet & P. B. Baltes (Eds.), *Life span developmental psychology: Research and theory.* New York: Academic Press, 1970.

Richardson, S. A. The influence of severe malnutrition in infancy on the intelligence of children at school age: An ecological perspective. In R. N. Walsh & W. T. Greenough (Eds.), *Environments as therapy for brain dysfunction.* New York: Plenum, 1976.

Rosenzweig, M. R. Effects of environments on development of brain and of behavior. In E.

Tobach., L. R. Aronson, & E. Shaw (Eds.), *the biopsychology of development*. New York: Academic Press, 1971.

Rosenzweig, M. R. Effect of environment on brain and behavior in animals. In E. Schopler & R. J. Reichler (Eds.), *Psychopathology and child development*. New York: Plenum, 1976.

Rosenzweig, M. R., & Bennett, E. L. Cerebral changes in rats exposed individually to an enriched environment. *Journal of Comparative and Physiological Psychology,* 1972, **80**, 304–313.

Rosenzweig, M. R., Bennett, E. L., & Diamond, M. C. Effects of differential environments on brain anatomy and brain chemistry. In J. Zubin & G. Jervis (Eds.), *Psychopathology of mental development*. New York: Grune & Stratton, 1967.

Rosenzweig, M. R., Bennett, E. L., & Diamond, M. C. Brain changes in response to experience. *Scientific American,* 1972, **226**, 22–29.

Rosner, B. S. Brain functions. In P. H. Mussen & M. R. Rosenzweig (Eds.), *Annual Review of Psychology* (Vol. 21). Palo Alto: Annual Reviews, 1970.

Rosvold, H. E., Mirsky, A. F., & Pribram, K. H. Influence of amygdalectomy on social behaviour in monkeys. *Journal of Comparative and Physiological Psychology,* 1954, **47**, 173–178.

Rudel, R.G., Teuber, H. L., & Twitchell, T. E. Levels of impairment of sensorimotor functions in children with early brain damage. *Neuropsychologia,* 1974, **12**, 95–108.

Rush, D., Stein, L., Christakis, G., & Susser, M. The prenatal project: The first 20 months of operation. In M. Winick (Ed.), *Nutrition and foetal development* (Vol. 2): *Current conceptions in nutrition*. New York: Wiley, 1974.

Rusk, H. A. Rehabilitation of the brain-injured patient. In A. E. Walker, W. F. Caveness, & M. Critchley (Eds.), *The late effects of head injury*. Springfield, Ill.: Thomas, 1969.

Rutter, M. Brain damage syndromes in childhood: Concepts and findings. *Journal of Child Psychology and Psychiatry,* 1977, **18**, 1–22.

Rutter, M., Graham, P., & Yule, W. *A neuropsychiatric study in childhood*. London: Spastics International Medical Publication, 1970.

Rutter, M., & Hersov, L. *Child psychiatry: Modern approaches*. London: Blackwell, 1976.

Sadick, T. L., & Ginsberg, B. E. The development of lateral functions and reading ability. *Cortex,* 1978, **14**, 3–11.

St. James-Roberts, I. *A reinterpretation of hemispherectomy data without functional plasticity of the brain:* I. Intellectual function. (Submitted-a)

St. James-Roberts, I. *A reinterpretation of hemispherectomy data without functional plasticity of the brain:* II. Sensory and Motor Function. (Submitted-b)

Sameroff, A. J. Early influences on development: Fact or fancy? *Merrill-Palmer Quarterly,* 1975, **21**, 267–294.

Sameroff, A. J., & Chandler, M. J. Reproductive risk and the continuum of caretaker casualty. In F. D. Horowitz (Ed.), *Review of child development* (Vol. 4). Chicago: University of Chicago Press, 1975.

Sarno, J. E., Sarno, M. E., & Levita, E. Evaluating language improvement after completed stroke. *Archives of Physical Medicine and Rehabilitation,* 1971, **52**, 73–78.

Sarno, M. T. The status of research in recovery from aphasia. In Y. Lebrun & R. Hoops (Eds.), *Recovery in aphasics*. Amsterdam: Swets & Zeitlinger, 1976.

Satz, P. Cerebral dominance and reading disability: An old problem revisted. In R. M. Knights & D. J. Bakker (Eds.), *The neuropsychology of learning disorders*. London: University Park Press, 1976.

Satz, P., & Fletcher, J. M. *Developmental changes in disabled readers: Implications for concepts of acquisition, arrest, and recovery*. Paper given at European Conference of the International Neuropsychology Society, Oxford, 1977.

Satz, P., Friel, J., & Rudegear, G. Differential changes in the acquisition of developmental skills in children who later become dyslexic. A three year follow-up. In D. G. Stein, J. J. Rosen, & N. Butters (Eds.), *Plasticity and recovery of function in the central nervous system.* New York: Academic Press, 1974.

Schmaltz, L. W., & Isaacson, R. L. The effects of preliminary training conditions upon DRL performance in the hippocampectomised rat. *Physiology and Behavior,* 1966, **1**, 175-182.

Schneider, G. E. Two visual systems: Brain mechanisms for localisation and discrimination are dissociated by tectal and cortical lesions. *Science,* 1969, **13**, 895-902.

Schneider, G. E., & Jhaveri, S. R. Neuroanatomical correlates of spared or altered function after brain lesions in the newborn hampster. In D. G. Stein, J. J. Rosen, & N. Butters (Eds.), *Plasticity and recovery of function in the central nervous system.* New York: Academic Press, 1974.

Schwartz, S. Effect of neocortical lesions and early environmental factors on adult rat behavior. *Journal of Comparative and Physiological Psychology,* 1964, **57**, 72-77.

Senf, G. Some methodological considerations in the study of abnormal conditions. In R. N. Walsh & W. T. Greenough (Eds.), *Environments as therapy for brain dysfunction.* New York: Plenum, 1976.

Shaffer, D. Brain injury. In M. Rutter & L. Hersov (Eds.), *Child psychiatry: Modern approaches.* London: Blackwell, 1976.

Shaffer, D., Chadwick, O., & Rutter, M. Psychiatric outcome of localised head injury in children. In R. Porter & D.Fitzsimons (Eds.), Ciba Foundation Symposium 34. *Outcome of severe damage to the central nervous system.* Amsterdam: Elsevier, 1975.

Shankweiler, D., & Liberman, I. Y. Exploring the relations between reading and speech. In R. M. Knights & D. J. Bakker (Eds.), *The neuropsychology of learning disorders.* London: University Park Press, 1976.

Slob, A. K., Snow, C. E., & Natris-Mathot, E., de. Absence of behavioral deficits following neonatal undernutrition in the rat. *Developmental Psychobiology,* 1973, **6**, 177-186.

Smith, A. Dominant and nondominant hemispherectomy. In M. Kinsbourne and W. L. Smith (Eds.), *Hemisphere disconnection and cerebral function.* Springfield, Ill.: Thomas, 1974.

Smith, A., & Sugar, C. Development of above normal language and intelligence 21 years after left hemispherectomy. *Neurology,* 1975, **25**, 813-818.

Smithells, R. W., Ankers, C., Carver, M. E., Lennon, D., Schorah, C. J., & Sheppard, S. *Maternal malnutrition,* 1977, **381**, 497-506.

Spinelli, D. N., Hirsch, H. V. B., Phelps, R. W., & Metzler, J. Visual experience as a determinant of the response characteristics of cortical receptive fields in cats. *Experimental Brain Research,* 1972, **15**, 289-304.

Spinelli, D. N., and Jensen, F. E. Plasticity: The mirror of experience. *Nature (London),* 1979, **203**, 75-78.

Spreen, D. Neuropsychology of learning disorders: Post-conference review. In R. M. Knights & D. J. Bakker (Eds.), *The neuropsychology of learning disorders.* London: University Park Press, 1976.

Stein, D. G. Some variables influencing recovery of function after central nervous system lesions in the rat. In D. G. Stein, J. J. Rosen, & N. Butters (Eds.), *Plasticity and recovery of function in the central nervous system.* New York: Academic Press, 1974.

Stein, D. G., Rosen, J. J., & Butters, N. (Eds.). *Plasticity and recovery of function in the central nervous system.* New York: Academic Press, 1974.

Stein, Z. A., & Susser, M. W. Prenatal nutrition and mental competence. In J. D. Lloyd-Still (Ed.), *Malnutrition and intellectual development.* Lancaster: MTP Press, 1976.

Stein, Z. A., Susser, M. W., Saenger, G., & Marolla, F. *Famine and human development: The dutch hunger winter of 1944-45.* New York and London: Oxford University Press, 1975.

Stenevi, U., Bjorklund, A., & Moore, R. Y. Growth of infant central adrenergic axons in the denervated lateral geniculate body. *Experimental Neurology*, 1972, **35**, 290-299.

Stern, P., McDowell, F., Miller, J. M., & Robinson, M. Factors influencing stroke rehabilitation. *Stroke*, 1971, **2**, 213-218.

Stewart, A. L., & Reynolds, E. O. R. Improved prognosis for infants of very low birthweight. *Pediatrics*, 1975, **54**, 724-735.

Stewart, D. L., & Riesen, A. H. Adult vs infant brain damage: Behavioural and electrophysiological effects of striatectomy in adult and neonatal monkeys. In G. Newton & A. H. Riesen (Eds.), *Advances in psychobiology*. New York: Wiley, 1972.

Stryker, M. P., & Sherk, H. Modification of cortical orientation selectivity in the cat by restricted visual experience: A re-examination. *Science*, 1975, **190**, 904-906.

Susser, M., Stein, Z. A., & Rush, D. Prenatal nutrition and subsequent development. In P. Mittler (Ed.), *Research to practice in mental retardation* (Vol. III): *Biomedical aspects*. London: University Park Press, 1977.

Tanaka, D. Sparing of an escape response following serial prefrontal decortication in the monkey. *Brain Research*, 1974, **65**, 195-201.

Taub, E., Perrella, P., & Barro, G. Behavioral development after forelimb deafferentiation on day of birth in monkeys with and without blinding. *Science*, 1973, **181**, 959-960.

Taub, H. B., Goldstein, K. M., & Capito, D. V. Indices of neonatal prematurity as discriminators of development in middle childhood. *Child Development*, 1977, **48**, 797-805.

Teasedale, G., & Jennett, B. Assessment of coma and impaired consciousness. *Lancet*, 1974, **2**, 81-84.

Tees, R. C. The effects of neonatal striate lesions and visual experience on form discrimination in the rat. *Canadian Journal of Psychology Review of Canadian Psychology*, 1975, **29**, 66-85.

Tees, R. C. Depth perception after infant and adult neocortical lesions in light and dark reared rats. *Developmental Psychobiology*, 1976, **9**, 223-235.

Teitelbaum, P., & Epstein, A. N. The lateral hypothalamic syndrome: Recovery of feeding and drinking after lateral hypothalamic lesions. *Psychological Review*, 1962, **69**, 74-90.

Teuber, H. K., & Rudel, R. G. Behavior after cerebral lesions in children and adults. *Developmental Medicine and Child Neurology*, 1962, **4**, 3-20.

Thomas, A., Chess, S., & Birch, H. G. *Temperament and behavior disorders in children*. New York: New York University Press, 1968.

Thompson, C. I., Bergland, R. M., & Towfighi, J. T. Social and nonsocial behaviours of adult rhesus monkeys after amygdalectomy in infancy or adulthood. *Journal of Comparative and Physiological Psychology*, 1977, **91**, 533-548.

Thompson, C. I., Harlow, H. F., Blomquist, A. J., & Schilz, K. A. Recovery of function following prefrontal lobe damage in rhesus monkeys. *Brain Research*, 1971, **35**, 37-48.

Thompson, R. Retention of a brightness discrimination following neocortical damage in the rat. *Journal of Comparative and Physiological Psychology*, 1960, **53**, 212-215.

Thomson, A. M. Diet in pregnancy. 2. Assessment of the nutritive value of diets, especially in relation to differences between social classes. *British Journal of Nutrition*, 1959, **13**, 190-195.

Tizard, J. Early malnutrition, growth, and mental development in man. In R. M. Gale & M. J. Keating (Eds.), *Development and regeneration in the nervous system. British Medical Bulletin*, 1974, **30**(2), 169-174.

Tjossem, T. D. *Intervention strategies for high risk infants and young children*, London: University Park Press, 1976.

Tsang, Y. C. Maze learning in rats hemidecorticated in infancy. *Journal of Comparative and Physiological Psychology*, 1937, **24**, 221-254. (a)

Tsang, Y. C. Visual sensitivity in rats deprived of visual cortex in infancy. *Journal of Comparative and Physiological Psychology,* 1937, **24**, 255-262. (b)

Ucko, L. E. A comparative study of asphyxiated and non-asphyxiated boys from birth to five years. *Developmental Medicine and Child Neurology,* 1965, **7**, 643-657.

Usdin, G. L., & Weil, M. L. Effect of apnea neonatorum on intellectual development. *Pediatrics,* 1952, **9**, 387-394.

Van Dongen, H. R., & Loonen, M. C. B. Factors related to prognosis of acquired aphasia in children. *Cortex,* 1977, **13**, 131-136.

Van Sluyters, R., & Blakemore, C. Experimental creation of unusual neuronal properties in visual cortex of kitten. *Nature (London),* 1973, **246**, 506-508.

Von Monakow, C. *Die Lokalisation in der Grosshirnrinde und der Abbau der Funktion durch Korticale Herde.* Wiesbaden: Bergmann, 1914.

Wachs, T. D., Uzgiris, I. C., & Hunt, J. McV. Cognitive development in infants of different age levels and from different environmental backgrounds: An explanatory investigation. *Merrill-Palmer Quarterly,* 1971, **17**, 283-317.

Walsh, R. N., & Cummins, R. A. Neural responses to therapeutic environments. In R. N. Walsh & W. T. Greenough (Eds.), *Environments as therapy for brain dysfunction.* New York: Plenum, 1976.

Warrington, E. Commentary on McFie. In N. O'Conner (Ed.), *Language, cognitive deficits and retardation.* London: Butterworth, 1975.

Wedell, K. Variations in perceptual ability among types of cerebral palsy. *Cerebral Palsy Bulletin,* 1960, **2**, 149.

Wetzel, A. B., Thompson, V. E., Horel, J. A., & Meyer, P. M. Some consequences of perinatal lesions of the visual cortex in the cat. *Psychonomic Science,* 1965, **3**, 381-382.

White, H. H. Cerebral hemispherectomy in the treatment of infantile hemiplegia. *Confinia Neurologica,* 1961, **21**, 1-50.

Wiener, G., Rider, R. V., Oppel, W. C., & Harper, P. A. Correlates of low birth weight: Psychological status at eight to ten years of age. *Pediatric Research,* 1968, **2**, 110-118.

Wiesel, T. N., & Hubel, D. H. Comparison of the effects of unilateral and bilateral eye closure on cortical unit responses in kittens. *Journal of Neurophysiology,* 1965, **28**, 1029-1040.

Will, B. E., Rosenzweig, M. R., Bennett, E. L., Hebert, M., & Morimoto, H. Relatively brief environmental enrichment aids recovery of learning capacity and alters brain measures after postweaning brain lesions in rats. *Journal of Comparative and Physiological Psychology,* 1977, **91**, 33-50.

Wilson, P. J. Cerebral hemispherectomy for infantile hemiplegia. *Brain,* 1970, **93**, 147-180.

Winick, M., & Noble, A. Quantitative changes in DNA, RNA and protein during prenatal and postnatal growth in the rat. *Developmental Biology,* 1965, **12**, 451-466.

Winick, M., Rosso, P., & Brasel, J. A. Malnutrition and cellular growth in the brain. *Bibliotheca Autritio et Dieta,* 1972, **17**, 60-68.

Witelson, S. F. Abnormal right hemisphere specialisation in developmental dyslexia. In R. M. Knights & D. J. Bakker (Eds.), *The neuropsychology of learning disorders.* London: University Park Press, 1976.

Zaidel, E. Unilateral auditory language compensation on the token test following cerebral commissurotomy and hemispherectomy. *Neuropsychologia,* 1977, **15**, 1-18.

AUTHOR INDEX

Numbers in italics refer to the pages on which the complete references are listed.

SUBJECT INDEX

Contents of Previous Volumes